QuickBooks 2000: The Official Guide

About the Author

Kathy Ivens has been a computer consultant and author since 1985. She is the author of *QuickBooks 99: The Official Guide,* and has written and contributed to more than forty other books, and hundreds of magazine articles. She also writes the Reader Challenge for *Windows 2000 Magazine* (formerly known as *Windows NT Magazine*).

QuickBooks 2000: The Official Guide

Kathy Ivens

Osborne/McGraw-Hill
Berkeley New York St. Louis San Francisco
Auckland Bogotá Hamburg London Madrid Mexico City Milan Montreal
New Delhi Panama City Paris São Paulo Singapore Sydney Tokyo Toronto

Osborne/**McGraw-Hill**
2600 Tenth Street
Berkeley, California 94710
U.S.A.

For information on translations or book distributors outside the U.S.A., or to arrange bulk purchase discounts for sales promotions, premiums, or fund-raisers, please contact Osborne/**McGraw-Hill** at the above address.

QuickBooks 2000: The Official Guide

34567890 AGM AGM 019876543210

ISBN 0-07-212320-6

Publisher	**Copy Editors**
Brandon A. Nordin	Claire Splan
	Bill McManus
Associate Publisher and	
Editor-in-Chief	**Proofreader**
Scott Rogers	Stefany Otis
Acquisitions Editor	**Indexer**
Joanne Cuthbertson	David Heiret
Project Editors	**Computer Designers**
Betsy Manini	Jim Kussow
Lisa Theobald	Dick Schwartz
Patty Mon	Roberta Steele
Acquisitions Coordinator	**Illustrators**
Stephane Thomas	Robert Hansen
	Beth Young
Technical Editor	Brian Wells
Michael Woodward	
	Series Design
	Peter F. Hancik

This book was composed with Corel VENTURA™ Publisher.

This book is dedicated to all my kids
(it's amazing how each one of them is so fantastically perfect):
Debby, Allen, Beverly, Bill, Judy, Mike, and Sarah.

Contents at a Glance

Part III
Using Time and Billing

Part IV
Managing QuickBooks

Part V
Appendices

Contents

Part II
Bookkeeping

Part III
Using Time and Billing

Part IV
Managing QuickBooks

Acknowledgments

The wonderful team at Osborne/McGraw-Hill that worked on this book is an author's dream team. Joanne Cuthbertson's dedication to making this book a winner is truly appreciated. Stephane Thomas, as always, proved she is one of the real gems of the editorial world. Betsy Manini kept us all organized and almost as efficient as she is. Michael Woodward, despite his own hectic schedule, responded to my pleas to provide technical editing I could rely on. Copy editors Claire Splan and Bill McManus used their considerable skills to make sure the world doesn't learn about my weaknesses in using the language correctly.

At Intuit, the support of Laurel Lee and Lynn Favor has been invaluable. The various technicians and project managers who assisted me did so with warmth, charm, and expertise, and I owe special thanks to Brian Niegocki, Larry Zacharczyk, Robert Sandstedt, and Vanlee Waters.

Kathy Ivens

Introduction

Different Ways to Use This Book

While I'd like to believe that writing this book was tantamount to writing a prize-winning novel, I really know that you won't read this book by starting at page 1 and continuing to the end. However, there is a progressive logic to the way the book is organized.

You can consult the **Table of Contents**, where you'll notice that the order of the chapters reflects the way you'll probably use your QuickBooks software. The tasks you perform often (and immediately upon installing the software) are covered before the tasks you perform less frequently.

The **Index** guides you to specific tasks and features, so when you absolutely must know immediately how to do something, it's easy to find the instructions.

However, there are some sections of this book you should read first, just because accounting software is truly more complex than most other types of software. You should read **Appendix A** to learn what information to have at hand in order to set up your accounting system properly. Then, you should read the first two chapters so you can configure your system properly. After that, read the chapter or section you need to in order to perform the tasks that have to be accomplished immediately.

Upgrading the Information in This Book

Like most software applications, QuickBooks is updated, tweaked, and improved over the course of time. In fact, during the year 2000, QuickBooks will be introducing new ways to perform tasks via its Web site.

As software features change, so do the contents of this book. To keep this book up to date you can visit this book's Web page, which is located at **http://www.cpa911.com.**

Besides upgraded instructions, this Web site has lots of tricks, tips, and shortcuts (hopefully, you'll add your own discoveries). There's also a lot of information for your accountant, explaining the technical accounting processes that go on behind the scenes as you use your QuickBooks software. Your accountant can also find information that helps him or her work with QuickBooks clients.

What's Provided in This Book to Help You

There are some special elements in this book that you'll find extremely useful:

- **Tips** give you some additional insight about a subject or a task. Sometimes they're shortcuts, and sometimes they're tricks I've learned working with clients.
- **Notes** provide extra information about a topic or a task. Sometimes they provide information about what happens behind the scenes when you perform a task, and sometimes they have additional information I think you might be curious about.
- **Cautions** are presented to help you avoid the traps you can fall into if a task has a danger zone.
- **Putting QuickBooks to Work** is a device for showing you how the tasks you're learning can be used in your business. In these supplementary sections, I've illustrated ways in which various businesses have actually used QuickBooks features. Within these stories, you'll find information aimed at helping you use certain features in a more creative and robust manner.

What's New in This Version of QuickBooks

If you've used previous versions of QuickBooks, here are the exciting new features you'll want to put to use:

- **Navigation Bar** The easiest one-click access to functions and features you've ever used! You can customize it to hold listings for all the features you use frequently.
- **Report Finder** All the reports you need, in one place, sorted by type.

- **Automatic Link Between Credits and Refund Checks**   No more need to create complicated transactions.
- **More Printing Power**   Print registers, journals entries, and more.
- **More Links to Software**   Synchronize contact information with Microsoft Outlook and Symantec ACT!

If You Have QuickBooks Pro

QuickBooks Pro is a special version of QuickBooks. It's designed for businesses that need job costing, estimating, or time tracking. In addition, QuickBooks Pro provides support for network use of the product. This book covers the QuickBooks Pro features.

You and Your Accountant

One of the advantages of double-entry bookkeeping software like QuickBooks is that a great many simple bookkeeping tasks are performed automatically. If you've been keeping manual books, or using a check-writing program such as Quicken, your accountant will probably have less work to do now that you're using QuickBooks.

Many accountants visit clients regularly, or ask that copies of checkbook registers be sent to the accountants' offices. Then, using the data from the transactions, a general ledger is created, along with a trial balance and other reports based on the general ledger (profit & loss statements and balance sheets).

If you've had such a relationship with your accountant, it ends with QuickBooks. Your accountant will only have to provide tax advice and business planning advice. All those bookkeeping chores are performed by QuickBooks, which keeps a general ledger and provides reports based on the data in the general ledger.

However, you'll want to check with your accountant as you set up your chart of accounts (the accounts that make up the general ledger), and also as you link tax forms to the accounts that are connected to your tax reports.

Throughout this book, I've provided information about general ledger postings as you create transactions in QuickBooks, and you'll also find references from me when I think specific information is going to be important to your accountant. Accountants tend to ask questions about how software handles certain issues (especially payroll, inventory, accounts receivable, and accounts payable) and I've had many years of experience working with accountants as I set up bookkeeping software. As a result, you'll see comments from me such as "your accountant will probably ask how QuickBooks handles this," followed by an explanation that you can give your accountant. There are also a number of places in this book in which I advise you to call your accountant before making a decision about how to handle a certain transaction.

Don't worry—your accountant won't complain about losing the bookkeeping tasks. Most accountants prefer to handle more professional chores, and they rarely protest when you tell them they no longer have to be bookkeepers. Their parents didn't spend all that money on their advanced, difficult educations for that.

Getting Started

The decision to use a software application for your bookkeeping and accounting needs is a momentous one. It will change your business life—for the better.

However, installing QuickBooks isn't the same as installing a word processor. With a word processor you can dive right in and begin using the program—sending letters to Mom or memos to the staff or writing the great novel of the century.

QuickBooks, on the other hand, has to be set up, configured, built one brick at a time. Otherwise, you can't use it properly as a foundation for your business activities. In fact, the first time you use QuickBooks you'll be asked to take part in an interview. The software has a slew of questions for you, all of them designed to help you configure your QuickBooks system properly.

In Part One of this book, you'll learn how to get through the interview. I'll explain what's really important, what can wait until later, and what you can do all by yourself instead of through the interview process. I'll even explain when it's okay to lie, and how to lie in a way that makes your QuickBooks database accurate. Part One also includes a chapter containing instructions and hints about putting all those boring details into your accounting system, like customers, vendors, and general ledger information. (Sorry, but these fine points are necessary; you cannot keep books without them.)

Before you read Part One, be sure you've looked at Appendix A, which I've titled "Do This First!" Take that title seriously; it'll make getting through all this setup stuff easier.

Using QuickBooks for the First Time

In this chapter, you will learn to...

- Open QuickBooks
- Go through the setup interview
- Decide whether to continue the interview
- Perform a manual setup
- Navigate the QuickBooks window

Chapter 1

The first time you launch QuickBooks, you have to introduce yourself and your company to the software by means of a rather substantial setup process. This process has a lot to wade through, but it's a one-time-only task.

Launching the Software

If you installed QuickBooks with the option of placing a shortcut to the software on your desktop, double-click that shortcut to get started. Otherwise, use the Start menu, where you'll find QuickBooks in the Programs menu. When QuickBooks opens, you see a Welcome screen, followed by the opening window.

There is no company file open.

- To create a new company, select New from the File menu.

- To open an existing company, select Open from the File menu.

Don't be confused by the offer to open an existing company; this refers to the fake company that QuickBooks provides, complete with data, for you to experiment with.

Starting the Setup Interview

The setup interview, which is called EasyStep Interview, is linked to the creation of a new company, so choose Set up a new data file for a company, and click OK. The EasyStep Interview window, shown in Figure 1-1, opens immediately. Click Next to begin the interview.

The Welcome Interview

The first section of the interview is the Welcome section. Click Next to display the first screen of the interview, which asks whether you're upgrading from another Intuit product (either an earlier version of QuickBooks or the sister product, Quicken). Answer the question and click Next. Then, you're given the opportunity to skip the interview altogether. If you do want to skip it, you can return later; you can also enter some of the information QuickBooks needs by

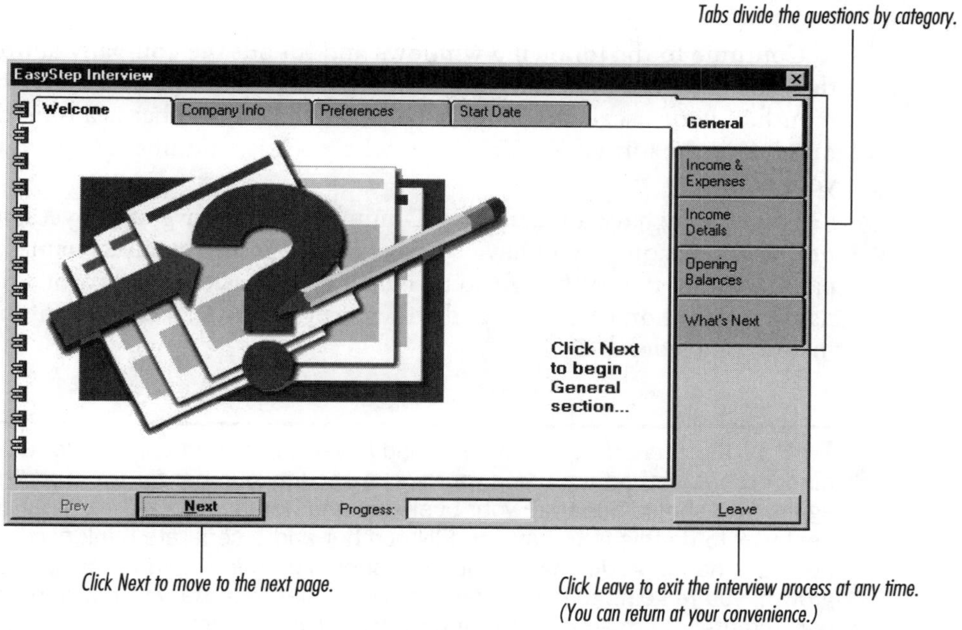

Tabs divide the questions by category.

Click Next to move to the next page.

*Click Leave to exit the interview process at any time.
(You can return at your convenience.)*

FIGURE 1-1 The EasyStep Interview provides an easy-to-follow method of creating a new data file

using the functions available on the menu bar. Chapter 2 has a great deal of information that will help you do this. Incidentally, even if you opt to skip the interview, you still have to answer several questions.

For now, however, move on with the interview so that you can learn more about it before making up your mind whether to pursue this setup step at this time.

The Company Info Interview

After you read, respond, and click Next to get through the pages of the Welcome section, the Company Info portion of the interview begins. Remember to click Next to keep chugging along throughout the entire interview process.

The next item of information QuickBooks needs is your company name, for which two entry fields are available. The first field is for the real company name, the one you do business as. The second entry is optional and is used only if the legal name of your company differs from the company name you use for doing business. For instance, if your company does business as WeAreWidgets, but the legal name or corporate name is WAW, Inc., you should fill out both name fields.

Continue to the following windows and fill out the company address, and then the basic tax information (your federal tax ID number and the starting month of your fiscal and tax year). The federal ID number is a nine-digit number in the format *XX-YYYYYYY*, where *XX* is a number assigned to your state.

You already have a federal tax ID number if you have employees, and you probably have one if you have a bank account in the business name. (Most banks require this, although some banks merely ask for a copy of a fictitious name registration certificate and will accept your social security number instead of a federal ID.)

TIP: If you are a sole proprietor and haven't bothered applying for a federal ID number, but instead are using your social security number for tax reporting, think again. You should separate your business and personal life/taxes/finances. The best way to do this is to have an EIN number and a separate bank account in your business name. Additionally, since you should be thinking in terms of business growth, you're going to need a federal ID number eventually to pay subcontractors, consultants, or employees. Get it now and avoid the rush.

QuickBooks also asks which tax form you use for your business. The common forms for small businesses are the following:

- 1120 for C Corporations
- 1120S for S Corporations
- 1065 for Partnerships
- 1040 for Proprietorships

Note that these are the tax forms on which income (loss) is reported, but there are lots of other tax forms you'll use in addition to these.

One interesting window in the Company Info portion of the EasyStep Interview is the one in which you tell QuickBooks the type of business you have (see Figure 1-2).

QuickBooks creates the company file you'll use when you work in the software. A Save As dialog box opens, asking for a filename. QuickBooks suggests a name based on the company name you've entered, so just click Save to use that filename.

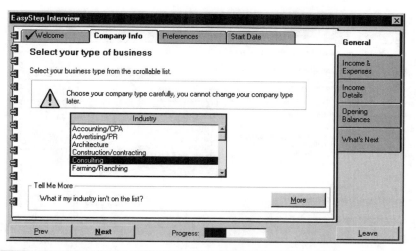

FIGURE 1-2 If you don't see an exact description of your business type, choose one that comes close

> **TIP:** It's a good idea to use a filename that reflects your company name, instead of choosing a name such as Myfiles. Then, if you start another business, you can choose another specific filename for your new venture. And, of course, you may end up using QuickBooks for your personal financial records, and you'll want a specific filename for that, too.

The response you make to the interview question regarding your type of business enables QuickBooks to design a partial chart of accounts that makes sense for your business type. When you save your company information, a chart of accounts is created for you (see Figure 1-3). In addition, business tips and information tidbits are available in the QuickBooks Help files for each particular type of business listed.

Continue to click Next to move through all the wizard windows. You're asked how many people will have access to your QuickBooks file (which really means the computer on which it resides). This is not connected to running QuickBooks on a network; it refers only to this QuickBooks software on this computer. Many small businesses permit multiple users access to the computer and accounting software, and if you plan to do so, you should tell QuickBooks about it. Then, you'll be able to determine who sees which part of your accounting records. This is a good way to keep payroll records away from everyone (except the person who enters payroll data) or to keep employees out of the general ledger (where the totals and profit/loss reports are).

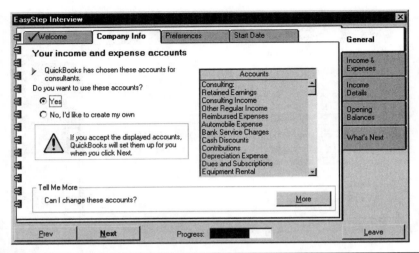

FIGURE 1-3 A chart of accounts based on your business is created. You can add, remove, or change accounts easily

Restrictions on users are implemented with the use of passwords that are attached to user names. The password feature is covered in Chapter 21.

T I P : The question about additional users is worded to mean "in addition to yourself," so if nobody but you uses your computer, zero is an appropriate answer.

Deciding Whether to Continue the Interview

At this point, you can continue the interview process or leave it. Everything else you do in the EasyStep Interview can be accomplished manually. To help you make the decision, this section reviews some things to consider.

In the setup interview, you will be asked about the features you need (such as inventory tracking, or collecting sales tax from customers). You can turn on these features manually, through the menu system, or take care of setting them up now. It's six of one and a half dozen of the other; there's no particular advantage to either approach.

The setup interview will ask for a starting date, which means you need to decide on the date your use of QuickBooks begins. Any activity that occurred in your system before that date is entered as a series of totals. For example,

QuickBooks asks you about the amount of money owed to you by customers as of that date, and you must fill out the customer information (and the balance as of the starting date) for each of those customers. The same process occurs for vendors and, in fact, for all the totals of your accounts (banks, liabilities, and so on) as of the starting date.

QuickBooks adds up all the customer balances and uses the total as the starting accounts receivable balance. You can enter customer invoices yourself manually, pretty much in your spare time. That's because QuickBooks is date-sensitive. If you tell QuickBooks your starting date is 3/30, entering customer invoices that predate that starting date (invoices that aren't yet paid) creates the same accounts receivable balance, but you have details about the invoices.

If it's early in the year, you can tell QuickBooks that your starting date is the first day of the year and enter all the transactions for the year. You don't have to enter them before you can begin using QuickBooks for current transactions; you can make your entries in your spare time. If it's November or December, you might want to wait until January to start using QuickBooks.

A major problem with doing all of this through the interview process is that you're forced to set up accounts in your chart of accounts during the procedure and you may want to use a different naming system than the one QuickBooks presents. Specifically, I'm talking about using numbers for your chart of accounts instead of names. Numbered accounts also have names, but the accounts are always sorted by numbers. You assign the first digit to reflect the type of account; for example, assets always start with 1, liabilities with 2, and so on. After you finish the interview process and begin to use QuickBooks, you can configure the software to use numbers. However, that choice isn't offered during the interview process, so you're stuck with names instead of numbers (you can switch later). Check with your accountant—I think you'll find that he or she is an enthusiastic advocate of numbered accounts.

Chapter 2 explains how to enter all the information QuickBooks needs manually, from customers to the chart of accounts. In the meantime, this section describes the interview process, so you can either follow along if you've decided to complete the interview, or read about it in order to make your decision about using it.

The Preferences Interview

The QuickBooks features you plan to use, and assorted other preferences, are determined in the Preferences section of the EasyStep Interview. Nothing you enter is etched in cement, and you'll probably change your mind about some of the responses you give here, because as you work in QuickBooks and get to know it better, you'll think of a better way to customize it for yourself.

Inventory Feature

The first feature you're asked about is whether or not you want to use inventory. Actually, you first are asked whether you maintain inventory in your business, and then you're asked whether you want to turn on the inventory features.

If you use inventory, answer Yes to the first question. Regarding the second question, about turning on the inventory feature, I can give you a good argument for either choice. If you do turn it on, you are walked through the process of entering all of your inventory items at the end of the interview. Personally, I think that is really onerous and I wouldn't do it. You can enter your inventory items later, perhaps one morning when the telephones aren't ringing and you've had plenty of sleep and several cups of coffee (and you haven't just gone through this long interview process). Inventory is one of those things that has to be entered accurately and precisely if the feature is going to work properly. If you stock only a few inventory items, you might want to complete this now; otherwise, wait a while, and when you're ready, start by reading Chapters 2 and 10, which cover entering inventory items.

Sales Tax Feature

If you collect sales tax from your customers, you have to tell QuickBooks about it so it can be added to your invoices. First, answer Yes to the question about whether or not you are responsible for collecting (and remitting) sales tax. Then, specify whether or not you collect a single tax or multiple taxes. Multiple taxes can be defined in several ways:

- You do business in more than one state and collect sales tax and remit it to the appropriate states.
- You do business in only one state, but different tax rates apply depending on the city in which your customer resides.
- You have both of the preceding situations.

If you do business in a state that has a different sales tax for one city than it does for other cities (for example, New York City has a higher tax rate than the rest of New York state, and Philadelphia has a higher tax rate than the rest of Pennsylvania), then be sure to read the tax law carefully. Some tax rates are determined by the address of the vendor (which is you), not the address of the customer. When Philadelphia raised its rate one percent higher than the rest of Pennsylvania, companies inside Philadelphia had to raise the rate for all customers (including those outside of Philadelphia), and companies outside of Philadelphia collected tax from their customers (including Philadelphia businesses) at the lower rate. Many businesses (and, sadly, many accountants) didn't understand this and spent hours changing tax rates on customer records based on customer addresses. Of course, later, when the details of the tax law became clearer, they had to change everything back again.

Invoice Form Preference

Choose the invoice form you prefer from the formats available in QuickBooks (see Figure 1-4). The form can be modified, so pick the one that comes closest to your own taste, and then read Chapter 3 (see the section called "Customizing Forms") to learn how to tweak it to a state of perfection.

Select a format to see a sample of that form in the window.

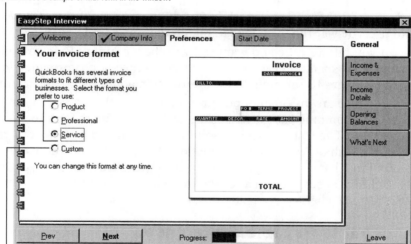

Select Custom if you want to build your own form.

FIGURE 1-4 Choose the invoice form that best suits your needs

Payroll Feature

If you have employees, QuickBooks wants to know about it, and also wants to know how many. Here are the guidelines for answering that question:

- An *employee* is someone you pay for whom you withhold taxes and issue a W-2 form at the end of the year.
- Subcontractors are not employees.
- If you write a payroll check and withhold taxes for yourself, you are an employee.
- If you write checks to yourself but don't withhold taxes, you are not an employee.

If you do have employees, you're asked whether you want to use the payroll feature. Say Yes, if that's the appropriate answer.

See Chapters 8 and 9 to learn everything about doing your own payroll.

Estimating, Invoicing, and Reports Preferences

If you provide estimates and then bill your customers according to a formula that tracks the progress of a job, QuickBooks has some features you may want to use. Answer the questions to match the way you do business.

If you bill for time and want to track the amount of time you or your employees spend on each job, an interview question is provided for that, also. See Chapters 18 through 20 for information about using this feature.

You also are given an opportunity to turn on the classes feature, which is a way to combine categories and accounts to create reports that produce an overview. The feature can be useful for tracking types of customers, jobs, or even branch offices. More information about setting up and using classes is found in Chapter 21. If you turn on the classes feature here, you must establish the classes at some point after the interview (or answer No now and turn on the feature when you're ready to set up the classes).

Accounts Payable Preferences

The next section in the interview process is the determination of the method for handling your bills from vendors. You have two choices and both offer advantages and disadvantages:

- Enter the checks directly.
- Enter the bills first and then enter the payments later.

If you opt to enter your checks directly, it means that as bills arrive in your office, you put them somewhere (an envelope, a folder, or a shoebox) until you're ready to pay them. Then, you just have to enter the checks in the

QuickBooks check register, place the checks in the envelopes, and attach a stamp. The advantage of this method is that it takes less time and less data entry. The disadvantage is that the only way to know how much money you owe at a given moment is to take the bills out of the container and to total them manually. Also, unless you specially mark and store those bills that offer a discount for timely payment, you might inadvertently miss a deadline and lose the discount.

If you decide to enter the bills first and then go through the process of paying them in QuickBooks, you can let the software remind you about due dates and you can get a current accounts payable total from the software. Another consideration when you opt to enter your bills into the software is that your accountant might have to make an adjustment when it's time to figure your taxes. Tracking accounts payable (and accounts receivable, for that matter) is called *accrual accounting*. If you file on a *cash basis* instead of an accrual basis, the accrued amount owing is not considered an expense and has to be subtracted from your total expenses. This isn't terribly unusual or difficult, but you should be aware of it. Most small businesses that don't have inventory file on a cash basis.

Reminders Preferences

QuickBooks has a feature which tracks the things you need to do and shows you a To Do list when you start the software. Included in the list are any due dates that exist (as a result of your data entry) in addition to any notes you wrote yourself and asked for a reminder about.

You can continue to let QuickBooks show you the reminder list when you open the software, or opt to display it manually through the menu. Make your decision based on the way you're most comfortable working. (You can always change it later.)

Cash or Accrual Reporting

QuickBooks has a specific interview question about the way you want to keep your books, offering cash or accrual options. Before you make the decision, check with your accountant. The smart way to do that is to ask your accountant to give a full explanation (don't just say "Which way?" and accept a one-word answer).

 N O T E : One important fact that both you and your accountant should be aware of is that when you use QuickBooks, the decision of accrual versus cash isn't as important as it is with some other accounting software programs. QuickBooks is capable of producing reports either way, regardless of the decision you make in the interview.

Here's a quick overview of what's really involved in this decision. (For details that apply specifically to your business, you should have a fuller discussion with your accountant.) In cash-based accounting, an expense doesn't exist until you write the check. Even if you enter the bill into the software and post it to an expense account in the general ledger, it isn't really an expense until the check is written. The same is true for revenue, meaning income isn't considered to be real until payment is received from your customer. Even though you enter an invoice and post it to a revenue account in the general ledger, it isn't revenue until it's paid.

In accrual-based accounting, as soon as you incur an expense (receive a bill from a vendor) or earn income (send an invoice to a customer), it's real.

Because most accounting software is accrual-based, most businesses, especially small businesses, keep accrual books and report to the IRS on a cash basis. Most accounting software is accrual-based because business owners want to know those accrued totals: "How much did I earn (bill customers for)?" and "How much do I owe?"

 TIP: If you have inventory, you'll probably file your business taxes using accrual accounting.

My own advice is that you should choose accrual-based reports in the QuickBooks interview so that you can obtain information about your earning and spending in greater detail.

The Start Date Interview

If today is the first day of your fiscal year (usually January 1) and your accountant has just completed all the accounting stuff for last year, and your numbers are pristine and perfect, you can keep going now. If any other situation exists, you should stop right here, right now, and read the section on selecting a start date in Appendix A. (You might also want to call your accountant.)

The start date you select has an enormous impact on the amount of detail your QuickBooks reports will have. In fact, it has an enormous impact on the accuracy of the numbers QuickBooks reports.

Without repeating all the information in Appendix A, the following is a quick overview of the choices you have:

- Choose the start date that represents the first day of your fiscal year and enter every transaction.

- Choose a start date that represents some accounting period, such as the end of a specific month or a specific quarter, enter totals as of that date, and then enter all the transactions since that date.
- Choose today (or some other non-meaningful date) and enter totals.

If the start date is not the first day of your fiscal year, you will have to enter the totals for each account in your chart of accounts as of the start date. This is called an *opening trial balance*.

 N O T E : In fact, even if today is the first day of your fiscal year, you'll need an opening trial balance, but it's a much smaller one (a balance sheet) and doesn't involve income and expenses incurred so far.

If you enter year-to-date totals, you won't have the details about how those totals were accrued in your QuickBooks file. That's not necessarily awful; it simply means that if you want to know how you reached a total income of a gazillion dollars by June 30, you'll have to go back to your manual records (or your old software) to get the information. If a customer calls and wants details about the billings, the individual bills won't be in your QuickBooks system and you'll have to walk to the filing cabinet and pull the paperwork.

If you're starting your QuickBooks software (and reading this book) in the first half of your fiscal year, I recommend using the first day of your fiscal year and entering each historical transaction. You don't have to enter all of them today, or even tomorrow; you can take your time.

 T I P : If other people in your office will be using QuickBooks, entering the historical transactions is a terrific way to learn how to use the software. Make sure everyone participates.

Ready? Okay, enter the date. As Figure 1-5 shows, you can enter a date directly, or use the calendar icon to move through the months and select a different date or month.

The Accounts Configuration Interview

Next on your interview agenda is the configuration of your income and expense accounts. Remember that QuickBooks entered a partial chart of accounts earlier in the interview process, when you indicated the type of business you have.

Enter a date directly, in the format mm/dd/yy.

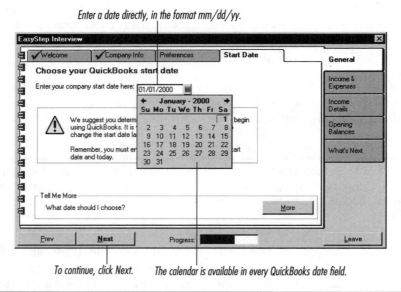

To continue, click Next.   The calendar is available in every QuickBooks date field.

FIGURE 1-5   Enter the start date for your QuickBooks system

Income Accounts Configuration

At this point, the income accounts are displayed and you're asked whether you want to add any income accounts. By default, the Yes option is selected.

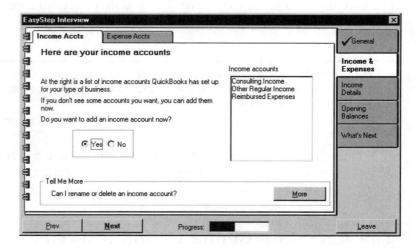

I suggest you switch the option to No, even if you do need more income account types; you can add those accounts later. Chapter 2 covers this process in detail.

Expense Accounts Configuration

The number of interview screens connected to configuring expense accounts is larger, because QuickBooks walks you through an explanation of accounts and subaccounts. Finally, the expense accounts already entered into your chart of accounts are displayed and you're offered the opportunity to add additional accounts. There's no particular reason to do this now, so answer No. When you're ready to add accounts, refer to Chapter 2 for directions.

The Income Details Interview

Here's where you set up the income and accounts receivable features you'll use in QuickBooks. Move through the questions and respond according to the way you do business. You'll be asked about the manner in which customer payments are made, and whether you send statements to customers.

Then, you're asked whether you want to set up the items for which you invoice customers. These items can be services or products. If you indicate that you're ready to set up your items, QuickBooks starts with service items and presents a dialog box to do so, as shown in Figure 1-6.

This is another one of those tasks that you can (and should) put off until later. This interview process is long and tiresome, and there's no reason to make it worse by entering all of this information now. When you decide to put these items into your system (which you can do any time before you send your first invoice to a customer), Chapter 2 will walk you through the process.

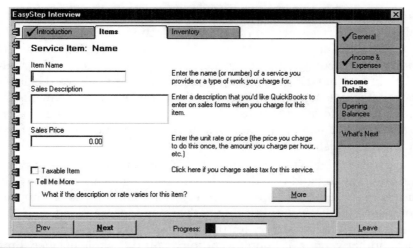

FIGURE 1-6   The services you provide for customers are considered items

The Items portion of this Income Details Interview continues with all the different types of items (noninventory and inventory). I advise you to respond No to each invitation to enter an item. You can do it later.

If you want to accomplish these tasks now (make that decision only if you have a small number of items that you'll be using to invoice customers), answer Yes and fill out the dialog boxes with the appropriate information.

The Opening Balances Interview

The next series of interview windows ask about balances—all sorts of balances.

Customer and Vendor Balances

QuickBooks wants to know about the balances owed by your customers as of the opening date. If you fill out the interview questions, be prepared to fill out the customer information as well as the balance due (and the revenue account you posted the balance to).

The balances you owe your vendors are also requested, requiring you to fill out vendor cards and the expense account that should be used for your purchases.

If you don't want to fill in these amounts now, just lie. Tell QuickBooks that none of your customers owe you money as of your start date. (I'm assuming that's a lie, unless you have a retail business, because it's normal to have customers with balances due.) Or, answer that you don't owe any money to vendors (wouldn't that be nice!).

Balance Sheet Balances

When the interview gets to the Accounts section, you're asked whether you want to set up credit card accounts. That means QuickBooks wants to track the money you spend via plastic for business expenses. It tracks the credit card as a liability, an outstanding loan. If you pay off your credit card balances each month, there is no reason to do this. If you make partial payments on your credit cards and frequently have a running balance, you can choose to track the credit card as a liability (although you don't have to do it during the interview; you can establish it later).

Personally, I don't understand why QuickBooks makes the assumption that the only way to handle credit cards with running balances is as a liability. It means that you have to open a credit card account to record your purchases and reconcile the account (filling in the finance charges and interest charges). I hate that—I'm far too lazy for that process. I like to treat my credit card as just another vendor. If I don't want to pay off the whole balance, I make a partial payment. I enter any finance charges as just another expense when I enter the vendor invoice.

 TIP: Credit card interest or finance charges you incur for a business are deductible. They are not deductible if the credit card is used for personal purchases.

This option has no right and wrong answer. I just want to point out that QuickBooks takes the liability account connection for granted, and you don't have to do it that way if you don't want to. You might want to discuss this with your accountant before making the decision.

This is also the place to set up loans (including lines of credit) and bank accounts.

The interview process next walks through all the different types of asset accounts you might have on your balance sheet, asking for the name of the account, the type of asset, and the balance as of your start date (see Figure 1-7).

The name should be specific, such as Furniture or Factory Equipment.

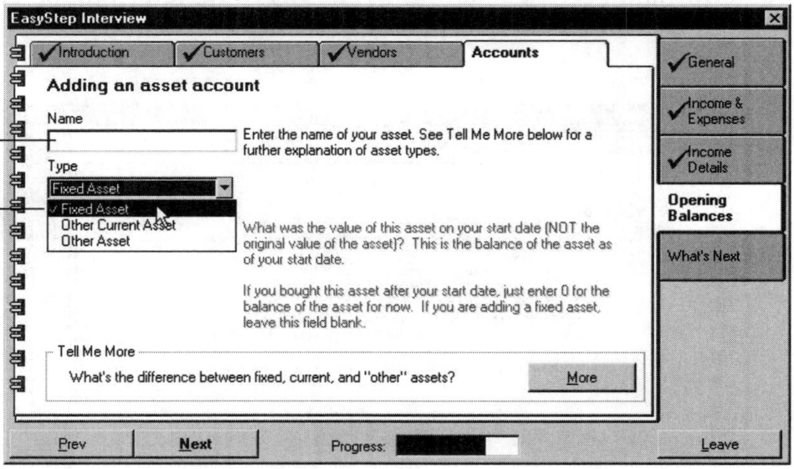

Choose the type of asset this account represents.

FIGURE 1-7 You can set up your asset accounts during the interview process

Following asset accounts is an interview section for equity accounts. These are the accounts that represent the worth of your business. Generally, your current equity is the difference between your income and your expenses (your profit or loss), along with the original capital you put into the business. If your business is a proprietorship or partnership, the money you've pulled out of the business as a draw is subtracted from that number (if you aren't on the payroll).

The What's Next Interview

The last section of the interview process is called What's Next, and it begins with a list of recommended actions, as shown in Figure 1-8.

As you click Next, each window displays instructions about how to accomplish the task it's recommending. You don't perform the task in the interview; these are just recommendations and reminders.

Finishing Up

Guess what? You're finished. This is the last window in the EasyStep Interview. If you failed to make entries in any section of the interview, no check mark appears on the tab to the right.

You can click any side tab to return to an interview section. If you can't face it now (and I can't blame you), you can always return to the EasyStep Interview by choosing File | EasyStep Interview from the menu system.

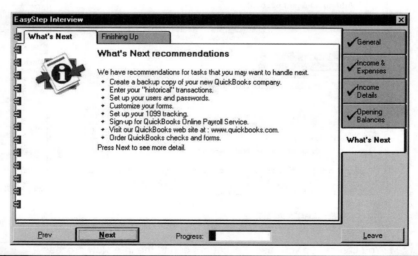

FIGURE 1-8   Here's a list of things you still need to do

Choose Leave to close the EasyStep Interview and start working in the QuickBooks window. (You may see some messages first, such as a reminder to set up users and passwords if you indicated that more than one person would work on this computer.)

Performing a Manual Setup

If you opt to leave the EasyStep Interview after the point at which you save your company data with a filename, you can use the QuickBooks menu system to turn on features and enter data.

This section reviews the method for turning on features. Then, in Chapter 2, you can learn how to enter the basic data that QuickBooks needs.

Choose Edit | Preferences from the menu bar to select the QuickBooks features you want to use. The Preferences dialog box appears, as shown in Figure 1-9.

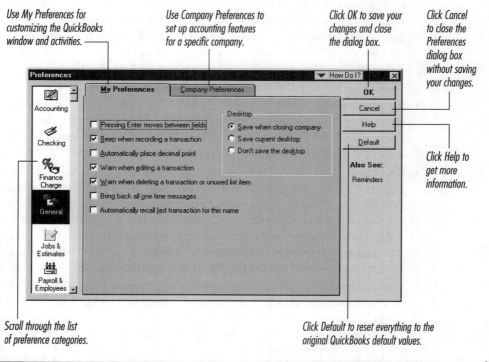

Use My Preferences for customizing the QuickBooks window and activities.

Use Company Preferences to set up accounting features for a specific company.

Click OK to save your changes and close the dialog box.

Click Cancel to close the Preferences dialog box without saving your changes.

Click Help to get more information.

Scroll through the list of preference categories.

Click Default to reset everything to the original QuickBooks default values.

FIGURE 1-9 Use the Preferences dialog box to select and deselect the features you want to use

For this discussion, you won't be using the My Preferences tab, but you can read Chapter 21 to learn how to set these preferences. In fact, the accounting preferences discussed here don't offer choices in the My Preferences tab. The following sections offer some guidelines for establishing the features you want to use in QuickBooks, using the Company Preferences tab.

- **Accounting Preferences**   Specify whether or not you want to use account numbers (a good idea). Also, you can indicate whether you want to use classes (see Chapter 21 for more information) and whether you want to keep an audit trail. An *audit trail* is a list of changes made to transactions, and if you turn this feature on, you may notice a small slowdown in the software. However, it's sometimes handy to track changes, particularly if you need to be reminded why some numbers have changed in your reports.

- **Checking Preferences**   You can choose what you want to print on check vouchers (stubs), and decide the way you want to date checks (when you fill in the data or when you actually print the check).

- **Finance Charge Preferences**   Use this dialog box to turn on finance charges for late-paying customers. You can set a default rate and the circumstances under which finance charges are assessed.

- **Jobs and Estimates Preferences**   This is the place to configure estimating and progress billing (billing a percentage of the price of a job as you reach a percentage of completion), if you need it. You can also configure the language you want to use for describing the status of jobs.

- **Purchases and Vendors Preferences**   Use this dialog box to turn on inventory and purchase orders. You have to enable both features; you can't pick only one of them, but you don't actually have to use purchase orders. You also configure the way you handle bills and bill paying.

- **Sales and Customers Preferences**   Here's where you establish your shipping preferences and the default markup on inventory products. In addition, you can configure the way you want to handle reimbursed expenses. One of the important preference options on this dialog box is whether or not you want to apply customer payments automatically or manually. This really means that if the feature is turned on, customer payments are applied starting with the oldest invoice first. I've found that this frequently doesn't work well, because customers skip invoices that they want to contend (the product didn't arrive, or it arrived damaged, or they think the price is wrong). I find that if you apply the payments against the invoices manually, you have a more accurate record of payments. Most customers are applying the payment to one of your specific invoices when they cut the check, so if you follow their lead, you and your customer will have identical payment records.

If you don't apply payments by invoice and use balance-forward billing, it's okay to leave the automatic application feature turned on.

- **Sales Tax Preferences**   This is the place to turn sales tax on (or off). You must also specify when you have to remit the sales tax to the taxing authority, as well as whether the tax is due when it's charged or collected (check the state law).
- **Tax 1099 Preferences**   If you pay subcontractors and need to send 1099 MISC forms at the end of the year, this is the dialog box to use for configuration (see Figure 1-10).

 C A U T I O N :   You cannot use the same account for multiple 1099 categories. You must select (or create) a specific account for each 1099 box you use.

After you configure your 1099 form, you must remember to specify the 1099 check box in each applicable vendor card. See Chapter 2 for information on setting up vendors.

As you go through the dialog boxes, each time you make a change and move to the next category, you're asked whether you want to save the changes in the

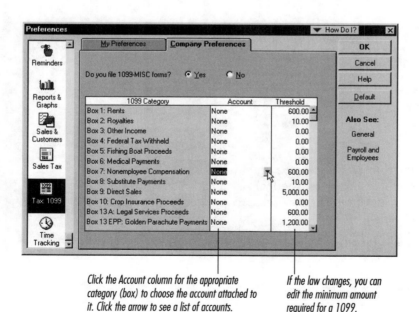

Click the Account column for the appropriate category (box) to choose the account attached to it. Click the arrow to see a list of accounts.

If the law changes, you can edit the minimum amount required for a 1099.

FIGURE 1-10   Configure your 1099 forms

category you just completed. Answer Yes. When you're finished with all the categories, choose OK to close the Preferences dialog box.

These are the important system categories, and if you've completed them, you're ready to finish your manual setup. Chapter 2 introduces you to all the lists you need to enter.

The QuickBooks Software Window

When the EasyStep Interview window closes, you're in the standard QuickBooks software window shown in Figure 1-11.

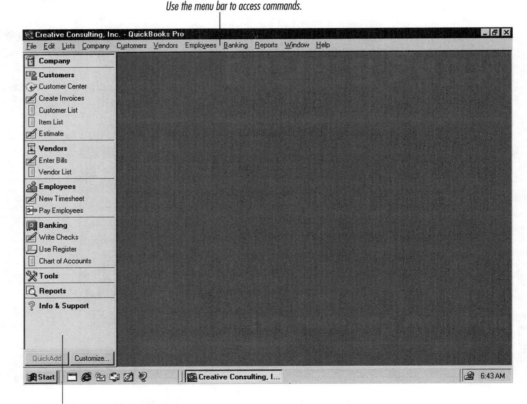

Use the menu bar to access commands.

Use the Navigation Bar to access features by category.

FIGURE 1-11 The QuickBooks window is designed for easy navigation

The Navigation Bar is divided into sections that correspond to the QuickBooks functions. The first listing in each section is bold, and clicking it opens a navigation window for that feature (see Figure 1-12). Selecting any other listing opens the appropriate window or dialog box.

You can add functions to the Navigation Bar quite easily. See Chapter 21 to learn how to customize the Navigation Bar. To exit QuickBooks, click the X in the upper-right corner or press ALT-F4.

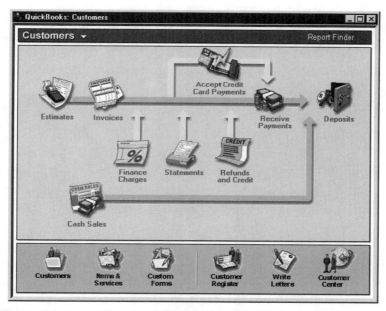

FIGURE 1-12 Select a bold listing to open a navigation window for that function

Setting Up Your Lists

In *this chapter, you will learn to...*

- Create a full chart of accounts

- Enter all your lists

- Invent your own fields to make your lists more useful

Chapter 2

In this chapter, we're going to cover a lot of basic chores. They aren't terribly exciting or creative, but if you don't do them now, you'll regret it later. That's because every time you enter a transaction or fill out a form, you'll have to enter some basic data at the same time. Talk about annoying! So take the time now to get the basic data into the system. This is the preparation stuff, the work that makes future work faster and more efficient.

 TIP: Each of the lists you create in QuickBooks has its own List window, and when you view the items in a list, you can sort the list by any column in the window. Just click the column heading to sort the list by the category of that column.

Creating a Full Chart of Accounts

The first priority is your chart of accounts. QuickBooks created some accounts for you during the initial setup of your company, but most people need lots of additional accounts in order to keep books accurately.

Using Numbers for Accounts

As we go through the entry of accounts, remember that I'm using numbers as the primary element in my chart of accounts. There's a title attached to the number, but the primary method of sorting my account list is the number. Even though the QuickBooks default is to use names, it's a simple matter to change the default and use numbers. Your accountant will be grateful and you'll find you have far fewer mistakes in posting to the general ledger.

To switch to a number format for your accounts, you just need to spend a couple of seconds changing the QuickBooks preferences:

1. Choose Edit | Preferences from the menu bar to bring up the Preferences dialog box.
2. Select the Accounting icon from the scroll box.
3. Click the Company Preferences tab to see the choices shown in Figure 2-1.

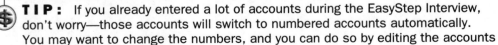 **TIP:** If you already entered a lot of accounts during the EasyStep Interview, don't worry—those accounts will switch to numbered accounts automatically. You may want to change the numbers, and you can do so by editing the accounts (which is covered here).

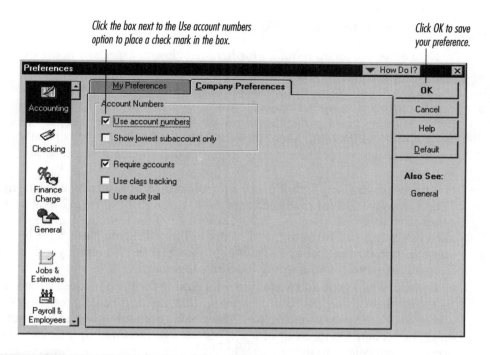

Click the box next to the Use account numbers option to place a check mark in the box.

Click OK to save your preference.

| **FIGURE 2-1** | Change the accounting options to enable numbers for your chart of accounts |

Now that you've set up numbered accounts, you have a more efficient chart of accounts, and you, your bookkeeper, and your accountant will have an easier time.

Numbers give you a quick clue about the type of account you're working with. As you enter the accounts, you must use the numbers intelligently, assigning numbers to account types. You should check with your accountant before finalizing the way you use the numbers, but there's a common approach that you might find helpful. You can have as many as seven numbers (plus a title) for each account and, in this example, I'll use four numbers:

- 1*xxx* Assets
- 2*xxx* Liabilities
- 3*xxx* Equity
- 4*xxx* Revenue
- 5*xxx* Expenses
- 6*xxx* Expenses
- 7*xxx* Expenses

- 8*xxx* Expenses
- 9*xxx* Other Revenue and Expenses

Notice the amount of room for further breakdowns, especially in the expenses. (You always need more expense categories than revenue categories.)

You can, if you wish, have a variety of expense types and reserve the starting number for specific types. Many companies, for example, use 5*xxx* for sales expenses (they even separate the payroll postings between the salespersons and the rest of the employees), then use 6*xxx* through 7*xxx* for general operating expenses, and 8*xxx* for other specific expenses that should appear together in reports.

Also, as an example, think about the breakdown of assets. You might use 1000 through 1099 for cash accounts, 1100 through 1199 for receivables and other current assets, then use 1200 through 1299 for tracking fixed assets such as equipment, furniture, and so on. Follow the same pattern for liabilities, starting with current liabilities, moving to long term. (It's also a good idea to keep all the payroll withholding liabilities together.)

Usually, you should add accounts by increasing the previous account number by ten, so that if your first bank account is 1000, the next bank account is 1010, and so on. For expenses (where you'll have many accounts), you might want to enter the accounts in intervals of five. This gives you room to squeeze in additional accounts that belong in the same general area of your chart of accounts when they need to be added later.

Using Names for Accounts

Okay, I didn't convince you, or your accountant is just as happy with names for accounts. Or, you've imported your accounts from another software application and you cannot bear the thought of changing all that data. Here's how to avoid the pitfalls that named accounts throw in your path: Make rules about naming and using accounts, and stick to those rules.

This means that when you name an account, you keep the naming convention consistent, and you use the same abbreviations and shortcuts all the time. I have been in too many offices where I found accounts with names such as these in one chart of accounts:

- Telephone Exp
- Exps-Telephone
- Tele Expense
- Telephone & Answering Serv
- Tele and Ans Service

You get the idea, and I'll bet you're not shocked to hear that every one of those accounts had amounts posted to them. That's because users "guess" at account names and point and click on whatever they see that seems remotely related. If they don't find the account the way they would have entered the name, they invent a new one. Avoid all of those errors by establishing rules about searching the account list before applying a transaction.

Adding Your List of Accounts

After you've done your homework, made your decisions, and checked with your accountant, entering a whole slew of accounts is a piece of cake:

1. Click the Chart of Accounts item in the Navigation Bar (or choose Lists | Chart of Accounts from the menu bar), which displays the Chart of Accounts List window, as shown in Figure 2-2.
2. Press CTRL-N to enter a new account. The New Account dialog box opens so you can begin entering information.
3. Click the down arrow to the right of the Type box and select an account type from the drop-down list.

The dialog box for entering a new account changes its appearance depending on the account type, because different types of accounts require different information. In addition, if you've opted to use numbers for your accounts, there's an extra field for the account number. (Figure 2-3 shows a blank New Account dialog box for an Expense account.)

Here are some guidelines for entering account information:

- Use consistent protocols for the account name, abbreviating words in the same manner throughout the entire list of accounts.

FIGURE 2-2 The Chart of Accounts List is a simple list of the accounts you're using for your QuickBooks system

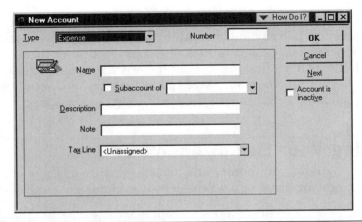

FIGURE 2-3 The only required entries for a new account are a number (if you're using numbers) and a name

- If you are using subaccounts, you can assign the subaccount to an existing account, or create a new parent account while you're configuring the subaccount.

- The Description field is optional, and I've found that unless there's a compelling reason to explain the account, it just makes your account lists busier and harder to read.

- Many of the balance sheet accounts have a field named Bank No., which you use to record the account number for the bank attached to that account. If the account is an asset or liability account that's unconnected to a bank, skip the field.

- Accounts that don't have a Bank No. field have a Note field, which I've never found a really good use for.

- The Tax Line field is used to assign an account to an IRS form and line number. You can assign a tax line during this entry process or wait until the end of the year and do it in one fell swoop (see Chapter 17).

  If you're not currently using this account, you can select the Account is Inactive option, which means the account won't be available for posting amounts. Entering a new account and marking it inactive immediately means you're really good at planning ahead. (Okay, I really wanted to say "you're compulsive.")

- Some account types (those connected to banks) have a field for an opening balance. Don't worry about it during this initial entry of new accounts.

The priority is to get all of your accounts into the system; you don't have to worry about balances now. In fact, the fastest and easiest way to put the account balances into the system is to enter an opening trial balance as a journal entry (see Appendix A).

As you finish entering each account, choose Next to move to another blank New Account dialog box. When you're finished entering accounts, click OK and then close the Chart of Accounts List window by clicking the X in the upper-right corner.

TIP: If you need to make changes to any of the account information, select the account and press CTRL-E. The Edit Account dialog box appears, which looks just like the account card you filled out. Just make your changes and click OK to save them.

Entering Your Customer List

In QuickBooks, customers and jobs are handled together. In fact, QuickBooks doesn't call the list a Customer List, it calls it a Customer:Job List. You can create a customer and consider anything and everything you invoice to that customer a single job, or you can have multiple jobs for the same customer.

The truth is that most small businesses don't have to worry about jobs; it's just the customer that's tracked. But if you're a building contractor or subcontractor, an interior decorator, or some other kind of service provider who usually bills by the job instead of at an hourly rate for an ongoing service, you might want to try tracking jobs. For example, I find it useful and informative to track income by jobs (books) instead of customers (publishers).

Jobs don't stand alone as an entity in QuickBooks; they are attached to customers, and you can attach as many jobs to a single customer as you need to. If you are going to track jobs, it's a good idea to enter all the customers first (now) and then attach the jobs later.

If you enter your existing customers now, when you're first starting to use QuickBooks, all the other work connected to the customer is much easier. It's annoying to have to stop in the middle of every invoice you enter to create a new customer record.

Entering a New Customer

Putting all of your existing customers into the system takes very little effort:

1. Press CTRL-J to open the Customer:Job List window, or click the Customer List entry in the Navigation Bar.
2. Press CTRL-N to open a blank customer card and fill in the information for the customer (see Figure 2-4).

Using the Customer Name Efficiently

Consider the Customer field a code rather than just the billing name. It doesn't appear on your invoices. (The invoices print the company name and the primary contact name.)

You must invent a protocol for this Customer field so that you'll enter every customer in the same manner. Notice the Customer field in Figure 2-4. This customer code entry has no apostrophe, even though the client name contains an apostrophe. Avoiding punctuation and spaces in codes is a good protocol for filling in code fields.

Your lists and reports use this field to sort your customer list, so if you want it alphabetized, you must make sure you use the last name if there's no company name. Each customer must have a unique entry in this field, so if you have a lot of customers named Jack Johnson, you may want to enter them as JohnsonJack001, JohnsonJack002, and so on.

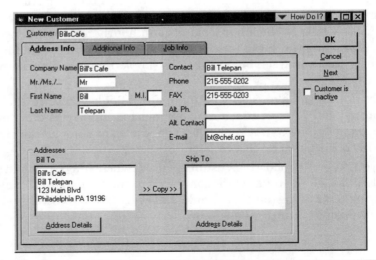

FIGURE 2-4   The customer card has plenty of fields for detailed information

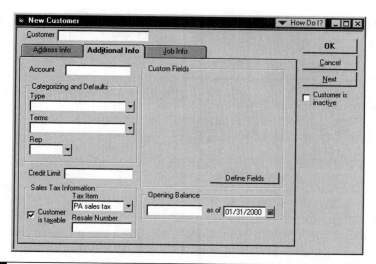

FIGURE 2-5 Entering additional information can make reports and analysis more accurate

Using the Additional Info Tab

The information you enter in the Additional Info tab of a customer card (see Figure 2-5) ranges from essential to convenient. It's worth spending the time to design some rules for the way data is entered. (Remember, making rules ensures consistency, without which you'll have difficulty getting the reports you want.)

Let's spend a minute going over the fields in this tab:

- **Account** is an optional field you can use to invent an account number for the customer. It's far easier to use the data in the Customer field, but you can invent account numbers if you wish.

- **Type** is an internal field you can use to sort your customers. For example, you may have wholesale and retail customers. To use the field, click the arrow to see a list of types that have been entered, along with an entry to create a new type.

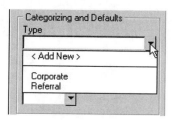

- **Terms** is, of course, payment terms. Click the arrow to the right of the text box to see the terms that are already defined, or define a new one.

TIP: You don't have to use the Terms box if you offer the same payment terms to every customer. Instead, you can have your terms printed on your invoice form (for example, "Payment due upon receipt" or "Pay within 10 days to avoid a finance charge").

- **Rep** means sales representative. If you pay commissions (or just want to know which employee is in charge of this customer), you can use the field. QuickBooks assumes the rep is an employee, so clicking the arrow to the right of the field brings up your Employee List (if you've entered it) or a blank employee card so you can record this rep as an employee. If your reps are not employees (an *employee* is defined as someone for whom you deduct taxes and report on to local and federal tax bureaus), you cannot use this field. In fact, if your reps are not employees and you send them 1099 forms, consider using the Type field for rep information (or create a custom field as described later in this chapter).
- **Credit Limit** is a way to establish a number that works as a threshold. If a customer places an order, and the new order, combined with any unpaid invoices, exceeds the threshold, you should reject the order (or ship it COD).

TIP: If you aren't going to enforce the credit limit, don't bother to use the field.

- **Sales Tax Information** uses several fields in this tab. If the customer is liable for sales tax, click the arrow to the right of the Tax Item box to select the sales tax authority and rate (if you collect multiple sales taxes). If no sales tax is entered, choose <Add New> to bring up a sales tax list blank form. If the customer does not pay sales tax, deselect the option and enter the Resale Number provided by the customer (handy to have when the state tax investigators pop in for a surprise audit).

- **Opening Balance** can be used to enter the balance due to you, and it's accompanied by a date field, which you can use to enter the date for which this balance due is valid. If you don't want to use this field, you can enter an invoice to represent the unpaid balance. In fact, you can enter multiple invoices if you want detailed records on the balance.

- **Custom Fields** are your opportunity to invent fields for sorting and arranging your QuickBooks lists. (See the section on using custom fields at the end of this chapter.)

When you have finished filling out the fields (remember, we're skipping the Job Info tab for now), choose Next to move to another blank customer card so you can enter the next customer. When you have finished entering all of your customers, click OK.

Editing Customer Records

You can make changes to the information in a customer record quite easily. Open the Customer List and select the customer record you want to change. Press CTRL-E to open the customer card.

When you open the customer card, you can change any information, or fill in data you didn't have when you first created the customer entry. In fact, you can fill in data you *did* have but didn't bother to enter. (Some people find it's faster to enter just the customer name and company name when they're creating their customer lists, and then fill in the rest at their leisure or the first time they invoice the customer.)

However, there are several things I want you to note about editing the customer card:

- Don't mess with the Customer field.
- Take notice that there's a button named Notes on the card.
- You can't enter an opening balance.

Unless you've reinvented the protocol you're using to enter data in the Customer field, don't change this data. Many high-end (translate that as "expensive and incredibly powerful") accounting software applications lock this field and never permit changes. QuickBooks lets you change it, so you have to impose controls on yourself.

Click the Notes icon to open a notepad that's dedicated to this customer, as shown in Figure 2-6. This is a useful feature, and I'll bet you use it frequently.

The notepad is a great marketing tool, because you can use it to follow-up on a promised order, track a customer's special preferences, and notify the customer when something special is available. Don't forget to use the To Do list to nag about unpaid invoices.

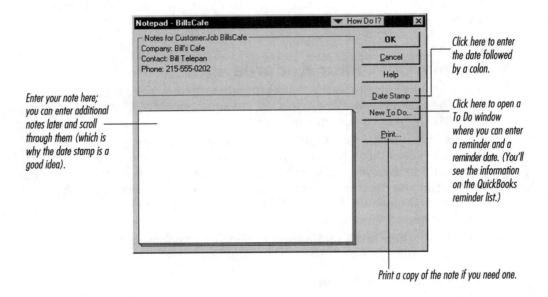

Enter your note here; you can enter additional notes later and scroll through them (which is why the date stamp is a good idea).

Click here to enter the date followed by a colon.

Click here to open a To Do window where you can enter a reminder and a reminder date. (You'll see the information on the QuickBooks reminder list.)

Print a copy of the note if you need one.

FIGURE 2-6   QuickBooks gives you a notepad for each customer, which you can use for all sorts of handy information and reminders

Configuring Protocols
for Customer Records

WeRWound is a manufacturer of videotape-rewinding machines. The people at WeRWound sell their products all over the country, and most of their customers are video stores. When they began planning their QuickBooks installation, there was major concern about tracking their customers accurately and easily.

The big problem was that they have thousands of customers, and 80 percent of them are named Video*SomethingOrOther*. There are lots of VideoHuts, VideoPalaces, and other similar incarnations.

Their manual invoicing system required lots of double-checking, which was time-consuming and frequently failed. Orders were taken over the phone by telemarketers, and then the orders had to be passed around the office, through the accounts receivable department, the sales department, and anyone else who could say "yes, that's the right VideoHut store." The telemarketers pulled an index card when the order came in, but the system's frequent failures resulted from the fact that sometimes the wrong card was pulled. Also, if the card couldn't be located quickly, telemarketers assumed that the customer didn't exist in the system, and a new index card was created. Now there were two sets of cards for the same customer, and the accounts receivable people went crazy trying to send invoices and statements, apply payments, and track credit limits.

The solution this company devised for using the customer code to assure accurate records is quite inventive. It's also foolproof. They use the customer's telephone number, including the area code. This is an absolutely unique identifier for any business (or for any individual). For example, a VideoHut in Philadelphia has a customer code similar to 215551234, VideoHut in Berkeley has the customer code 5105559876, and so on.

No matter who calls to place the order, that person knows his or her telephone number. (Have you ever asked a customer if they know their customer number with your company?) If an order arrives by mail, the WeRWound order form (which is mailed out as part of their marketing mailings and also appears in trade magazine ads) has a line for the telephone number that is marked "required information."

Entering Your Vendor List

The vendors you purchase goods and services from have to be entered into your QuickBooks system, and it's far easier to do it now. Otherwise, every time you want to write a check, you'll have to go through the process of establishing the vendor and entering all the important information.

Choose Vendor List from the Navigation Bar to open the Vendor List window, and then press CTRL-N to open a New Vendor card and fill out the fields (see Figure 2-7).

As with customers, you should have a set of rules about entering the information in the Vendor field. This field doesn't appear on checks or purchase orders; it's used to sort and select vendors when you need a list or a report. Think of it as a code. Notice that in Figure 2-7, the code is a telephone number, but the vendor is the telephone company. This is how I create separate checks for each telephone bill I receive.

The Address field is important if you're planning to print checks. You can purchase window envelopes, and when you insert the check in the envelope, the vendor name and address is in the right spot.

The Additional Info tab for vendors has only three really important categories:

- **Payment terms**   Enter the terms for payment this vendor has assigned to you.
- **1099 status**   If appropriate, select the check box for Vendor Eligible for 1099.
- **Account**   Enter your account number with this vendor (to the vendor, it's your customer number) and the number will appear in the memo field of printed checks.

The other fields are optional.

After you fill in the information, choose Next to move to the next blank card and enter the next vendor. When you're finished, click OK.

Later, when you view or edit a vendor card, you'll find a Notes icon just like the one in the customer card.

Entering the Payroll Lists

If you plan to use QuickBooks for payroll, you must enter all of your employees, including their pertinent tax information. In order to do that, you have to define the tax information, which requires you to define the items that make up the payroll check. This means you have two lists to create—the payroll items and the employees. I'm assuming all the vendors who receive checks from the payroll system have been entered into your Vendor List (the IRS, the insurance companies,

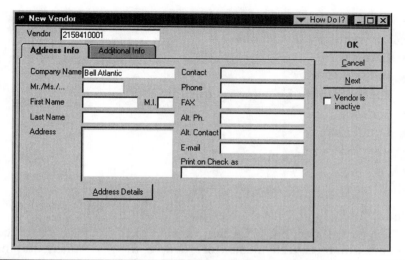

FIGURE 2-7 Vendor cards are less complicated than customer cards

and so on). And your chart of accounts should have all the accounts you need in order to post payroll items.

 TIP: If you've neglected to add a vendor or account, you can add whatever you need while you're entering the payroll lists. Just select <Add New> from any drop-down list.

Entering Payroll Items

The number of individual elements that go into a paycheck may be larger than you thought. Consider this list, which is typical of many businesses:

- Salaries
- Wages (hourly)
- Overtime
- Doubletime
- Federal tax withholdings (including FIT, FICA, and Medicare)
- State tax withholdings
- State unemployment and disability withholdings
- Local tax withholdings
- Pension plan deductions

- Medical insurance deductions
- Life insurance deductions
- Garnishes
- Union dues
- Reimbursement for auto expenses
- Bonuses
- Commissions
- Vacation pay
- Sick pay
- Advanced Earned Income Credit

Whew! And you may have some other element that I haven't listed.

Each payroll item has to be defined and linked to the chart of accounts. The vendors who receive payments (for example, the government and insurance companies) have to be entered and linked to the payroll item. Oh yes, don't forget about employer payments (FICA, Medicare, SUTA, and FUTA).

To create or add to your list of payroll items (you may have some items listed as a result of your EasyStep Interview), choose Lists | Payroll Item List from the menu bar.

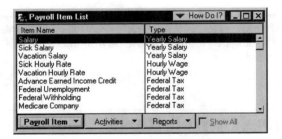

 TIP: You can add the Payroll Item List (or any other task) to your Navigation Bar. See Chapter 21 to learn how.

Scroll through the list, and if anything is missing, add it now by pressing CTRL-N to open the Add new payroll item wizard shown in Figure 2-8.

There are some tricks and tips you should be aware of as you fill out the wizard windows to enter payroll items:

- Many state taxes are already listed in the wizard.
- You'll have to enter your local (city or township) taxes manually.

- For deductions, the wizard will ask about the vendor who receives this money. (It's called an agency, but it's a vendor.)
- If you want the employer contributions to pension, health insurance, life insurance, and so on to appear on the payroll check stubs, you must enter those items as payroll items.
- When you enter a pension deduction, you must make sure to specify the taxes that are *not* calculated (I said *calculated*, not *deducted*) before you deduct the new payroll item. If you forget one, the paychecks and deductions may be incorrect. Figure 2-9 shows the Taxes window presented by the wizard, which assumes a pre-tax deduction. Some plans permit employees to choose between pre- and post-tax deductions. Some states have pre-tax deduction allowances. Just check with your accountant before checking off additional taxes.

When you have entered all your payroll items, you're ready to move on to the next step in entering your payroll information.

Create a Template

There is a great deal of information to fill out for each employee, and some of it is probably the same for all or most of your employees. You may have many employees who share the same hourly wage, or the same deductions for medical insurance.

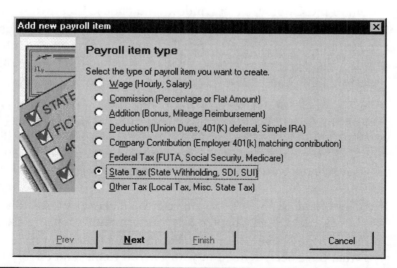

FIGURE 2-8 Select the type of item you want to add, and then click Next to kick off the wizard

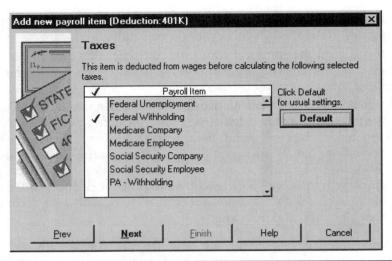

FIGURE 2-9 Check off the taxes that are not calculated before this deduction

To avoid entering the same information over and over, you can create a template and then apply the information to all the employees who match that data. You'll save yourself lots of time, even if some employees require one or two entries that differ from the template.

To get to the template, you have to start with the Employee List. Choose Lists | Employee List from the menu bar. Then click the Employee button at the bottom of the Employee List window, and choose Employee Defaults.

When the Employee Defaults window opens (see Figure 2-10), you can enter the data that applies to most or all of your employees. The information you put into the template is used in the Payroll Info tab for each employee (discussed in the next section).

- Enter the **Pay Period**. Use the arrow to the right of the field to see a list of choices and select your payroll frequency. The available choices are Daily; Weekly; Biweekly; Semimonthly; Monthly; Quarterly; and Yearly. That should suffice, but if you're planning to pay your employees with some unusual scheme, you're out of luck, because you cannot create a new choice for this field.

- The **Class field** can be used if you've created classes for tracking your QuickBooks data. (See Chapter 21 for information on using classes.)

- In the top **Item Name column,** click the arrow to see a list of earnings types that have been defined in your Payroll Items, and choose the one that is suitable for a template.

- In the **Hour/Annual Rate column**, enter a wage or salary figure if there's one that applies to most of your employees. If there's not, just skip it and enter each employee's rate on the individual employee card.
- If you're using **QuickBooks' time-tracking features** to pay your employees, check that box. See Chapter 19 to learn how to transfer time tracking into your payroll records.
- If all or most of your employees have the same additional adjustments (such as insurance deductions, 401(k) deductions, or reimbursement for car expenses), click the arrow in the **Item Name column** to select the appropriate adjustments.
- Click the **Taxes button** to see a list of taxes and select those that are common and therefore suited for the template (usually all or most of them).
- Click the **Sick/Vacation button** to set the terms for accruing sick time and vacation time if your policy is broad enough to include it in the template.

When you are finished filling out the template, click OK to save it and return to the Employee List window.

Entering Employees

Finally, you're ready to tell QuickBooks about your list of employees. Press CTRL-N to bring up a New Employee form (see Figure 2-11).

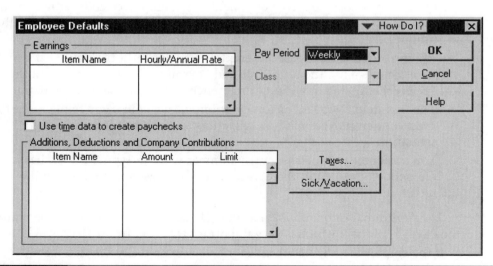

FIGURE 2-10 Use the template to avoid the boredom of entering the same information over and over again when you enter your employees

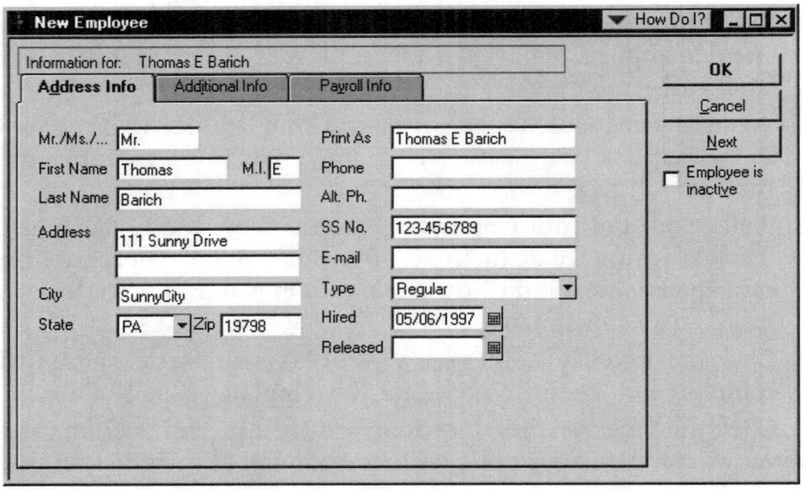

FIGURE 2-11 Enter employee information carefully, because there's no room for error here

Entering Basic Information

The tabs on the employee card have lots of fields, not all of which are necessary. It's probably a good idea for me to indicate what's unimportant, important, and incredibly important on the employee record card:

- QuickBooks does not give you a field for an employee code. However, the payroll list is kept by social security number (which is, of course, totally unique).

- When you need reports about employees, you can sort by either the first or last name—use the Employee and Payroll preferences section of the Preferences dialog box (Edit | Preferences) to make that determination.

- The first field (Mr./Ms.) is totally unimportant unless you're planning to send your employees mail-merge letters and you need the title for the salutation.

- You can enter the social security number without typing the dashes; QuickBooks will enter them as soon as you press TAB to move to the next field.

The Additional Info tab is sparse and self-explanatory, so let's move on to the Payroll Info tab, which is very important (see Figure 2-12).

If the employee's pay matches the information already filled in from the template, you can skip the earnings and deductions columns. However, if the employee has additional compensation or deductions on his or her paycheck, fill them in now. For example, there may be a commission due every week. Or, there may be a deduction for a garnish or a loan from the company.

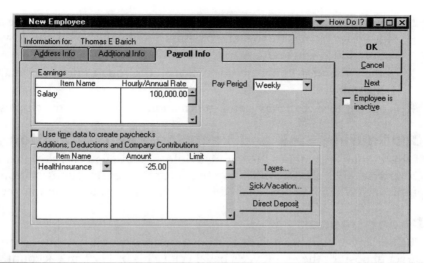

FIGURE 2-12 The stuff from my template is already filled in, so there's almost nothing to do

If the amount of the additional income or the deduction is the same every week, enter an amount. If it differs from week to week, don't enter an amount on the employee card. (You'll enter it when you create the payroll check.)

Configuring Employee Tax Status

If the employee tax status matches the template you created, you don't have to reenter the data, but you should check the data to make sure.

1. Click the Taxes button to open the Taxes dialog box, which starts with federal tax information, as shown here.

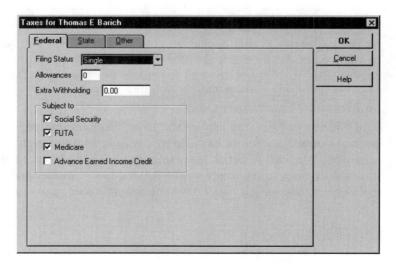

2. Move to the State tab and configure the employee's status for the state. This varies from state to state, of course, and you should check with your accountant if you aren't sure of something you find there.

3. In the Other tab, apply any local payroll tax you've entered that applies to this employee.

4. Click OK to save the tax status information and return to the employee card.

Configuring Sick and Vacation Pay Information

If this employee matches the template information, you can skip this section. Otherwise, click the Sick/Vacation button and enter the configuration for this employee. When you are finished, click OK to return to the employee card.

Direct Deposit

The employee card has a Direct Deposit button, which you can use to establish direct deposit of the employee's paycheck to his or her bank account. The button won't work until you've set up direct deposit as an online feature. See Chapter 8 to learn how to use direct deposit.

Click Next to move to the next blank card and enter the next employee. When you've entered all of your employees, click OK. Congratulations, you did it!

Entering Items

If you are a service business, this is going to be a snap. If you sell a few items, it'll be pretty easy. If you have a large inventory, get a cup of coffee or a soda or take a bathroom break, because this is going to take some time.

Understanding Items

Items are the things that appear on your invoices when you send an invoice to a customer. If you think about it, that's a bit more complicated than it might appear. Do you charge sales tax? If you do, that's an item. Do you subtotal sections of your invoices? That subtotal is an item. Do you show prepayments or discounts? They're items, too.

While you can issue an invoice that says "Net amount due for services rendered" or "Net amount due for items delivered," your customers aren't going to be very happy with the lack of detail. More important, when you try to analyze your business in order to see where you're making lots of money and where you're making less money, you won't have enough information to determine the facts.

This is another setup chore that requires some planning. Each of your items must have a code, a unique identification (QuickBooks calls that the Item Name or Number). Try to create a system that has some logic to it, so your codes are recognizable when you see them listed.

Understanding Item Types

It isn't always clear how and when some of the item types are used (or why you must define them). Here are some guidelines you can use as you plan the names for your items:

- **Service**   A service you provide to a customer. You can create services that are charged by the job or by the hour.
- **Non-inventory Part**   A product you don't stock in inventory, or don't track even though it's in your inventory warehouse. Most of the time, you use this item type to buy products that you don't sell, such as office supplies. It's only needed if you use purchase orders when you order these items, and if you only use purchase orders for inventory items, you don't have to create any items of this type.

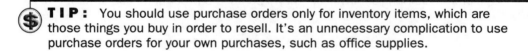

TIP: You should use purchase orders only for inventory items, which are those things you buy in order to resell. It's an unnecessary complication to use purchase orders for your own purchases, such as office supplies.

- **Other Charge**   You'll need this item type for things like shipping charges, or other line items that appear on your invoices. In fact, some people create one for each method of shipping.
- **Subtotal**   This item type adds up everything that comes before it. It's used to give a subtotal before you add shipping charges, or subtract any discounts or prepayments.
- **Group**   This item type is a clever device. You can use it to enter a group of items (all of which must exist) at once. For example, if you frequently have a shipping charge and sales tax on the same invoice, you can create a group item that includes those two items.
- **Discount**   You can't give a customer a discount as a line item if the item type doesn't exist. You may have more than one item that falls within this item type; for example, a discount for wholesale customers and a discount

for a volume purchase. When you enter the item, you can indicate a percentage as the rate.

TIP: I have a revenue item in my chart of accounts called "customer discounts," and items are posted there as discounts instead of as expenses. (This system gives me a better picture of my revenue.) Check with your accountant about the best method for posting discounts.

- **Payment** If you receive a prepayment (either a total payment or a deposit), you must indicate it as a line item. You can use this item type to do that (or you can create a prepayment item as a discount if you prefer).
- **Sales Tax Item** Create one of these item types for each sales tax authority for which you collect.
- **Sales Tax Group** This is for multiple sales taxes that appear on the same invoice.

REMEMBER: Even though I've described all of the item types in terms of their use on your invoices, they'll be used on your purchase orders, too.

Entering the Data for Items

To put your items into the system, choose Lists | Item List from the menu bar. When the Item List window opens, any items that were created during your EasyStep Interview are listed.

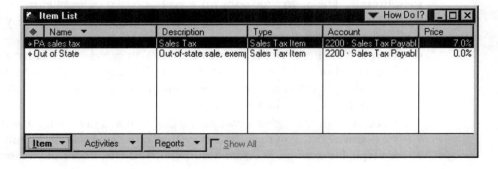

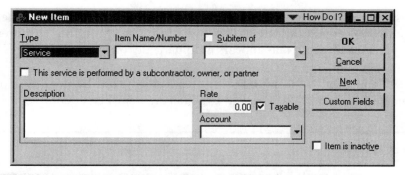

FIGURE 2-13 All the information you need to buy, sell, and generate reports about the item is contained in the fields

To create an item, press CTRL-N. The New Item window opens, as shown in Figure 2-13.

Click the arrow next to the Type field and choose a type from the drop-down list. The list includes calculation items in addition to actual items.

NOTE: The fields in the New Item window may change, depending on the item type you select.

The Item Name/Number field is the place to insert a unique identifying code for the item. When you are filling out invoices (or purchase orders), this is the listing you see in the drop-down list.

After you've created an item, you can create subitems. For example, if you sell shoes as an item, you can create subitems for dress shoes, sneakers, boots, and so on. Or, use the subitems to describe a parent item that comes in a variety of colors.

You can enter a rate for those items that you've priced, and leave the rate at zero for the items you want to price when you are preparing the invoice (usually service items). You can also create a rate that's a percentage, and QuickBooks will calculate it. Don't worry; nothing is etched in stone—you can change any rate that appears automatically on an invoice.

When you complete the window, choose Next to move to the next blank New Item window. Don't forget to create at least one item for each of the calculation items. When you finish entering items, click OK.

Entering Jobs

If you plan to track jobs, you can enter the ones you know about during this setup phase. Or, you can enter them as they come up.

Jobs are attached to customers; they can't stand alone. To create a job, press CTRL-J or choose Customer List from the Navigation Bar. When the Customer:Job List window opens, select the customer for whom you're creating a job. Click the Customer:Job button at the bottom of the Customer:Job List window and choose Add Job from the drop-down menu. This opens the New Job window, shown in Figure 2-14.

Create a name for the job (you can use up to 29 characters) and make it descriptive enough for both you and your customer to understand it.

The Additional Info tab is related to the customer (in fact, it *is* the Additional Info tab for the customer card), so you can skip it.

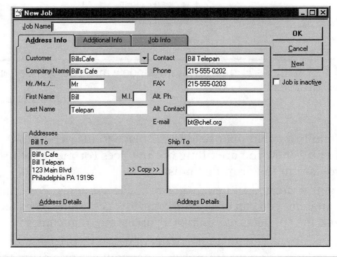

FIGURE 2-14 You only have to create a job name; everything else is filled in from the customer data

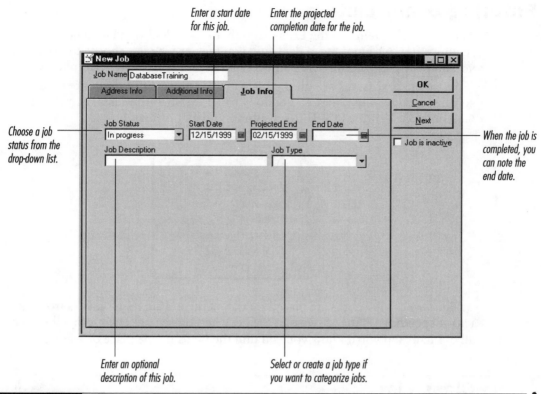

Enter a start date for this job.

Enter the projected completion date for the job.

Choose a job status from the drop-down list.

When the job is completed, you can note the end date.

Enter an optional description of this job.

Select or create a job type if you want to categorize jobs.

FIGURE 2-15 The important stuff about a job is on the Job Info tab

Move to the Job Info tab (see Figure 2-15) to begin configuring this job.

When you finish entering all the data, choose Next if you want to create another job for the same customer. Otherwise, click OK to close the New Job window and return to the Customer:Job List window. The jobs you create for a customer become part of the customer listing.

• Entering Other Lists

There are a few items on the Lists menu that I haven't covered in detail. They don't require extensive amounts of data, and you may or may not choose to use them. If you do plan to use them, here's an overview of the things you need to know.

Some of these items are on the Lists menu and some of them are on a submenu called Customer & Vendor Profile Lists (in the Lists menu). Your Customer & Vendor Profile Lists submenu may not match mine.

```
Sales Rep List
Customer Type List
Vendor Type List
Job Type List
Terms List
Customer Message List
Payment Method List
Ship Via List
```

The way the list items are placed on the menu and submenu differs from user to user, depending on the answers in the EasyStep Interview. Therefore, I'll just cover all of them, and you'll know you can find the items in one place or another.

Class List

The Class List command appears on the Lists menu only if you've enabled the classes feature. Classes provide a method of organizing your activities (income and disbursement activities) to produce reports that you need. Many times, a well-designed chart of accounts will eliminate the need for classes, but if you do want to use them, you can create them ahead of time through the Lists menu.

It's a better idea to work with QuickBooks for a while and then, if you feel you need a report that can only be produced with the use of classes, create the class at that point. Chapter 21 covers the use of classes.

Other Names List

QuickBooks provides a list called Other Names, which is the list of people whose names come up but whose activity you don't want to track. This list will appear when you write checks, but the names are unavailable for invoices, purchase orders, and any other QuickBooks transaction type.

If there are several partners in your business, use this list for the checks you write to the partners' draw. If your business is a proprietorship, put yourself on the list to make sure your name is listed when you write your draw check.

When you open a New Name window, there are fields for the address (handy for printing checks), telephone numbers, and other contact information.

 TIP: Many people over-use this category and end up having to move these names to the Vendors List because they do need to track the activity. It's totally possible to use QuickBooks efficiently for years without using this list.

Memorized Transaction List

This list (which isn't really a list, but rather a collection of transactions) should be built as you go, instead of creating it as a list. QuickBooks has a nifty feature that memorizes a transaction you want to use again and again. Paying your rent is a good example. You can tell QuickBooks to memorize the transaction at the time you create it, instead of filling out this list in advance.

Customer Type List

When you created your customer list, you may have used the Customer Type field as a way to categorize the customer. This gives you the opportunity to sort and select customers in reports, perhaps to view the total income from specific types of customers.

You can predetermine the customer types you want to track by opening this list item and creating the types you need during setup. (Oops, it's too late if you've followed this chapter in order.) Or you can create them as you enter customers (as we did here).

Vendor Type List

See the previous paragraphs, substituting the word "vendor" for the word "customer."

Job Type List

You can set up categories for jobs by creating job types. For example, if you're a plumber, you may want to separate new construction from repairs.

Terms List

QuickBooks keeps all payment terms in one list, so your vendor terms and customer terms are all available when you need to enter terms in an invoice or a purchase order.

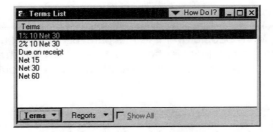

To enter a new terms listing, press CTRL-N to open the New Terms window, shown in Figure 2-16.

Customer Message List

If you like to write messages to your customers when you're creating an invoice, you can enter a bunch of appropriate messages ahead of time and

Give the new terms a
descriptive name.

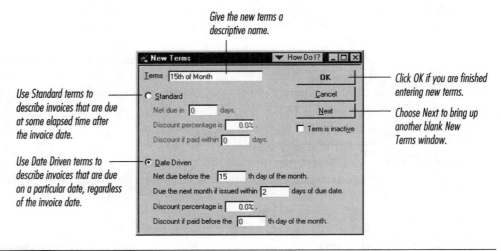

Use Standard terms to
describe invoices that are due
at some elapsed time after
the invoice date.

Use Date Driven terms to
describe invoices that are due
on a particular date, regardless
of the invoice date.

Click OK if you are finished
entering new terms.

Choose Next to bring up
another blank New
Terms window.

FIGURE 2-16 Name the new terms item and then configure it so QuickBooks can calculate it

then just select the one you want to use. In fact, QuickBooks provides some for you.

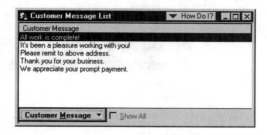

Press CTRL-N to enter a new message to add to the list. You just have to write the sentence—this is one of the easier lists to create.

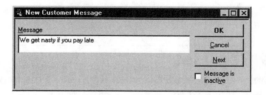

Payment Method List

You can track the way payments arrive from customers. This not only provides some detail (in case you're having a conversation with a customer about invoices and payments), but also allows you to print reports on payments that are subtotaled by the method of payment, such as credit card, check, cash, and so on. (Your bank may use the same subtotaling method, and that makes it easier to reconcile the account.)

QuickBooks provides some payment methods for you. In fact, you probably won't have to add any new methods unless you have customers who pay you with groceries or some other strange currency substitution.

Ship Via List

To describe the way you ship goods on your invoices, QuickBooks provides a list of the common carriers.

If you use any other method of delivery, press CTRL-N to add a new Ship Via entry to the list.

Sales Rep List

QuickBooks also provides a Sales Rep List. This is not quite as straightforward as the other lists you maintain. A sales rep is a person who receives a commission on a sale. If you want to track sales for reps by putting the rep name on the customer card, the rep must be an employee. In fact, the rep must be entered in your employee list before you can enter him or her as a sales rep.

If you want to maintain a list of sales reps who are not employees, each sales rep must be entered in your system as a vendor before adding him or her as a sales rep. You cannot enter a non-employee sales rep on the customer card.

To enter a new sales rep, press CTRL-N and open the drop-down list in the Sales Rep Name field to select the name of an employee or vendor.

Using Custom Fields

If you're brave, adventurous, and comfortable with computers, you can add fields to the customer, vendor, employee, and item records. In fact, even if you're not any of those things, you can add your own fields, because it isn't very difficult. You can create custom fields for names (customers, vendors, and employees) and for items.

Custom fields are useful if there's information you just have to track, but QuickBooks didn't provide a field for it. For example, if it's imperative for you to know what color eyes your employees have, add a field for eye color. Or, perhaps you have two offices and you want to attach your customers to the office that services them. Add an Office field to the customer card. If you maintain multiple warehouses, you can create a field for items to indicate which warehouse stocks any particular item.

Adding a Custom Field for Names

Open one of the names lists (Customers:Job, Vendors, or Employees) and then take these steps:

1. Select any name on the list.
2. Click the menu button at the bottom of the List window and choose Edit from the drop-down list.
3. Move to the Additional Info tab.
4. Click the Define Fields button.
5. When the Define Fields dialog box opens, name the field and indicate which list you want to use the new field with (see Figure 2-17).

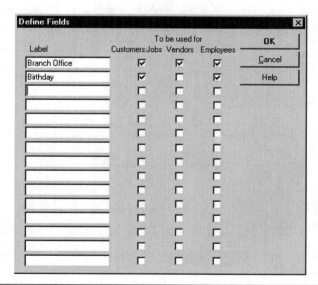

FIGURE 2-17 You can track any information you need (or are curious about) with custom fields

That's all there is to it, except you must click OK to save the information. When you do, QuickBooks flashes a message reminding you that if you customize your templates (forms for transactions, such as invoices), you can add these fields.

Click OK to make the message disappear (and select the option to stop showing you the message, if you wish).

The Additional Info tab for the lists you attached the fields to now shows those fields (see Figure 2-18).

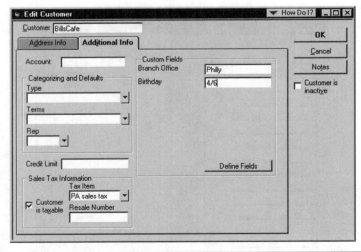

FIGURE 2-18   The new fields are on the Additional Info tab, and you can enter the appropriate data

Adding a Custom Field for Items

You can add custom fields to your items in much the same manner as for names:

1. Open the Item List.
2. Select an item.
3. Press CTRL-E.
4. Click the Custom Fields button.
5. When a message appears telling you that there are no custom fields yet defined, click OK.
6. When the Custom Fields dialog box appears, it has no fields on it (yet). Choose Define Fields.
7. When the Define Custom Fields for Items dialog box opens, enter a name for each field you want to add.
8. Click the Use box to use the field. (You can deselect the box later if you don't want to use the field any more.)

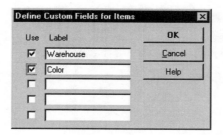

9. Click OK.

You can enter the data for the custom fields now, or wait until later.

Your QuickBooks setup is complete, and now it's time to start entering transactions. The following chapters cover all the things you'll be doing in QuickBooks.

Bookkeeping

Now we're getting into the good stuff. Part Two is a series of chapters about the day-to-day bookkeeping chores you'll be performing in QuickBooks. The chapters are filled with instructions, tips, and explanations. There's even a lot of information that you can pass along to your accountant, who will want to know about these things.

The chapters in Part Two take you through everything you need to know about sending invoices to your customers and collecting the money they send back as a result. You'll learn how to track and pay the bills you receive from vendors. There's plenty of information about dealing with inventory; buying it, selling it, counting it, and keeping QuickBooks up-to-date on those figures. Payroll is discussed, both for in-house payroll systems and outside services.

All the reports you can generate to analyze the state of your business are covered in Part Two. So are the reports you run for your accountant—and for the government (tax time is less of a nightmare with QuickBooks).

Finally, you'll learn about budgets, general ledger adjustments, and all the other once-in-a-while tasks you need to know to accomplish to keep your accounting records finely tuned.

Invoicing

In this chapter, you will learn to...

- Create and edit invoices

- Create and edit credit memos

- Print invoices and credit memos

- Use invoices for sales orders

- Create pick lists and packing slips

- Customize your invoices

For many businesses, the way to get money is to send an invoice (the exception is retail, of course). Creating an invoice in QuickBooks is easy once you understand what all the parts of the invoice do, and why they're there.

Creating Standard Invoices

To begin creating invoices, select the Create Invoices item on the Navigation Bar. This opens the Create Invoices window, which is really a blank invoice form (see Figure 3-1).

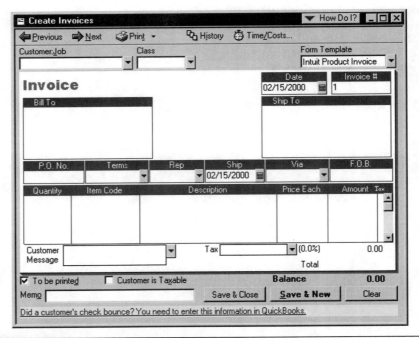

FIGURE 3-1   The invoice template you chose during the EasyStep interview is presented when you first open an invoice form

There are several invoice templates built into QuickBooks and you can use any of them (as well as create your own, which is covered later in this chapter in the section "Printing Invoices and Credit Memos"). The first thing to do is decide whether or not the displayed template suits you, and you should probably look at the other templates before settling on the one you want to use. To do that, click the arrow next to the Form Template box and select another invoice template.

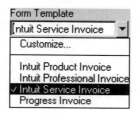

The Professional and Service templates are almost identical. There's a difference in the order of the columns and the Service template has a field for a purchase order number. The Product template has more fields and columns because it contains information about the items in your inventory. The Progress template, which is covered later in this chapter, is designed specifically for progress billing against a job estimate.

For this section I'll use the Product template; if you're using any other template you'll be able to follow along, even though your invoice form lacks some of the fields related to products.

The top portion of the invoice is for the basic information (sometimes called the *invoice heading*), the middle section is where the billing items (also called *line items*) are placed, and the bottom contains the totals. Each section of the invoice has fields into which you must enter data.

Entering Heading Information

Start with the customer, or the customer and job. Click the arrow to the right of the Customer:Job field to see a list of all your customers. If you've attached jobs to any customers, those jobs are listed under the customer name. Select the customer or job for this invoice.

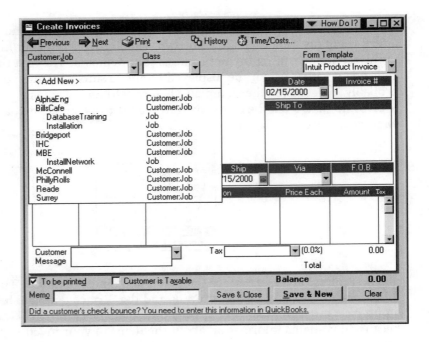

TIP: If the customer isn't in the system, choose <Add New> to open a new customer window and enter all the data required for setting up a customer. Read Chapter 2 for information on adding new customers.

In the Date field, the current date is showing, which usually suffices. If you want to change the date, you can either type in a new date, use the calendar icon, or employ one of the nifty date entry shortcuts built into QuickBooks. (Just inside the front cover of this book, you'll find all the shortcuts for entering dates.)

TIP: For service businesses, it's a common practice to send invoices on the last day of the month. If you have such a regular invoicing date, you can start preparing your invoices ahead of time and set the invoice date for the scheduled date. That way, the actual billing day isn't a zoo as you scramble to put together your information and enter the invoices.

The first time you enter an invoice, fill in the invoice number you want to use as a starting point. Hereafter, QuickBooks will increment that number for each ensuing invoice.

The Bill To address is taken from the customer card, as is the Ship To address. Only the Product invoice template has a Ship To field.

If you have a purchase order from this customer, enter the P.O. Number.

The Terms field is filled in automatically with the terms you entered for this customer when you created the customer. You can change the terms for this invoice if you wish. If terms don't automatically appear, it means you didn't enter that information in the customer record. If you enter it now, when you finish the invoice, QuickBooks offers to make the entry permanent by adding it to the customer card.

TIP: In fact, if you enter any information about the customer such as a new address or a shipping address, QuickBooks offers to add the information to the customer card. Just click the Yes button in the dialog box that displays the message. This saves you the trouble of going back to the customer record to make the changes.

The Rep field is for the salesperson attached to this customer. If you didn't indicate a salesperson when you filled out the customer card you can click the arrow next to the field and choose a salesperson from the list of employees that appears.

TIP: If you use the invoice form as a sales order and track the order taker with the Rep field, don't fill in the rep on any customer cards, and don't let QuickBooks update the field in the customer card when you enter a rep. To learn how to use invoices as sales orders, read the section on creating sales orders later in this chapter.

The Ship field is for the ship date (which also defaults to the current date).

The Via field is for the shipper. Click the arrow next to the field to see the carriers you entered in your Ship Via list. See Chapter 2 for information about creating this list.

The FOB field is used by some companies to indicate the point at which the shipping costs and the assumption of a completed sale takes place. (That means, if it breaks or gets lost, you own it.) If you use FOB terms, you can insert the applicable data in the field; it has no impact on your QuickBooks records and is there for your convenience only.

Entering Line Items

Now you can begin to enter the items for which you are billing this customer. Click in the first column of the line item section.

If you're using the Product invoice template, that column is Quantity. Enter the quantity of the first item you're billing for.

Press TAB to move to the Item Code column. An arrow appears on the right edge of the column—click it to see a list of the items in your inventory. (See Chapter 2 to learn how to enter items.) Select the item you need. The description and price are filled in automatically, using the information you provided when you created the item.

QuickBooks does the math and the Amount column displays the total of the quantity times the price. If the item and the customer are both liable for tax, the Tax column displays a "T."

Repeat this process to add all the items that should be on this invoice. You can add as many rows of items as you need; if you run out of room, QuickBooks automatically adds additional pages to your invoice.

You can make adjustments to the total with discounts or credits due this customer. These are entered as line items. Before you enter a discount, use a line to enter a subtotal item (which you should have created when you created your items). Then add the discount line items section and the discount will be applied to the subtotal. Doing it this way makes it very clear to the customer.

Checking the Totals

When you're finished entering all the line items, you'll see that QuickBooks has kept a running total, including taxes (see Figure 3-2).

If you want to add a message, click the arrow in the Customer Message field to see all the available messages. You can create a new message if you don't want to use any of the existing notes.

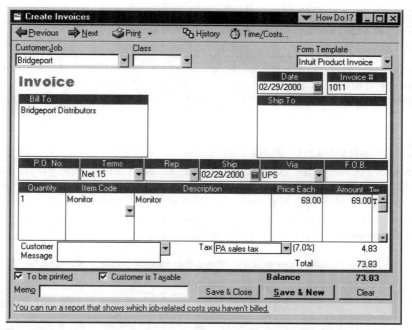

FIGURE 3-2 The invoice is complete, and there are no mathematical errors because QuickBooks does the addition

Saving the Invoice

Choose Save & New to save this invoice and move on to the next blank invoice form. If you have a sound card, you'll hear the sound of a cash register ringing. You can print the invoice before you start the next one, or wait until you've finished creating all your invoices. Information about printing invoices (one at a time or in batches) is found later in this chapter. Incidentally, if there's some reason that you aren't ready to print this invoice, not even later on when you print a whole batch of invoices, click the To be printed check box to remove the check mark. The invoice won't be printed until you check that box again.

When you are finished creating all the invoices you need, click Save & Close.

Creating Progress Billing Invoices

If you work with estimates and job tracking in QuickBooks, you can use the Progress invoice template to invoice your customers as each invoicing plateau arrives. This feature is only available in QuickBooks Pro. See the section "Creating Estimates," later in this chapter, to learn how to use estimates.

Choosing the Job

Progress invoices are connected to jobs. Choose the job for which you're creating the progress invoice. QuickBooks checks to see if you've recorded an estimate for this job, and asks if you want to create the invoice based on the information in the estimate. Answer Yes. Then fill out the dialog box that asks you to specify what you want to include on the invoice.

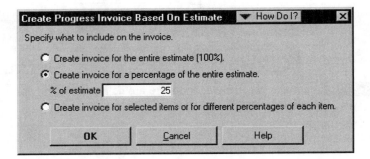

Selecting the Invoice Method

There are several approaches you can use to invoice a customer based on a contract or a job. Here are some guidelines for using progress invoices:

- You can bill for the whole job, 100% of the estimate. When the line items appear, you can edit any individual items. In fact, you can bill for a higher amount than the original invoice (you should have an agreement with your customer regarding overruns).
- You can create an invoice for a specific percentage of the estimate. The percentage usually depends upon the agreement you have with your customer. For example, you could have an agreement that you'll invoice the job in a certain number of equal installments, or you could invoice a percentage that's equal to the percentage of the work that's been finished.

- You can create an invoice that covers only certain items on the estimate, or an invoice that has a different percentage for each item on the estimate. This is the approach to use if you're billing on completed work for a job that has a number of distinct tasks. Some of the work listed on the estimate may be finished, other work not started, and the various items listed on the estimate may be at different points of completion.
- After you've created the first invoice for an estimate, a new option appears on subsequent invoices. That option is to bill for all remaining amounts in the estimate. This is generally reserved for your last invoice and it saves you the trouble of figuring out which percentages of which items have been invoiced previously.

As far as QuickBooks is concerned, the estimate is not etched in cement; you can change any amounts or quantities you wish while you're creating the invoice. Your customer, however, may not be quite so lenient and your ability to invoice for amounts that differ from the estimate depends on your agreement with the customer.

Entering Progress Line Items

Choose your method and click OK to begin creating the invoice. QuickBooks automatically fills in the line item section of the invoice, based on the approach you've selected (see Figure 3-3).

Changing the Line Items

To change the percentages or amounts that are billed on this invoice, click the Progress Detail button to open a dialog box that allows configuration of the line items, as seen in Figure 3-4.

In order to change any figures, you must display them in this dialog box. Using this method keeps the history of your estimate and invoices intact (as opposed to making changes directly on the invoice form).

Select Show Quantity and Rate to display those columns from the estimate. The quantity and rate for previously billed items are also displayed. Then click the QTY column for any line item to highlight the default number that's been used to calculate the invoice (see Figure 3-5). Replace the number with the amount you want to use for the invoice. You can also change the rate, but generally that's not cricket unless there are some circumstances that warrant it (and that you and the customer have agreed upon).

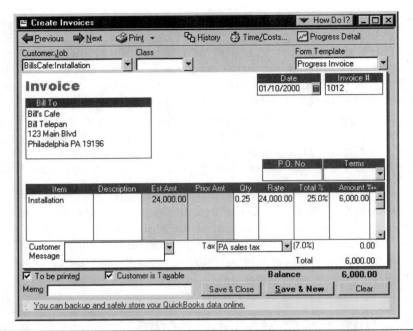

FIGURE 3-3 Progress invoices are filled in automatically

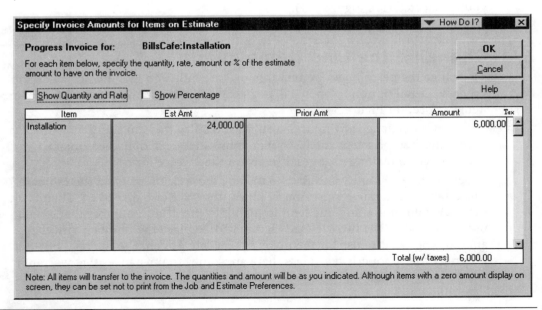

FIGURE 3-4 You can alter the amounts that are automatically placed on the invoice

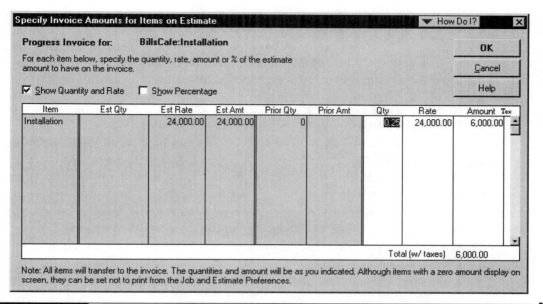

FIGURE 3-5 Change the quantity of items you want to include on this invoice

Select Show Percentage to add a column that displays the percentage of completion for this and previous billings. The percentages compare the dollar amounts for invoices against the estimated total. Click the Curr% column to change the percentage for any line item.

Click OK when you have finished making your adjustments. You return to the invoice form where the amounts on the line items have changed to match the adjustments you made.

Click Save & New to save this invoice and move on to the next invoice, or click Save & Close to save this invoice and finish your invoicing chores.

Editing Invoices

If you want to correct an invoice (perhaps you charged the wrong amount or forgot you'd promised a different amount to a particular customer), you can do so quite easily.

Editing the Current Invoice

Editing the invoice that's currently on the screen is quite easy. Click on the field or column that requires changing and make the changes (you've probably already figured this out).

Editing a Previously Entered Invoice

You can open the Create Invoices window (or perhaps you're still working there) and click the Prev (which means Previous) button to move through all the invoices in your system. However, if you have a great many invoices it might be faster to take a different road:

1. Press CTRL-A to bring up the Chart of Accounts list.
2. Select the Accounts Receivable account (that's where invoices are posted).
3. Press CTRL-R to use the A/R account register. This is the keyboard equivalent to clicking the Activities button at the bottom of the list window and choosing Use Register.
4. When the A/R account register opens, find the row that has the invoice you want to edit and click anywhere on the row to select the invoice.
5. Click the Edit Transaction button to open the Create Invoices window with the selected invoice displayed.
6. Make your changes and click OK. Then close the A/R register.

If you've printed the invoices, when you finish editing be sure to check the To be printed box so you can reprint it with the correct information.

If you've mailed your invoices, it's too late—you can't edit them. Instead, issue a credit memo (discussed later in this chapter).

Voiding and Deleting Invoices

There's an enormous difference between voiding and deleting an invoice. Voiding an invoice makes the invoice nonexistent to your accounting and the customer balance. However, the invoice number continues to exist so you can account for it (missing invoice numbers are just as frustrating as missing check numbers).

Deleting an invoice removes all traces of it—it never existed, you never did it, the number is gone, and a couple of months later you probably won't remember why the number is gone. You have no audit trail, no way to tell yourself (or your accountant) why the number is missing.

C A U T I O N : If you choose to ignore my advice (perhaps you have the memory of an elephant and when someone questions the missing number you'll be able to explain no matter how much time has passed), do not ever delete an invoice to which a customer payment has been attached. Straightening out that mess is a nightmare.

Voiding an invoice isn't difficult:

1. Press CTRL-A to bring up the Chart of Accounts list.
2. Select the Accounts Receivable account (that's where invoices are posted).
3. Press CTRL-R to use the A/R account register. This is the keyboard shortcut that is the same as clicking the Activities button at the bottom of the list window and choosing Use Register.
4. When the A/R account register opens, find the row that has the invoice you want to edit and right-click anywhere on the row to display the shortcut menu.
5. Choose Void Invoice from the shortcut menu. The word "VOID" appears in the memo field. (If you've entered a memo, the word "VOID" is placed in front of your text.)
6. Close the register by clicking the X in the upper-right corner. QuickBooks asks you to confirm the change you made.

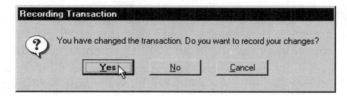

If you want to delete an invoice, follow steps 1 through 3 above. Then click the row that has the invoice you want to delete and press CTRL-D. You'll have to confirm the deletion.

Understanding the Postings

It's important to understand what QuickBooks is doing behind the scenes, because everything you do has an impact on your financial reports. Let's look at the postings for an imaginary invoice that has several line items:

- $500.00 for services rendered
- $30.00 for sales tax

Since QuickBooks is a full, double-entry bookkeeping program, there is a balanced posting made to the general ledger. For this invoice, the following postings are made to the general ledger:

ACCOUNT	DEBIT	CREDIT
Accounts Receivable	530.00	
Sales Tax		30.00
Revenue—Services		500.00

If the invoice includes inventory items, the postings are a bit more complicated. Let's post an invoice that sold ten widgets to a customer. The widgets cost you $50.00 each and you sold them for $100.00 each. This customer was shipped ten widgets, and also paid tax and shipping.

ACCOUNT	DEBIT	CREDIT
Accounts Receivable	1077.00	
Revenue—Sales of Items		1000.00
Sales Tax		70.00
Shipping		17.00
Cost of Sales	500.00	
Inventory		500.00

There are some things to think about as you look at these postings:

- To keep accurate books, you should fill out the cost of your inventory items when you create them. That's the only way to get a correct posting to the cost of sales and the balancing decrement in the value of your inventory.
- You don't have to separate your revenue accounts (one for services, one for inventory items, and so on) to have accurate books. In the bottom line, revenue is revenue. However, you may decide to create accounts for each type of revenue if you want to be able to analyze where your revenue is coming from.

TIP: Some people think it's a good idea to have two revenue items, one for revenue liable for sales tax, and one for revenue that's not taxable. They find it easier to audit the sales tax figures that way.

- There are two theories on posting shipping: Separate your shipping costs from the shipping you collect from your customers or post everything to the shipping expense. To use the first method, in addition to the shipping expense, create a revenue account for shipping and attach that account to the shipping item you insert in invoices. If you use the latter method, don't be surprised at the end of the year if you find your shipping expense is reported as a negative number, meaning that you collected more than you spent for shipping. You won't have a shipping expense to deduct from your revenue at tax time, but who cares—you made money.

Issuing Credits and Refunds

Sometimes you have to give money to a customer. You can do this in the form of a credit against current or future balances, or you can write a check and refund money you received from the customer. Neither is a lot of fun, but it's a fact of business life.

Creating Credit Memos

A credit memo reduces a customer balance. This is necessary if a customer returns goods, has been billed for goods that were lost or damaged in shipment, or wins an argument about the price of a service you provided.

The credit memo itself is printed to let the customer know the details about the credit that's being applied. The totals are posted to your accounting records just as the invoice totals are posted, except there's an inherent minus sign next to the number.

Creating a credit memo is similar to creating an invoice:

1. Click Customers on the Navigation Bar.
2. Click the Refunds and Credit icon to bring up a blank Credit Memo window, as seen in Figure 3-6.
3. Select a customer or job, and fill out the rest of the heading.

> **TIP:** By default, the credit memo number is the next available invoice number. If you change the number because you want a different numbering system for credit memos, you'll have to keep track of numbers manually. QuickBooks will use the next number (the one after this credit memo) for your next invoice. Therefore, use the default procedure of having one set of continuous numbers for invoices and credit memos.

4. Move to the line item section and enter the quantity and rate of the items for which you're issuing this credit memo.
5. Remember to insert all the special items you need to give credit for, such as taxes, shipping, and so on.
6. You can use the Customer Message field to add any short explanation that's necessary.
7. Click Save & Close to save the credit memo (unless you have more credit memos to create—in which case, click Save & Next).

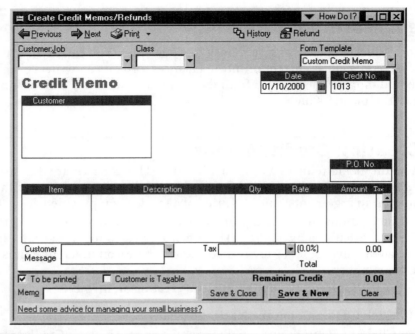

FIGURE 3-6 The Credit Memo form has all the fields you need to provide details about the reason the credit is being given

See the section on printing, later in this chapter, to learn about printing credit memos.

Issuing Refunds

If a customer has paid up and has no existing invoices against which a credit is desired (and has indicated no desire to have a floating credit against future purchases), you'll have to send that customer a refund.

Refunds start as credit memos, then they keep going, requiring a few extra steps to write the check and post the totals to your general ledger properly.

Follow the steps for creating a credit memo, through step 6. Then click the Refund button at the top of the Credit Memo window. This opens a Write Checks window, as seen in Figure 3-7.

Make sure that everything on the check is the way it should be. (The only thing you may want to change is the date; everything else should be accurate.) Then either print the check or click OK to save it. If you're not printing the check now, make sure the To be printed check box is checked so you can print it later. Information about check printing is in Chapter 7.

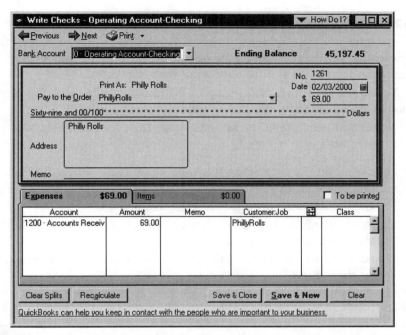

FIGURE 3-7 The check takes the information from the credit memo, so everything is already filled out

You're returned to the Credit Memo window where you should either print the credit memo or click OK to save it for later printing.

QuickBooks automatically links the check to the credit memo. This means the credit memo is no longer in the customer record, decrementing the balance. If you've updated to QuickBooks 2000 from a previous version, it also means you don't have to go through all the steps to link the check to the credit manually, as you did in earlier versions.

Printing Invoices and Credit Memos

You have all sorts of choices about printing invoices and credit memos. You can use blank paper, preprinted forms on a single sheet of paper, preprinted multipart forms, or your company letterhead.

Setting Up the Printer

A setup process has to be performed, but once you complete it you don't have to do it again. There are several steps involved in setting up a printer but they're not terribly difficult.

Selecting the Printer and Form

If you have multiple printers attached to your computer or accessible through a network, you have to designate one of them as the invoice printer. If you use multipart forms you should have a dot matrix printer.

Your printers are already set up in Windows (or should be) so QuickBooks, like all Windows software, has access to them.

Now you have to tell QuickBooks about the printer and the way you want to print invoices:

1. Choose File | Printer Setup from the menu bar to open the Printer Setup dialog box seen in Figure 3-8.
2. In the Form Name drop-down list select Invoice.
3. If you have multiple printers available, click the arrow next to the Printer name box to choose a printer.
4. Make sure the data in the Printer type box matches the type of printer you selected.
5. In the bottom of the dialog box, select the type of form you're planning to use.

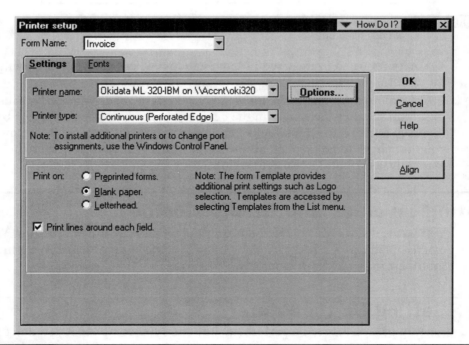

FIGURE 3-8 This QuickBooks system is on a network and uses a network printer; if your printer is attached to your computer, the printer name won't include a network path

After you've selected the form type, you have to fine-tune the settings so everything prints in the right place. Click to place a check mark next to one of these three form types:

- **Preprinted forms** are templates with all your company information, field names, and row and column dividers already printed. These forms need to be aligned to match the way your invoice prints. If you purchase the forms from a company that knows about QuickBooks' invoice printing formats, everything should match just fine. Selecting this option tells QuickBooks that only the data needs to be sent to the printer because the fields are already printed.

- **Blank paper** is easiest, but may not look as pretty as a printed form. Some of us don't care about pretty—we just want to ship invoices and collect the payments. But if you care about image this may not be a great choice. On the other hand, if you don't need multipart printing, you can use the fonts and graphic capabilities of your laser printer to design a professional-looking invoice that prints to blank paper. Selecting this option tells QuickBooks that everything, including field names, must be sent to the printer. Select the option to print lines around each field to make sure the information is printed in a way that's easy to read.

- **Letterhead** is another option, and it means your company name and address is preprinted on paper that matches your company's "look." Selecting this option tells QuickBooks not to print the company information when it prints the invoice. Also, select the option to print lines around each field to make sure the information is printed in a way that's easy to read.

Setting Up Form Alignment

You have to test the QuickBooks output against the paper in your printer to make sure everything prints in the right place. To accomplish this, click the Align button in the Printer Setup dialog box to bring up the Align Printer dialog box, seen here.

Choose the invoice template you're using and click OK.

QuickBooks presents another dialog box that explains how to fix any alignment problems. That dialog box differs depending on the type of printer you've selected.

Aligning Dot Matrix Printers

If you're using a continuous feed printer (dot matrix using paper with sprocket holes), you'll see the dialog box shown here.

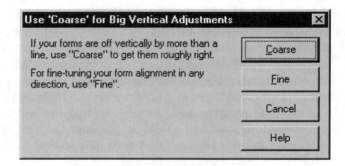

Start by clicking the Coarse button. A dialog box appears telling you that a sample form is about to be printed and warning you not to make any physical adjustments to your printer after the sample has printed. QuickBooks provides a dialog box where you can make any necessary adjustments. Make sure the appropriate preprinted form, letterhead, or blank paper is loaded in the printer. Click OK.

The sample form prints to your dot matrix printer. Take the paper out of your printer and read the Coarse Alignment dialog box that now appears on your QuickBooks window.

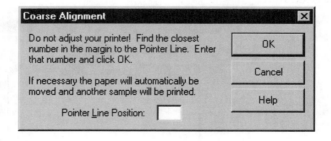

The Pointer Line referred to in the dialog box is found at the top of the printed sample. Follow the instructions and make any adjustments needed. (I can't give specific instructions because I can't see what your sample output looks like.) QuickBooks displays a message telling you to note the position of the form now that it's printing correctly. If you want to tweak the alignment, choose Fine. (See the information on using the Fine Alignment dialog box that follows this section.) Otherwise, choose OK.

 TIP: Here's the best way to note the position of the forms in your dot matrix printer: Get a magic marker and draw an arrow with the word "invoice" at the spot on the printer where the top of the form should be. I have mine marked on the piece of plastic that sits above the roller.

Aligning Laser and Inkjet Printers

If you're using a page printer you'll see this Fine Alignment dialog box.

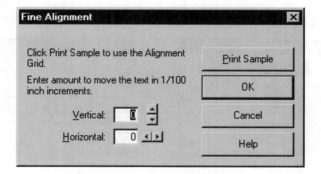

Click Print Sample to send output to your printer. Then, with the output page in your hand, make adjustments to the alignment in the dialog box. Use the arrows next to the Vertical and Horizontal boxes to move the positions at which printing occurs.

Click OK, then click OK in the Printer Setup dialog box. Your settings are saved and you don't have to go through this again.

Batch Printing

If you didn't click the Print button to print each invoice or credit memo as you created them, and you made sure that the To be printed check box was selected on each of them, you're ready to start a print run:

1. Place the correct paper in your printer and, if it's continuous paper, position it properly.
2. Choose File | Print Forms | Invoices.
3. In the Select Invoices to Print window (see Figure 3-9), all your unprinted invoices are selected with a check mark. If there are any you don't want to print at this time, click the check mark to remove it.
4. If you need to print mailing labels for these invoices, you must print them first (see the next section).
5. Click OK to print your invoices and credit memos.

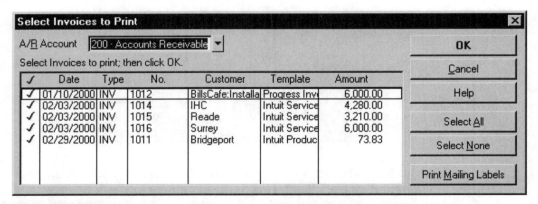

FIGURE 3-9   Batch printing is quick and you can select all the invoices or just print specific invoices

Printing Mailing Labels

If you need mailing labels, QuickBooks will print them for you. Click the Print Mailing Labels button to bring up the Select Mailing Labels to Print dialog box, seen here.

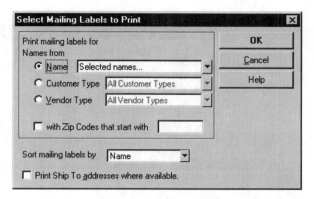

Fill out the fields to match your needs, and click OK.

The Print Labels dialog box appears (see Figure 3-10), assuming that you've loaded Avery labels into your printer. Select the appropriate printer and specify the Avery label format you use and choose Print.

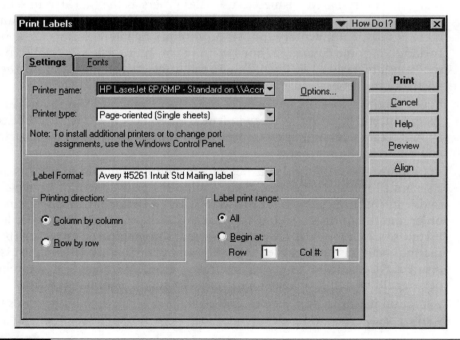

FIGURE 3-10   Set up your label printing options

After the labels are printed you're returned to the Select Invoices to Print dialog box. Choose Print. Then check the print job to make sure nothing went wrong (the printer jammed, you had the wrong paper in the printer, whatever). If anything went amiss you can reprint the forms you need when the following dialog box appears. (Use the invoice number as the form number.)

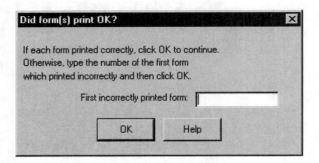

If everything is hunky-dory, click OK.

Creating Sales Orders

Many inventory-based businesses use sales orders as the first step in selling products to a customer. A *sales order* is a tentative document, on hold until there is sufficient inventory to fill it or until prices and discounts are approved. In addition, some companies don't want to consider a sale as a final step until the items are packed, weighed, and on the truck. Nothing on a sales order is posted to the general ledger.

QuickBooks does not have a sales order form, nor does it really have a sales order concept. However, you can imitate this protocol if you need it. I discovered I could set up sales order processing in QuickBooks by using a little imagination and a couple of keystrokes.

In more robust (and more expensive) accounting software, the sales order is a separate form and a separate menu choice. It's printed along with a *pick list* (a document that's printed for the warehouse personnel, listing the items in bin order, omitting prices), then there's a menu item that converts sales orders to invoices. When the sales order is converted, shipping costs are added (because the shipment has been packed and weighed by now) and a packing list is printed. *Packing lists* do not display prices because it's none of the warehouse personnel's business what an owner pays for goods that are received.

I found it easy to duplicate all the steps I needed for small businesses that wanted sales order and pick slip functions in their QuickBooks software.

Creating a sales order is just a matter of creating an invoice and then taking the additional step of marking the invoice as pending. Here's how:

1. Create an invoice as described earlier in this chapter.
2. Choose Edit | Mark Invoice as Pending from the QuickBooks menu bar. The Pending notice is placed on the invoice (see Figure 3-11).
3. Print the invoice and send it to the warehouse as a pick slip, or send it to a supervisor to approve the pricing (or both).

TIP: Some of my clients purchase multipart invoice forms that have areas of black on the last form, covering the columns that hold the pricing information. They use this copy as the pick list and the packing list. Other clients have created pick lists and packing lists by customizing the invoice template. See information on customizing later in this chapter.

4. When the order is through the system, bring the invoice back to the window and add the shipping costs.

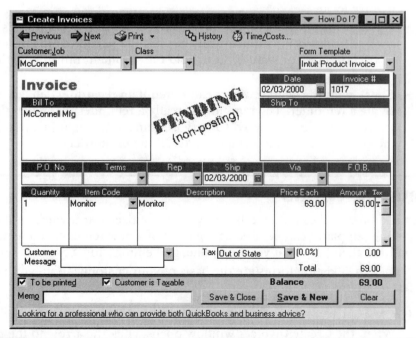

FIGURE 3-11   There's no mistaking the fact that this invoice isn't ready to send

5. Choose Edit | Mark Invoice as Final. Now you have a regular invoice and you can proceed accordingly.

If you have a service business, the sales order protocol can be handy for noting specific jobs or tasks that customers request. It's a good first step, even before the estimating process (if there is one).

Creating Backorders

If you're selling inventory, there's nothing more frustrating than getting a big order when you're out of some or all of the products being ordered. You can ship the items you do have in stock, and consider the rest of the items a backorder. The problem is that there's no Backorder button on a QuickBooks invoice, nor is there a backorder form.

Use the Pending Invoice feature described in the previous section. Here are some guidelines for making this work:

- As the items arrive in your warehouse, remove them from the Backorder form (and save the pending invoice again) and place them on a regular invoice form.
- Use the Notes feature on customer cards to indicate whether this customer accepts backorders, automatically cancels the portion of the order that must be backordered, or wants you to hold the shipment until the entire order can be sent.
- Check with the vendor of a backordered item regarding delivery date and create a reminder. The reminder is really a reminder that when those items arrive, they're backordered (otherwise somebody might just put them onto the shelves without remembering to fill the backorder).

Customizing Forms

QuickBooks makes it incredibly easy to customize your invoices. All the existing templates can be used as the basis of a new template, copying what you like, changing what you don't like, and eliminating what you don't need.

Since the existing forms are the basis of your customization, you need to start in an invoice window:

1. Choose Create Invoices from the Navigation Bar.
2. When the Create Invoices window opens, click the arrow to the right of the Custom Form box to display the drop-down list. Instead of choosing one of the invoice templates, choose Customize.

3. The Customize Template dialog box opens, as seen in Figure 3-12.
4. Choose the QuickBooks template that comes closest to the form you want to design.
5. Choose the action you want to use to customize your form.

Editing an Existing Form

You can make minor changes to an existing form by choosing Edit in the Customize Template dialog box. This is commonly done to make a small change in one of the existing QuickBooks templates in order to match your company's needs or your own taste. After a message appears to tell you that this Edit process has limited features (remember, I said it was for minor adjustments), the Customize Invoice dialog box appears, as seen in Figure 3-13.

If your printer setup indicated you were using blank paper, the options to print the company name and address are selected. If you want to remove one or both of them (because you're switching to preprinted forms or letterhead),

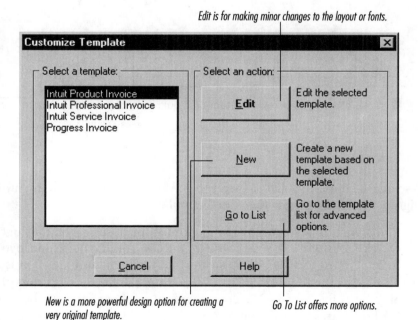

Edit is for making minor changes to the layout or fonts.

New is a more powerful design option for creating a very original template.

Go To List offers more options.

FIGURE 3-12 There are several methods of customizing forms

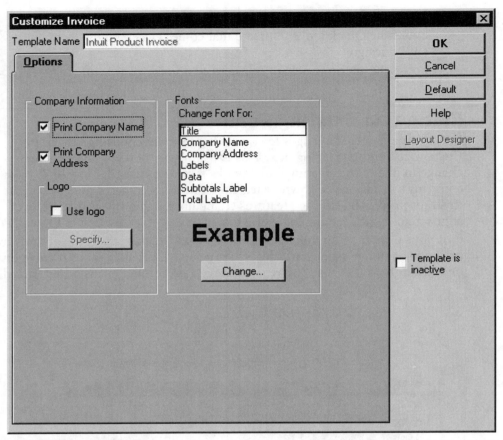

FIGURE 3-13 Make changes to an existing template quickly by choosing the Edit method

deselect the option(s). Don't forget to go through a new setup, including alignment, when you use the edited template.

- If you want to add a logo to your printed form, select the Use logo option. QuickBooks will ask you where to find the graphic file. Your logo must be in bitmapped format, which means that the filename extension is .bmp.
- To change the font for any title element in the form, select the title element and then click Change. Select a new font or change the attributes of a font (or both) using this dialog box.

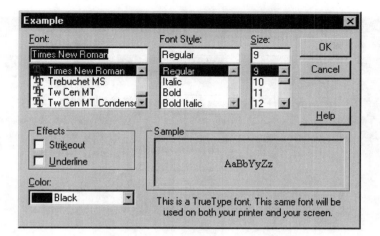

Click OK in the dialog box to return to the Customize Invoice dialog box. Then click OK to save your customized template. If you changed the name of the form it will appear on the drop-down list when you next work with this form.

Designing a New Form

Choose New in the first Customize Template dialog box to design a form of your own. The Customize Invoice dialog box opens with a whole raft of choices (see Figure 3-14).

Notice that this time, QuickBooks doesn't enter the name of the template you're using as a model in the Template Name box. That's because the changes you make here are more sweeping than a minor edit and you should give the template a name to create a new form (instead of replacing the QuickBooks form). Enter a name for the form—something that reminds you of the format (such as "bigtypeface" or "FootersAdded") or just call it "ProductInvoice2."

Move through the tabs to make changes, deletions, or additions to the various parts of the form.

 TIP: Many of the various tabs include an option to remove an element from the screen and the printed version, but some elements can only be removed from the printed version of the form.

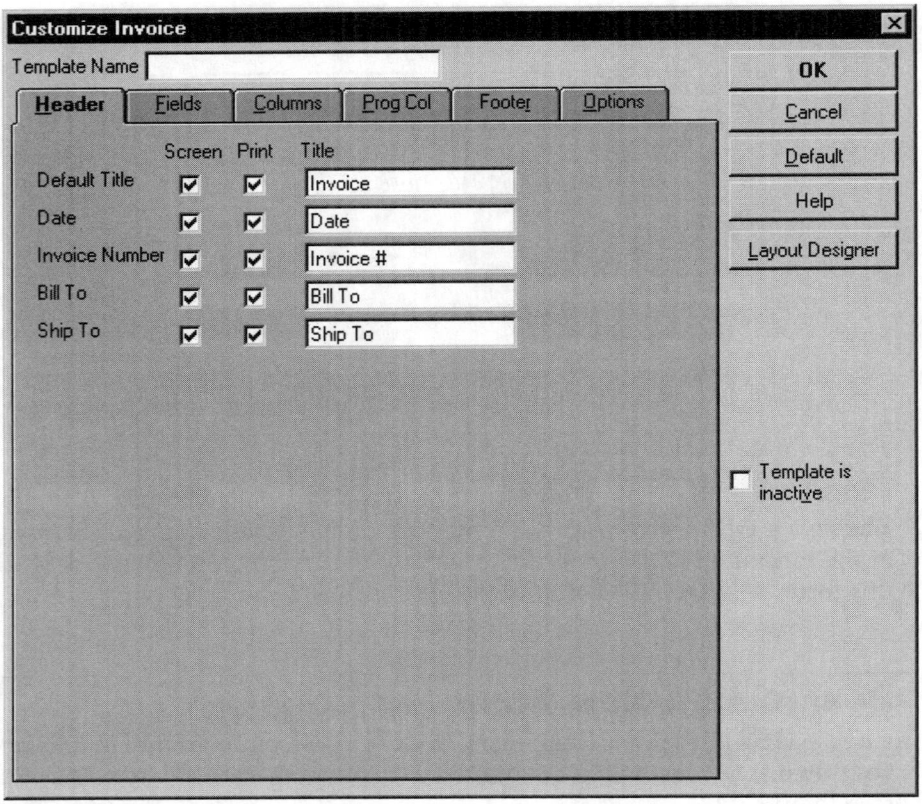

FIGURE 3-14 Each tab has specific customization options available

If you're comfortable with designing forms (or if you like to live on the edge), click the Layout Designer button on the Customize window. The Layout Designer window opens (see Figure 3-15) and you can plunge right in, moving elements around, changing margins, and building your own layout. In this example, I've selected the option to show the window envelope placement so I don't accidentally move the customer address somewhere outside the window area.

1. Select the Show envelope window option if you use window envelopes to mail your invoices.

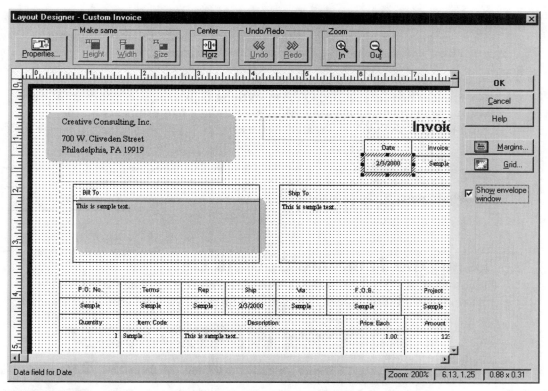

FIGURE 3-15 Move components around to create your own style for an invoice form

2. Select any element to put a frame around it, then perform an action on the frame:
   - Position your pointer on one of the sizing handles on the frame, then drag the handle to change the size of the element.
   - Position your pointer inside the frame and when your pointer turns into a four-headed arrow, drag the frame to move the element to a different position on the form.
   - Double-click the frame to see a dialog box that permits all sorts of option changes for the selected element.
3. Click the Margins button to change the margins.

4. Click the Grid button to eliminate the dotted line grid or change its size.
5. Use the toolbar buttons to align and zoom into the selected elements. There's also an Undo/Redo choice, thank goodness.

When you finish with the Layout Designer, click OK to move back to the Customize Invoice window. Once everything is just the way you want it, save your new template by clicking OK. This template name appears on the drop-down list when you create invoices.

 T I P : You can now use this new template as the basis for other customizations.

Using the Template Options List

If you choose Go to List in the original Customize Template dialog box, a Templates window opens listing all the forms in your system.

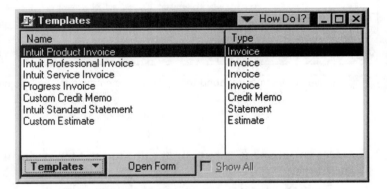

Select the form you want to work with, then click the Templates button at the bottom of the window to see the options available. You can edit the selected template or build a new form based on the selected template. In addition you can duplicate or remove a form.

Creating Pick Slips and Packing Slips

Marty Mogul's business is growing fast—it seems the whole world wants his special occasion balloons. He decided he needs pick slips for the warehouse staff and packing slips for the boxes, instead of having his salespeople create a list in a word processor (which takes far too much time) or write the list by hand (which nobody can read). He designed the pick slips, which also function as packing slips.

Marty opened the Create Invoices window and selected Customize as the template to use. When the Customize Template dialog box appeared, he selected the Intuit Product Invoice as the template, then he clicked New to create a new template based on the product invoice template.

He named the new template Pick/Packing Slip. On the Columns tab he eliminated the Rate and Amount columns from the printed version. Then he clicked OK to save the new template.

Now, when an order is taken, this template is used. The Rate and Amount columns are on the screen so the order can be filled out accurately, but they don't print. The invoice is marked "Pending" (choose Edit | Mark Invoice as Pending) and is then printed to a dot matrix printer with multipart paper.

When the warehouse workers have filled the order, boxed it (with the packing slip inside), and weighed it, they call the Accounts Receivable office to tell them the shipping cost. By the way, next year, when Marty installs a network, the warehouse workers will be able to bring the invoice up on their own computer screens and fill in the shipping cost line item.

The A/R person does the following things:

1. He brings the pending invoice onto the screen and adds the shipping cost as a line item.
2. He clicks the arrow to the right of the Custom Template box and switches to the standard Product Invoice template (thus creating an invoice form while all the items remain the same).
3. He selects Edit | Mark Invoice as Final to get rid of the pending status.
4. He saves, prints, and mails the invoice to the customer.

The ability to switch templates without disturbing the contents of the invoice is the secret behind Marty's ingenious plan.

Using Memorized Invoices

If you have a recurring invoice (most common if you have a retainer agreement with a customer), you can automate the process of creating it. Recurring invoices are those that are sent out at regular intervals, with the same total.

Create the first invoice, filling out all the fields. If there are any fields that will change each time you send the invoice, leave those fields blank and fill them out each time you send the invoice. Then press CTRL-M to tell QuickBooks to memorize the invoice.

When the Memorize Transaction dialog box opens (see Figure 3-16), fill it in using these guidelines:

- Change the title in the Name box to reflect what you've done. It's easiest to add a word or two to the default title (the customer name or job), such as "Customer Retainer."
- Choose Remind Me and specify how and when you want to be reminded in the How Often and Next Date fields. The reminder will appear in the automatic QuickBooks Reminder window.
- Choose Don't Remind Me if you have a great memory.

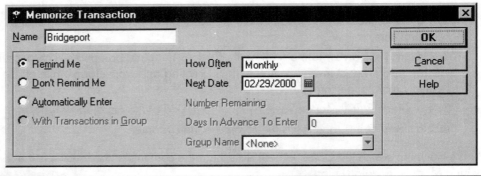

FIGURE 3-16   Select a reminder to make recurring invoices even more efficient

- Choose Automatically Enter if you want QuickBooks to issue this invoice automatically. If you opt for automatic issuing of this invoice, you must fill in the fields so that QuickBooks performs the task accurately.

- The How Often field is where you specify the interval for this invoice, such as monthly, weekly, or so on. Click the arrow to see the drop-down list and choose the option you need.

- The Next Date field is the place to note the next instance of this invoice.

- The Number Remaining field is a place to start a countdown for a specified number of invoices. This is useful if you're billing a customer for a finite number of months because you only have a one-year contract.

- The Days In Advance To Enter field is for specifying the number of days in advance of the next date you want QuickBooks to create the invoice.

Click OK when you have finished filling out the dialog box. Then click OK in the Invoice window to save the transaction.

Creating Estimates

If you're using QuickBooks Pro, you have the ability to create estimates. An estimate isn't an invoice, but it can be the basis of an invoice (you can create multiple invoices to reflect the progression of the job).

Creating an estimate doesn't impact your financial condition. When you indicate that you use estimates in your QuickBooks preferences, a non-posting account named Estimates is added to your chart of accounts. The amount of the estimate is posted to this account (invoices, on the other hand, are posted to the Accounts Receivable account).

To create an estimate, choose Estimate from the Navigation Bar, which opens an Estimate form. As you can see in Figure 3-17, the form is very much like an invoice form. Fill out the fields in the same manner you use for invoices.

Estimates permit you to invoice customers with a markup over cost. This is often the approach used for time and materials on bids. Just enter the cost and indicate the markup in dollars or percentage. Incidentally, if you decide to change the total of the item, QuickBooks will change the markup so your math is correct.

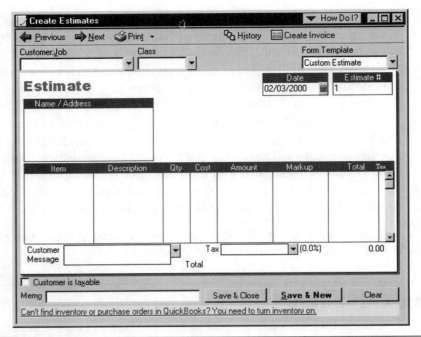

FIGURE 3-17 Estimates provide a way to bill customers for partial completion of work

You can only create one estimate for a job, so if you need multiple estimates you must create multiple jobs for the customer. Use a naming scheme for the job that indicates what you're doing, such as Phase1, Phase2, and so on.

The more accurate your invoices are, the fewer questions you'll have from your customers. This increases the likelihood that your customers will send checks right away.

Receiving Payments

In this chapter, you will learn to...

- Handle payments on customer invoices
- Handle cash sales
- Issue receipts for cash sales
- Deposit payments and cash sales into your bank account
- Apply credits and discounts to invoices
- Customize the cash sales receipt

Chapter 4

Receiving Invoice Payments

As you create invoices and send them to your customers, there's an expectation that money will eventually arrive to pay off those invoices. And, in fact, it almost always works that way. In accounting, there are two ways to think about the cash receipts that pay off invoices:

- **Balance forward**   This is a system in which you consider the total of all the outstanding invoices as the amount due from the customer and you apply payments against that total. It doesn't matter which particular invoice is being paid, because it's a running total of payments against a running total of invoices.
- **Open item**   This is a system in which payments you receive are applied to specific invoices. Most of the time, the customer either sends a copy of the invoice along with the check or notes the invoice number that is being paid on the check stub to make sure your records agree with the customer's records.

QuickBooks assumes you're using a balance forward system, but you can override that default easily. In fact, applying payments directly to specific invoices is just a matter of a mouse click or two.

 NOTE: QuickBooks refers to the process of handling invoice payments from customers as "Receive Payments." The common bookkeeping jargon for this process is "cash receipts," and you'll find I use that term frequently throughout this chapter (it's just habit).

Recording the Payment

When checks arrive from customers, follow these steps to apply the payments:

1. Click the Customers listing on the Navigation Bar and then click the Receive Payments icon to bring up a blank Receive Payments window, as shown in Figure 4-1.
2. Click the arrow to the right of the Customer:Job field to display a list of customers, and select the customer who sent the check. If the check is for a job, select the job. The current balance for this customer or job automatically appears.

Receive Payments ▼ How Do I? _ □ ✕

⬅ Previous ➡ Next ⧉ History ✏ Print Credit Memo

Customer Payment

	Date	Balance
	02/03/2000 🔲	0.00

Customer:Job [▼]   Amount   0.00
                                         Pmt. Method   [▼]
Memo _____   Check No.   _____

☐ Apply Existing Credits?   Existing Credits   0.00

Outstanding Invoices/Statement Charges

✓	Date	Type	Number	Orig. Amt.	Disc. Date	Amt. Due	Payment

	Totals	0.00	0.00

[Discount Info] [Auto Apply]   Total to Apply   0.00
                                      Unapplied Amount   0.00

◉ Group with other undeposited funds

○ Deposit To [▼] [Save & Close] [**Save & New**] [Clear]

Did you know you can run a report that shows all the bank deposits you've made?

FIGURE 4-1   All sorts of details have to be filled in when you receive a customer payment

3. In the Amount field, enter the amount of this payment.

4. Click the arrow to the right of the Pmt. Method field and select one of these methods.

< Add New >

American Express
Cash
Check
Discover
Master Card
VISA

5. In the Check No. field, enter the check number.

6. The Memo field is optional and I've never come across a reason to use it, but if there's some important memorandum you feel you must attach to this payment record, feel free.

Applying the Payment

QuickBooks offers two options for depositing your cash receipts: Group with other undeposited funds, and Deposit To (which you can use to name a specific bank account). By default, the first option is selected. There are two ways to interpret what QuickBooks is doing here.

Some say that the choices are there to make it easier for you to read your bank statement. If you select the second option, each check you deposit is listed separately in your QuickBooks reports. If your bank lists each check you deposit separately, your reports and the bank statement will match. If you select the first option, today's receipts are written to the Undeposited Funds account and transferred to the real bank account when you tell QuickBooks you've made the deposit. The total deposit is placed in your bank account instead of the individual checks. If your bank lists your total deposits for a particular date on the statement, then your report and the bank statement will duplicate each other.

On the other hand, it's tempting to use the logic of the English language as you consider these options. If you deposit all of your payments in the same bank account, use the first option. If you deposit cash receipts into different bank accounts (perhaps you have a bank account you use only for credit card receipts, or you use one bank on odd-numbered days and another bank on even-numbered days, or you have some other scheme you like to use), you can specify the account into which you're depositing the current payment.

Actually, almost all businesses deposit cash receipts into the same account, even if the company maintains multiple accounts (they transfer money between accounts later). Having such a regular protocol is a good idea. One notable exception is law firms, which frequently must deposit some checks into escrow accounts.

Make your decision according to the way you use your bank accounts.

Now you have to apply the payment against the customer invoices. This is done at the bottom of the Receive Payments window, where the customer's open invoices are listed. As you can see in Figure 4-2, QuickBooks automatically applies the payment to the oldest invoice.

I can apply any existing credit to an invoice in addition to this payment. Usually, customers let you know how they want credits applied, and it's not unusual to find a note written on the copy of the invoice that the customer sent along with the check.

In this case (referring to Figure 4-2), the payment is less than the amount of the oldest invoice, and even applying the existing credit doesn't pay off the invoice. Partial payments like this aren't unusual in business. When I click the option to apply existing credits, the amount of the check that's applied remains the same, but the balance due on the invoice is reduced by the credit.

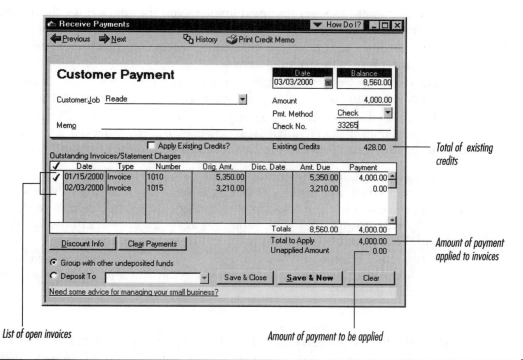

List of open invoices

Total of existing credits

Amount of payment applied to invoices

Amount of payment to be applied

FIGURE 4-2   A check mark indicates which invoice is being paid (QuickBooks automatically picks the oldest invoice)

If the check is for the same amount as a later invoice, you can assume that you should apply the payment to that later invoice. To do so, click the check mark next to the oldest invoice (the one that QuickBooks automatically selected) to remove the check mark. Then, click the check mark column next to the invoice that's being paid with this payment.

NOTE: Customers frequently enclose a copy of the invoice being paid along with the check, or note the invoice number on the check stub. You can also assume that the customer either forgot about the first invoice or has a problem with it (perhaps the goods arrived damaged or didn't arrive at all). Either way, you should call the customer and straighten it out.

You could face several scenarios when receiving customer payments:

• The customer has one unpaid invoice and the check is for the same amount as that invoice.

- The customer has several unpaid invoices and the check is for the amount of one of those invoices.
- The customer has one or more unpaid invoices and the check is for an amount lower than any single invoice.
- The customer has several unpaid invoices and the check is for an amount greater than any one invoice, but not large enough to cover two invoices.
- The customer has one or more unpaid invoices and the check is for a lesser amount than the current balance. However, the customer has a credit equal to the difference between the payment and the customer balance.

You have a variety of choices for handling any of these scenarios, but for situations in which the customer's intention isn't clear, the smart thing to do is to call the customer and ask how the payment should be applied. You can manually enter the amount you're applying against an invoice in the Payment column. You must, of course, apply the entire amount of the check.

If you are not tracking invoices, but are using a balance forward system, just let QuickBooks continue to apply payments to the oldest invoices (or a portion of the oldest invoice).

Applying Discounts for Timely Payments

If you offer your customers terms that include a discount if they pay their bills promptly (for instance, 2% 10 net 30), you must apply the discount to the payment if it's applicable.

Figure 4-3 shows the Receive Payments window for a customer who has been offered a discount for timely payment and has taken it by reducing the amount of the payment.

What's missing is any way to make up the difference, to avoid having a balance due on this invoice. Unfortunately, QuickBooks doesn't make this an automatic process. Instead, you must click the Discount Info button to see the discount information for this invoice.

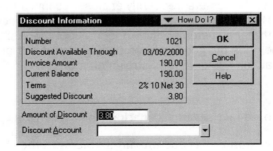

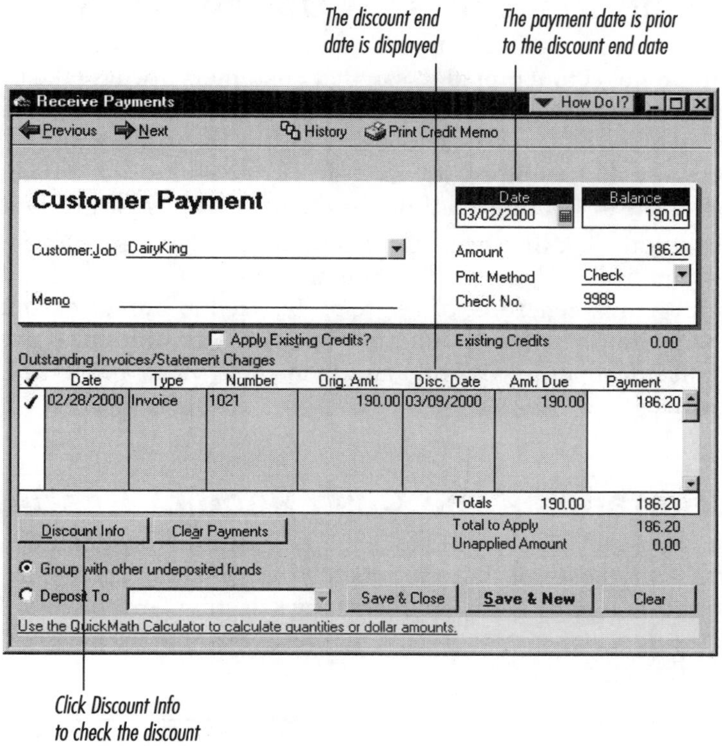

The discount end
date is displayed

The payment date is prior
to the discount end date

Click Discount Info
to check the discount

FIGURE 4-3 The fields in the Receive Payments form change to reflect the fact that this customer has been configured for discounts for timely payment

A summary of the invoice and discount terms appears and QuickBooks inserts the amount of the discount, based on the information in the invoice. Accept the amount of discount or change it, and then click OK. When you return to the Receive Payments window, you'll see that QuickBooks has changed the Amt. Due column to reflect the discount. The original amount column remains the same.

To track the amount of money you've given away with discounts, you can create a specific account in your chart of accounts. You should make the account an income account (I call mine Discounts Given). You can also use the standard revenue accounts, which will be reduced every time you apply a discount. The math is right, but the absence of an audit trail bothers me. If there's an account named "Discounts" in the part of your chart of accounts that's devoted to expenses, don't use that account for your customer discounts, because it's there to track the discounts you take with your vendors.

Applying Discounts for Untimely Payments

Sometimes, customers take the discount even if the payment arrives after the discount date. (I'm tempted to say that customers *always* take the discount even if the payment arrives later than the terms permit.) You can apply the payment to the invoice and leave a balance due for the discount amount that was deducted by the customer, if you wish. However, most companies give the customer the discount even if the payment is late, as part of "good will."

When you click the Discount Info button in that case, QuickBooks does not automatically fill in the discount amount—it's too late, and QuickBooks is not forgiving, generous, or aware of the need to humor customers to preserve good will. Simply enter the amount manually (the amount is available on the Discount Information window) and then click OK to apply the discount to the invoice.

Understanding the Cash Receipt Postings

When you receive money in payment for customer invoices, QuickBooks automatically posts all the amounts to your general ledger. Here are the postings if you opt to hold payments, by selecting Group With Other, and make the deposit separately (covered in the section "Depositing Cash Receipts," later in this chapter).

ACCOUNT	DEBIT	CREDIT
Undeposited Funds	Total of cash receipts	
Accounts Receivable		Total of cash receipts

The Undeposited Funds account is an asset, just like your regular bank account is an asset. In fact, it's a cash asset and belongs in the same section of your chart of accounts as your bank accounts. The only difference between the amount in the Undeposited Funds account and the amount in your bank account is that you cannot write checks or otherwise spend the funds in the former.

When you make the actual deposit, QuickBooks automatically posts the following transaction:

ACCOUNT	DEBIT	CREDIT
Bank	Total of deposit	
Undeposited Funds		Total of deposit

Here are the postings for a customer who takes a discount. Let's assume the sale was for $100.00. The original sale posted the following amounts:

ACCOUNT	DEBIT	CREDIT
Accounts Receivable	$100.00	
Income		$100.00

The customer was entitled to (and took) a 1% discount. When you enter the customer payment, which is in the amount of $99.00, the following postings occur:

ACCOUNT	DEBIT	CREDIT
Undeposited Funds	$99.00	
Accounts Receivable		$100.00
Discounts Given	$1.00	

Handling Cash Sales

Cash sales are the same as invoiced sales insofar as an exchange of money for goods or services occurs. The difference is that there's no period of time during which you have money "on the street." You can have a cash sale for either a service or a product, although it's far more common to sell products for cash. Most service companies use invoices.

I'm assuming that cash sales is not your normal method of doing business (you're not running a candy store). If you are running a retail store, the cash sale feature in QuickBooks isn't an efficient way to handle your cash flow. You should either have specialized retail software (that even takes care of opening the cash register drawer automatically) or use QuickBooks only to record your daily totals of bank deposits as a journal entry (check with your accountant about the offset income account).

 N O T E : Don't take the word "cash" literally, because a cash sale can involve a check or a credit card.

There are two efficient methods for handling cash sales in QuickBooks:

- Record each cash sale as a discrete record
- Record sales in batches (usually one batch for each business day)

Recording each cash sale is useful for tracking sales of products or services to customers with whom you don't have an ongoing relationship and regular invoicing cycles. It provides a way to maintain records about those customers.

Recording cash sales in batches is useful for tracking income and inventory decrements when you have no desire to maintain customer information.

Recording a Cash Sale

To record a cash sale, click the Customers listing on the Navigation Bar and then click the Cash Sales icon. The Enter Cash Sales window appears, as shown in Figure 4-4.

Enter a name in the Customer:Job field or select the name from the drop-down list. If the customer information doesn't exist, you can add it by choosing <Add New>.

TIP: If you have customers who always pay at the time of the sale, you might want to consider creating a customer type for this group (Cash seems an appropriate name for the type). You can separate this group for reports or for marketing and advertising campaigns.

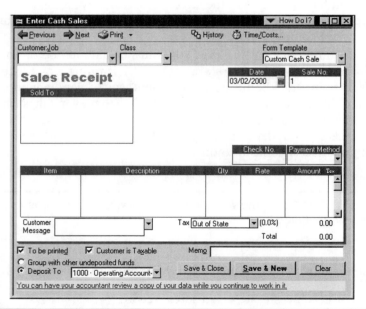

FIGURE 4-4 The Enter Cash Sales form is an invoice, a payment form, and a receipt, all rolled into one

Every field in the Enter Cash Sales window works exactly the way it works for invoices and payments. Just fill in the information. To save the record, click Save & New to bring up a new blank record, or click Save & Close to stop using the Enter Cash Sales window.

Printing a Receipt for a Cash Sale

Many cash customers want a receipt. Click the Print button in the Enter Cash Sales window to display the Print One Sales Receipt window, shown in Figure 4-5.

 T I P : If the customer wants a receipt with a name on it, use the Sold To block in the Enter Cash Sales window and avoid the need to enter a new customer into your system.

If you're not printing to a dot-matrix printer with multipart paper and you want a copy of the receipt for your files, be sure you change the specification in the Number of Copies check box.

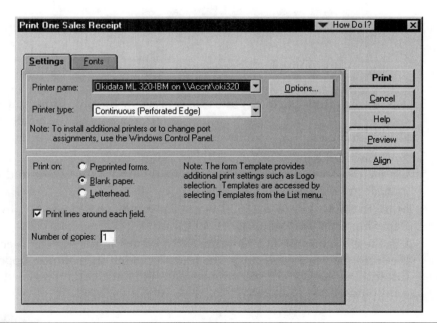

FIGURE 4-5 Choose the options you need to print a receipt

Customizing the Cash Sales Form

I think a lot is missing from the form QuickBooks presents for cash sales. For example, there's no place for a sales rep, which is needed if you're paying commissions on cash sales. There's no Ship To address if the customer pays cash and wants delivery. In fact, there's no Ship Via field.

The solution is to customize the Enter Cash Sales form. Here's how to do that:

1. Click the arrow next to the Form Template box in the upper-right corner of the form and choose Customize from the drop-down list.
2. The Customize Template dialog box opens with several choices.

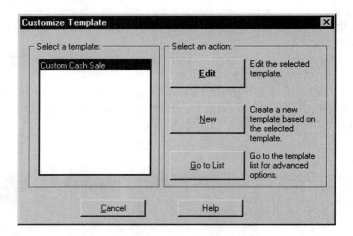

3. There aren't multiple forms to use as a basis for the new form, so Custom Cash Sale is selected. Click New to open the Customize Cash Sale window, shown in Figure 4-6.
4. Give the form a name in the Template Name box.
5. On the Header tab, select the Ship To field for both the Screen and the Print forms.
6. Move to the Fields tab and add any fields you need. It's common to need Rep, Ship Date, and Ship Via.
7. Use the Columns tab to add or remove columns in the line item section of the form. You can also change the order in which the columns appear. (For instance, perhaps you'd rather have Qty in the first column instead of the Item number.)

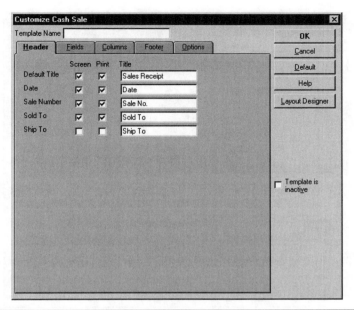

FIGURE 4-6   Build your own, more useful, form for cash sales

After you finish making the changes you need, click OK. You're returned to the Enter Cash Sales window, and your new form is ready to use (see Figure 4-7).

Handling Batches of Cash Sales

If you sell products or services and receive instant payment on a more frequent basis, you might want to consider batching the transactions. This works only if you don't care about maintaining information about the customers, and no customer expects a receipt. This technique also works if you have a business in which sales and service personnel return to the office each day with customer payments in hand.

Create a customized form, using the steps described in the previous section, with the following guidelines:

- Name the form appropriately (for example, Batch Sales or Sales Batch).
- In the Header tab, keep only the Date and Sale Number fields in the heading.
- In the Fields tab, deselect all the optional fields.
- In the Footer tab, remove the Message field.

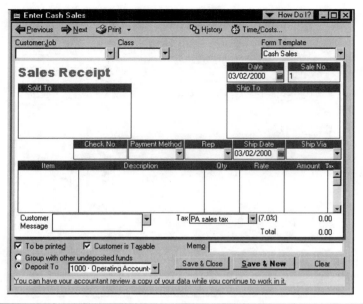

FIGURE 4-7 Now the form works for any type of cash sale

To batch-process cash sales, use the Enter Cash Sales window with the following procedures:

- Use a customer named Cash or CashSale, or skip the Customer:Job field.
- In the line item section, use a new line for each sale, regardless of whether the same customer is purchasing each item, each item is purchased by a different customer, or there's a combination of both events.
- Use the Save & Close button at the end of the day.

If you use this technique, you cannot track the method of payment, and all receipts are treated as "money in."

N O T E : The QuickBooks Help files provide a method for using a Summary approach to cash sales that involves creating templates based on the method of payment and pre-entering all the items available for sale. You might want to try using that method if you think it suits your business. I tested it and found it inconvenient and prone to user errors, but perhaps your business model would make it efficacious.

Understanding the Cash Sale Postings

QuickBooks treats cash sales in the simplest, most logical manner. If you've sold a service instead of an inventory item for cash (perhaps a service call for a one-time customer you don't want to invoice), the postings are very straightforward:

ACCOUNT	DEBIT	CREDIT
Undeposited Funds	Total cash sales	
Revenue		Total cash sales

If the cash sale involved inventory items, here are the postings:

ACCOUNT	DEBIT	CREDIT
Undeposited Funds	Total cash sales	
Income		Total cash sales
Cost of Sales	Total cost of items sold	
Inventory		Total cost of items sold

Now, I'm going to suggest you make it a bit more complicated, but don't panic, because it's not difficult, and in the long run, my suggestions will make your bookkeeping chores easier. There's also a chance you'll make your accountant happier.

The Enter Cash Sales window provides two choices for posting the cash you receive:

- Group With Other Undeposited Funds
- Deposit To (you're expected to enter the bank account into which you place your cash receipts)

If you use the Deposit To option, your sales won't appear in the Payments to Deposit window when you tell QuickBooks you're taking your cash receipts to the bank. (See the section "Depositing Cash Receipts," later in this chapter.) In fact, your bank account will be incremented by the amount of cash you post to it from cash sales, even though the money isn't really there until you make the trip to the bank.

I have two suggestions for tracking receipts from cash sales; pick the one that appeals to you:

- Opt to post the receipts to the Undeposited Funds account, but make those deposits separately when you work in the QuickBooks Payments to Deposit window.
- Opt to post the receipts to a new account called Undeposited Till (or something similar) and manually deposit the money into your bank account via a journal entry.

If you want to use the Undeposited Funds account, when you use the Make Deposits window, select only the cash receipts for deposit and then return to the Make Deposits window to deposit the remaining cash receipts in a separate transaction. Details on the procedures are found in the "Depositing Cash Receipts" section, later in this chapter.

If you want to create an account to which you post cash in the Enter Cash Sales window, make the new account a type Other Current Asset.

If you deal in real cash and have a cash register, you need to fill the till to make change. Write a check from your operating account (the payee should be Cash) and post the amount to the new account (which I call Undeposited Till). This produces the following posting (assuming $100.00 is allocated for change):

ACCOUNT	DEBIT	CREDIT
Checking		$100.00
Undeposited Till	$100.00	

When it's time to go to the bank, leave the original startup money (in this example, $100.00) in the till, count the rest of the money, and deposit that money into your checking account. When you return from the bank, make the following journal entry:

ACCOUNT	DEBIT	CREDIT
Checking	Amt of deposit	
Undeposited Till		Amt of deposit

In a perfect world, after you make the deposit and the journal entry, you can open the register for the Undeposited Till account and see a balance equal to your original startup cash. The world isn't perfect, however, and sometimes the actual amount you were able to deposit doesn't equal the amount collected in the Enter Cash Sales transaction window. To resolve this, see the section "Handling the Over and Short Problem," later in this chapter.

Incidentally, if you want to raise or lower the amount you leave in the till for change, you don't have to do anything special. Just deposit less or more money, and the remainder (in the register for the Undeposited Till account and also in the physical till) just becomes the new base.

Depositing Cash Receipts

With all of those checks you've received for invoice payments, and the cash hanging around from the cash sales, it's time to go to the bank. Wait, don't grab those car keys yet! You have to tell QuickBooks about your bank deposit. Otherwise, when it's time to reconcile your checkbook, you'll have a nervous breakdown.

Choosing the Payments to Deposit

As you've been filling out the payment and cash sales forms, QuickBooks has been keeping a list it calls "Undeposited Funds." That list remains designated as Undeposited Funds until you clear it by depositing them.

To tell QuickBooks to make a deposit, choose Banking | Make Deposits from the QuickBooks menu bar, which brings up the Payments to Deposit window, shown in Figure 4-8.

Notice that the Payments to Deposit window displays information about the items in the Type column: Customer payments are indicated by PMT, and cash sales receipts are indicated by RCPT.

You may have other deposits to make, perhaps refund checks from vendors, checks representing loans you've been approved for, checks representing a capital infusion from you, or some other type of deposit. Don't worry, you can

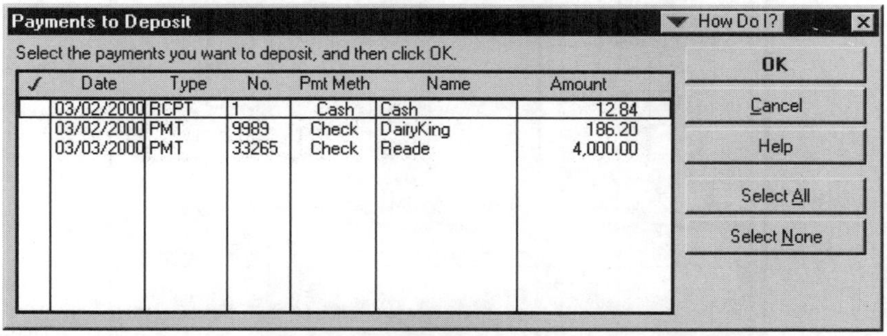

FIGURE 4-8 All the money you've received since your last bank deposit is listed in the Payments to Deposit window

tell QuickBooks about them in the next transaction window—this window is only displaying the cash receipts you've entered into QuickBooks through the Payments and Cash Sales transaction windows.

Click Select All to select all the payments for deposit. If you want to hold back the deposit of any item, deselect it by clicking in the check mark column. Only the items that have a check mark will be cleared from the undeposited payments list. There are several reasons to deselect deposit items:

- You received a payment in advance from a customer and don't want to deposit it until you're sure you can fill the order.
- You've accepted a post-dated check and it cannot yet be deposited.
- You want to separate the transactions for depositing customer payments and cash sales.

After you make your selections, click OK.

Filling Out the Deposit Slip

Clicking OK in the Payments to Deposit window brings up the Make Deposits window, shown in Figure 4-9.

If you were paying attention when you looked at Figure 4-8, you'll notice that, in this case, I'm separating the deposit of customer payments from the

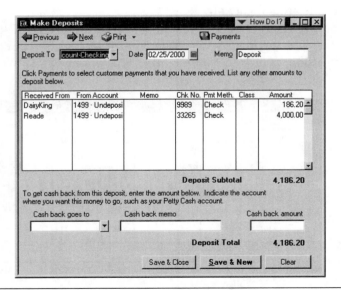

FIGURE 4-9   The Make Deposits window is a virtual deposit slip

deposit of receipts from cash sales. This is a common practice when depositing cash, because sometimes the bank notifies you that their automatic counting machine produced a different total from the total on your deposit slip (you probably counted the cash by hand instead of purchasing counting machines for coins and paper money). If that happens, you can edit the cash sales deposit item in your bank register, and the cause of the edit will be obvious (I'm a stickler for good audit trails).

Select the bank account you're using for this deposit. Then, make sure the date matches the day you're physically depositing the money. (If you're doing this at night, use tomorrow's date so your records match the bank statement.)

Adding Items to the Deposit

If you decide to add a payment you deselected in the previous window, click the Payments button at the top of the window to return to the Make Deposits window and select it.

If you want to add deposit items that weren't in the Make Deposits window, click anywhere in the Received From column to make it accessible, and select an existing name by clicking the arrow, or click <Add New> to enter a name that isn't in your system. If the source of the check is a bank, or yourself, or any other entity that isn't a customer or vendor, use the Other classification for the type of name.

Press TAB to move to the From Account column and enter the account to which you're posting this transaction. For example, if the check you're depositing represents a bank loan, use the liability account for that bank loan (you can create it here by choosing <Add New> if you didn't think to set up the account earlier). If the check you're depositing represents an infusion of capital from you, use the Owner's Capital account. If the check is a refund for an expense (perhaps you overpaid someone and they're returning money to you), post the deposit to that expense.

Use the TAB key to move through the rest of the columns, which are self-explanatory.

Getting Cash Back from Deposits

If you're getting cash back from your deposit, you can tell QuickBooks about it right on the virtual deposit slip, instead of making a journal entry to adjust the total of collected payments against the total of the bank deposit.

Enter the account to which you're posting the cash (usually a petty cash account); optionally, enter a memo as a note to yourself and enter the amount of cash you want back from this deposit. Even though you can put the cash in your pocket, you must account for it, because these are business funds. As you spend the cash for business expenses, post the expense against a petty cash account with a journal entry.

If you're keeping the money for yourself, use the Draw account to post the cash back.

 T I P : Many banks will not cash checks made out to a company, so your ability to get cash back may be limited to checks made out to you, personally.

Printing Deposit Slips

If you want to print a deposit slip or a deposit summary, click the Print button in the Make Deposits window. QuickBooks asks whether you want to print a deposit slip and summary, or just a deposit summary.

If you want to print a deposit slip that your bank will accept, you must order printable deposit slips from Intuit. Call 800-433-8810 to order personalized deposit slips that have your name, address, and bank information, or visit the Web site at www.intuitmarket.com.

The deposit slips from Intuit are guaranteed to be acceptable to your bank. You must have a laser printer or inkjet printer to use them. When you print the deposit slip, there's a tear-off section at the bottom of the page that has a deposit summary. Keep that section for your own records and take the rest of the page to the bank along with your money.

If you don't have Intuit deposit slips, select Deposit Summary and fill out your bank deposit slip manually. A Print dialog box appears so you can change printers, adjust margins, or even print in color. Choose Print to send the deposit information to the printer. When you return to the Make Deposits window, click OK to save the deposit.

 T I P : If you're printing real deposit slips and your bank requires multiple copies, change the Number of Copies specification in the Print dialog box.

Handling the Over and Short Problem

If you literally take cash for cash sales, when you count the money in the till at the end of the day, you may find that the recorded income doesn't match the cash you expected to find in the till. Or, you may find that the money you posted to deposit to the bank doesn't match the amount of money you put into the little brown bag you take to the bank. This is a common problem with cash, and, in fact, it's an occasional problem in regular accrual bookkeeping. One of the ensuing problems you face is how to handle this in your bookkeeping system. QuickBooks is a double-entry bookkeeping system, which means the left side of the ledger has to be equal to the right side of the ledger. If you post $100.00 in cash sales, but only have $99.50 to take to the bank, how do you handle the missing 50 cents? You can't just post $100.00 to your bank account (well, you could, but your bank reconciliation won't work and, more importantly, you're not practicing good bookkeeping).

The solution to the Over/Short dilemma is to acknowledge it in your bookkeeping procedures. Track it. You'll be amazed by how much it balances itself out—short one day, over another. (Of course, if you're short every day, and the shortages are growing, you have an entirely different problem, and the first place to look is at the person who stands in front of the cash register.) To track Over/Short, you need to have some place to post the discrepancies, which means you have to create some new accounts in your chart of accounts.

Create two new accounts as follows:

1. Click the Chart of Accounts listing in the Navigation Bar to open the Chart of Accounts window.
2. Press CTRL-N.
3. In the New Account window, select an account type of Income.
4. If you're using numbered accounts, choose a number that's on the next level from your regular Income accounts; for example, choose 4290 if your regular Income accounts are 4000, 4010, and so on.
5. Name the account **Over**.
6. Click Next and repeat the processes, using the next number and naming the account **Short**.
7. If you want to see a net number for Over/Short (a good idea), create three accounts. Name the first account (the parent account) **Over-Short**, and then make the Over and Short accounts subaccounts of Over-Short.

In addition, you need items to use for your overages and shortages (remember, you need items for everything that's connected with entering invoices and cash sales).

Now create new items as follows:

1. Click the Item List entry on the Navigation Bar to open the Item List window.
2. Click the Item button and choose New from the menu.
3. Create a noninventory part item named Overage.

4. Don't assign a price.
5. Make it nontaxable.
6. Link it to the account named Over that you just created.
7. Click Next to create another new noninventory part item.
8. Name this item Short and link it to the account named Short.
9. Click OK to close the Item List window.

Now that you have the necessary accounts and items, use the Over and Short items right in the Cash Sale window to adjust the difference between the amount of money you've accumulated in the Cash Sale transactions and the amount of money you're actually depositing to the bank. Remember to use a minus sign before the figure if you're using the Short item.

Tracking Accounts Receivable

In this chapter, you will learn to...

- Set up finance charges

- Send customer payment reminders

- Print customer statements

- Run A/R aging

Collecting your money is one of the largest headaches in running a business. You have to track what's owed and who owes it and then expend time and effort to collect it. All of the effort you spend on the money your customers owe you is called "tracking A/R."

Using Finance Charges

One way to speed up collections is to impose finance charges for late payments. Incidentally, this isn't "found money"; it probably doesn't cover its own cost. The amount of time spent tracking, analyzing, and chasing receivables is substantial.

To use finance charges you have to establish the rate and circumstances under which they're assessed.

Configuring Finance Charges

Your company's finance charges are configured as part of your company preferences. Choose Edit | Preferences to open the Preferences window. Then click the Finance Charge icon on the left pane and select the Company Preferences tab (see Figure 5-1).

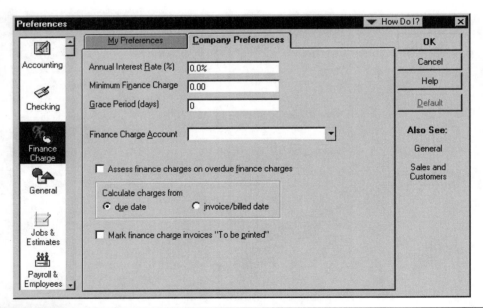

FIGURE 5-1   Configure your finance charges

Here are some guidelines for filling out this window:

- Notice that the interest rate is annual. If you want to charge 1% a month, enter 12% in the Annual Interest Rate field.

- You can assess a minimum finance charge for overdue balances. QuickBooks will calculate the finance charge and if it's less than the minimum, the minimum charge is assessed.

- Use the Grace Period field to enter the number of days after a bill is considered eligible for finance charges (usually the due date) before finance charges are assessed.

- During setup, QuickBooks probably created an account for finance charges. If so, it's displayed in this window. If not, enter (or create) the account you want to use to post finance charges.

- The issue of assessing finance charges on overdue finance charges is a sticky one. By default, it's selected in this window, but it's illegal in many states. Selecting this option means that a customer who owed $100.00 last month and had a finance charge assessed of $2.00 now owes $102.00. Now, the next finance charge is assessed on a balance of $102.00 (instead of on the original overdue balance of $100.00). Regardless of state law, the fact is that very few businesses opt to use this calculation method. To change the default, click to remove the check mark for this option.

- You can tell QuickBooks to calculate the finance charge from the due date or the invoice date.

- QuickBooks creates an invoice when finance charges are assessed in order to have a permanent record of the transaction. By default, these invoices aren't printed; they're just accumulated along with the overdue invoices so they'll print out on a monthly statement. You can opt to have the finance charge invoices printed, which you should do only if you're planning to mail them as a reminder.

Click OK to save your settings after you've filled out the window.

Assessing Finance Charges

You should assess finance charges just before you calculate and print customer statements. Choose Customers | Assess Finance Charges to open the Assess Finance Charges window with a list of all the customers with overdue balances (see Figure 5-2).

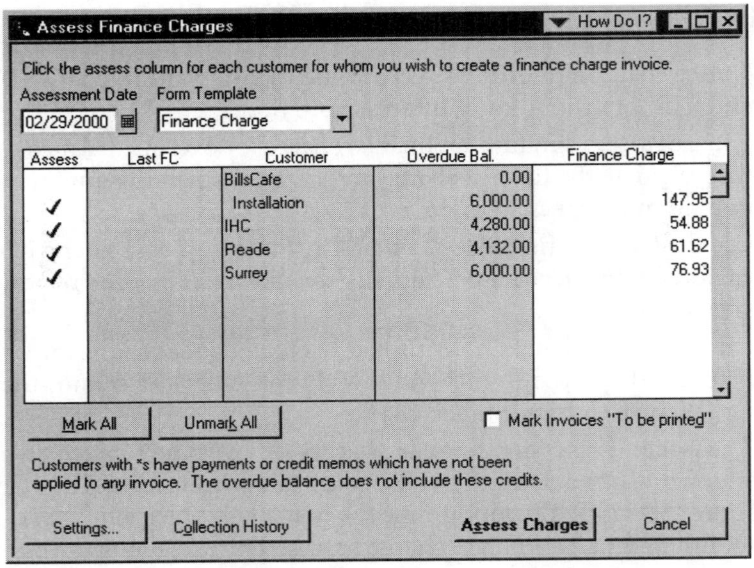

FIGURE 5-2 QuickBooks automatically calculates the finance charges as of the current date

There are some things you should know about the figures you see in the window:

- Credit memos that haven't been applied to an invoice (thus reducing the amount of the invoice and, therefore, reducing the finance charge) are not subtracted from the total due. Customers with that condition extant are marked with an asterisk. If this is a problem (your customers may think it is), you can apply the credit memos to invoices in order to reduce the balance. (See Chapter 4 to learn how to apply credit memos.)
- QuickBooks calculates the finance charge on a daily basis, starting with the invoice date or due date (whichever you specified in the settings).

Choosing the Assessment Date

Change the Assessment Date field to the date on which you want the finance charge to appear on customer statements. It's common to assess finance charges on the last day of the month. When you press the TAB key to move out of the date field, the finance charges are recalculated to reflect the new date.

Selecting the Customers

You can eliminate a customer from the process by clicking in the Assess column to remove the check mark. QuickBooks, unlike many other accounting software packages, does not have a finance charge assessment option on each customer card. Therefore, all customers with overdue balances are included when you assess finance charges. It can be time consuming to deselect each customer, so if you have only a few customers for whom you reserve this process, choose Unmark All, then reselect the customers you want to include.

Changing the Amounts

You can change the calculated total if you wish (a good idea if there are credit memos floating around). Just click on the amount displayed in the Finance Charge column to activate that column for that customer. Then enter a new finance charge amount. If you need to calculate the new figure (perhaps you're giving credit for any floating credit memos), press the equal sign (=) to use the built-in QuickMath calculator.

Checking the History

When you select the Finance Charge column for a customer, you've also selected the customer. Now you can use the Collection History button to see the selected customer's history in a Collections Report. As you can see in the following illustration, your mouse pointer turns into a magnifying glass with the letter "z" (for "zoom") in it when you position it over a line item. Double-click the line item to display the original transaction window if you need to examine the details.

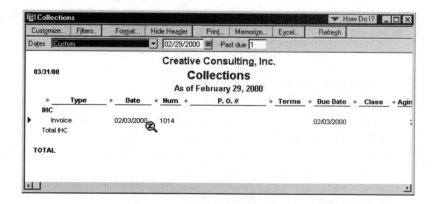

Selecting Printing Options

If you want to print the finance charge invoices (they really are invoices since they add charges to the customer balance), be sure to select the check box named Mark Invoices To Be Printed. You can send the printed copies to your customers as a nagging reminder. If you just want the customer to see the finance charge on the monthly statement, deselect that option.

To print the finance charge invoices, choose File | Print Forms | Print Invoices. The list of unprinted invoices appears, and unless you have regular invoices you didn't print yet, the list includes only the finance charge invoices. If the list is correct, click OK to continue on to the printing process. Chapter 3 has detailed information about printing invoices.

Saving the Finance Charge Invoices

Click Assess Charges in the Assess Finance Charges window when all the figures are correct. If you've opted to skip printing, there's nothing more to do. When you create your customer statements, these charges will appear.

Sending Statements

On a periodic basis you should send statements to your customers. (Most statements are sent monthly.) They serve a couple of purposes: They remind customers of outstanding balances and they insure that your records and your customers' records reflect the same information.

If you're coming to QuickBooks from a manual system, statements will seem like a miraculous tool, because creating statements from manual customer cards is a nightmare. As a result, companies without software generally don't even bother to try.

Creating the Statements

Before you start creating your statements, be sure that all the transactions that should be included on the statements have been entered into the system. Did you forget anything? Credit memos? Payments from customers? Finance charges?

Choose Customers | Create Statements to display the Select Statements to Print window, shown in Figure 5-3.

Selecting the Customers

It's normal procedure to send statements to all customers, but if that's not the plan you can change the default selection.

There's only one format for printing unless you create one of your own

Select the period the statement covers

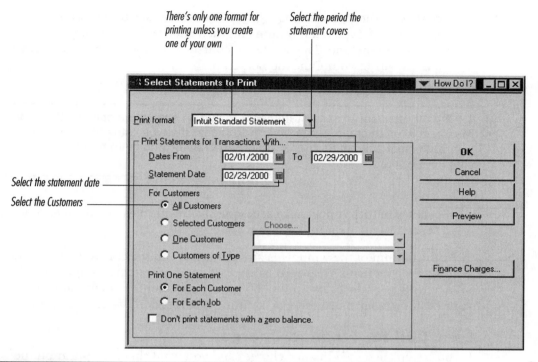

Select the statement date

Select the Customers

FIGURE 5-3   Statements start with configuration options

- If you're sending a statement to one customer only, select One Customer and then click the arrow next to the text box to scroll through the list of your customers and select the one you want.
- If you want to send statements to a group of customers, click the Selected Customers option to activate the Choose button that's next to it. Then click the Choose button to bring up a list of customers and click each customer you want to include.

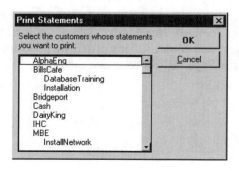

- Another method of selecting a group of customers is to select the Customers of Type radio button and then choose the customer type you want to include. This works, of course, only if you created customer types as part of your QuickBooks setup.

 TIP: If you want to send statements to certain customers only, that's a good reason in itself to create a customer type (name the type "stmnts"). Then link your statement customers to that type. See Chapter 2 to learn how to set up customer types.

- Specify whether you want to send one statement to each customer or send a separate statement for each job.

At the bottom of the window is an option you can select if you don't want to send statements that have a zero balance. If you use statements only to collect money, you can select this option. If you use statements to make sure you and your customers have matching accounting records, don't select the option.

Last Call for Finance Charges

If you haven't assessed finance charges and you want them to appear on the statements, click the Finance Charges button. The Assess Finance Charges window opens (see Figure 5-4), but this time no customers are selected and the charges are not yet assessed.

If you've already assessed finance charges for the selected time period, this window won't re-assess them (whew!). You'll be told that the finance charge for this customer is zero. This screen is useful only if you haven't already run the finance charge assessment for the period.

Previewing the Statements

Before you commit the statements to paper, you can click the Preview button to get an advance look (see Figure 5-5). This is not really just to see what the printed output will look like; it's also a way to look at the customer records. Click the Next Page button to move through all the statements. If you see a

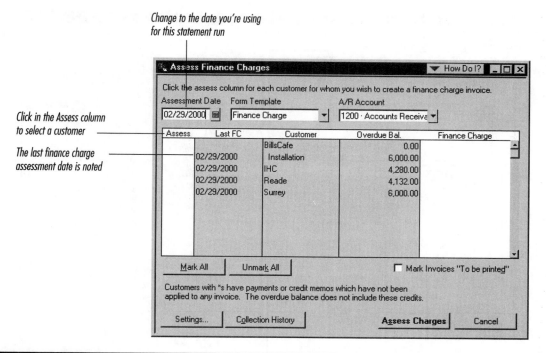

Change to the date you're using for this statement run

Click in the Assess column to select a customer

The last finance charge assessment date is noted

FIGURE 5-4 You can run a last-minute finance charge assessment just before you print statements

statement that seems "funny," you can drill down to the transactions and check everything.

Printing the Statements

When everything is just the way it should be, print the statements by clicking the Print button in the Print Preview window, or clicking OK in the original Select Statements to Print window.

If you use the Print button in the Print Preview window, the statements print using the printer and printing options of your last print job, because no Print window is displayed. If you return to the Select Statements to Print window and click OK, the Print Statement(s) window appears (as seen in Figure 5-6), and you can change the printing options.

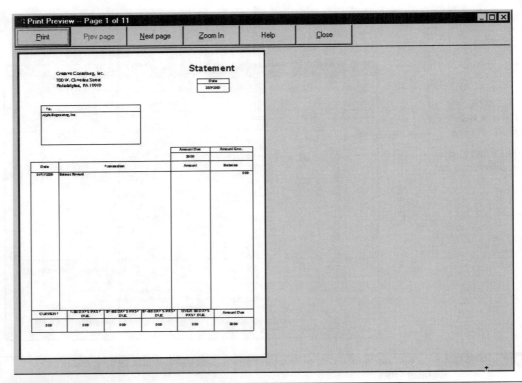

FIGURE 5-5 The Print Preview window provides a quick check before you print and mail the statements

Customizing the Statements

You don't have to use the standard statement form—you can design your own. To accomplish this, in the Select Statements to Print window click the arrow to the right of the Print Format box and choose Customize to open the Customize Template window. Choose New in that window to open the Customize Statement window. This window has five tabs, but the only one that contains options that merit consideration for change is the Fields tab, shown in Figure 5-7.

Here are the fields you might want to think about changing:

- **Terms** It doesn't seem fair to tell a customer of amounts past due without reminding the customer of the terms.
- **Amount Due** This field isn't really necessary, because the same field and its data are positioned at the bottom of the statement page.
- **Amount Enc.** If you use statements as bills, or expect payment for the amount of the statement, this field is supposed to contain an amount filled

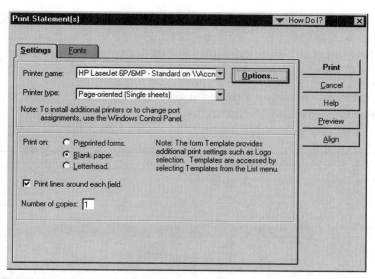

FIGURE 5-6   Change any options you need to, and then click Print

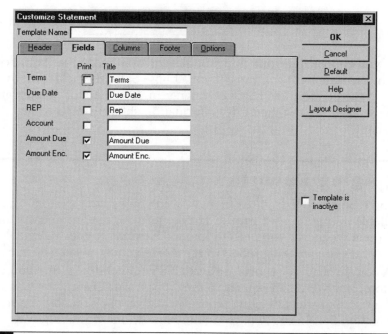

FIGURE 5-7   You may want to change the fields that appear on top of the columns in the statement

in by the customer. (The amount is supposed to match the amount of the check that's returned with the statement.) If you mail invoices and use statements as reminders (and your customers never send checks attached to the statements), you may not want to use this field.

You must also supply a name for this new template, because you cannot save the new design with the existing name.

 N O T E : When you add fields to a template, QuickBooks may issue a warning that the fields overlap existing fields.

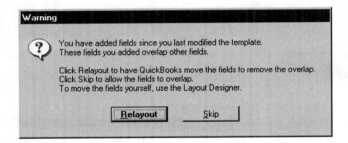

If you choose Relayout, QuickBooks will attempt to fit all the fields onto the top of the statement columns. If you choose Skip, the fields will overlap; you should then choose the Layout Designer in the Customize Statement window to make everything neat and tidy. Information about using the Layout Designer is in Chapter 3.

Running Aging Reports

Aging reports are lists of the money owed you by your customers, and they're available in quite a few formats. They're for you, not for your customers. You run them whenever you need to know the extent of your receivables. Many companies run an aging report every morning, just to keep an eye on things.

A couple of aging reports are available in QuickBooks, and you can also customize any built-in reports so they report data exactly the way you want it. To see the variety of aging reports available, click the Reports item on the Navigation Bar. In the Report Finder window, make the following selections:

1. In the Select a Type of Report box, select Customers & Receivables.
2. Choose A/R Aging Summary or A/R Aging Detail.

3. In the Set the Date Range box select This Fiscal Year-To-Date.
4. Click Display to see your aging report.

Using Summary Aging Reports

The quickest way to see how much money is owed to you is to select A/R Aging Summary, which produces a listing of customer balances (see Figure 5-8).

Let's pause a moment and talk about the importance of the number for that A/R asset. In fact, banks give lines of credit and loans using the A/R balance as collateral.

When your accountant visits, you can bet one of the things he or she will ask to see is this report. Incidentally, your accountant should be visiting regularly, not just at tax time. Having your accountant look at your books quarterly or semi-annually is important because it means you'll receive analysis and planning advice that helps you keep your business on track.

When your accountant asks for an aging report, another safe bet is that you'll receive a request to see the amount posted to A/R in your general ledger. The general ledger A/R balance and the total on the aging report must be the same (for the same date)—not close, not almost, but *exactly* the same. If the figures are not identical, your general ledger isn't "proved" (jargon for "I'm sorry, we can't trust your general ledger figures because they don't audit properly.").

Creative Consulting, Inc.
A/R Aging Summary
As of February 29, 2000

	1 - 30	31 - 60	61 - 90	> 90	TOTAL
BillsCafe					
Installation	0.00	6,000.00	0.00	0.00	6,147.95
Total BillsCafe	0.00	6,000.00	0.00	0.00	6,147.95
Bridgeport	0.00	0.00	0.00	0.00	73.83
DairyKing	0.00	0.00	0.00	0.00	190.00
IHC	4,280.00	0.00	0.00	0.00	4,334.88
Reade	3,210.00	4,922.00	0.00	0.00	8,193.62
Surrey	6,000.00	0.00	0.00	0.00	6,076.93
TOTAL	**13,490.00**	**10,922.00**	**0.00**	**0.00**	**25,017.21**

FIGURE 5-8 A/R totals for each customer are displayed in an aging summary report

My own experience tells me that when the general ledger doesn't "prove," it almost always means that somebody made a journal entry that involved the A/R account. Don't do that—it's unacceptable bookkeeping. The only way the A/R account should change is via transactions involving customers: invoices, discounts, and credits.

> **TIP:** If you file your business taxes on a cash basis, your accountant may make a journal entry involving the A/R account and the Revenue account(s). It's a reversing entry, and it takes effect on the last day of your fiscal year. The next day it must be reversed. (Your accountant will give you specific explanations and instructions.)

To ascertain whether your A/R account matches your aging total, set the date of the aging report to the last day of the current month and click the Refresh button. Then, with the aging report still on the screen, choose Lists | Chart of Accounts from the menu bar. When the Chart of Accounts list opens, double-click the Accounts Receivable account listing. Both windows are on your screen (see Figure 5-9) and the totals should be identical.

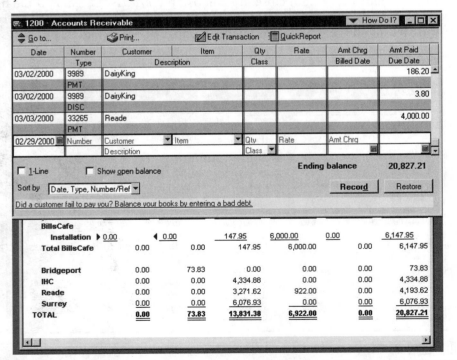

FIGURE 5-9 You can see the totals from both the account listing and the A/R report, and they must match

Using Aging Detail Reports

If you choose Aging Detail from the Accounts Receivable reports menu, you see a much more comprehensive report, such as the one seen in Figure 5-10.

The report is organized by dates, showing individual transactions, including finance charges, for each aging period.

Customizing Aging Reports

If you don't use (or care about) all of the columns in the aging detail report, or you'd prefer to see the information displayed in a different manner, you can customize the report before you print it.

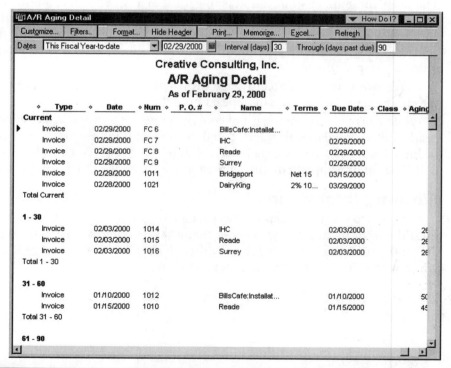

FIGURE 5-10   Use the scroll bars to see all the information on a detailed aging report

Start by clicking the Customize button on the report to see the Customize Report window.

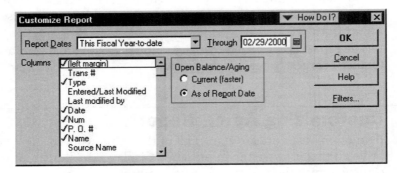

Customizing the Columns

The most common customization is to get rid of any column you don't care about. For example, if you don't use classes for categorizing transactions (or you do use classes, but don't care about that information in your aging report), get rid of the column. Or you might want to get rid of the Terms column since it doesn't impact the totals.

To remove a column, scroll through the list of columns and click it to remove the check mark. The column disappears from the report.

While you're looking at the list of column names, you may find a column heading that's not currently selected, but that contains information you'd like to include in your report. If so, click that column listing to place a check mark next to it. The column appears on the report and the data linked to it is displayed.

Filtering Information

If you want to produce a report that isn't a straight aging report, you can easily filter the information that appears so that it meets criteria important to you. To filter your aging report, click the Filters button in the Customize Report window to bring up the Report Filters window.

Select a filter and then set the limits for it. (Each filter has its own specific type of criteria.) For example, you can use this feature if you want to see only those customers with receivables higher than a certain figure, or older than a certain aging period.

Customizing the Appearance

Click the Format button in the report window to see this Format Report window.

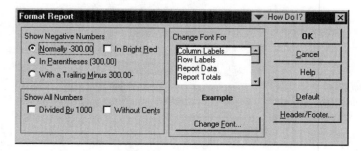

You can change the way negative numbers are displayed and you can change the fonts for any or all the individual elements in the report.

Printing Aging Reports

Whether you're using the standard report or one you've customized, you'll probably want to print the report. Click the Print button in the report window to bring up the Print Reports window (see Figure 5-11). You can use the Fonts and Margins tabs to make changes to the printed output.

Memorizing Aging Reports

If you've customized a report and have the columns, data, and formatting you need, there's no reason to re-invent the wheel the next time you need the same information. Instead of going through the customization process again next month, memorize the report as you designed it. Then you can fetch it whenever you need it.

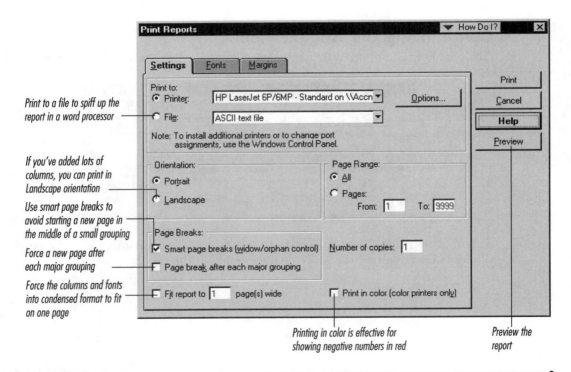

Print to a file to spiff up the report in a word processor

If you've added lots of columns, you can print in Landscape orientation

Use smart page breaks to avoid starting a new page in the middle of a small grouping

Force a new page after each major grouping

Force the columns and fonts into condensed format to fit on one page

Printing in color is effective for showing negative numbers in red

Preview the report

FIGURE 5-11 You can set printing options before sending the report to the printer

Click the Memorize button in the report window. When the Memorize Report window appears, enter a new name for the report and click OK.

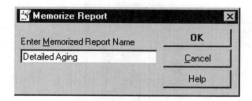

From now on, this report name will be on the list of memorized reports you can select from when you choose Reports | Memorized.

 N O T E : When you use a memorized report, you're generating it, not printing it the way it looked when you memorized it. "Generating" means that you enter a new aging date and the data is fetched from the QuickBooks transaction records, so you get current, accurate information.

Running Customer and Job Reports

Customer and job reports are like aging reports, but they're designed to give you information about the customers instead of concentrating on financial totals. There are several customer reports available from the menu that appears when you choose Customers & Receivables as the report type in the Report Finder window:

- **Open Invoices Report** Lists all unpaid invoices, sorted and subtotaled by customer and job.
- **Collections Report** A nifty report for nagging. Includes the contact name and telephone number, along with details about invoices with balances due.
- **Customer Balance Summary Report** Lists current total balance owed for each customer.
- **Customer Balance Detail Report** Lists every transaction for each customer, with a net subtotal for each customer.
- **Accounts Receivable Graph** Shows a graphic representation of the accounts receivable. For a quick impression, there's nothing like a graph (see Figure 5-12).

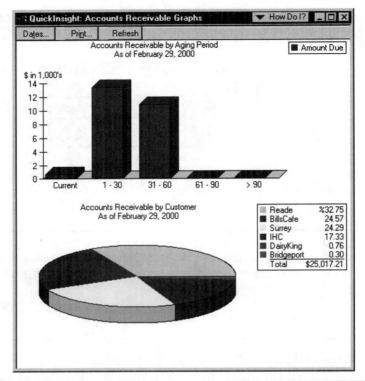

FIGURE 5-12 You can see a lot at a glance with a graph; double-click a pie slice to see the details

TIP: If you're using job costing, you can also create an Unbilled Costs by Job report.

Using Reports to Make Collections

Martin Miser, the corporate controller at Buford Button Corp., is a fanatic about keeping the accounts receivables balances at the lowest possible number. The collection rate at Buford Buttons is quite good, thanks to the techniques Martin has instigated. No customer has terms longer than 30 days, and any customer more than 60 days overdue is put on a C.O.D. basis until checks are received to reduce the balance.

Buford does most of its sales by telephone, fax, or e-mail, and none of the company's sales reps work outside the office. To keep the receivables down, Martin has invented a number of protocols, some of which involve the sales reps.

He prints an aging summary report every morning at 9:00 A.M. (it sets his mood for the day). When the accounts receivable clerk completes the entry of payments that arrived in the mail (usually by noon), a collections report is printed. However, Martin did something clever with this report—he customized it to include a REP column. When the report is distributed, it's easy for each sales rep to find the right customers to call.

The reps are trained to ask for specific dates by which the customer promises to catch up. In addition, they ask the customers to send a series of post-dated checks. The company holds the checks and deposits them according to a schedule worked out between the rep and the customer.

Every Monday morning Martin prints another customized report, which is a collection report that he filters so that it shows only customers over a certain amount. That report is given to the A/R department head for Monday morning phone calls. By 2:00 P.M., Martin himself is on the telephone with those customers the department head feels weren't cooperating.

If a customer is constantly behind in payments, a customer type "DUN" is applied to the customer and the dunning starts as statements are sent weekly instead of monthly to all customers of that type.

Entering Accounts Payable Bills

n this chapter, you will learn to...

- Enter vendor bills
- Enter inventory item purchases
- Enter vendor credit memos
- Use purchase orders
- Track reimbursable expenses
- Enter recurring bills

Chapter 6

Entering your bills and then paying them through QuickBooks is *accrual accounting*. That means an expense is posted to your Profit & Loss statement when you enter the bill, not when you actually pay the bill. The total of unpaid bills is the amount posted to the Accounts Payable account. However, if your taxes are filed on a cash basis (an expense isn't posted until you pay the bill), be assured (and assure your accountant) that QuickBooks understands how to report your financial figures on a cash basis. (See Chapter 15 for information on financial reports.)

Recording Vendor Bills

When the mail arrives, after you open all the envelopes that contain checks from customers (I always do that first), you should tell QuickBooks about the bills that arrived. Don't worry; QuickBooks doesn't automatically pay them. You decide when to do that.

The best way to enter your bills is to click the Enter Bills listing on the Navigation Bar. (You could also use the register for the Accounts Payable account, but you get more tracking information if you use the Enter Bills window.)

When the Enter Bills window opens (see Figure 6-1), you can fill out the information from the bill you received. If the vendor, the terms, or the general ledger expense account you need isn't yet in your system, choose <Add New> to put in the information. (See Chapter 2 for information about adding data to your QuickBooks lists.)

Easy One-Account Posting

In the Vendor field, click the arrow to choose a vendor from the list that appears. If the vendor isn't on the list, choose <Add New> to add this vendor to your QuickBooks vendor list. Then fill out the rest of the bill as follows:

1. Enter the bill date.
2. Enter the vendor's invoice number in the Ref. No. field.
3. In the Terms field, click the arrow to display a list of terms, and select the one you need. If the terms you have with this vendor aren't available, choose <Add New> to create a new Terms entry.
4. If there's some reason to do so, change the Bill Due date. (QuickBooks fills in the due date by using the bill date and performing a calculation that uses the Terms field.)
5. When you click in the Account column, an arrow appears. Click the arrow to display a list of your accounts. Then, select the general ledger account to which this bill is assigned.

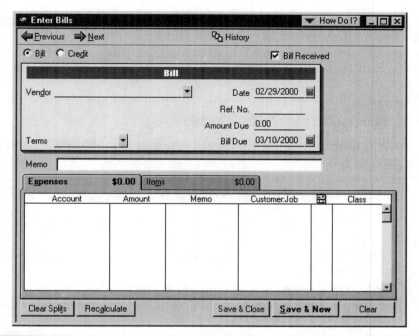

FIGURE 6-1 The Enter Bills window has a heading section and a details section

6. When you're finished, click Next to save this bill and bring up another blank Enter Bills window. When you've entered all your bills, click OK.

Splitting Expenses

Some bills aren't neatly assigned to one account in your general ledger; instead, they're split among multiple accounts. The most common example is a credit card bill.

To split a bill among multiple general ledger accounts:

1. Click in the Account column to display the arrow you use to see your chart of accounts.
2. Select the first account to which you want to assign this bill.
3. QuickBooks has already applied the entire amount in the Amount column. Replace that data with the amount you want to assign to the account you selected.
4. Click in the Account column to select the next account, and enter the appropriate amount in the Amount column.

As you add each additional account to the column, QuickBooks assumes that the unallocated amount is assigned to that account (see Figure 6-2). Repeat the process of changing the amount and adding another account until the split transaction is completely entered.

Entering Reimbursable Expenses

A reimbursable expense is one that you incurred on behalf of a customer. Even though you pay the vendor bill, there's an agreement with your customer that you'll send an invoice to recover your costs.

There are two common ways to encounter the issue of reimbursable expenses:

- *General expenses, such as long-distance telephone charges, parking and tolls, and other incidental expenses incurred on behalf of a client.* Those portions of the vendor bill that apply to customer agreements for reimbursement are split out when you enter the bill.
- *Purchase of specific goods or services on behalf of the customer.* The entire bill that arrives for this type of reimbursable expense is generally charged to the customer.

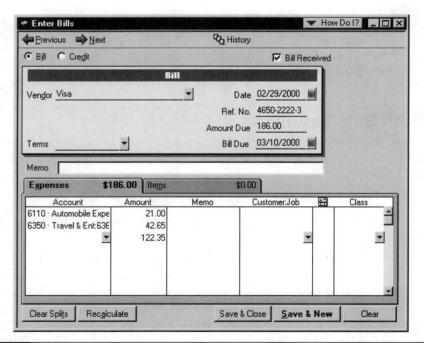

FIGURE 6-2 QuickBooks keeps recalculating, making it easy to enter split transactions

Recording the Reimbursable Expense

If you want to be reimbursed by customers for parts of bills you're entering, you must enter the specific amounts you're charging to each customer:

1. In the Amount column, enter the portion of the bill that you're charging back to a customer or job.
2. In the Customer:Job column, choose the appropriate customer or job.
3. Repeat to include any additional reimbursable expenses (see Figure 6-3).
4. Of course, if the entire vendor bill is for a purchase you made on behalf of the customer, you don't have to go through all the steps of splitting the total amount; just select the customer and apply the entire amount of the bill.

The column with the strange-looking icon (to the right of the Customer:Job column) is a selection feature. The icon is supposed to represent an invoice. You can click the column to put an X through the icon if you don't want to bill the customer for the expense. The expense is associated with the customer in your records, but the amount isn't available for automatic billing to the customer.

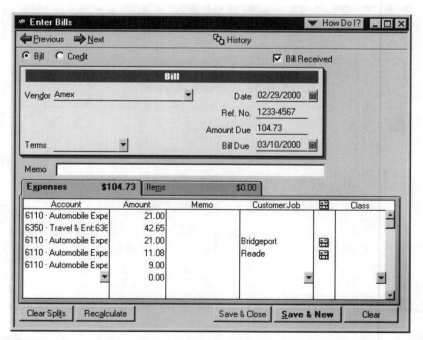

FIGURE 6-3 You can create multiple reimbursable expense lines from a single vendor bill

Invoicing the Customer for Reimbursable Expenses

When you save the vendor bill, the amounts you linked to a customer are saved in the customer file. When you next invoice the customer, you can add those amounts to the invoice. Here are the special steps to take during customer invoicing (see Chapter 3 for complete information about creating invoices for customers):

1. As you're creating the invoice, click the Time/Costs icon at the top of the Create Invoices window.
2. When the Choose Billable Time and Costs window opens, move to the Expenses tab, which displays the reimbursable amounts you posted when you entered vendor bills.
3. Click in the Use column to select the expenses you want to include on the invoice you're currently creating (see Figure 6-4).
4. Click OK to move the item to the invoice, where it appears in the line item section.
5. Add any other invoice items for this customer and then save the invoice.

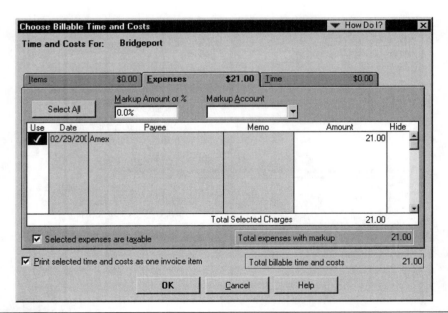

FIGURE 6-4 Click the expense(s) you want to add to the invoice you're currently preparing

Entering Inventory Item Bills

If the vendor bill you're recording is for inventory items, you need to take a different approach, because the accounting issues (the way you post amounts) are different. Two steps are involved when you buy items for your inventory:

1. You receive the inventory products.
2. You receive the bill for the inventory.

Once in a while, the bill comes before the products, and sometimes both events occur at the same time. (In fact, you may find the bill pasted to the carton or inside the carton.)

Another twist to all of this is the change in procedures if you've used purchase orders. In this section, I'll go over all the available scenarios, including how to track purchase orders.

Using Purchase Orders

If you want, you can use purchase orders to order inventory items from your suppliers. However, it's not a great idea to use purchase orders for goods that aren't in your inventory—that's not what they're intended for.

Creating and saving a purchase order has no effect on your general ledger. No amounts are posted to an account, because purchase orders exist only to help you track what you've ordered against what you've received.

Here's how you can create a purchase order:

1. Click the Purchase Order item on the Navigation Bar, which opens a blank Create Purchase Orders window.
2. Fill in the purchase order fields, which are easy and self-explanatory (see Figure 6-5).
3. Click Save & New to save the purchase order and move on to the next blank form, or click Save & Close if you have created all the purchase orders you need right now.

TIP: If you're using job tracking, you can use the Customer column to keep track of your purchases for jobs.

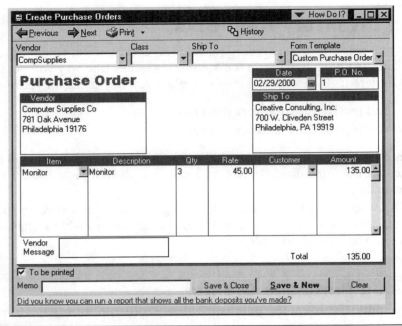

FIGURE 6-5 A purchase order looks like a bill, but you don't incur any accounts payable liability

You can print the purchase orders as you create them, by clicking the Print button as soon as each purchase order is completed. If you'd prefer, you can print them all in a batch by choosing File | Print Forms | Purchase Orders.

Later, when the inventory items and the bill for them are received, you can use the purchase order to check those transactions and automate the receiving process.

Receiving Inventory Items

Since this chapter is about accounts payable, we must cover the steps involved in paying for the inventory items. However, you don't pay for items you haven't received, so receiving the items merits some mention.

If the inventory items arrive before you receive a bill from the vendor, you must tell QuickBooks about the new inventory. Here's how:

1. Choose Vendors | Receive Items from the menu bar to open a blank Create Item Receipts window (see Figure 6-6).

2. Enter the vendor name, and if open purchase orders exist from this vendor, QuickBooks notifies you.

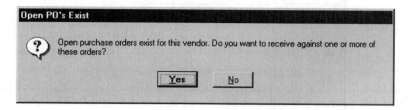

3. If you know there isn't a purchase order for this shipment, click No. Then, fill out the Create Item Receipts window.

4. If you're not sure, or you know there is a purchase order, click Yes. QuickBooks displays all the open purchase orders for this vendor. Select the appropriate PO (check the paperwork that arrived with the shipment to find the PO number).

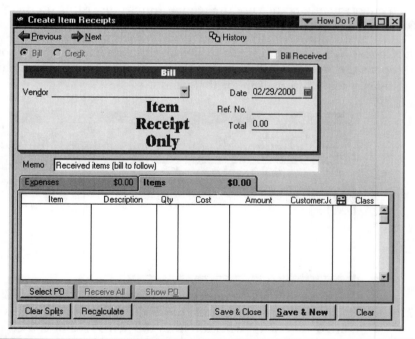

FIGURE 6-6   Items that arrive at the warehouse aren't officially in the inventory (and can't be sold) until you receive them

QuickBooks fills out the Create Item Receipts window using the information in the PO. If there isn't a PO that matches this shipment, click Cancel on the Open Purchase Orders listing to return to the receipts window. Remember to check the shipment against the PO.

5. Click Save & New to receive the next shipment into inventory, or click Save & Close if this takes care of all the receipts of goods.

 TIP: You can link this shipment to a purchase order as soon as you open the Create Item Receipts window by clicking the Select PO button. Find the right PO, and QuickBooks fills in the receipt information automatically.

Recording Bills for Received Items

After you receive the items, eventually the bill comes from the vendor.

To enter the bill, do not use the regular Enter Bills listing on the Navigation Bar. Instead, do the following:

1. Choose Vendors | Enter Bills for Received Items from the menu bar. This opens the Select Item Receipt window. Choose a vendor to see the current items receipt information for that vendor.

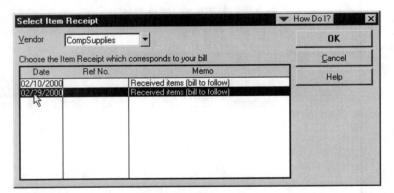

2. Select the appropriate listing and click OK to open an Enter Bills window (see Figure 6-7). The information from the items receipt is used to fill in the bill information.

Now the bill is due and owing; it's okay to pay it, because you've received the items.

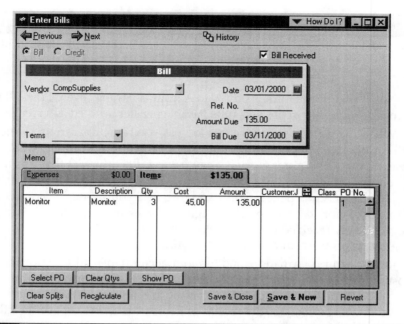

FIGURE 6-7 The transaction for the receipt of items automatically becomes a bill

Receiving Items and Bills Simultaneously

If the items and the bill arrive at the same time (sometimes the bill is in the shipping carton), you must tell QuickBooks about those events simultaneously. To do this, choose Vendors | Receive Items and Enter Bill from the menu bar. This opens the standard Enter Bills window, but when you fill it out, QuickBooks receives the items into inventory in addition to posting the bill.

Understanding the Postings

You need to explain to your accountant (or warn your accountant) about the way QuickBooks posts the receipt of goods and the bills for inventory items. It seems a bit different from standard practices if you're a purist about accounting procedures, but as long as you remember to use the correct commands (as described in the preceding sections), it works fine.

QuickBooks makes the same postings no matter how, or in what order, you receive the items and the bill. Let's look at what happens when you receive $400.00 worth of items:

ACCOUNT	DEBIT	CREDIT
Accounts Payable		$400.00
Inventory	$400.00	

Notice that the amount is posted to Accounts Payable, even if the bill hasn't been received. The entry in the Accounts Payable register is noted as a receipt of items.

When the vendor bill arrives, as long as you remember to use Vendors | Enter Bill for Received Items, the amount isn't charged to Accounts Payable again; instead, the A/P register entry is changed to reflect the fact that it is now a bill. If you use the standard Enter Bills listing, QuickBooks will warn you that this vendor has receipts pending bills and instructs you to use the correct command if this bill is for that receipt. If you ignore the listing, and the bill is indeed for items already received into QuickBooks, you'll have double entries for the same amount in your Accounts Payable account.

Just for your information, and for your accountant's information, here's the posting you could expect from the receipt of $400.00 worth of items if you take the purist approach. In fact, most accounting software systems do use this two-step method, which separates the receipt of items from the receipt of the bill from the vendor. This approach requires an account in your chart of accounts that tracks received items. (It's usually placed in the Liabilities section of the chart of accounts; you can call it whatever you wish.)

ACCOUNT	DEBIT	CREDIT
Inventory	$400.00	
Receipts holding account		$400.00

Then, when the vendor bill arrives, a separate posting is made to the general ledger:

ACCOUNT	DEBIT	CREDIT
Receipts holding account	$400.00	
Accounts Payable		$400.00

Because the postings to the receipts holding account are washed between the receipt of goods and the receipt of the bill, the bottom-line effect to your general ledger is the same when QuickBooks does it. The only thing missing in QuickBooks is the ability to look at the amount currently posted to the receipts holding account to see where you stand in terms of items in but bills not received (or vice versa). As long as you use the correct commands to enter bills, you shouldn't have a problem. I'm covering this so you can reassure your accountant (who will probably want to know why QuickBooks didn't put a receipts holding account in your chart of accounts when you indicated you were using the inventory feature).

Recording Vendor Credits

If you receive a credit from a vendor, you must record it in QuickBooks. Then, you can apply it against an open vendor bill or let it float until you next order from the vendor. (See Chapter 7 for information about paying bills, which includes applying vendor credits to bills.)

QuickBooks doesn't provide a discrete credit form, nor a listing for vendor credits on the Navigation Bar. Instead, a vendor bill form can be changed to a credit form with a click of the mouse:

1. Click the Enter Bills listing on the Navigation Bar.
2. When the Enter Bills window appears, select Credit, which automatically deselects Bill and changes the available fields in the form (see Figure 6-8).
3. Choose the vendor from the drop-down list that appears when you click the arrow in the Vendor field.
4. Enter the date of the credit memo.
5. In the Ref. No. field, enter the vendor's credit memo number.
6. Enter the amount of the credit memo.
7. If the credit is not for inventory items, use the Expenses tab to assign an account and amount to this credit.
8. If the credit is for inventory items, use the Items tab to enter the items, along with the quantity and cost, for which you are receiving this credit.

REMEMBER: If you've agreed that the vendor pays the shipping costs to return items, don't forget to enter that amount in the Expenses tab.

9. Click Save & Close to save the credit (unless you have more credits to enter—in which case, click Save & New).

Here are the postings to your general ledger when you save a vendor credit:

ACCOUNT	DEBIT	CREDIT
Inventory		Amount of returned items
Applicable expense accounts		Amounts of expenses in the credit
Accounts Payable	Total credit amount	

 TIP: Don't use an RA (Return Authorization) number from your vendor as the basis for your credit. Wait for the credit memo to arrive so your records and the vendor's records match. This makes it much easier to settle disputed amounts.

Entering Recurring Bills

You probably have quite a few bills that you must pay every month. Commonly, the list includes your rent or mortgage payment, payments for assets you purchased with a loan (such as vehicles or equipment), or a retainer fee

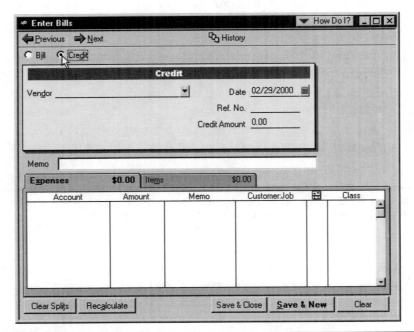

| **FIGURE 6-8** | Use the same QuickBooks window for bills and credits—the Terms and Due Date fields disappear when you are entering a credit |

(for an attorney, accountant, or subcontractor). You might even need to order inventory items on a regular basis.

You can make it easy to pay those bills every month without reentering the bill each time. QuickBooks provides a feature called *memorized transactions,* and you can put it to work to make sure your recurring bills are covered.

Creating a Memorized Bill

To create a memorized transaction for a recurring bill, first fill out the bill, as shown in Figure 6-9.

TIP: If the recurring bill isn't always exactly the same—perhaps the amount is different each month (your utility bills, for instance)—it's okay to leave the Amount Due field blank.

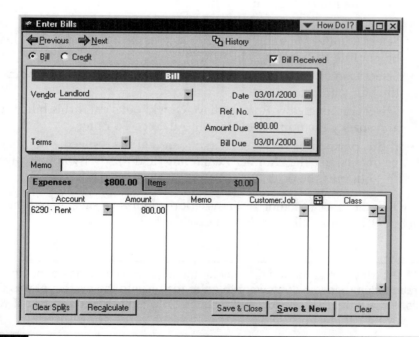

FIGURE 6-9   Enter a transaction once and then memorize it to use it again and again

After you fill out the form, but before you save it, memorize it. To accomplish this, press CTRL-M (or choose Edit | Memorize Bill from the main QuickBooks menu bar). The Memorize Transaction window opens.

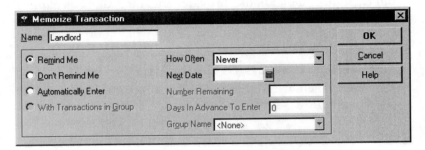

Use these guidelines to complete the Memorize Transaction window:

- Use the Name field to enter a name for the transaction. (It doesn't have to match the vendor or the expense.) Use a name that describes the transaction so you don't have to rely on your memory.
- Enter the interval for this bill in the How Often field.
- Enter the Next Date this bill is due.
- Select Remind Me to tell QuickBooks to issue a reminder that this bill must be put into the system to be paid.
- Select Don't Remind Me if you want to forego getting a reminder and enter the bill yourself.
- Select Automatically Enter to have QuickBooks enter this bill as a payable, and specify the number of Days In Advance To Enter.
- If this payment is finite, such as a loan that has a specific number of payments, use the Number Remaining field to specify how many times this bill must be paid.

Click OK in the Memorize Transaction window to save it, and then click OK again in the Enter Bills window to save the bill.

 TIP: If you created the bill only for the purpose of creating a memorized transaction, and you don't want to enter the bill into the system at this time, close the Enter Bills window and respond No when QuickBooks asks if you want to save the transaction.

Using a Memorized Bill

If you've opted to enter the memorized bill yourself (either by asking QuickBooks to remind you to do this, or by trusting your memory), you must bring it up to make it a current payable.

To use a memorized bill, press CTRL-T (or choose Lists | Memorized Transaction List). This opens the Memorized Transaction List window.

Select the transaction you want to use, and click the Enter Transaction button at the bottom of the window. This opens the bill in the usual Enter Bills window, with the next due date showing. Click OK to save this bill, so it becomes a current payable and is listed when you pay your bills. (See Chapter 7 for information about paying bills.)

Creating Memorized Groups

If you have a whole bunch of memorized transactions to cover all the bills that are due the first of the month (rent, mortgage, utilities, car payments, whatever), it's silly to convert them to a real bill one at a time. You can create a group and then invoke actions on the group (automatically invoking the action on every bill in the group).

The steps to accomplish this are easy:

1. Press CTRL-T to display the Memorized Transaction List.
2. Click the Memorized Transaction button at the bottom of the List window to display the menu.
3. Choose New Group.
4. In the New Memorized Transaction Group window, give this group a name.
5. Fill out the fields to specify the way you want the bills in this group to be handled.

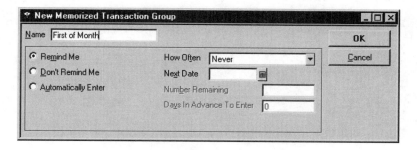

6. Click OK to save this group.

Now that you've created the group, you can add memorized transactions to it:

1. In the Memorized Transaction List window, select the first memorized transaction you want to add to the group.
2. Click the Memorized Transaction button at the bottom of the window to open the menu.
3. Choose Edit from the menu.
4. When the Schedule Memorized Transaction window opens with this transaction displayed, select the option named With Transactions In Group. Then, select the group from the list that appears when you click the arrow next to the Group Name field.

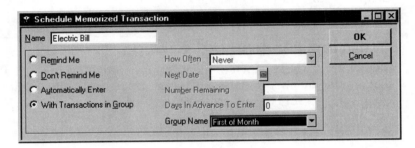

5. Click OK and repeat this process for each bill in the list.

As you create future memorized bills, just select the same With Transactions In Group option.

If you have other recurring bills with different criteria (perhaps they're due on a different day of the month), create groups for them and add the individual transactions to the group.

Now that all of your vendor bills are in the system, you have to pay them. Chapter 7 covers everything you need to know about accomplishing that.

Memorizing Zero-Based Bills for Later Use

Fred is president of his own company, for which he has procured two company credit cards. He uses the AMEX card for travel and entertainment, which includes plane or train tickets, car rentals, and taking customers to dinner. He uses the Visa card for office supplies and charges for his Internet connection.

To make life easier and his work in QuickBooks faster, Fred clicked the Enter Bills listing on the Navigation Bar and created a bill for each credit card. He left the Amount field blank and then moved to the Expenses tab at the bottom of the form. For AMEX, he selected the Travel account, and then immediately clicked in the Account column again and selected the Entertainment account. He didn't fill in any other information, which means that the amounts posted to those accounts were zero.

He pressed CTRL-M to memorize the bill, and asked to be reminded monthly. He made the next due date a few days hence (which is when the current AMEX bill is actually due). He clicked OK and then canceled the original bill when he returned to that window. Then, he repeated the process for the Visa card, entering the appropriate accounts for that card.

When the bills were due, he selected each bill from the Memorized Transaction List, and when the Enter Bills window opened, everything was already filled in except for the amounts. A nifty and easy way to make bookkeeping easier. Congratulations, Fred.

Paying Bills

*I*n this chapter, you will learn to...

- Choose the bills to pay
- Apply discounts and credits
- Write the checks
- Make direct disbursements
- Set up sales tax payments

The expression "writing checks" doesn't have to be taken literally. You can let QuickBooks do the "writing" part by buying computer checks and printing them. Except for signing the check, QuickBooks can do all the work.

Choosing What to Pay

You don't have to pay every bill that's entered, nor do you have to pay the entire amount due for each bill. Your current bank balance and your relationships with your vendors have a large influence on the decisions you make.

There are all sorts of rules that business consultants recite about how to decide what to pay when money is short, and the term "essential vendors" is prominent. I've never figured out how to define "essential," since having electricity is just as important to me as buying inventory items.

Having worked with hundreds of clients, however, I can give you two rules to follow that are based on those clients' experiences:

- The government (taxes) comes first. Never, never, never use payroll withholding money to pay bills.
- It's better to send lots of vendors small checks than to send gobs of money to a couple of vendors who have been applying pressure. Vendors hate being ignored much more than they dislike small payments on account.

Incidentally, I'm not covering the payment of payroll tax obligations in this chapter, so be sure to read Chapter 9 to stay on top of those accounts payable items.

Viewing Your Accounts Payable

Start by examining the bills that are due. The best way to see that list is to click the Reports listing on the Navigation Bar. Select Vendors & Payables as the type of report and choose the Unpaid Bills report. All of your outstanding vendor bills are displayed, as shown in Figure 7-1.

You can filter the report to display only certain bills. For example, you may want to see only one of the following types of bills:

- Bills that are due today (or previously), eliminating bills due after today
- Bills that are more or less than a certain amount
- Bills that are more than a certain number of days overdue

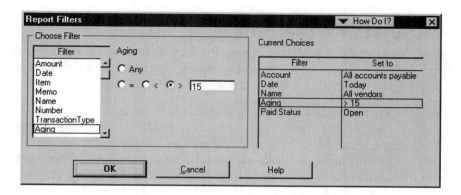

Print the report, and if you're short on cash, work on a formula that will maintain good relationships with your vendors.

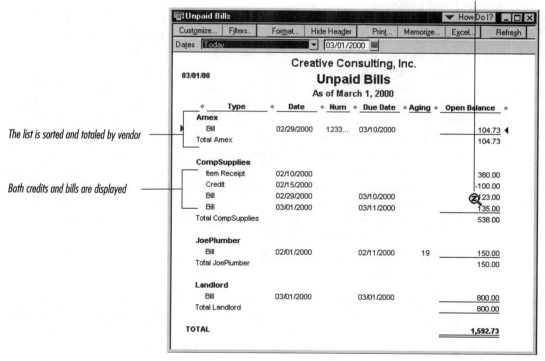

Double-click with the magnifying glass pointer to see the original transaction

The list is sorted and totaled by vendor

Both credits and bills are displayed

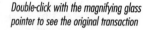

FIGURE 7-1   All of your current bills are listed in the Unpaid Bills report

Selecting the Bills

When you're ready to tell QuickBooks which bills you want to pay, choose Vendors | Pay Bills from the menu bar. The Pay Bills window appears (see Figure 7-2) and you can begin to make your selections.

- **Payment Date**   The date that you want to appear on your checks. By default, the current date appears in the field, but if you want to predate or postdate a check (or multiple checks), you can change that date. If you merely select the bills today and wait until tomorrow (or later) to print the checks, the payment date set here still appears on the checks. You can tell QuickBooks to date checks by the day of printing by changing the Checking Preferences (see Chapter 21 to learn about Preferences).

- **Show Bills Due On Or Before**   Displays all the bills due within ten days, by default, but you can change the date to display more or fewer bills. If you have discounts for timely payments with any vendors, this selection is more important than it seems (see the section "Applying Discounts," later in this chapter).

- **Show All Bills**   Shows all the bills in your system, even those due after the default due date. This option is more important than it seems (see the section "Applying Discounts," later in this chapter).

- **Sort Bills By**   Determines the manner in which your bills are displayed in QuickBooks. By default, the list of bills is displayed according to the due date, starting with the earliest due date. Click the arrow to the right of the field to choose another sort scheme. The other choices are Discount Date, Vendor, or Amount Due.

- **Pay By**   Offers two methods of payment: check or credit card. If you are paying by check and QuickBooks prints your checks, be sure the To Be Printed option is selected. If you're using manual checks, click that selection to make the check mark disappear. Actually, if you've configured your checking account for online banking, you'll see a third choice: Online Payment. See Chapter 16 for more information.

- **Payment Account**   The checking or credit card account you want to use for these payments.

After you've made changes to the data in the fields, your list of bills to be paid may change. If all the bills displayed are to be paid either in full or in part, you're ready to move to the next step. If there are still some bills on the list that you're not going to pay, you can just select the ones you do want to pay.

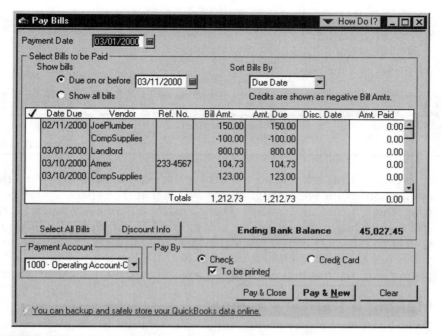

FIGURE 7-2 The job of paying bills starts in the Pay Bills window

Selecting a bill is simple—just click the leftmost column to place a check mark in it.

 TIP: I've found it best to change the way bills are sorted after all the other configuration options are set the way I want them. I sort them by vendor so I can see at a glance whether there's a credit (indicated by a minus sign on the bill amount) mixed in with the bills. That way, I can apply the credits easily.

Selecting the Payment Amounts

If you want to pay all the bills that are listed in the Pay Bills window in full, and there aren't any credits or discounts to worry about, the easiest thing to do is to click the Select All Bills button. This selects all the bills for payment (and the

Select All Bills button changes its name to Clear Payments, so you have a way to reverse your action).

Here's what happens in your general ledger when you make straight payments of your bills:

ACCOUNT	DEBIT	CREDIT
Accounts Payable	Total bill payments	
Bank		Total bill payments

I've had clients ask why they don't see the expense accounts when they look at the postings for bill paying. The answer is that the expenses were posted when they entered the invoices. That's a major difference between entering bills and then paying them, or writing checks without entering the bills into your QuickBooks system. If you just write checks, you enter the accounts to which you're assigning those checks. For that system (the cash-based system) of paying bills, the postings debit the expense and credit the bank account.

Making a Partial Payment

If you don't want to pay a bill in full, you can easily adjust the amount:

1. Click the check mark column on the bill's listing to select the bill for payment.
2. Click in the Amt. Paid column and replace the amount that's displayed with the amount you want to pay. The total will change to match your payment when you save the window.

When the transaction is posted to the general ledger, the amount of the payment is posted as a debit to the Accounts Payable account (the unpaid balance remains in the Accounts Payable account) and as a credit to your bank account.

Applying Discounts

QuickBooks doesn't pay sufficient attention to the matter of vendor discounts. The default due date for showing bills to pay on the Pay Bills window is 10 days hence, but QuickBooks reads only the amount of days for net, not discount, when deciding which bills to show. If your terms with a vendor are for a discount within 10 days and net within 30 days, the 10-day discount period could be looming but the bill doesn't appear in the window. Always make one of the following changes to avoid missing discounts:

- Change the date in the Due On Or Before field to 30 days hence—60 days if you have any vendors with terms that give you a discount within 10 days, net within 60.

- Select the Show All Bills option instead of the Due On Or Before option.

The appropriate bills are displayed in the Pay Bills window, and you can ignore the Date Due column and scan the information in the Disc. Date column as you decide which bills to pay.

When you want to take advantage of discounts for timely payment, the amount displayed in the Amt. Due column (or the Amt. Paid column if you've selected the bill for payment) doesn't reflect the discount. You have to apply it:

1. Select the bill by clicking the check mark column.
2. Click the Discount Info button.
3. When the Discount Information window appears, it displays the amount of the discount based on the terms for this bill. You can accept the amount or change it, and then click OK to apply it.

TIP: It's probably not "cricket" to tell you this, but lots of businesses fill in the discount amount even if the discount period has expired. The resulting payment, with the discount applied, is frequently accepted by the vendor. Businesses that practice this protocol learn which vendors will accept a discounted payment and which won't. Seeing that the discount you mistakenly took has been added back in the next statement you receive is a pretty good hint that you're not going to get away with it. In fact, you may have customers to whom you extend discounts for timely payment who take the discount regardless of whether or not the payment is made within the allotted time frame. Do you charge them back for the unearned discount they took?

Understanding the Discount Account

Notice that the Discount Information window has a field for the Discount Account. This account accepts the posting for the amount of the discount. If you don't have an account for discounts taken (not to be confused with the account for discounts given to your customers), you can create one now by clicking the arrow to the right of the field and choosing <Add New>.

The account for the discounts you take (sometimes called *earned discounts*) can be either an income or expense account. There's no right and wrong here, although I've seen accountants get into heated debates defending a point of view on this subject. If you think of the discount as income (money you've brought into your system by paying your bills promptly), make the account an income account. If you think of the discount as a reverse expense, make the account an expense account. It posts as a minus amount, which means it reduces total expenses.

In fact, if the only vendors who offer discounts are those from whom you buy inventory items, you may want to put the discount account in the section of your chart of accounts that holds the Cost of Goods Sold account. It's best to check with your accountant.

Here's what posts to your general ledger when you take a discount. For example, suppose the original amount of the bill was $484.00 and the discount was $9.68 (therefore, the check amount was $474.32).

ACCOUNT	DEBIT	CREDIT
Accounts Payable	$484.00	
Bank		$474.32
Discounts Taken		$9.68

Applying Credits

If the list of bills to be paid includes credits, you can apply the credits to the bills by selecting both the bills and the credits. If there's a credit showing, but no bill from the same vendor, don't select the credit (wait for the next time a bill is due to that vendor).

Saving the Pay Bills Information

There are two ways to save information about paying bills: save as you go or save at the end. You can select a bill, make adjustments (make a partial payment, apply a discount), and then click Pay & New to save that bill payment. That bill disappears from the list if it's paid in total, and reappears with the balance owing if it's partially paid. Or you can select each bill, making the appropriate adjustments. When you're finished applying all the credits, discounts, and partial payments, click Pay & Close.

Regardless of the approach, when you're finished selecting the bills to pay, QuickBooks transfers all the information to the general ledger and fills out your checkbook account register (or credit card account register) with the payments.

After you've paid the bills, the bills aren't really paid. Even though QuickBooks considers them paid bills, your vendors won't agree until they receive the checks. You can write manual checks or print checks.

When you click Pay & Close in the Pay Bills window, all the bills you paid are turned into checks, albeit unwritten checks. You can see those checks in the bank account register, as shown in Figure 7-3 (choose Lists | Chart of Accounts and double-click the listing for your bank). If you indicated in the Pay Bills window that you would be printing checks (by selecting the To Be Printed option), your bank account register displays To Print as the check number. See the section "Printing Checks," later in this chapter.

If you deselect the To Be Printed option in the Pay Bills window, your bank account register uses the next available numbers for the checks. See the following section, "Writing Manual Checks."

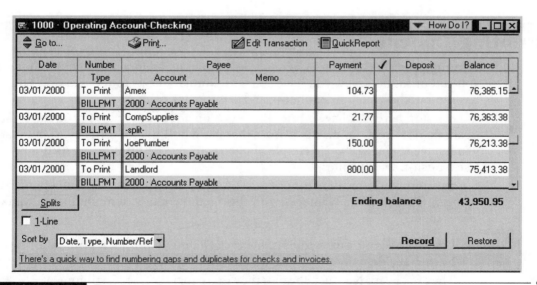

FIGURE 7-3 The checks for paying bills are already listed in your bank account

Writing Manual Checks

If you're not printing checks, you must make sure the check numbers in the register are correct. In fact, it's a good idea to print the register and have it with you as you write the checks. To accomplish that, with the register open in the QuickBooks window, click the Print icon at the top of the register window. When the Print Register window opens, select the date range that encompasses these checks (usually they're all dated the same day), and click OK to print.

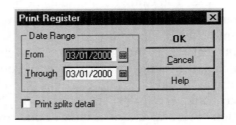

Then, as you write the checks, note the correct check numbers on the printout. If they're different from the check numbers that were entered by QuickBooks, make the necessary corrections in the register.

Printing Checks

Printing your checks is far easier and faster than using manual checks. Before you can print, however, you have some preliminary tasks to take care of. You have to purchase computer checks and set up your printer.

Let's stop here and have a brief conversation about dot matrix printers. First of all, do not use a dot matrix printer that has a pull tractor for checks, because you'll have to throw away a couple of checks to get the print head positioned. Use a push-tractor printer.

I use dot matrix printers for checks (I use my laser printer for QuickBooks reports). I gain a few advantages with this method, and you might like to think about them:

- I never have to change paper. I never accidentally print a report on a check. I never accidentally print a check on plain paper.
- They're cheap. Not just cheap—they're frequently free. Gazillions of companies have upgraded to networks and can now share laser printers. As a result, all of those dot matrix printers that were attached to individual computers are sitting in storage bins in the basement. Ask around. They're cheap to run (you replace a ribbon every once in a while) and they last

forever. I have clients using old printers (such as an OKI 92) that have been running constantly for about 15 years. And I mean constantly—dot matrix printers are great for warehouse pick slips and packing slips, and some of my clients pick and pack 24 hours a day, seven days a week.

I have two dot matrix printers, both connected to a second printer port that I installed in my computer (the first printer port is connected to my laser printer). The second port is connected to a switch box, which switches between the printers. One switch position is marked "company checks" and the other is marked "personal checks." Printer ports cost less than $10 and are easy to install.

In fact, I really have three checking accounts and still never have to change paper. I have one of those dot matrix printers (an OKI 520) that holds two rolls of paper at the same time; one feeds from the back and the other from the bottom. You flip a lever to switch between paper (in my case, to switch between checking accounts). When I move the switch box to the "personal checks" position, I also flip the lever to feed the checks from the appropriate personal account (I have two personal checking accounts).

I have clients who wanted the additional security of making copies of printed checks. You can buy multipart checks, where the second page is marked "copy" so nobody tries to use it as a check. Law firms, insurance companies, and other businesses that file a copy of a check appreciate multipart checks, which require a dot matrix printer.

End of dot matrix lecture.

 C A U T I O N : Lock the room that has the printer with the checks in it when you're not there.

Purchasing Computer Checks

You have several places to look for computer checks, and my own experience has been that there's not a lot of difference in pricing or the range of styles. Computer checks can be purchased for dot matrix printers (the check forms have sprocket holes) or for page printers (laser and inkjet).

Computer checks come in several varieties:

- Plain checks
- Checks with stubs (QuickBooks prints information on the stub)
- Checks with special stubs for payroll information (current check, and year-to-date information about wages and withholding)

- Wallet-sized checks

There is also a wide range of colors and designs for the checks.

You have several choices for purchasing computer checks:

- Intuit, the company that makes QuickBooks, sells checks through its Internet marketplace, which you can reach at http://www.intuitmarket.com
- Business form companies (there are several well-known national companies)
- Your bank (some banks have a computer-check purchasing arrangement with suppliers)

If you purchase checks from any supplier except Intuit, you just have to tell them you use QuickBooks. All check makers know about QuickBooks and offer a line of checks that are designed to work perfectly with the software.

Setting Up the Printer

Before you print checks, you have to go through a setup routine. Take heart; you only have to do it once. After you select your configuration options, QuickBooks remembers them and prints your checks without asking you to reinvent the wheel each time.

Your printer needs to know about the type of check you're using, and you supply the information in the Printer Setup window. To get there, choose File | Printer Setup from the menu bar. Click the arrow next to the Form Name drop-down list and choose Check/Paycheck. Your Printer Setup window should look similar to Figure 7-4.

Choosing a Check Style

You have to select a check style, and it has to match the check style you purchased, of course. Three styles are available for QuickBooks checks, and as you select each style, a sample page appears in the window to show you what the style looks like:

- **Standard checks** are just checks. They're the width of a regular business envelope (usually called a *#10 envelope*). If you have a laser printer, there are three checks to a page. A dot matrix pin-feed printer just keeps rolling, since the checks are printed on a continuous sheet with perforations separating the checks.
- **Voucher checks** have additional paper attached to the check form. QuickBooks prints voucher information if you have voucher checks, including the name of the payee, the date, and the individual amounts of the bills being paid by this check. The voucher is attached to the bottom of the check. The check is the

same width as the standard check (it's longer, of course, so you have to fold it to put it in the envelope).

- **Wallet checks** are narrower than the other two check styles (so they fit in your wallet). The paper size is the same as the other checks (otherwise, you'd have a problem with your printer), but there's a perforation on the left edge of the check, so you can tear off the check.

Changing Fonts

You can click the Fonts tab in the Printer Setup window and choose different fonts for the check information or for the payee's address block (or both).

Click the appropriate button and then choose a font, a font style, and a size from the dialog box that opens. Figure 7-5 shows font changes for the payee's address block.

Handling Partial Check Pages on Laser and Inkjet Printers

If you're printing to a laser or inkjet printer, you don't have the advantage that a pin-fed dot matrix printer provides—printing the check and stopping, leaving

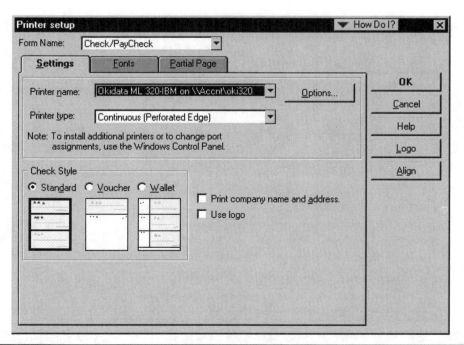

FIGURE 7-4 Use the Printer Setup window to configure check printing

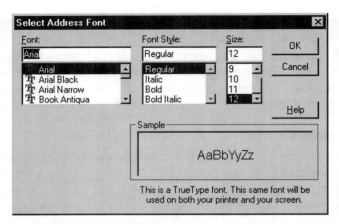

FIGURE 7-5   You can change the font style for elements of the check

the next check waiting for the next time you print checks. QuickBooks has a nifty solution for this problem, found on the Partial Page tab (see Figure 7-6). Click the selection that matches your printer's capabilities.

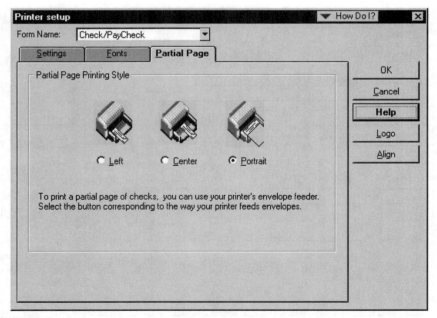

FIGURE 7-6   The QuickBooks partial page solution is based on the way your printer handles envelopes

Adding a Logo

If your checks have no preprinted logo and you have a bitmapped file of your company logo (the filename has a .bmp extension), you can select the Use Logo box and then tell QuickBooks where to find the file. There's also a selection box for printing your company name and address, but when you buy checks, you should have that information preprinted.

Printing the Checks

After your printer is configured for your checks, click OK in the Printer Setup window to save the configuration data. Now you can print your checks.

Choose File | Print Forms | Checks from the menu bar to bring up the Select Checks To Print window, shown in the following illustration.

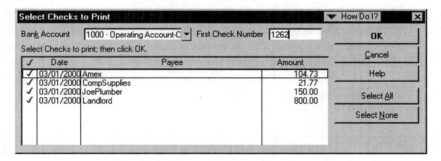

By default, all the unprinted checks are selected for printing. The first time you print checks, the first check number is 1; just replace that number with the first check number in the printer. Click OK when everything is correct.

The Print Checks window opens; everything should be correct, so just choose Print. If you're not using a dot matrix printer, QuickBooks asks how many checks are on the first page (in case you have a page with a check or two remaining). Fill in the number and place the page with leftover checks in the manual feed tray (QuickBooks prints those checks first). Then, let the printer pull the remaining check pages from your standard letter tray. If you indicate there are three checks on the page, printing starts with the checks in the standard letter tray.

Click Print to begin printing your checks.

Reprinting in Case of Problems

Sometimes, things go awry when you're printing. The paper jams, you run out of toner, the ribbon has no ink left, the dog chews the paper as it emerges, the paper falls off the back tray and lands in the shredder—all sorts of bad things can occur. QuickBooks knows this and checks the print run before it finalizes the printing process.

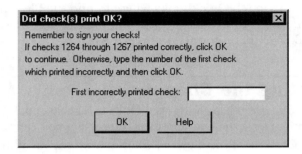

If everything is fine, click OK. If anything untoward happened, enter the number of the first check that is messed up. Put more checks into the printer (unless you're using a dot matrix printer, in which case you don't have to do anything). Then click OK to have QuickBooks reprint all the checks from the first bad one on to the end of the check run.

After your checks have printed properly, put them in envelopes, stamp them, and mail them. *Now* you can say your bills are paid.

 TIP: Just for the curious: Open the register for your bank account and you'll see that the checks are numbered to match the print run.

Using Direct Disbursements

A *direct disbursement* is a disbursement of funds (usually by check) that is performed without matching the check to an existing bill. This is check writing without entering bills.

If you're not entering vendor bills, this is how you'll pay your vendors. Even if you are entering vendor bills, you sometimes need to write a quick check without going through the process of entering the invoice, selecting it, paying it, and printing the check. For example, the UPS delivery person is standing in front of you waiting for a C.O.D. check and doesn't have time to wait for you to go through all those steps.

Writing Direct Manual Checks

If you use manual checks, you can write your checks and then tell QuickBooks about it later. Or you can bring your checkbook to your computer and enter the checks in QuickBooks as you write them. You have two ways to enter your checks in QuickBooks: in the bank register or in the Write Checks window.

Using the Register

To use the bank register, press CTRL-A to open the Chart of Accounts window, and then double-click the listing for the bank account. When the account register opens, you can enter the check on a transaction line (see Figure 7-7).

1. Enter the date.
2. Press the TAB key to move to the Number field. QuickBooks automatically fills in the next available check number.
3. Press TAB to move through the rest of the fields, filling out the name of the payee, the amount of the payment, and the expense account you're assigning to the transaction.
4. Click the Record button to save the transaction.
5. Repeat the steps until all the manual checks you've written are entered into the register.

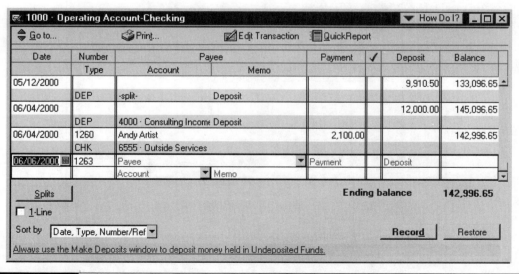

FIGURE 7-7   Enter the check information in the fields on the transaction line

Using the Write Checks Window

If you prefer a graphical approach, you can use the Write Checks window. To get there, press CTRL-W (or choose Banking | Write Checks from the menu bar).

When the Write Checks window opens (see Figure 7-8), select the bank account you're using to write the checks. Then, make sure the To Be Printed option box is not checked (if it is, click it to toggle the check mark off).

Fill out the check, posting amounts to the appropriate accounts. If the check is for inventory items, use the Items tab to make sure the items are placed into inventory. When you finish, click Save & New to open a new blank check. When you're through writing checks, click Save & Close to close the Write Checks window. All the checks you wrote are recorded in the bank account register.

Printing Direct Checks

You can print checks immediately, whether you normally enter bills and print the checks by selecting bills to pay or you normally print checks as direct disbursements.

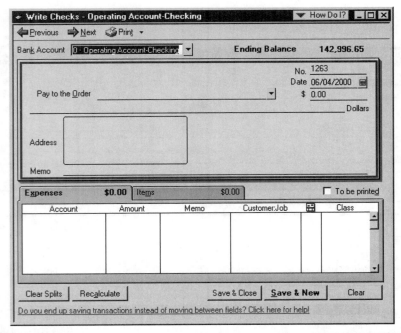

FIGURE 7-8   Use the TAB key to move through the fields, or just click the field you need

If you usually enter your vendor bills, but you need a check for which there is no bill in the system, you can use the Write Checks window to print an individual check quickly:

1. Press CTRL-W to open the Write Checks window. Make sure the To Be Printed option is selected.
2. Fill out the fields in the check and, when everything is ready, click Print.
3. The Print Checks window opens and displays the next available check number. Make sure that number agrees with the next number of the check you're loading in the printer, and then click OK.
4. When the Print Checks window opens, follow the instructions for printing described earlier in this chapter.
5. When you're returned to the Write Checks window, click Save & New to write another check, or click Save & Close if you're finished printing checks.

If you don't enter vendor bills but instead pay your bills as direct disbursements, you can print checks in a batch instead of one at a time. To do so, open the Write Checks window and make sure the To Be Printed option is selected:

1. Fill out all the fields for the first check and click Save & New to move to the next blank Write Checks window.
2. Repeat step 1 for every check you need to print.
3. Click Save & Close when you are finished filling out all the checks.
4. Choose File | Print Forms | Checks from the menu bar.
5. Follow the instructions for printing checks described earlier in this chapter.

The postings for direct disbursements are quite simple:

ACCOUNT	DEBIT	CREDIT
Bank account		Total of all checks written
An expense account	Total of all checks assigned to this account	
Another expense account	Total of all checks assigned to this account	
Another expense account (as many as needed)	Total of all checks assigned to this account	

Remitting Sales Tax

If you collect sales tax from your customers, you have an inherent accounts payable bill, because you have to turn that money over to the state taxing authorities. The same thing is true for payroll withholdings; those payments are discussed in Chapter 9.

Selecting the Sales Tax Payment Basis

There are two ways to remit sales tax to the taxing authorities:

- **Accrual-basis method**   When the customer is charged (the invoice date).
- **Cash-basis method**   When the customer pays.

Check with your accountant (and the state law) to determine the method you need to use. Then, choose Edit | Preferences from the menu bar. Click the Sales Tax icon in the left pane and select the Company Preferences tab to see the window shown in Figure 7-9.

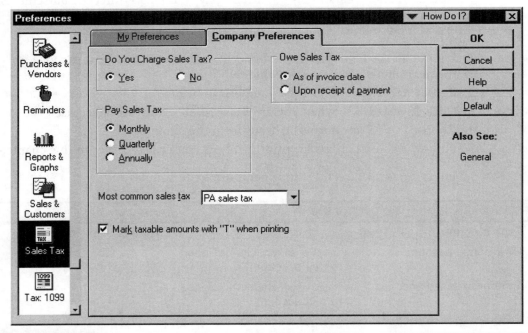

FIGURE 7-9   Be sure the specifications for remitting sales tax are correct, because QuickBooks goes on autopilot using these choices

C A U T I O N : If you collect taxes for more than one taxing authority and the rules are different for each, you're in for some additional work. QuickBooks does not permit separate configuration options for each state tax. You'll have to run detailed reports (see the next section) and calculate your payments outside of QuickBooks.

You also must indicate the frequency of your remittance to the state. Many states base the frequency on the amount of tax you collect, usually looking at your returns for a specific period of time (perhaps one specific quarter). If your sales tax liability changed dramatically during the examined period, you may receive notice from the state that your remittance interval has changed. (They'll probably send you new forms.) Don't forget to return to the Preferences window to change the interval.

Running Sales Tax Reports

If you collect sales tax for more than one state, or have to report separately on different rates (city and state), you must run sales tax reports to make sure your remittances are correct. Even if you only remit to one state, you should run a report to check your liability.

Click the Reports listing on the Navigation Bar and choose Vendors & Payables as the report type. Select the Sales Tax Liability report and use the Date Range box to select an interval that matches the way you report to the taxing authorities. By default, QuickBooks chooses the last interval (as configured in Preferences). Figure 7-10 shows a Sales Tax Liability report for a monthly filer who reports to one state. Figure 7-11 shows a Sales Tax Liability report for a monthly filer who reports to multiple states.

Paying the Sales Tax

After you check the figures (or calculate them, if you have multiple reports with different standards of calculation), it's time to pay the tax:

1. Choose Vendors | Pay Sales Tax from the QuickBooks menu bar.
2. In the Pay Sales Tax window select the bank account to use, if you have more than one.

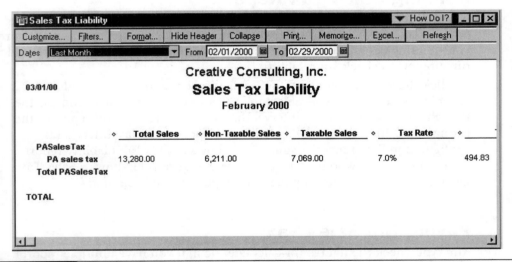

3. Check the date that's displayed in the field named Show Sales Tax Due Through. It must match the end date of your current reporting period (for instance, monthly or quarterly).

FIGURE 7-10   The Sales Tax Liability report always shows the nontaxable sales figure, because most states require that information

N O T E : QuickBooks doesn't ask for a start date, because it uses the current period as defined in your Preferences window.

4. If you report to multiple taxing authorities, every one of them is listed in the report. Click in the Pay column to insert a check mark next to those you're paying now. If you're lucky enough to have the same reporting interval for all taxing authorities—it never seems to work that way, though—just click the Pay All Tax button.

5. If you're going to print the check, be sure the To Be Printed selection box is checked. Click OK when you've completed filling out the information.

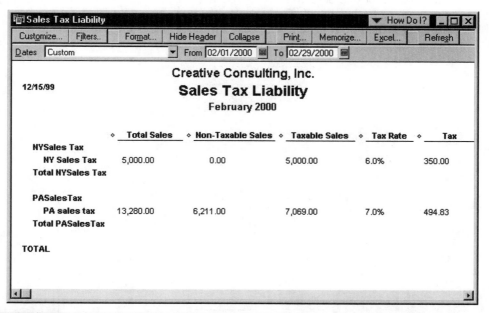

FIGURE 7-11 If you collect sales tax for more than one location, all of your sales tax liability figures are displayed

The next time you print or write checks, the sales tax check is in the group waiting to be completed.

TIP : If you have customers in a state other than the state in which you do business, you might be able to use another approach to sales tax. Technically, some states call this tax a Sales & Use tax, and the "use" part of the title means that the customer is responsible for remitting the tax. If the state permits it, you can skip the sales tax charge (and therefore skip the need to fill out forms and remit payments) and leave it up to the customer. The customer has to tell his or her state taxing authority that he or she purchased taxable goods from an out-of-state vendor (that's you), and remit the appropriate amount. Businesses that take advantage of this usually print a message on the invoice that says "Sales taxes for this purchase are not collected by us and are your responsibility" or something to that effect. The truth is, you have no legal obligation to warn the customer if the out-of-state taxing authority is willing to let you skip sales tax collections, but it's nice to do.

Paying Sales Tax to Multiple Tax Authorities

Mary Mulligan has a garden supply business with customers in Pennsylvania and New Jersey. She has to collect and report sales tax for both states and they have different rules: Pennsylvania collects monthly on collected taxes, New Jersey collects quarterly on billed taxes. Her QuickBooks preferences are set for Pennsylvania (she does more business there). Here's how she customized her QuickBooks system to make sales tax reporting easier.

She created three customer types and assigned a type to every customer:

- PA for taxable customers with Pennsylvania addresses
- NJ for taxable customers with New Jersey addresses
- NT for nontaxable customers

Then, she customized and memorized the Tax Liability Report:

1. She ran the report and clicked the Customize button on the report button bar.
2. When the Customize Report window opened, she clicked Filters.
3. In the Report Filters window, she selected Customer Type as the filter and then selected PA as the customer type to filter for.
4. She memorized the report as PATax.
5. She repeated the procedure for New Jersey-taxable customers.

Now she uses these memorized reports (choosing Reports | Memorized Reports from the menu bar) before she runs her Pay Sales Tax routine. She can select the taxing authorities and correct the numbers when necessary, because she has the information she needs.

Running Payroll

In this chapter, you will learn to...

- Check tax status, deductions, and other employee information

- Sign up for QuickBooks payroll services

- Enter historical data

- Write payroll checks

- Send direct deposit and withholding remittances to QuickBooks

If you plan to do your own payroll, rather than paying a payroll company, you'll find all the tools you need in QuickBooks. However, you can't use the payroll features unless you have an Internet connection, because you need to sign up for and implement payroll services from the QuickBooks Web site. All the information you need to set up and run payroll is covered in this chapter.

Fine-Tuning Your Setup

Before you run the first payroll, all your setup tasks must be completed. You can't produce accurate payroll checks unless QuickBooks knows everything there is to know about the payroll taxes you have to withhold, the payroll taxes you have to pay as an employer, and the deductions you need to take for benefits, garnishes, union dues, or any other reason. And, of course, you need to configure each employee for dependents and deductions.

Checking the Payroll Items

A QuickBooks payroll item is any element that is part of a payroll check. That means the elements that go into determining the gross amount of the payroll check (salary, wages, bonuses, and commissions), as well as the elements that determine the net amount of the payroll check (withheld taxes, deductions for benefits, and any other deductions).

You must create each payroll item (although QuickBooks creates many of them during your EasyStep Interview when you indicate you'll be using payroll). Each item you create has to be linked to an account in your chart of accounts. And, since all of the money you deduct is turned over to somebody else (the government, an insurance company, or a pension administrator), you must have vendors associated with each deduction.

Before you run your first payroll, it's a good idea to check your Payroll Item List to make sure everything you need has been entered, and also to double-check the links to accounts and vendors. Read Chapter 2 for step-by-step instructions about adding items to your Payroll Item List.

Open your list of payroll items by choosing Lists | Payroll Items from the menu bar. Every item that's used to generate a paycheck must exist in the Payroll Item List.

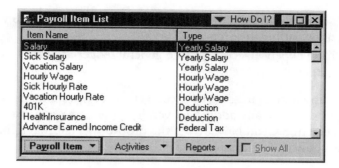

Double-click each item to make sure it's linked properly. Double-clicking puts the item in edit mode, which brings up a wizardlike series of windows. The first window is for the name of the item, the way it appears on the payroll check stub. Click Next to move to the next window, which contains the links (see Figure 8-1).

• The agency is the vendor to whom checks are drawn to pay the employer expense or remit withholdings.

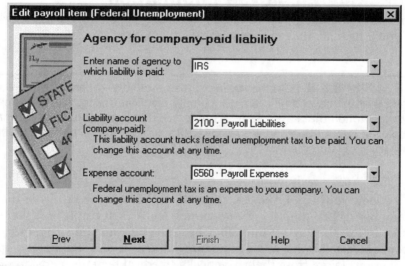

FIGURE 8-1   Be sure all the information is there, and be sure it's correct

- The liability account is the general ledger account to which the liability amount for this item is posted.
- The expense account is the general ledger account to which the employer expense is posted.

If any item is missing or incorrect, you must make the necessary entries. You can create any additional vendor or general ledger accounts you need by selecting <Add New> from the drop-down list that appears when you click the arrow to the right of the field.

 TIP: Some payroll items have only two wizard windows; others have more because there's additional information needed about the item. If you come across anything you don't understand or don't know, it's best to call your accountant.

Checking Employee Information

The information about your employees must be perfectly, pristinely accurate or you'll hear about it in a very unfriendly manner.

 REMEMBER: Make sure you pass around W-4 Forms every year and insist that employees fill them out completely. Don't accept blank forms back with a notation that says "same as before." This is your bible for entering employee information and it's important to be able to prove that you entered data from the horse's mouth.

To view your employee list, choose Lists | Employee List from the menu bar. When the list appears, double-click each employee's listing and move to the Payroll Info tab. Check the information against the W-4 Form and also against any documents that employees sign to have specific deductions taken from their paychecks (medical benefits, pension plans, and so forth).

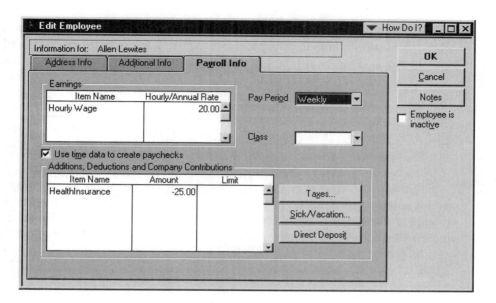

Click the Taxes button to check the tax status for this employee against the W-4 Form.

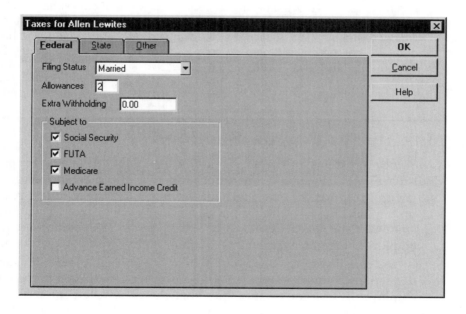

Click OK to return to the Payroll Info tab. The Sick/Vacation button, which is where you establish your sick and vacation day policies, is discussed in Chapter 2. The Direct Deposit button is used if you've signed up for direct deposit services with QuickBooks.

TIP: Most employees have all taxes withheld, but there are some exceptions to the rules. The employees who qualify for those exceptions usually know about it and their W-4 Forms will reflect their special status. Here are some of the exceptions you might encounter: For Federal Income Tax, there is a low-income exemption that is commonly used by students. FICA and Medicare exceptions can be taken by non-resident alien employees. Also, a child under the age of 18 who is employed by a parent in an unincorporated business can claim exemption from these withholding amounts. The parent must own more than half of the business for the child to qualify.

TIP: If your business is a corporation, you must separate compensation for corporate officers from the other employee compensation when you file your business taxes. To avoid having to perform all sorts of calculations outside of QuickBooks to determine these amounts, create a separate payroll item called Officer Compensation. Assign it to its own account (which you'll also have to create). Then open the Employee card for each officer and change the Earnings item to this new payroll item.

Signing Up for Payroll Services

You cannot do payroll within QuickBooks without signing up for payroll services. Actually, you can perform some payroll chores, such as generating gross payroll data by entering employee hours. However, unless you've signed up for QuickBooks payroll services, no calculations occur against the gross amount of the paycheck. No withholding appears, no amounts are posted to employee and employer liability accounts, and there is no net amount.

You can, if you wish, use your own printed tax table and calculate the deductions manually, and then issue a paycheck for the net amount to each employee. If you don't want to face that chore, however, you must sign up for payroll services. QuickBooks offers two payroll service plans: Basic Payroll Services and Deluxe Payroll Services. In addition, you can sign up for direct deposit with either plan. I'll discuss the details for each plan in this section.

QuickBooks Basic Payroll Services

The QuickBooks Basic Payroll Service keeps your tax table up to date. You pay a small monthly fee (automatically deducted from a credit card), and each time you run your payroll you connect to the Internet to check the status of the tax tables and your service agreement. If everything is fine, the software engine that calculates paychecks is unlocked. The calculations are performed locally, on your computer, not on the Internet (you can disconnect your Internet connection before proceeding with payroll tasks). No employee information is exposed to the Internet during this process. If the tax table has changed, a new tax table is downloaded to your computer before the calculation engine is turned on.

QuickBooks Deluxe Payroll Services

The Deluxe Payroll Service includes all the functions in the Basic Payroll Service and then adds the following features:

- Automatic payment, by electronic transfer, of your federal and state withholdings
- Automatic electronic filing of all the federal and state forms required throughout the year
- Preparation of W-2 Forms for each employee
- Preparation of W-3 Forms for transmitting W-2 Forms

 N O T E : If you live in Indiana, QuickBooks cannot file your state forms because they're linked to local taxes, which are not handled by the software.

QuickBooks Direct Deposit Services

With either the Basic or Deluxe Payroll Service, you can easily add direct deposit services for your employees. QuickBooks imposes a sign-up fee followed by a small charge for each direct deposit transaction. Employees must sign a form giving permission for direct deposit, and they can deposit their entire paychecks into one bank account, or split the amount between two bank accounts.

Signing Up for QuickBooks Payroll Services

When you sign up for the payroll services, you must be connected to the Internet. The sign-up procedure and subsequent payroll service processes all take place via the QuickBooks Web site.

Special Online Procedures for Network Users

You should always communicate with QuickBooks payroll services from the computer that's used to process payroll. If your payroll person is working from a QuickBooks installation on a computer that does not have Internet access, you can configure the QuickBooks network system to let that person have access to the files. To do so, from the computer that has Internet access choose File | Update QuickBooks. Click the Options link to see the window shown in the following illustration. Select On for the Share Download option so other network users can access the downloaded files. Then click Save and close the window.

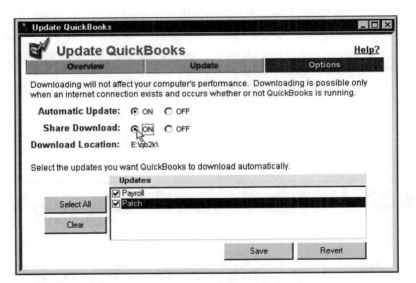

Applying for Payroll Services

To sign up for either service, choose Employees | Set Up Payroll Services, then choose either Basic Payroll Sign-up or Deluxe Payroll Sign-up from the submenu. Follow the onscreen instructions, which ask you for information about your company.

• For Basic Payroll Services you can complete your application online.

- For Deluxe Payroll Services, you must first fill out some forms and receive a Personal Identification Number from QuickBooks. You'll use the PIN in the onscreen sign-up window. Call QuickBooks at 800-332-4844 to get started.

The first 60 days are free, but in order to make sure your payroll processes aren't interrupted after the trial period, you must fill in information about your credit card. You can cancel at any time if you change your mind. When the sign-up process is completed, QuickBooks downloads the files you need to run payroll.

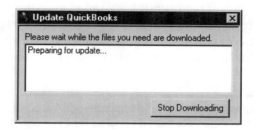

The new files are automatically added to your QuickBooks system; you don't have to do anything to install them. Because this is the first time you've received payroll update files, the current tax table is added to your system.

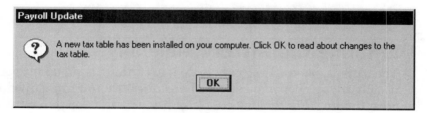

Signing Up for Direct Deposit Services

When you're signing up for either the Basic or Deluxe Payroll Services, you can also sign up for direct deposit services. Call QuickBooks at 800-332-4844. QuickBooks sends a package of information to you, and you must fill out the forms and return them. You're given a special key (PIN) to use during the setup of direct deposit services. Choose Employees | Set Up Payroll Services from the QuickBooks menu bar and repeat the steps you took to sign up for payroll services, except click Next instead of Sign Up Now if you're using Basic Payroll Services. Enter your PIN in the window that appears and fill in the information requested in the ensuing windows.

N O T E : The direct deposit package you receive also includes a sample form you can use to have employees authorize you to deposit paychecks directly into their banks. These forms are for your own records and aren't returned to QuickBooks.

Entering Historical Data

If you're not starting your use of QuickBooks at the very beginning of the year, you must enter all the historical information about paychecks. This is the only way to perform the tasks that are required at the end of the year. You cannot give your employees two W-2 Forms, one from your manual system and another from QuickBooks. Nor can you file your annual tax reports on any piecemeal basis.

T I P : No matter what your fiscal year is, your payroll year is the calendar year. Even though you can start using payroll for the current period before you enter the historical data, remember that the absence of historical data may affect some tax calculations. If there are withholding amounts that cease after a certain maximum (perhaps your state only requires SUI for the first $8,000.00 in gross payroll), you'll have to adjust those current paychecks manually to remove the withholding.

Entering the History Manually

The truth is, payroll is so easy to do if everything is set up properly that I usually advise clients to enter each historical payroll run individually. It's great training. For the first couple of pay periods, stop to look at the details and compare them to your manual records before saving the payroll. This gives you an opportunity to understand what QuickBooks is doing, in addition to checking accuracy.

If it's late in the year when you first begin using QuickBooks, I usually advise waiting until next year. If it's somewhere around the middle of the year, you may decide that my suggestion is crazy and refuse to go through the process of entering 26 or 30 weeks of payroll runs. I can understand your reluctance (although there's no such thing as being too careful when it comes to payroll), so read on to learn how to enter historical data in big batches.

Using the QuickBooks Payroll Data Wizard

QuickBooks provides assistance for entering prior payroll records in the form of a wizard. Click the Employees listing on the Navigation Bar to open the Employees

Navigator window, then click YTD Amounts. The introductory wizard window opens. Read the information and then click Next to proceed to your task. The wizard walks you through all the necessary steps. Remember that if you haven't gathered all the information you need, this won't go smoothly.

Set the Dates for Payroll History

The initial wizard questions are about the dates you're using to begin entering historical data (see Figure 8-2). QuickBooks needs to know when to post the historical totals to your accounts.

If you've been entering payroll information to accounts because you've had a payroll service, or you've been doing manual payroll and posting the amounts in account registers, you don't want QuickBooks to enter those amounts again. Specify the starting date for posting amounts, which may not be the same starting date for the historical data. For example, in Figure 8-2 the date to begin posting amounts is the first day of the year. That's because, in this instance, payroll has been handled manually but the amounts were never posted in QuickBooks. If you're performing this task later in the year, the odds are you *have* posted amounts to QuickBooks. Perhaps you've entered the paychecks and the vendor checks that transmitted withholdings and employer contributions. In that case, enter the first payroll date for which you have not yet entered transactions in QuickBooks (probably the current week).

The next wizard window asks for the date on which you plan to go "live" with payroll. QuickBooks defines historical data as any data that precedes this date.

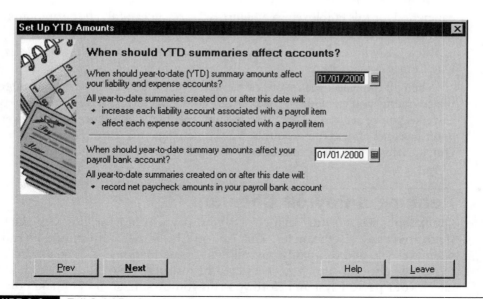

FIGURE 8-2   Tell QuickBooks when to post information to your accounts

It's important to understand how the dates you enter affect the task in front of you. Payroll records are summarized quarterly, because your 941 reports are due quarterly. In fact, your tax withholding may be remitted quarterly, depending on the rules of your local and state tax authority (generally, the larger the amount of withholding, the more frequently you have to remit the money).

You can't enter summarized data for the quarter that's current (the quarter that today's date falls in). Instead, for the current quarter, you must enter data for each individual pay period (which is weekly for many businesses). For previous quarters, you can enter quarterly totals. You have to enter data by pay period (which is weekly for many businesses). For previous quarters, you enter quarterly totals.

For example, if you tell QuickBooks that you want to start posting amounts and producing live paychecks as of any date in the first quarter, you will have to go through each pay period for the quarter. If your employees are configured for weekly pay periods, and you're performing this task in the last month of any quarter after the first quarter (June, September, or December), after you enter quarterly totals for the previous quarter(s), you have to enter each paycheck for the current quarter. That's a lot of work. To avoid the work, you may want to wait to implement payroll until the next quarter starts.

Enter Employee History

In the next window, a list of employees is displayed; now it's time to enter the year-to-date information. You perform this task one employee at a time. Select the first employee and click Enter Summary. QuickBooks presents a screen with the pay period for this employee (see Figure 8-3) so you can fill out the amounts and then click Next Period to move to the next pay period for this employee.

Click OK when you have finished with this employee. You're returned to the list of employees, where you select the next employee and repeat the process.

When all the employee records are entered, you can use the wizard to enter all the payments you've made to remit withholding, pay taxes, and so on. QuickBooks assumes you've accounted for these in your opening trial balance, so whatever you enter does not affect your accounts. You can change that assumption by instructing QuickBooks to post these amounts to the appropriate accounts.

Running a Payroll Checkup

QuickBooks has a feature that checks your payroll configuration to make sure there aren't any discrepancies. This Payroll Checkup feature should be run whenever you add or modify payroll items or deductions. It's also a good idea to run the checkup after you've entered historical data so that QuickBooks can check your payroll system before you run your first payroll. If QuickBooks

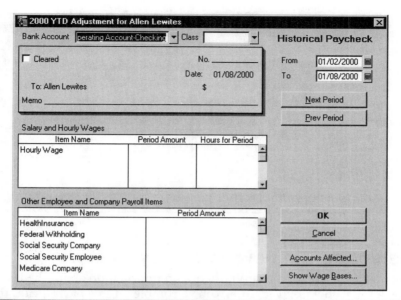

FIGURE 8-3   Enter the totals for the indicated time period for this employee

finds discrepancies or problems, you're told about them, and no changes are made to your system unless you make those changes manually.

Choose Employees | Run Payroll Checkup and click Run Checkup to begin the process. It takes a few seconds to check your system, then a window opens to display the results. You can scroll through the window to read the information, print the information (click the Print This Log button), or look at the file by opening it in a word processor or text editor (QuickBooks displays the file location in the results window).

Investigate, and if necessary fix, any problems. Then run the checkup again.

Running Payroll

It's payday. All the historical data is entered. It's time to run the payroll. Let's go!

If you're using direct deposit services you need a two-day lead before the actual payday. If only some of your employees use direct deposit, you have two choices:

- Do all your payroll data entry two days before payday and hold the printed checks until payday (date the checks appropriately).
- Run the payroll procedure twice, using the appropriate employees for each run.

Click the Pay Employees listing on the Navigation Bar to begin. The Select Employees To Pay window opens with a list of your employees displayed.

```
┌─────────────────────────────────────────────────────────────────────────┐
│ ≡. Select Employees To Pay                        ▼ How Do I? │_│□│X│    │
│                                                                           │
│ Bank Account │1020 · Payroll Account    ▼│   ⊙ Enter hours and preview check    Create    │
│                                             before creating.                             │
│ ┌──────────────────────────┐            ○ Create check without preview    Print Paychecks │
│ │ ☑ To be printed          │              using hours below and last quantities.          │
│ └──────────────────────────┘                                              Leave          │
│                                                                                          │
│ Check Date │04/13/2000│ ▦   Pay Period Ends │04/13/2000│ ▦            Mark All           │
│                                                                                          │
│ ✓    Employee       Pay Period        Rate          Hours         Last Date             │
│ ┌──────────────────────────────────────────────────────────────────────┐               │
│   Allen Lewites     Weekly           20.00          0:00                 ▲              │
│   Thomas E Barich   Weekly        1,923.08          0:00                                │
│                                                                                         │
│                                                                          ▼              │
│ · You can backup and safely store your QuickBooks data online.                          │
└─────────────────────────────────────────────────────────────────────────┘
```

Selecting Employees to Pay

The first time you run payroll, there's no information about the last payroll check for each employee. After you've completed this payroll run, that information will be available.

- For salaried employees, the information usually remains the same so you can create the checks without previewing information about hours.
- For hourly wage employees, if the number of hours are the same as the last check, you can repeat checks as if the employee were on salary.

For this first payroll, however, you must check the details before printing payroll checks:

1. Select the bank account you want to use for this payroll run.
2. Select the To be printed check box. This holds the check printing until everything is completed.
3. Select the option labeled "Enter hours and preview check before creating."
4. Select the employees to be paid by clicking in the check mark column. If all employees are included in this payroll run (they're all direct deposit, or all printed checks) click the Mark All button.
5. Specify the check date and the end date for this payroll period.
6. Click Create to begin entering paycheck information.

NOTE: If you separate the payroll run between corporate officers and employees, you'll need to select each group separately (and change the posting account appropriately).

Filling Out the Paycheck Information

The first employee's Preview Paycheck window opens (see Figure 8-4). If the employee is on an hourly wage, everything is blank until you fill in the Hours column. If the employee is salaried, the amounts are displayed.

Complete the following steps:

1. Make any corrections necessary. Perhaps you need to add an additional pay item such as a bonus or enter a one-time deduction.
2. When everything is correct, click Create.
3. The next employee's record appears so you can repeat the process.
4. Continue to move through each employee.
5. When the last employee check is created, you're returned to the original Select Employees To Pay window. Click Leave.

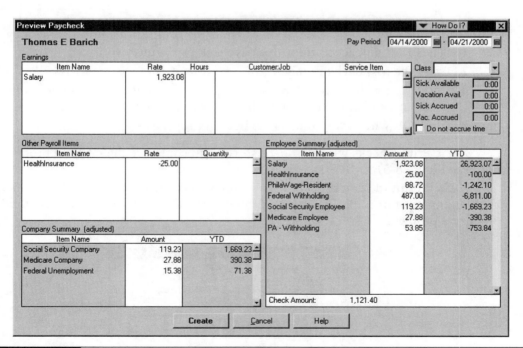

FIGURE 8-4 The details for payroll calculations are displayed in the Preview Paycheck window

Printing the Paychecks

When all the checks have been created, you must print the paychecks. Load the right checks in your printer (don't use your standard bank account checks if you have a separate payroll account).

Choose File | Print Forms | Paychecks to open the Select Paychecks to Print window.

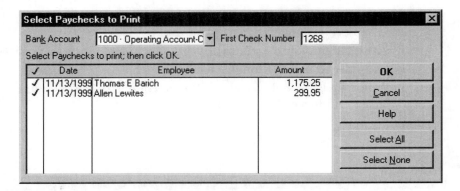

1. Select the bank account for this paycheck print run.
2. Enter the first check number.
3. Deselect any check you don't want to print at this time by clicking in the check mark column to remove the existing check mark.
4. Click OK when everything is configured properly.

The Print Checks window opens so you can configure the printing process (see Figure 8-5).

Click Print to print the paychecks. QuickBooks displays a window in which you must confirm that everything printed properly or reprint any checks that had a problem.

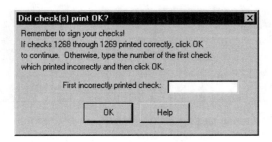

Select the printer.

If you have a partial page of checks for your laser or inkjet printer, supply that information in the Partial Page tab.

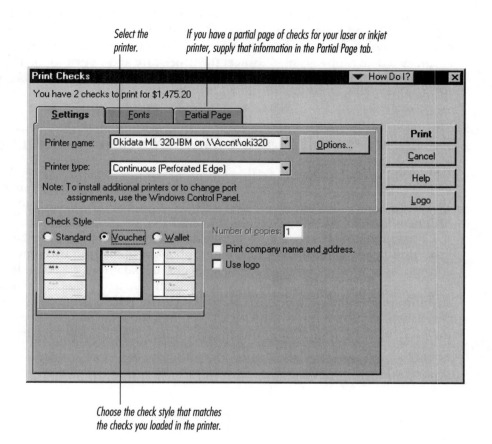

Choose the check style that matches the checks you loaded in the printer.

FIGURE 8-5 Configure the printer properties for this print job

---

If everything is fine, click OK. If there's a problem, enter the number of the first check that had a problem and QuickBooks will reprint as necessary, starting with the next available check number.

Sending Direct Deposit Information

If you use direct deposit services, you still go through the payroll process for the employees who opted for this service. You just don't print the checks. Instead, you notify QuickBooks to deposit the checks.

To make the direct deposit, open your Internet connection and then choose Employees | Send Payroll Data from the QuickBooks menu bar. A window opens to display the data you're about to upload, and you must confirm its accuracy. (If anything is amiss, cancel the procedure and return to the Pay Employees procedure to correct the information.) Click Go Online to begin the data transfer and follow the onscreen instructions.

Sending Payroll Liability Information to Deluxe Payroll Services

If you've signed up for Deluxe Payroll Services, you must upload the information about the payroll run you just completed so that the service can remit your withholding to the appropriate government agencies.

Choose Employees | Send Payroll Data from the QuickBooks menu bar. A window opens to display the data you're about to upload, and you must confirm its accuracy. Click Go Online to begin the data transfer, and follow the onscreen instructions. When the information is received by QuickBooks, a confirmation window appears to show you the transactions that are being performed (remittance of withholding taxes) and the fees charged. The transactions are automatically entered in your checking account register.

Handling Unusual Deductions

One of the employees at Bill's Diner has a garnishment for child support that has to be deducted and remitted to the local authorities. The garnishment order says that the employee must pay $30 if his paycheck is over $280 net, or 10% of his net pay if his net paycheck is below $280.

Since this is a choice, there's no way to create this deduction for automatic withholding. Here's what Bill has to do during the payroll process:

1. When the employee's Preview Paycheck window appears, enter the hours.
2. Note the Check Amount number that's displayed at the bottom of the window.
3. In the Other Payroll Items section of the window, click in the Name column.
4. Choose the garnishment deduction (which must be entered in the Payroll Item List).
5. Enter the appropriate amount for this deduction.

This works because Bill created a separate garnishment payroll item for each type of garnishment order, without indicating an amount or percentage. Each remittance check is separate (even if Bill has multiple employees with the same type of garnishment order) in order to track everything more efficiently.

When he created the deduction for the employee, he had two choices:

- Enter the $30 amount and then correct it if the current amount is less.
- Leave the amount blank and enter it each week.

The issue of garnishment is becoming more significant to employers because government agencies are using it more frequently to collect child support payments and overdue student loans.

Government Payroll Reporting

In this chapter, you will learn to...

- Make tax deposits
- Remit withheld amounts and employer taxes
- Prepare quarterly and annual returns
- Print W-2 Forms

Doing payroll in-house means having a lot of reports to print, forms to fill out, and checks to write. There's a logical order to these tasks, although the logic differs depending on the state and city (or town) you're in. In this chapter, we'll go over the procedures in the order in which most businesses have to perform the tasks.

If you've signed up for QuickBooks Deluxe Payroll services, you don't have to worry about the sections in this chapter that are concerned with remitting federal and state withholdings. You do, however, have to remit your local payroll tax withholding yourself.

 C A U T I O N : If you are in Indiana, QuickBooks Deluxe Payroll services does not handle your state payroll taxes.

Making Federal Payroll Tax Deposits

The federal government requires you to deposit the withholding amounts, along with the matching employer contributions, at a specified time. That time period is dependent upon the size of the total withholding amount you've accumulated. You may be required to deposit monthly, semi-monthly, weekly, or within three days of the payroll. Check the current limits with the IRS or your accountant.

There's a formula for determining the size of the deposit check—it is the sum of the following amounts:

- Total of all federal withholding
- Total of all FICA withholding
- Total of all Medicare withholding
- Matching FICA contribution from employer
- Matching Medicare contribution from employer

You don't have to do the math—QuickBooks does it for you. But it's a good idea to know what the formula is so you can check the numbers yourself.

Select the Liabilities for the Deposit Check

To prepare the check, choose Employees | Pay Payroll Liabilities from the QuickBooks menu bar. Select a date range for the check.

For a federal deposit, the date range must match your deposit frequency, which is determined by the amount of withholding. For most small businesses, monthly deposits are common. However, if your federal withholding amounts are very large, you may have to make a federal deposit within several days of each payroll. If your withholding amounts are relatively small, you may be able to file quarterly. Check Circular E, which is mailed to employers every year, or ask your accountant.

When you click OK, the Pay Liabilities window seen in Figure 9-1 appears.

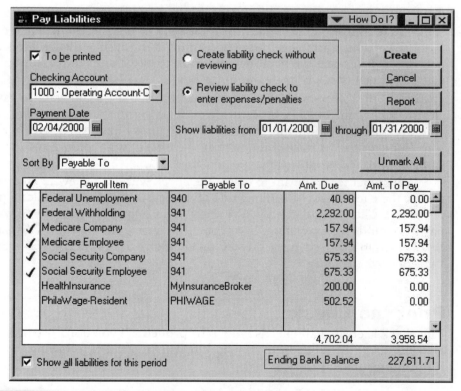

FIGURE 9-1 Select the items that are part of your federal deposit

In Figure 9-1, note that the name of the payee is the vendor code, not the name that prints on the check. For example, 941 is the code I use for my bank (federal deposits are made to the bank that has the account on which you draw payroll). I chose 941 as the code because the deposits are made against the total due on the 941 quarterly report. I draw other checks to my bank, including the federal unemployment (the vendor code is 940) and loan payments (the vendor code is Loan1). All those vendors have the same payee—my bank. If I'd used the bank as the vendor, whenever I have more than one payment type going to the bank at the same time (I frequently make the loan payment the same day I make the federal withholding deposit), QuickBooks would add up all the money due the bank and issue one check. That, of course, won't work. This is a good way to design vendor names, which do not have to be the same as the name that prints on checks.

You could select everything and write all the checks (whether they're due at the moment or not) just to get them out of the way. I don't do that. I select only those liabilities that are due now. Besides, this section is about the federal deposit check.

To make it easier, click the arrow to the right of the Sort By field and choose Payable To, which arranges the list according to the agency that receives the payment. Then select the liabilities you want to pay. For example, my federal payroll deposit check is made out to my bank.

Click in the check mark column to select the liabilities you want to pay. Notice that when you choose Medicare or Social Security, selecting the employee liability automatically selects the company liability (or vice versa). This is, of course, because you must pay the total of withholding and employer contributions at the same time.

Specify whether you want to create the check without reviewing it, or to review the check before finalizing it (I review everything before making payroll deposits!). Click Create when you've selected the liability payments you want to pay for your deposit payment. If you opted to review the check, it's displayed. If you need to make changes, do so (you shouldn't need to). Then click Save & Close to save the data.

Print the Check

The check is created and needs only to be printed. (If you don't use printed checks, just go ahead and use the check register instead of following these steps for printing.) This is the easy part:

1. Choose File | Print Forms | Checks from the menu bar.
2. When the Select Checks to Print window opens, select the bank account you use for payroll.

3. Be sure all the payroll liability checks you need to write are selected.

4. Click OK to bring up the Print Checks window so you can print the checks.

The federal government sent you a book of coupons (Form 8109) you must use when you deposit the funds you owe. Fill out a coupon and take it, along with your check, to the bank in which you have your payroll account. Make the check payable to the bank, unless you've been given different instructions by the bank or your accountant.

 N O T E : Don't forget to fill in the little bullets: one to indicate this is a 941 deposit, the other to indicate the quarter for which this payment is remitted.

Remitting State and Local Liabilities

Your state and local payroll liabilities vary, depending upon where your business is located and where your employees live (and pay taxes). Besides income taxes, you are probably liable for unemployment taxes as well. And many states have withholding for disability.

State and Local Income Taxes

Most states have some form of an income tax, which might be calculated in any one of a variety of ways:

- A flat percentage of gross income
- A sliding percentage of gross income
- A percentage based on the federal tax for the employee

Local taxes are also widely varied in their approach:

- Some cities have different rates for employees of companies that operate in the city. There may be one rate for employees who live in the same city and a different rate for non-residents.
- Your business might operate in a city or town that has a payroll head tax (a once-a-year payment that is a flat amount per employee).
- You may have a head tax for the town in which your business operates and still be required to withhold local taxes for employees who live in a nearby city.

State and local taxing authorities usually provide coupons to use for remitting income tax withholding. The frequency with which you must remit might depend on the size of your payroll, or might be quarterly, semi-annual, or annual regardless of the amount.

To remit the withheld income tax for your state and local taxing authorities, choose Employees | Pay Payroll Liabilities from the QuickBooks menu bar. Select the date range this payment covers and click OK to open the Pay Liabilities window shown in Figure 9-2.

Locate the state and local income tax liabilities and mark them by clicking in the check mark column, then click Create. Follow the steps to print the checks as described earlier. Mail them, along with your coupon, to the appropriate addresses.

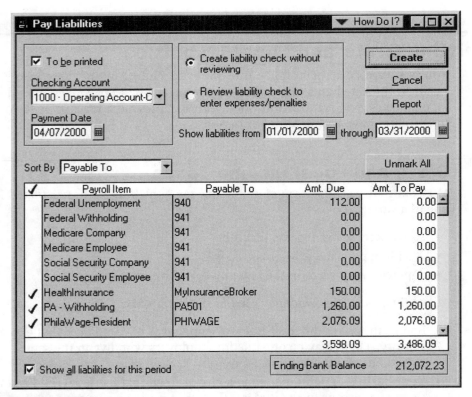

FIGURE 9-2 Choose the liabilities you need to send to the state and local tax authorities

Note that in Figure 9-2, there are no amounts due for federal tax liabilities. That's because each month I create that check, including the third month of the quarter. Then, at the end of the quarter, I perform a separate transaction to create the checks for the state and the city. I could easily skip creating the third month federal check discretely and include it in the quarterly liabilities payments; it's just habit.

 T I P : Deselect the Show All Liabilities for This Period option to eliminate all the zero-based liabilities on this window.

Other State Liabilities

If your state has SUI or SDI or both, you have to pay those liabilities when they're due. Commonly, these are quarterly payments. Even if the payee name is the same as the payee that receives the income tax withholding, don't select these liabilities at the same time you select your income tax withholding liabilities. If you do, QuickBooks will cut one check for the grand total, and the SUI and SDI should be sent with a different form (and frequently to a different address).

 T I P : It's a good idea to create a different payee name for SUI, SDI, and income tax withholding to make sure you don't accidentally send checks to the wrong place for the wrong thing.

Not all states have SUI or SDI, and some have one but not the other. Some states collect SUI from the employee and the company; some collect only from the company. Check the rules for your state.

Use the same process described earlier of selecting the amounts due from the Pay Liabilities window when it's time to pay your state liabilities.

Remitting Other Payroll Liabilities

The rules for remitting the paycheck deductions you take for other reasons, such as health benefits, pension, and so on, are specific to your arrangements with those vendors.

There are a great many ways to handle how these payments are posted, and you have to decide what makes sense to you (or to your accountant). For example, if you pay a monthly amount to a medical insurer, you may want to post the deductions back to the same expense account you use to pay the bill. That way, only the net amount is reported as an expense on your taxes. Or you can track the deductions in a separate account and calculate the net amount at tax time.

Then, you have to perform the steps to make sure the vendors get the right amount. For example, before you write the check to the medical insurance company, you must enter a regular vendor bill for the difference between the deducted amounts and the actual bill. That difference is your company contribution, of course. Then, when you write the check, both bills will be in the hopper and the check will be in the correct amount.

Preparing Your 941 Form

Every quarter you must file a 941 Form that reports the total amount you owe the federal government for withheld taxes and employer expenses. If you have been paying the deposits regularly, no check is remitted with the 941. Instead, it's a report of amounts due and amounts paid, and they should match.

The 941 is concerned with:

- Gross wages paid
- Federal Income Tax withholding
- FICA (Social Security) withholding and matching employer contributions
- Medicare withholding and matching employer contributions

Many people fill out the 941 Form they receive in the mail. You can gather the information you need from a QuickBooks report to do that, or have QuickBooks print the 941 Form for you.

 NOTE: The Federal Government is encouraging telephone filing, and instructions for that feature arrives with your 941 Form every quarter. This is certainly an easy way to file. You can expect the government to begin encouraging online filing via the Internet very soon.

Creating the 941 Form

QuickBooks will prepare your 941 report, using the information in your QuickBooks registers. To prepare the report, follow these steps:

1. Choose Employees | Process Payroll Forms from the QuickBooks menu bar.
2. Select the option to Create Form 941.
3. Follow the onscreen instructions to complete the form and print it.

The printed form can be sent to the IRS if you use these printing criteria:

- It must be printed with black ink on white or cream paper.
- The paper must be 8" × 11" or 8.5" × 11".
- The paper must be 18 lb. weight or heavier.

The printed report doesn't look exactly like the blank form you received, but it's close. More importantly, it's perfectly acceptable to the government.

You could also use the information in the printed report to fill in the blank 941 Form you receive, or to transmit the information via telephone, saving your QuickBooks printout as your copy.

Creating 941 Reports from the Internet

At some point during the calendar year 2000, QuickBooks will change the way you prepare 941 reports. If you're reading this book (and just starting to use QuickBooks) after the beginning of the year, the change may already be in effect.

When QuickBooks changes the way Form 941 is created, your system will be able to handle the transformation automatically. When you connect to the Internet to run your payroll checks, QuickBooks will automatically download the necessary changes to your software.

Then, the next time you create the 941 report, open your Internet connection and follow these steps:

1. Choose Employees | Process Payroll Forms from the QuickBooks menu bar.
2. On the QuickBooks 941 Web page, follow the instructions to complete the form.
3. Print the form and either file it or use it as the source for manually filling in your 941 Form (or for using the 941 telephone reporting feature).

Other QuickBooks Internet Report Services

QuickBooks will probably implement the ability to create quarterly and year-end reports for many states on the Internet. As these features are added, they'll be accessible from the Web page you load in your browser when you choose Employees | Process Payroll Forms from the QuickBooks menu bar.

Upgrading the Contents of This Book

As the 941 and state reporting Internet services are implemented, you'll be able to obtain detailed instructions on using them. Anyone reading this book has access to free upgrades to the contents of this book by going to http://www.cpa911.com. We'll be upgrading the book contents whenever QuickBooks changes the way any feature works.

 TIP: We'll also be upgrading the book contents with tricks and tips from our own experiences and also from users. If you discover shortcuts or tips you want to pass along to other QuickBooks 2000 users, be sure to add them to this site.

Preparing Annual Returns

All the taxing authorities want annual returns. The feds, state, and local folks need reports and forms. Some of them need checks. You can get all the information you need from QuickBooks. In fact, all the usual QuickBooks reports work just fine, as long as you remember to set the Dates field to the entire year.

Preparing State and Local Annual Returns

The state and local taxing authorities usually send you a form that asks for a reconciliation for the year. You may have to present quarterly totals as you fill out the form, which you can accomplish by changing the date range in the QuickBooks payroll reports.

Finish your State Unemployment annual report as soon as possible, because the payments you make to the state are relevant to the Federal Unemployment report (Form 940). Incidentally, for many states, the year-end State Unemployment report doesn't require a check because there's a limit to the wages that are eligible for applying the unemployment contribution rate.

Preparing the 940 Report

For small businesses, the 940 report is usually filed annually, along with a check. The 940 is the Federal Unemployment report (FUTA) and it's an employer expense.

To create your Form 940, choose Employees | Process Payroll Forms from the QuickBooks menu bar. Select the option to create the 940 Form and follow the instructions that appear on the screen. Many small businesses qualify for Form 940EZ (which is shorter and easier).

QuickBooks will probably move Form 940 to the Internet when the 941 Form changes go into effect. Your software will be updated automatically and detailed instructions for using the new feature will be available at http://www.cpa911.com.

Printing W-2 Forms

You must print W-2 forms for your employees, the government agencies, and your own files. Everybody needs them.

Choose Employees | Process W-2s from the QuickBooks menu bar to open the Process W-2s window.

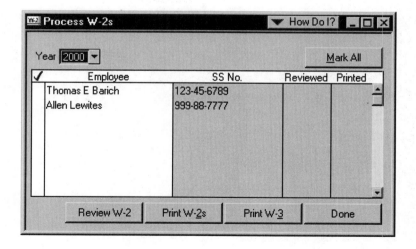

Click Mark All to select all the employees, then choose Review W-2. Each employee's W-2 Form is presented on screen. If there is non-financial data missing (such as an address or zip code), you must fill it in.

Click Next to move through all the employee forms. When everything is correct, load your W-2 Forms in the printer and choose Print W-2s. The Print W-2s window opens so you can choose a printer and print the forms.

You must also print the W-3 Form, which is a summary of your W-2 Forms. It must be in the package you send to the IRS when you transmit the W-2 Forms. You cannot preview the W-3 Form.

All these payroll reports are a bit time-consuming, but you have no choice; these tasks are legally necessary. At least QuickBooks keeps the records and does the math.

Configuring and Tracking Inventory

n this chapter, you will learn to...

- Add items
- Deal with physical inventory counts
- Adjust the count
- Create pre-builds
- Use backorders

For many businesses the warehouse is a source of frustration, bewilderment, rage, and erroneous information. I'm using the term "warehouse" generically to indicate the place where you store inventory (which may not be a discrete building that looks like a warehouse).

Creating Inventory Items

Inventory items are part of the items list in your QuickBooks system. That list contains all the elements that might ever appear on a customer invoice, a purchase order, or a vendor bill. If you track inventory, many of the items in your items list are the things you sell to customers from stock.

Creating New Items

Complete instructions for adding items to the items list are found in Chapter 2, but it's worth taking a moment here to go over the steps briefly.

Choose Lists | Items from the menu bar to open the Item List window, where all your inventory items are listed along with all the other types of items.

Name ▲	Description	Type	Account	On Hand	Price
◆ Administration		Service	4020 · Other Regula		0.00
◆ Cable	Cable	Inventory Part	4010 · Sales	8	0.00
◆ Consulting		Service	4000 · Consulting In		0.00
◆ Fin Chg	Finance Charges on	Other Charge	4050 · Finance Char		18.0%
◆ Installation		Service	4000 · Consulting In		0.00
◆ Keyboard	Keyboard	Inventory Part	4010 · Sales	15	29.00
◆ Modem	Modem	Inventory Part	4010 · Sales	6	95.00
◆ Monitor	Monitor	Inventory Part	4010 · Sales	6	69.00
◆ NY Sales Tax	NY Tax	Sales Tax Item	2200 · Sales Tax Pa		6.0%
◆ Overage		Non-inventory Pa	4290 · Over-Short 4		0.00
◆ PA sales tax	Sales Tax	Sales Tax Item	2200 · Sales Tax Pa		7.0%

The inventory items can be distinguished easily because they have their own type: Inventory Part. To see all the inventory items in a group, click the Type column heading to sort the list by type.

If you want to add a new item to your inventory items list, press CTRL-N while the Item List window is displayed. When the New Item window opens, fill in the information (see Figure 10-1 for an example).

You can also enter the current Qty On Hand in this window. If you're entering inventory as part of your original configuration of QuickBooks, that might be a suitable way to do it. If you've already started QuickBooks with an opening balance sheet from your accountant, you may want to enter the quantity on hand

The item name is really
your code for this item.

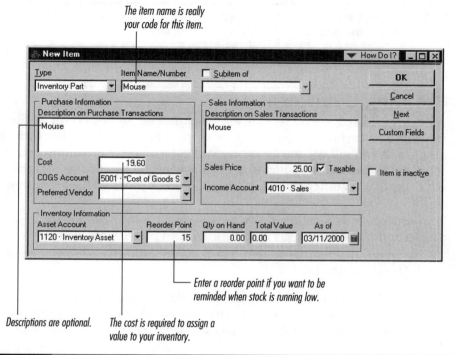

Descriptions are optional.   The cost is required to assign a
value to your inventory.

Enter a reorder point if you want to be
reminded when stock is running low.

FIGURE 10-1   The item record holds all the important information about each inventory item

through the inventory adjustment tool, discussed later in this chapter. In fact, you should ask your accountant for his or her advice on making the inventory adjustment before you start performing the tasks noted here.

The reason for the accountant query is the way inventory value is posted in QuickBooks. If you enter the quantity on hand through the New Item window, the value of that quantity is entered into your inventory asset account, and the balancing entry is made to your current equity.

If you use the inventory adjustment window, the balancing entry is made to an account of your choice. When you're performing standard adjustments (after a physical count of the inventory), the account you use is the inventory adjustment account. However, you can invent and use any account for offsetting the inventory adjustment and your accountant may want to use an equity account you've invented for prior years or some other balance sheet account instead of touching the preconfigured equity balance. See the detailed explanations for using the inventory adjustment window later in this chapter and discuss this issue with your accountant.

TIP: To edit an item, open the Item List and double-click the item you want to change. Make the necessary changes and click OK.

Creating Subitems

Subitems are used when there are choices for items and you want all the choices to be part of a larger hierarchy so you can track them efficiently. For instance, if you sell widgets in a variety of colors, you may want to create a subitem for each color: red widget, green widget, and so on. Or perhaps you sell widgets from different widget manufacturers: Jones widgets, Smith widgets, and so on.

In order to have a subitem, you must have a parent item. Figure 10-2 shows a new item that has been specifically created as a parent item.

Having created the parent item, subitems are easy to create by opening a blank New Item window:

1. In the Item Name field, enter the code for this item. It can be an item, a color, a manufacturer name, or any other code that specifies this subitem as compared to other subitems under the same parent item. For instance, the

A description isn't necessary (it doesn't carry over to subitems).

Item code is generic because the item is a parent.

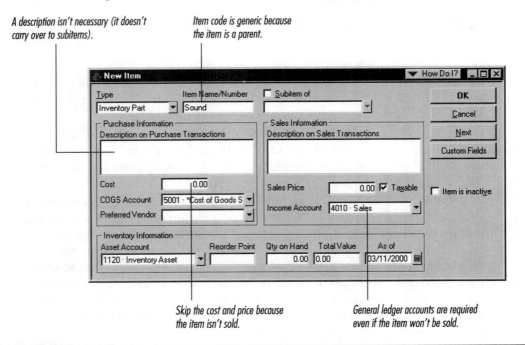

Skip the cost and price because the item isn't sold.

General ledger accounts are required even if the item won't be sold.

FIGURE 10-2 This item won't be sold to customers; it exists only as a parent item

first subitem I created under the parent item shown in Figure 10-2 was named Speakers.

2. Check the box named Subitem of, and then select the parent item from the drop-down list that appears when you click the arrow to the right of the field.

3. Enter the descriptions you want to appear on purchase orders and invoices.

4. Enter the general ledger account information.

5. Enter the cost and price.

6. Enter the reorder point if you're using that feature.

Continue to add subitems to each parent item in your system.

Making Items Inactive

Sometimes you have inventory items that you aren't buying or selling at the moment. Perhaps they're seasonal, or the cost is too high and you want to delay purchasing and reselling the item until you can get a better price.

As long as you're not using the item, you can make it inactive. It doesn't appear on the items list, which means that the list is shorter and easier to scroll through when you're creating an invoice. And you won't be nagged with reorder reminders.

To declare an item inactive, open the Item List window and select the item. Then click the Item button at the bottom of the window and choose Make Inactive from the menu.

When an item is inactive, it's not just invisible on the list of items for sale that appears during invoice data entry; it doesn't even appear on the Item List window. However, you can change the appearance of the Item List window to display inactive items.

When you make any item inactive, the Show All check box becomes activated in the Item List window. If no items are marked inactive, the Show All option is grayed out and inaccessible. Click the Show All check box to display the inactive items along with the active items. Any inactive item is displayed with an icon that looks like a hand to the left of the item listing (see Figure 10-3).

To make an inactive item active again, choose the Show All option so you can see the inactive items, and then click the hand icon.

CAUTION: You can make any individual subitem inactive, but if you make a parent item inactive all of its subitems are also made inactive.

A hand means the item is currently inactive.

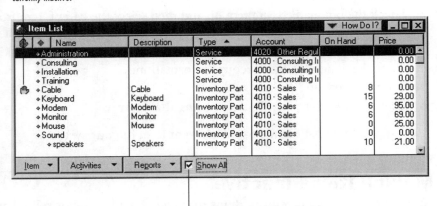

Click the Show All check box to toggle the display of inactive items on and off.

FIGURE 10-3 Inactive items remain in your system; they can be displayed if you need to see a complete items list

Running Inventory Reports

You'll probably find that you run reports on your inventory status quite often. For most businesses, tracking the state of the inventory is the second most important and frequently run set of reports (right behind reports about the current accounts receivable balances).

QuickBooks provides several useful, significant inventory reports, which you can access by choosing Reports on the Navigation Bar. In the Report Finder window, select Inventory as the report type to see the available reports, which are discussed later in this section.

Activating All Items

If you make an item inactive, QuickBooks pretends it doesn't exist. An inactive item doesn't show up in any inventory report. Worse, all calculations about the worth of your inventory, including reports that aren't directly connected to inventory (such as your balance sheet reports), fail to include any amounts connected to inactive items.

You must activate all inventory items, except those that have never been received into stock and never sold, before running any reports on inventory. You should also activate all inventory items before running financial statements.

Inventory Valuation Summary Report

This report gives you a quick assessment of the value of your inventory. By default, the date range is the current fiscal year to date. Each item is listed along with the following information displayed in columns:

- **Number on Hand** The net number of received items and sold items. Because QuickBooks permits you to sell items you don't have in stock (at least you haven't used QuickBooks transaction windows to bring them into stock), it's possible to have a negative number in this column.
- **Average Cost** Each receipt of inventory transaction is used to calculate this figure.
- **Asset Value** The value posted to your Inventory account in the general ledger. The value is calculated by multiplying the number on hand by the average cost.
- **% of Total Asset** The percentage of your total inventory assets that this item represents.
- **Sales Price** The price you've set for this item. This figure is obtained by looking at the item's configuration window. If you entered a price when you set up the item, that price is displayed. If you didn't enter a price (because you chose to determine the price at the time of sale), $0.00 displays. QuickBooks does not check the sales records for this item to determine this number.
- **Retail Value** The current retail value of the item, which is calculated by multiplying the number on hand by the retail price (which may be $0.00).
- **% of Retail Value** The percentage of the total retail value of your inventory that this item represents.

Inventory Valuation Detail Report

To be honest, I'm puzzled by this report, and I don't know how to describe it. In fact, I'm not sure why you would display it. The word "detail" in this report title means transaction detail, but the word is misleading (see Figure 10-4). Amounts involved in sales of the items are missing.

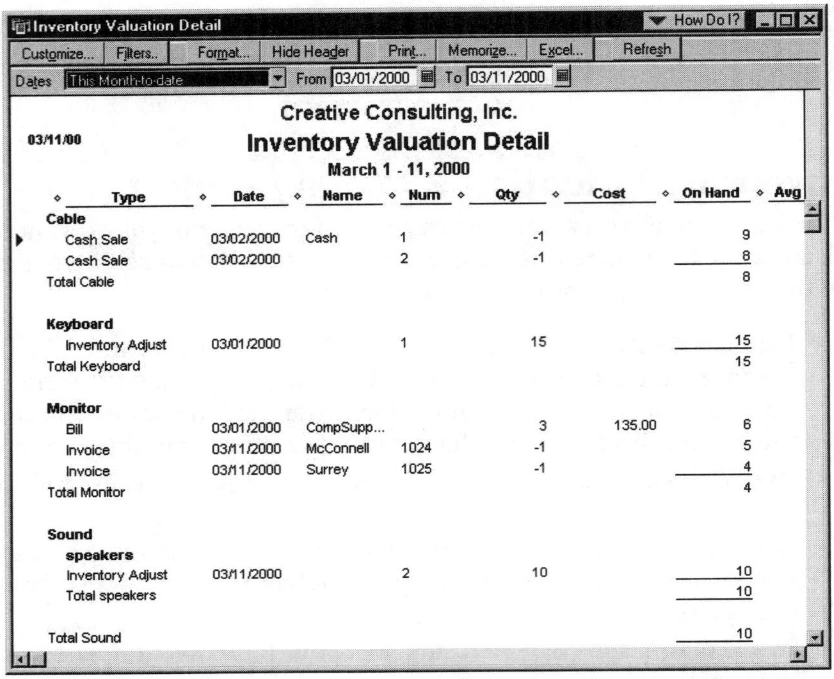

FIGURE 10-4 No details about sales amounts are on this report, even though the sales transactions are listed

You can, of course, double-click any sales transaction line to see the details, but there are faster and easier ways to obtain that information (see the section "Getting Quick Inventory Reports," later in this chapter).

Stock Status

Use the Stock Status reports to get quick numbers about inventory items, including the following important information:

- The reorder point
- The number currently on hand
- The number currently on order (purchase order exists but stock has not yet been received)
- The average number of units sold per week

There are two Stock Status reports: By Item and By Vendor. The information is the same in both reports, but the order in which information is arranged and subtotaled is different.

NOTE: Very few customization options are available for inventory reports—you can change the date range and filter some of the items, but you cannot add or remove columns.

Getting Quick Inventory Reports

QuickBooks provides a reporting feature called QuickReports that provides valuable information about an individual inventory item or all inventory items. QuickReports are available from the Item List window (click the Item List object in the Navigation Bar, or choose Lists | Item List from the QuickBooks menu bar). In the Item List window, select an item and press CTRL-Q (or click the Reports button and choose QuickReport) to open the QuickReport shown in Figure 10-5. Click any line to drill down to the transaction details.

Plenty of other reports are available from the Reports menu that appears when you click the Report button on the Item List window. You can get sales and purchase reports for all inventory items. The sales report shown in Figure 10-6 is a good example of the kind of information these reports offer.

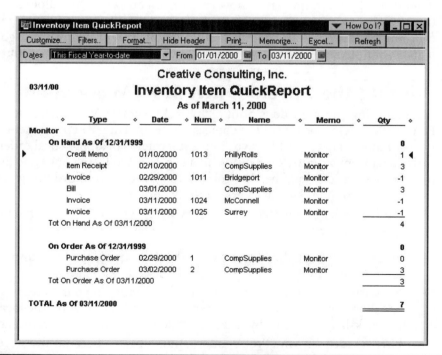

| **FIGURE 10-5** | A QuickReport is an activity report for an item |

	Sales by Item Detail								

Creative Consulting, Inc.

03/11/00

Sales by Item Detail

March 1 - 11, 2000

Type	Date	Num	Name	Memo	Qty	Sales Price	Amount	B:
Inventory								
Cable								
Cash Sale	03/02/20...	1	Cash	Cable	1	12.00	12.00	
Cash Sale	03/02/20...	2		Cable	1	10.00	10.00	
Total Cable							22.00	
Monitor								
Invoice	03/11/20...	1024	McConnell	Monitor	1	69.00	69.00	
Invoice	03/11/20...	1025	Surrey	Monitor	1	69.00	69.00	
Total Monitor							138.00	

FIGURE 10-6   For transaction details like this, double-click on the transaction line

Counting Inventory

I can hear the groans. I know—there's nothing worse than doing a physical inventory. However, no matter how careful you are with QuickBooks transactions, no matter how pristine your protocols are for making sure everything that comes and goes is accounted for, you probably aren't going to match your physical inventory to your QuickBooks figures. Sorry about that.

Printing the Physical Inventory Worksheet

The first thing you must do is print a Physical Inventory Worksheet (see Figure 10-7), which is one of the choices on the Inventory Reports menu in the Report Finder. This report lists your inventory items in alphabetical order, along with the current quantity on hand, which is calculated from your QuickBooks transactions. In addition, there's a column that's set up to record the actual count as you walk around your warehouse with this printout in hand.

If you have a large number of inventory items, you may have some problems with this worksheet:

- You cannot change the way the worksheet is sorted, so you cannot arrange the items to match the way you've laid out your warehouse.
- If you use bins, rows, or some other physical entity in your warehouse, QuickBooks has no feature to support it, so you cannot enter the location on this worksheet (and sort by location, which is an extremely useful method).
- I have no idea why the Pref Vendor column exists, because I've never experienced a physical inventory in which that information was used.

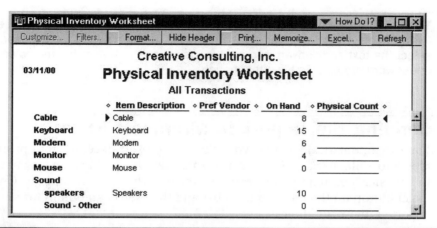

FIGURE 10-7 The worksheet's most important column is the one with the blank lines that you use to enter the physical count

If you stock by manufacturer, the manufacturer's name is referred to in the code or description. However, you cannot get rid of it.

Click the Print button in the worksheet window to bring up the Print Reports window. In the Number Of Copies box, enter as many copies as you need (one for each person helping with the count).

 T I P : Don't hand every person a full report—cut the report to give each person the pages he or she needs, and keep one full copy to use as a master.

Exporting the Report to a File

You can also export the worksheet, which is useful if you want to print additional columns or rearrange the way the report is sorted. Exporting is accomplished by printing to a file instead of the printer:

1. In the Print Reports window, select File in the Print To field.
2. Click the arrow to the right of the File text box and select a format for the file. Then click Print.
3. In the Create Disk File dialog box, select a folder to hold this file and give the file a name. Then click OK to save the file.
4. Open the appropriate software and manipulate the file to make a worksheet that fits your exact needs.

> **TIP:** If you want to send the file to a word processor and use the Table feature, select Tab Delimited as the file type. Then, in the word processor, select the text and convert it to a table, using tabs to determine the columns (most word processors have this option).

Sending the Report to Microsoft Excel

You can automatically export your file to Microsoft Excel without printing the report to a file. Because Excel is a spreadsheet, this gives you a way to record the physical count and then rearrange the way the numbers appear. Click the Excel button on the report button bar and then select an option for saving this exported file. Your choices are:

- Create a new Excel spreadsheet file
- Add the current data to an existing Excel spreadsheet file

For even more control, click the Advanced button and select the options you want to take advantage of (see Figure 10-8).

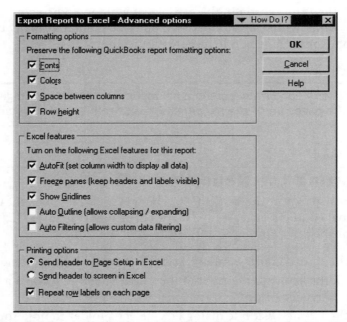

FIGURE 10-8 Select the formatting features and Excel features you want to use

N O T E : For information on using QuickBooks 99 with Microsoft Office applications, see Appendix C.

Planning the Physical Count

QuickBooks lacks a "freeze" feature like the one found in some inventory-enabled software. *Freezing inventory* means that after you've printed the worksheet and begun counting, any transactions involving inventory are saved to a holding file in order to avoid changing the totals. When you've finished your physical count, you unfreeze the inventory count and print a report on the holding file. Make your adjustments to the count using the information in that file, and then make the final adjustments to the count.

You can perform these actions manually. After you print the worksheet (which you don't do until you're ready to start counting), be sure that all sales invoices will be handled differently until after the inventory count is adjusted. There are a couple of ways to do this:

- Print an extra copy of each invoice and save the copies in a folder. Don't pick and pack the inventory for the invoices until after the count.
- Prepare a form for sales people to fill out the name and quantity of inventory items sold during the freeze, and delay picking and packing the inventory until after the count.
- Delay entering invoices until after the count is over. (This is not a good idea if counting takes a couple of days.)
- Don't receive inventory in QuickBooks (don't fill out a Receive Items or Receive Bill form) until after the count.
- If inventory arrives in the warehouse, don't unpack the boxes until after the count.

When you start counting the inventory, be sure there's a good system in place. The most important element of the system is having *somebody in charge*. One person, with a master inventory worksheet in hand, must know who is counting what. When each counter is finished, his or her sheet should be handed to the person in charge and the numbers should be duplicated onto the master inventory worksheet. (This is why you print multiple copies of the worksheet.) Note the date and time the count was reported.

After the count, bring in any inventory that's arrived during the count. Then start picking and packing your orders so you can generate income again.

Making the Inventory Adjustments

After you've finished counting the inventory, you may find that the numbers on the worksheet don't match the physical count. Most of the time the physical count is lower than the QuickBooks figures. This is called "shrinkage." *Shrinkage* is jargon for "stuff went missing for an unexplained reason," but most of the time the reason is employee theft. Sorry, but that's a well-documented fact. Another reason for shrinkage is breakage, but most of the time that's reported by employees, and you can adjust your inventory because you know about it. When you don't know about it, suspect the worst, because statistics prove that suspicion to be the most accurate.

Adjusting the Count

You have to tell QuickBooks about the physical count, and you accomplish that by choosing Vendors | Inventory Activities | Adjust Quantity/Value On Hand from the menu bar.

The Adjust Quantity/Value On Hand window opens, which is shown in Figure 10-9. Here are some guidelines for filling out this window:

- Enter the date (usually inventory adjustments are made at the end of the month, quarter, or year but there's no rule about that).

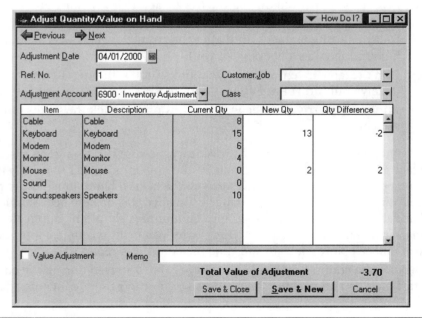

FIGURE 10-9 Straighten out your inventory numbers by adjusting the quantities after you complete the physical count

- Use an optional Ref. number to track the adjustment. The next time you enter an adjustment, QuickBooks will increment the Ref. number by one.
- Enter the inventory adjustment account in your chart of accounts. Click the arrow to see a display of all your accounts, and if you don't have an inventory adjustment account, choose Add New and create one.

 TIP: An inventory adjustment account must exist in order to adjust your inventory. Usually it's an expense account.

- The Customer:Job field is there in case you're sending stuff to a customer (or for a job) but not including the items on any invoices for that customer or job. QuickBooks provides this feature to help you when you do that (which is usually as a result of a job-costing scheme you're using). The inventory is changed and the cost is posted to the job.
- Use the Class field if you've created classes that affect inventory reports.
- Use either the New Qty column or the Qty Difference column to enter the count (depending on how you filled out the worksheet and calculated it). Whichever column you use, QuickBooks fills in the other column automatically.

When you have completed entering all the information, click OK to save the adjustments.

Adjusting the Value

When you complete the entries, the total value of the adjustment you made is displayed in the window. That value is calculated by using the average cost of your inventory. For example, if you received ten widgets into inventory at a cost of $10.00 each, and later received ten more at a cost of $12.00 each, your average cost for widgets is $11.00 each. If your adjustment is for minus one widget (what *did* happen to it?), your inventory asset value is decreased by $11.00.

You can be more precise about your inventory valuation by eliminating the average valuation and entering a true value:

1. Click the Value Adjustment check box.
2. A column named New Value opens in the window (see Figure 10-10).
3. The value of the total adjusted count is displayed for each item, and you can change the value to eliminate the effects of averaging costs.

Of course, to do this, you must have the information you need, and then make the appropriate calculations in order to enter the correct total value.

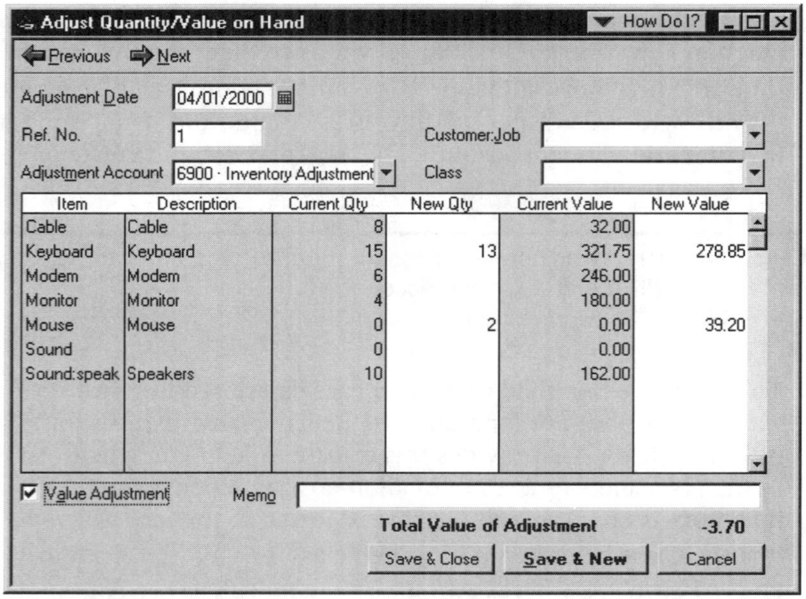

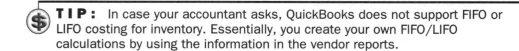

Adjust Quantity/Value on Hand
How Do I?
Previous
Next
Adjustment Date
04/01/2000
Ref. No.
1
Customer:Job
Adjustment Account
6900 · Inventory Adjustment
Class
Item
Description
Current Qty
New Qty
Current Value
New Value
Cable Cable 8 32.00
Keyboard Keyboard 15 13 321.75 278.85
Modem Modem 6 246.00
Monitor Monitor 4 180.00
Mouse Mouse 0 2 0.00 39.20
Sound 0 0.00
Sound:speak Speakers 10 162.00
Value Adjustment
Memo
Total Value of Adjustment
-3.70
Save & Close
Save & New
Cancel

FIGURE 10-10 You can manually change the current total value of any inventory item

In the Item List window, click the Reports button. Then choose Reports on All Items | Purchases | Purchases By Vendor Detail to see a history of your purchases, and then make the necessary calculations.

> **TIP:** In case your accountant asks, QuickBooks does not support FIFO or LIFO costing for inventory. Essentially, you create your own FIFO/LIFO calculations by using the information in the vendor reports.

When you've finished making your changes, click OK to save your new inventory numbers.

Understanding the Posting

When you adjust the inventory count, you're also changing the value of your inventory asset. When you save the adjustment, the inventory asset account is changed to reflect the differences for each item (see Figure 10-11).

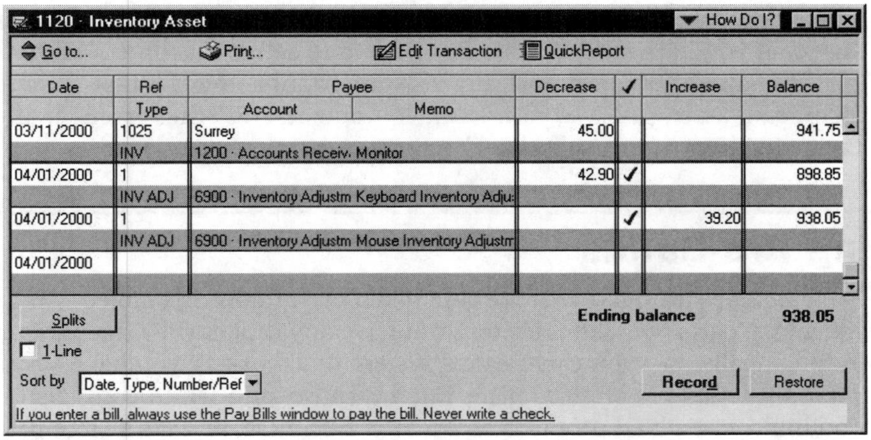

Date	Ref	Payee		Decrease	✓	Increase	Balance
	Type	Account	Memo				
03/11/2000	1025	Surrey		45.00			941.75
	INV	1200 · Accounts Receiv·	Monitor				
04/01/2000	1			42.90	✓		898.85
	INV ADJ	6900 · Inventory Adjustm	Keyboard Inventory Adju				
04/01/2000	1				✓	39.20	938.05
	INV ADJ	6900 · Inventory Adjustm	Mouse Inventory Adjustm				
04/01/2000							

Ending balance 938.05

Sort by Date, Type, Number/Ref

If you enter a bill, always use the Pay Bills window to pay the bill. Never write a check.

FIGURE 10-11 Notice the two entries of the type INV ADJ, indicating an adjustment of inventory instead of a sale or receipt of goods

But this is double-entry bookkeeping and that means there has to be an equal and opposite entry somewhere else. For example, when you sell items via customer invoices, the balancing entry to the decrement of your inventory account is made to cost of sales. When you're adjusting inventory, however, there is no sale involved (nor is there a purchase involved). In this case, the balancing entry is made to the inventory adjustment account, which must exist in order to adjust your inventory.

If your inventory adjustment lowers the value of your inventory, the inventory account is credited and the adjustment account receives a debit in the same amount. If your adjustment raises the value of your inventory, the postings are opposite.

Making Other Adjustments to Inventory

You can use the Adjust Quantity/Value On Hand window to make adjustments to inventory at any time and for a variety of reasons:

- Breakage or other damage
- Customer demo units
- Gifts or bonuses for customers (or employees)
- Removal of inventory parts in order to create pre-built or pre-assembled inventory items. See the upcoming section on pre-building inventory.

The important thing to remember is that tracking inventory isn't just to make sure that you have sufficient items on hand to sell to customers (although that's certainly an important point). Equally important is the fact that inventory is a significant asset, just like your cash, equipment, and other assets. It affects your company's worth in a substantial way.

Creating Pre-Builds

Pre-builds are products that are assembled or partially assembled using existing inventory parts. QuickBooks does not have any capacity for tracking pre-builds automatically, but you can create a system that works if you have a couple of pre-built items you want to place into inventory and sell to your customers. If you build assembled products as a matter of course, and it's a large part of your business, QuickBooks is not the software for you.

Software that supports pre-builds automates all the processes, using the following steps:

1. Permits the creation of a pre-built inventory item, asking which inventory parts (and how many of each) are used.
2. Receives the pre-built item into inventory (after you physically build it), automatically removing the individual parts from inventory.
3. Automatically creates a cost for the new pre-built item based on the cost of the individual parts.

 TIP: Most software that supports pre-builds also permits a labor charge to be added as part of the cost.

Each of these steps can be performed manually in QuickBooks and, although it's more time-consuming, you can create pre-builds yourself.

Creating the Pre-Built Item

Start by putting the item into your items list, as seen in Figure 10-12.

Making Checkbook Adjustments

In this chapter, you will learn to...

- Make deposits

- Transfer funds between accounts

- Deal with bounced checks

- Void disbursements

- Track ATM transactions

- Understand petty cash

- Balance credit card statements

Before you started using accounting software, did your checkbook register have things crossed out? Pencil notes next to inked-in entries? Inked notes next to penciled-in entries? Transactions that were made in April entered in the middle of a string of June transactions ("The statement came—I forgot about that transaction")? Lots of corrections for math errors?

If so, don't relax; the only thing QuickBooks can take care of for you is the last problem—the math errors. Computers don't make math mistakes. Even with QuickBooks, you still have to enter your transactions. The advantage is that most of your transactions (your customer payments and the checks you write) are entered for you automatically.

Making a Deposit

Even though QuickBooks automatically enters deposits into your bank account when you record customer payments, there are times when you receive money that's unconnected to a customer sale.

Entering a deposit (one that's not a customer payment) into your QuickBooks check register isn't much different than entering a deposit into a manual checkbook register. In fact, it's easier because you don't have to make any calculations—QuickBooks takes care of that.

Click the Use Register item in the Navigation Bar and choose the account you want to work with.

Fill in the date and then click in the deposit column to enter the amount (see Figure 11-1). Assign the deposit to an account. You should use the memo field for an explanation, because your accountant will probably ask you about the deposit later (and sometimes create a journal entry to re-assign the amount). Click the Record button. That's it!

Usually, the account you assign is an income account, because you're receiving revenue, even though it may not be from a sale to a customer. You can use a miscellaneous revenue account or create a revenue account specifically for this type of income. However, if you're making a deposit that's a refund from a vendor, you can post the amount to the expense account that was used for the original expense. If you're depositing your own money into the business, that's capital and you should use the capital account (it's an equity account), or establish a liability account if you're making a loan to your company. When in doubt, post the amount to the most logical place, and call your accountant. You can always edit the transaction later, or make a journal entry to post the amount to the right account.

Date	Number	Payee		Payment	✓	Deposit	Balance
	Type	Account	Memo				
05/12/2000						9,910.50	149,350.57
	DEP	-split-	Deposit				
06/04/2000						12,000.00	161,350.57
	DEP	4000 · Consulting Income	Deposit				
06/04/2000	1260	Andy Artist		2,100.00			159,250.57
	CHK	6555 · Outside Services					
06/10/2000	Number	Payee		Payment		1,000.00	
	DEP	7030 · Other Income	Memo				

Window title: **1000 · Operating Account-Checking**   ▼ How Do I?

Toolbar: ⬍ Go to...   🖨 Print...   ✍ Edit Transaction   📋 QuickReport

Splits   □ 1-Line   Sort by [Date, Type, Number/Ref ▼]

Ending balance   159,250.57

Record   Restore

Use alerts to stay on top of deadlines and events that affect your business.

FIGURE 11-1 The simplest way to record a deposit is to use only the required fields: date and amount

TIP: It's a good idea to set up accounts for transactions that you're unsure how to post. I have two such accounts. For income about which I want to ask my accountant, I use account #9998, titled MiscIncome. Account #9999 is titled MiscExpense. If the account has a balance, it means I should call my accountant and find out where to post the income or expense I temporarily "parked" in that account. A journal entry puts the money into the right account.

If you want more detail, you can use the Payee column to enter the name of the source of the deposit. If the name isn't on any of your QuickBooks lists, you're asked how you want to add it.

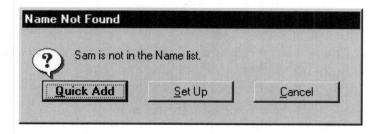

- Choose Quick Add to select the list to which this name should be assigned. Then choose OK. Later, you can open the record and fill in more information. See Chapter 2 for detailed information about adding entries to your QuickBooks lists.
- Choose Set Up to access a blank Name form in which you enter all the necessary data about this name.

Transferring Funds Between Accounts

Moving money between accounts is a common procedure in business. If you have a bank account for payroll you have to move money out of another account into your payroll account every payday. Some people deposit all the customer payments into a money market account and then transfer the necessary funds to an operating account when it's time to pay bills. Law firms deposit some funds into an escrow account and then transfer the portion that belongs to them into the operating account. The rest of the escrow deposit goes to the client.

The difference between a regular deposit and a transfer isn't clear if you think about the end result as being nothing more than "money was disbursed from one account and deposited into another account." However, that's not the way to think about it. When you work with accounting issues, every action has an effect on your general ledger, which means there's an effect on your financial reporting (and your taxes). A transfer isn't a disbursement (which is an expenditure that's assigned to a specific account), and it isn't a regular deposit (income received).

 TIP: If you don't use the transfer protocol, you run the risk of posting a deductible expense or taxable income to your profit and loss reports.

To make a transfer, follow these steps:

1. Choose Banking | Transfer Funds to open the Transfer Funds Between Accounts window.
2. Fill out the fields (see Figure 11-2).
3. Click OK. QuickBooks posts the transaction (you'll see it marked as Transfer in both bank accounts if you open their registers) without affecting any totals in your financial reports. All the work is done on the balance sheet, but the bottom line of your balance sheet doesn't change.

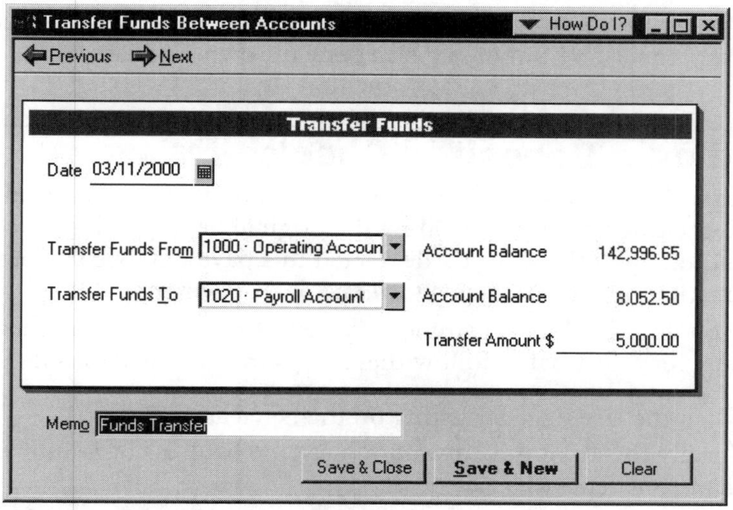

Transfer Funds Between Accounts How Do I?

Previous Next

Transfer Funds

Date 03/11/2000

Transfer Funds From 1000 · Operating Accoun   Account Balance   142,996.65

Transfer Funds To 1020 · Payroll Account   Account Balance   8,052.50

Transfer Amount $ 5,000.00

Memo Funds Transfer

Save & Close   **Save & New**   Clear

FIGURE 11-2 It doesn't get any easier than this!

ACCOUNT	DEBIT	CREDIT
Sending Bank Account		Amount of Transfer
Receiving Bank Account	Amount of Transfer	

 TIP: In order to facilitate a transfer of funds, you really should have both of the accounts set up in your QuickBooks system. Although you can create accounts during the transfer procedure, it's always quicker and easier to have everything set up in advance.

Handling Bounced Checks

Customer checks sometimes bounce. When that happens, you have several tasks in front of you:

- Deducting the amount of the bounced check from your checking account
- Recording any bank charges you incurred from your checking account
- Removing the payment credit applied to the customer invoice
- For a cash sale, creating an invoice to recover the money from the customer

In addition, you might want to collect a service charge from the customer (at least for the amount of any charges your own bank assessed).

Voiding a Deposited Check

The first thing you must do is deduct the amount of the bounced check from your checking account by voiding the original deposit. This procedure varies, depending upon the way you deposited this payment. See Chapter 4 for detailed information on making deposits of customer payments.

If you deposited this customer payment directly into your checking account (usually for a cash sale), follow these steps to void the deposit:

1. Click the Use Register listing on the Navigation Bar.
2. Specify the account you want to use (the bank account into which you made the deposit).
3. When the account register is on your screen, find the check that bounced and click anywhere on its row to select that transaction.
4. Right-click and choose Void Check.

The transaction is marked VOID and the amount of the check is deducted from your balance. In addition, the check is marked as cleared so it won't show up on the list of items to reconcile when you reconcile your bank statement. (See Chapter 12 to learn about reconciling your bank account.) The income account to which you posted the cash sale is also adjusted by the amount of the voided check.

You must also invoice the client for the bounced check, because the original invoice was not paid by a standard payment (using the Receive Payments window). See the section "Invoicing Customers for Bounced Checks" later in this chapter.

Removing the Bounced Payment from a Payment Deposit

If you used the Receive Payment window to deposit the customer payment, and then made the deposit, it's a bit more complicated. The deposit that appears in your bank register could be made up of a number of different customer checks. You must remove the bounced check from the group of checks that was deposited, then you can reverse the bounced check.

1. Choose Lists | Chart of Accounts and double-click the undeposited funds account to open its register.
2. Choose the deposit that contains the bounced check, which has a type of DEP in the register (see Figure 11-3).
3. Click the Edit button in the register window. This opens the Make Deposits window where all the payments for that deposit are listed.
4. Click on the line that contains the check that bounced (see Figure 11-4).
5. Choose Edit | Delete Line from the QuickBooks menu bar.
6. Click Save & Close to re-record the deposit, minus the payment you deleted. QuickBooks asks you to confirm the action, so click Yes. You're returned to the undeposited funds account register, where this payment no longer has an entry for a deposit; it's still a payment, but it's undeposited.
7. Select the payment (it has a PMT type).
8. Choose Edit | Delete Payment from the QuickBooks menu bar. QuickBooks wants you to confirm the deletion.

Payments increase the balance of the undeposited funds account.

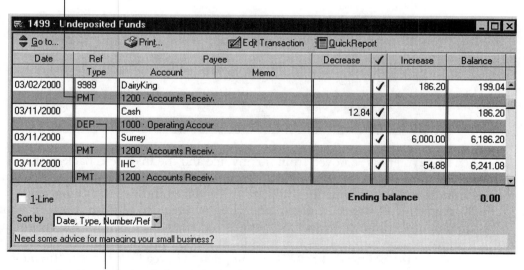

Depositing payments into a bank account decreases the balance of the undeposited funds account.

FIGURE 11-3   The undeposited funds account displays the check details for each deposit you've made

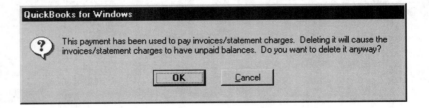

FIGURE 11-4 The original deposit window is available so you can eliminate a check that bounces

The payment is removed from the invoice and the invoice is back in the system, once again due and owing. If you run a Customer Balance Detail report from the A/R Reports menu, you'll see the invoice (and you'll no longer see the payment). If you send statements, you don't have to send an invoice for the amount of the bounced check (although you should call or write the customer to explain what happened). You should, however, bill the customer a service charge for the bounced check. To accomplish that, read the section "Invoicing Customers for Bounced Checks" later in this chapter.

Recording Bank Charges for Bounced Checks

If your bank charged you for a returned check, you have to enter the bank charge. To do so, start by opening the register for your bank account. Then fill out the fields, pressing the TAB key to move from one field to the next:

1. Click the Date field in the blank line at the bottom of the register and enter the date that the bank charge was assessed.

2. In the Number field, QuickBooks automatically fills in the next available check number. Delete that number and press TAB. QuickBooks fills in the word "Number."

3. In the Payee field, type the words **Returned Check Charges** (or any other similar phrase). That payee probably doesn't exist, so after you press the TAB key you'll see a Name Not Found message.

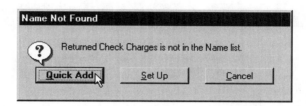

4. Click Quick Add and then select Other as the type of name in the next dialog box. Click OK.

5. In the Payment field, enter the amount of the service charge for the returned check.

6. In the Account field, assign this transaction to the account you use for bank charges.

7. Click the Record button in the register window to save the transaction.

Your bank account balance is reduced by the amount of the service charge. You should charge the customer for this, and in the following sections I'll cover the steps you need to take to accomplish that.

Setting Up Items for Bounced Checks

If you want to bill your customers for the amount due you as a result of a bounced check, and for a service charge for the bounced check, you have to set up your system. There are a couple of items you must add to your items list in order to have them appear on the invoices you send to customers who send rubber checks.

1. Choose Lists | Items from the menu bar and when the Item List window appears, press CTRL-N to enter a new item.

2. Create an item of the type Other Charge to use when you invoice a customer for a bounced check (see Figure 11-5).

3. Click Next to move to another blank item window so you can enter a new item for the service charge you want to assess on your customer.

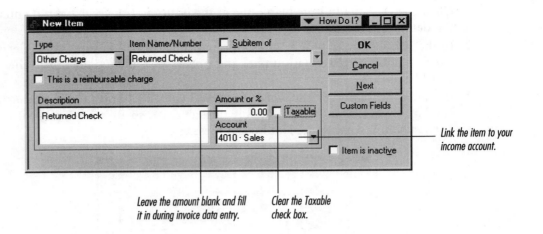

Link the item to your
income account.

Leave the amount blank and fill
it in during invoice data entry.

Clear the Taxable
check box.

FIGURE 11-5 Create an invoice item for recovering bounced checks from cash sale
customers

4. Fill out the bounced check service charge item (see Figure 11-6), leaving
the amount blank and assigning the item to an account that's established
for collecting this type of income.
5. Click OK to save your new items.

Now that these items are in your QuickBooks system, you can use them to
create invoices.

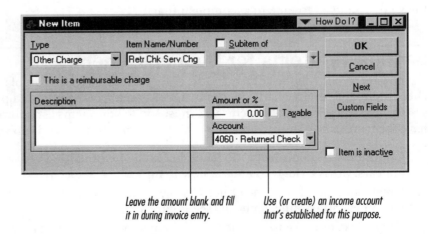

Leave the amount blank and fill
it in during invoice entry.

Use (or create) an income account
that's established for this purpose.

FIGURE 11-6 Create another item to collect a service charge for bounced checks

Incidentally, for the bounced check item, if you have multiple income accounts, create a new, general income account for this item (call it "bounced checks" if you wish). Later, you can do a journal entry to move the income from the general account to the specific account that was used at the time of the cash sale.

The QuickBooks "Official Instructions" on a Bounced Check Item

QuickBooks provides instructions on how to create the bounced check item so you can bill customers for the amount of the bounced check. They, like I, suggest you create a separate item for the service charge and bill it separately, but that item is not at issue here.

I have personal reservations about using the QuickBooks setup configuration for a bounced check item, and since you'll see the instructions in the QuickBooks Help file, I think it's only fair to explain to you why I showed you how to create the item in a different manner.

The difference between my approach and the "official" QuickBooks approach is merely a matter of bookkeeping practices and audit trails. Whether you use my instructions or the QuickBooks instructions, the bottom line (financially) is the same.

My Approach to Bounced Checks

In the instructions I gave in the preceding section, I told you to take two steps:

1. Void the check in the bank account register.
2. Create an item called "bounced check" and associate it with an income account.

Here's what happens to your QuickBooks system and your general ledger when you follow these instructions:

- When you void the check, the word VOID appears on the check entry in the account register. This is a clear indication of the history of this check; there's no question about what happened.
- When you void the check, the check is automatically cleared so it won't appear on the Reconcile Bank window.
- When you void the check, the offsetting income account is also adjusted and the revenue disappears.

The original cash sale had the following effect on your general ledger:

ACCOUNT	DEBIT	CREDIT
Bank	Amount of Sale	
Income		Amount of Sale

When you use my instructions to void the bounced check, the following occurs in the general ledger:

ACCOUNT	DEBIT	CREDIT
Bank		Amount of Bounced Check
Income	Amount of Bounced Check	

This "washes" the original posting, leaving behind a clear message that the check bounced, via the word VOID in the transaction line.

When you send the customer an invoice, the following posting takes place in the general ledger:

ACCOUNT	DEBIT	CREDIT
Accounts Receivable	Amount of Bounced Check	
Income		Amount of Bounced Check

I believe this is exactly the state you're in: You have an outstanding receivable, and the item you sold was "recovery of a bounced check." (See "Invoicing Customers for Bounced Checks," a bit later in this chapter.)

QuickBooks Approach to Bounced Checks

For a bounced check from a cash sale, QuickBooks tells you not to void the check. Instead, they suggest you only send a bill for the bounced check to the customer. The instructions tell you to link the bounced check item to your bank account instead of an income account. When you send the bill, the following posting occurs in the general ledger:

ACCOUNT	DEBIT	CREDIT
Bank		Amount of Bounced Check
Accounts Receivable	Amount of Bounced Check	

Financially, the end result is the same: You've added this amount to your outstanding receivables, and your bank account is credited (decremented) by the same amount.

The difference is in the audit trail. If you open the bank account register and look at this transaction, you'll see that it is treated as a payment, the type of transaction is an invoice, and the payment is posted to Accounts Receivable. Six months from now, you may not remember why on earth you had an invoice payment with no check number attached to the transaction. When your accountant looks at the transaction, he or she will have a lot of questions about why you would have posted a payment to Accounts Receivable. There are not a lot of good audit trail standards at work here.

In the end, because the bottom line is the same, it doesn't matter financially if you use the instructions given here, or the instructions in the QuickBooks Help files. I just wanted to explain why there's a difference.

Invoicing Customers for Bounced Checks

When you voided the check you didn't remove the payment that was linked to the original invoice. That invoice is still considered paid, but the customer owes you the money. Therefore you need to issue a new invoice to get your money:

 TIP: You might want to select the Service Invoice—which I find is easier and "cleaner" for this type of invoice—from the Custom Template box, but you don't have to.

1. Click the Create Invoices listing on the Navigation Bar.
2. When the Create Invoices window opens, enter the name of the customer who gave you the bad check.
3. Enter the date on which the check bounced.
4. Click in the Item column and select the item you created for returned checks.
5. Enter the amount of the returned check. If you want to, you can add another line item for a service charge for the bounced check (discussed next).
6. Click Print so you can send the invoice to the customer, then click Save & Close to save the invoice.

Invoicing Customers for Service Charges

If your bank charges you a fee for handling the customer's bounced check, you should collect it from the customer by invoicing for that amount. In fact, you might want to invoice the customer for a handling charge even if your bank doesn't charge you.

Follow the steps for invoicing the customer to recover the amount of a bad check, but use the item you created for service charges instead of the returned check item. Then print and save the invoice.

Voiding Disbursements

Sometimes you have to void a check that you've written. Perhaps you decided not to send it for some reason, or perhaps it was lost in the mail. Whatever the reason, if a check isn't going to clear your bank you should mark it void.

The process of voiding a check is quite easy, and the only trouble you can cause yourself is deleting the check instead of voiding it. Deleting a check removes all history of the transaction, and the check number disappears into la-la land. This is not a good way to keep financial records. Voiding a check keeps the check number, but sets the amount to zero.

To void a check, open the bank account register and click anywhere on the check's transaction line. Right-click to see the shortcut menu and choose Void Check. The corresponding entry in the expense account (or multiple expense accounts) to which the check was written is also adjusted.

Tracking ATM Transactions

Aren't those ATM gadgets wonderful? They're everywhere, even at the supermarket checkout! It's so easy to take cash out of your bank account.

And it's so easy to forget to enter the transaction in your account register. You must create a system for yourself that insures your ATM withdrawals are accounted for. Having said that, I'll move on to the accounting procedures involved with ATM transactions, because QuickBooks cannot help you remember to enter transactions.

TIP: I have one of those consoles with a flip-up lid between the front seats of my car and the only use I ever make of it is as a receipts container. I keep ATM, gas station, credit card, and bank deposit receipts in it. Every so often I bring everything in the console into the office and enter the ATM amounts. (I get a monthly bill for the gas I put into my car and the credit card bills, and I save the receipts because my accountant insists on it.) Then I put all the receipts into a large manila envelope. If I need to check anything when a bill comes in, I look in the envelope. At the end of the year, the envelope is filed away with my copy of my tax returns. I'm ready if they audit me!

When you withdraw cash from an ATM machine there's an assumption that you need the cash for a business expense. (Don't withdraw cash from a business bank account for personal spending.) In effect, you're taking a petty cash advance and you have to account for it. That means you have to account for the portion of it you spend, and the portion that's still in your pocket. The way to track expenses for which you've taken money in advance is to use a petty cash account.

Using a Petty Cash Account

If you spend cash for business expenses, your chart of accounts should have a petty cash account. This account functions like a cash till: You put money in it, then you account for the money that's spent, leaving the rest in the till until it, too, is spent. Then you put more money into the till. The petty cash account doesn't represent a real bank account; it just represents that portion of the money in the real bank account that you've put into the till.

If you don't have a petty cash account in your chart of accounts, create one:

1. Choose Lists | Chart of Accounts from the menu bar.
2. When the Chart of Accounts window appears, press CTRL-N to open a blank New Account window.
3. Fill in the account information using the following guidelines:
   - The Account Type is Bank.
   - If you number your accounts, use a number that places your new petty cash account near the other (real) bank accounts in your chart of accounts.
   - There's no tax association; the money you spend from this account is posted to existing expense accounts.
   - Leave the opening balance at zero.

Now that you have the petty cash account, you can use it to track your ATM withdrawals.

Putting ATM Money into Petty Cash

When you withdraw money from your bank account with your ATM card, it's not an expense; it's just cash. You've put cash into a till (literally, the till is your pocket, but to your accounting system it's a petty cash container). It becomes an expense when you spend it (and get a receipt so you can enter the expense into your system).

Putting QuickBooks to Work

Tracking Petty Cash

Sally and Sarah are partners in a consulting firm. They have one employee, a salesperson named Susan. There's a constant need for petty cash as all three of them pursue their work: parking fees, tolls, cab fare, and so on.

They established a petty cash system that makes each person accountable for the money she receives and also automatically replenishes the cash as it's spent. Here's what they did to start this system:

- They established a separate petty cash account for each person in the chart of accounts.
- They wrote three checks to cash ($100.00 each), posting each check to an individual petty cash account.

Now, each woman has $100.00 in cash. During the course of each day, that money is spent and receipts are saved. (This means everyone has to remember to ask for a receipt, because the policy is "no receipt, no cash.")

Every week, usually on Friday, each woman fills out an expense account form. (Sarah created it in a word processor and printed a whole bunch of copies.) Each type of expense is listed and subtotaled. Receipts are attached to the form. Then the following tasks are completed:

- A check is written to each person for the total amount on the expense account form. This means each woman is now back at $100.00 because the check amount is the difference between the original $100.00 and the expenditures.
- Sally opens the petty cash account registers and records the information from the expense account forms, assigning the correct expense accounts to each subtotal.
- The forms, with the attached receipts, are filed in case they're ever needed (such as for an IRS audit).

This is a terrific, efficient system, and Sally and Sarah have made their accountant very happy.

Bring the ATM receipt and receipts for the stuff you purchased with the ATM cash back to the office. In QuickBooks, perform the procedures necessary to track the cash you spent and the cash you didn't spend.

Transfer the Withdrawal to Petty Cash

The first thing you have to do is take the cash out of your QuickBooks bank account, because you stood in front of an ATM dispenser and took cash out of your actual bank account. However, this is double-entry bookkeeping and there has to be an equal and opposite posting to another account. That's what the petty cash account is for.

1. Choose Banking | Transfer Funds from the menu bar.
2. In the Transfer Funds Between Accounts window, fill out the information needed, which is just the two accounts and the amount. Then click Save & Close.

The money in your petty cash account is the same as the money in your pocket, and you're responsible for it. As you spend it, you must explain what you're spending it on. In the next section, I'll show you how to record your expenditures.

Enter the Cash Disbursements

As you spend the money you withdraw via an ATM transaction, you must record those expenditures in the petty cash account. There are a couple of valid methods for accomplishing this, all of which start with opening the petty cash account register.

When you open the petty cash account register, the next available transaction line is highlighted automatically. Now you can enter the amount of cash you actually spent, using either of the methods described here:

- Enter each individual cash transaction you made. You can invent a payee named Cash for each transaction, or enter a real payee for each transaction (Joe's Hardware Store, Mary's Office Supplies, and so on). QuickBooks uses automatic numbering, thinking each entry is a check. It's OK to let those numbers stand (you never reconcile this account with a bank statement). Enter the appropriate expense account for each transaction.
- Enter one large transaction, splitting the transaction among all the appropriate expense accounts, as described next.

Entering a Split Disbursement

If you want to enter one transaction and split it, after you enter the amount and move to the Account field, click the Splits button in the register window. This opens a Splits window in the account register (see Figure 11-7).

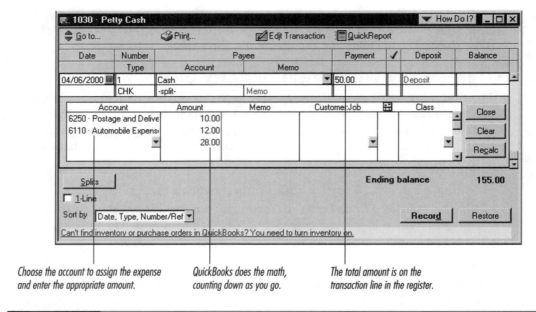

Choose the account to assign the expense and enter the appropriate amount.

QuickBooks does the math, counting down as you go.

The total amount is on the transaction line in the register.

FIGURE 11-7 Split a disbursement among multiple accounts with the Splits feature

When you finish entering accounts for the split transaction, click Record. The transaction appears in the register with an indication of a split in the Account field (see Figure 11-8).

Working with Credit Cards

When you use a business credit card, you have a number of choices for tracking and paying the credit card bill. First of all, you can either pay the entire bill every month, or pay part of the bill and keep a running credit card balance. Secondly, you can choose between two methods of handling credit card purchases in QuickBooks: Treat the credit card bill as an ordinary vendor and deal with the bill when it arrives, or treat the credit card bill as a liability and track each transaction as it's made instead of waiting for the bill. You can use either choice even if you keep a running balance.

Treating Credit Cards as Vendors

You can set up the credit card as an ordinary vendor and enter the bill into QuickBooks when it arrives. Most of the time, the bill is posted to a variety of accounts, so the credit card bill transaction is a split transaction (see Figure 11-9).

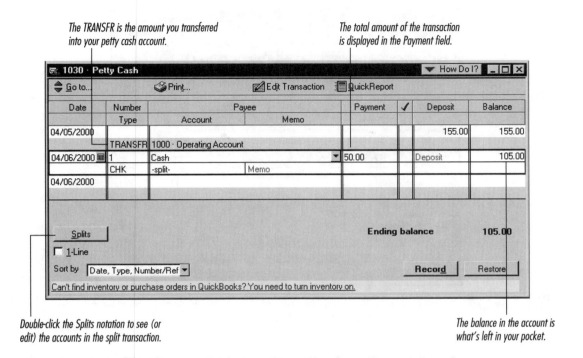

The TRANSFR is the amount you transferred into your petty cash account.

The total amount of the transaction is displayed in the Payment field.

Double-click the Splits notation to see (or edit) the accounts in the split transaction.

The balance in the account is what's left in your pocket.

FIGURE 11-8 A split transaction is easy to spot

If you maintain a running balance, be sure to enter any current interest charges for late payment so your current balance is accurate. The current balance is part of your Accounts Payable balance.

When you pay the credit card bill, you can enter the amount you want to pay against each bill in the system. Always start with the oldest bill, making a partial payment or paying it in full. Then move to the next oldest bill, making a partial payment or paying it in full (see Figure 11-10). You can use the memo field to note the name of the vendor if you wish.

Treating Credit Cards as Liability Accounts

You can also treat credit cards as liability accounts, tracking each transaction against the account as it occurs. Then, when the bill arrives, you match the transactions against the bill and decide how much to pay. Your running balance is tracked specifically against the credit card, instead of being part of your Accounts Payable balance.

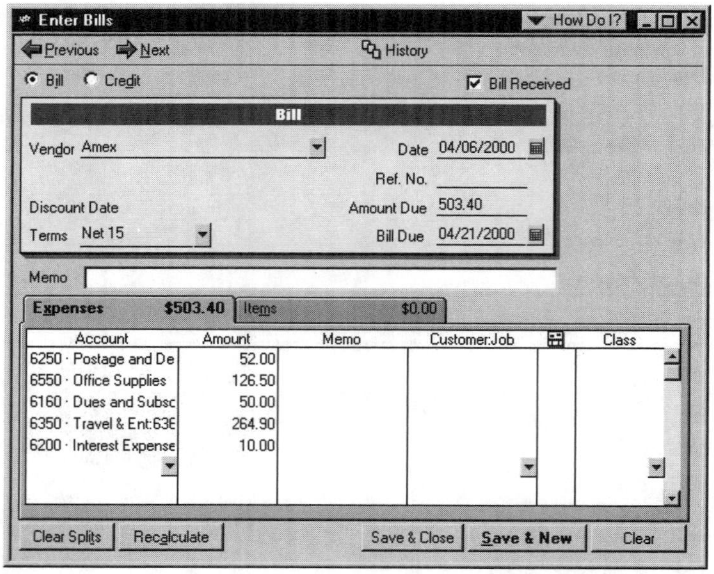

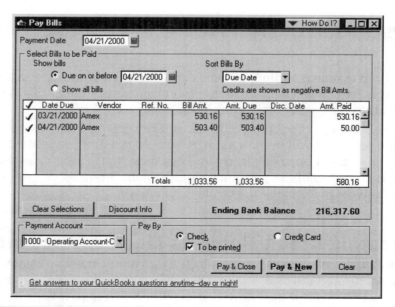

FIGURE 11-9 The credit card bill usually has multiple accounts, including any charges for the balance you previously failed to pay off

FIGURE 11-10 This bill payment transaction pays off the previous bill and makes a partial payment on the current bil

Creating a Credit Card Account

To use credit cards in this manner, you must have an account for each credit card in your chart of accounts. If you don't have such an account as a result of the EasyStep Interview, you can create one now, using an account type of Credit Card. Check out Chapter 2 for information about adding items to your chart of accounts.

 CAUTION: QuickBooks arranges the chart of account by account types. If you're using numbers for your accounts, the numbering is ignored in favor of account types. To make sure your credit card account is displayed in the right order, use a number that fits in with current liabilities. Don't use a number that falls in the asset range (where your bank accounts are).

Entering Charges on the Credit Card Account

If you want to track your credit card charges as they're assumed, instead of waiting for the bill, you have to treat your credit card transactions like ATM transactions—enter them as you go. QuickBooks has a built-in feature to help you accomplish this.

1. Choose Banking | Enter Credit Card Charges from the QuickBooks menu bar to open the Enter Credit Card Charges window seen in Figure 11-11.
2. Select the appropriate credit card account.
3. Fill in the fields, using the store receipt as a reference document.
4. Click Save & Next to save the record and move to another blank window, or click Save & Close if you're finished entering credit card charges.

 TIP: You can also enter these charges directly in the register of your credit card account. (Some people find it faster to work in the register.)

Reconciling the Credit Card Bill

Eventually, the bill arrives. You have some work to do and decisions to make:

- Reconciling the bill against the entries you recorded.
- Deciding whether to pay the entire bill or just a portion of it.
- Writing a check.

Enter a real vendor, or use a generic
vendor for credit card transactions.

Record the receipt
reference number.

Select Credit if this
transaction was a return.

If you use a generic vendor
for credit card transactions,
use the Memo field to note
the name of the store.

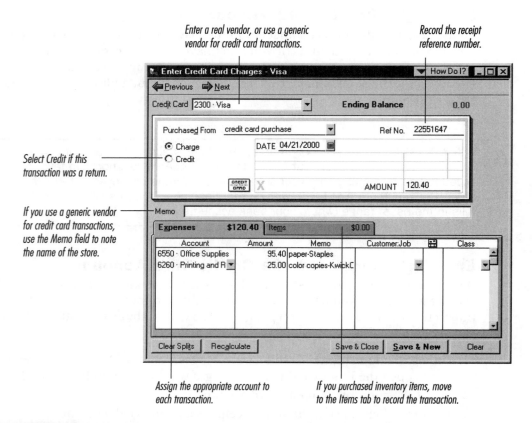

Assign the appropriate account to
each transaction.

If you purchased inventory items, move
to the Items tab to record the transaction.

FIGURE 11-11   Credit card transactions can be entered in their own transaction window

Choose Banking | Reconcile from the QuickBooks menu bar to open the
Reconcile Credit Card window shown in Figure 11-12.

NOTE: The first time you do this, there won't be an opening balance for this
credit card. If you don't pay the entire bill you'll see an opening balance the next
time you use this window. Also, the payment you make this time will appear the
next time you reconcile the bill.

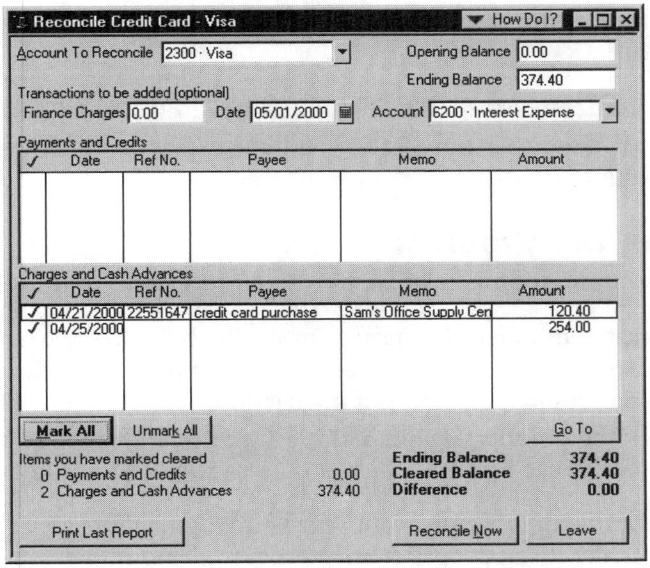

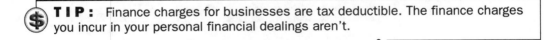

FIGURE 11-12 Check the credit card bill against the transactions you entered

1. Select the credit card account you want to reconcile.
2. Enter the ending balance from the credit card bill.
3. Click the check mark column for each transaction on your window that has a matching transaction on the credit card bill (make sure the amounts match, too). That includes payments, credits, and charges.
4. Add any transactions which you forgot to enter earlier to the window if they appear on the bill.
5. Enter any finance charges on the bill in the Finance Charges box, along with the date on which the charges were assessed.

> **TIP:** Finance charges for businesses are tax deductible. The finance charges you incur in your personal financial dealings aren't.

6. Choose the account you use to post finance charges (or create one if you don't have one—it's an expense).

Now look at the box at the bottom of the window, where the totals are displayed:

- If the difference is $0.00, congratulations! Everything's fine. Click Done.
- If the difference is not $0.00, you have to figure out the problem and make corrections.

Finding the Problem

If your account doesn't balance, try these procedures to find a solution:

- Count the number of transactions on the bill and make sure the same number of transactions appear in your window. Don't forget to count the finance charge entry as a transaction.
- Check the numbers again, making sure that the amount you originally entered for each transaction matches the amount on the bill.

Usually, one of these problems exists in an unbalanced account. If this is the case, make the appropriate correction in the window.

Deferring the Problem

If you can't figure it out and you just don't have time to work on it now, click Leave. QuickBooks will keep the transaction information you've entered thus far and it will be waiting for you when you return to finish reconciling the account.

Adjusting the Difference

If there's a difference you just cannot resolve and you want to finalize the reconciliation, you can make an adjusting entry. Then, later, if you find the transaction that caused the problem you can delete the adjusting entry and record the correct transaction.

To accomplish this, click Reconcile Now even though the difference isn't $0.00. QuickBooks displays this Reconcile Adjustment window.

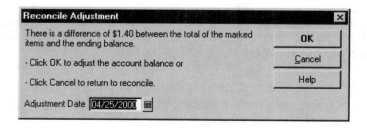

Click OK to let QuickBooks create an adjustment entry. Later, if you figure out what the problem was, open the credit card account register and remove the adjusting entry. Replace it with a real entry that solves the problem.

Paying the Credit Card Bill

When you click Reconcile Now in the Reconcile Credit Card window, QuickBooks moves on to pay the bill by asking you whether you want to write a check now, or create a vendor bill that you'll pay the next time you pay your bills.

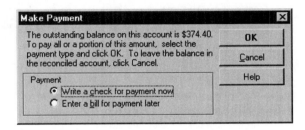

Select the appropriate response and complete the transaction. All the detailed information you need to create vendor bills is found in Chapter 6, and everything about writing checks is in Chapter 7.

If you don't want to pay the entire bill, change the amount. The unpaid amount will appear as an opening balance the next time you reconcile the account.

TIP: My plastic includes more than the traditional credit card companies, because I have business charge accounts at several office supply stores and computer retail stores. If you have the same situation, don't forget to create accounts for those credit cards, too.

Reconciling Bank Accounts

In this chapter, you will learn to...

- Enter data from your bank statement
- Clear transactions
- Reconcile the differences
- Make adjustments

Reconciling bank accounts is fancy terminology for "I have to balance my checkbook," which is one of the most annoying tasks connected with financial record keeping.

 NOTE: The first time you reconcile your bank accounts in QuickBooks, there's a bit more work involved than you'll find in subsequent reconciliations.

Entering Data from the Statement

After your bank statement arrives, you must find some uninterrupted moments to compare it to the information in the QuickBooks account register.

If your bank sends your canceled checks in the envelope along with the statement (some banks don't include the physical checks), you can arrange the checks in numerical order before you start this task. However, instead of sorting and collating the physical checks, use the list of check numbers on your statement. They appear in numerical order. An asterisk or some other mark usually appears to indicate a missing number (a check that hasn't cleared yet, or perhaps a voided check).

Choose Banking | Reconcile to open the Reconcile window and select the account to reconcile. The first time you do this, the amount of information displayed in the window may seem overwhelming (see Figure 12-1), but it's not difficult to get a handle on what's what.

Entering Bank Balances

Check the Opening Balance field in your window against the opening balance on the bank statement. (Your bank may call it the *starting balance*.) If this is the first time you've reconciled this account in QuickBooks, a difference probably exists. You cannot change this figure. See the suggestions that follow if this is the first reconciliation you're performing.

Enter the ending balance from your statement in the Ending Balance field.

Resolving First-Time Balance Problems

The reason the opening balance doesn't match the first time is that your QuickBooks opening balance includes the initial entry you made for this bank account during setup. The number may have been derived from an opening

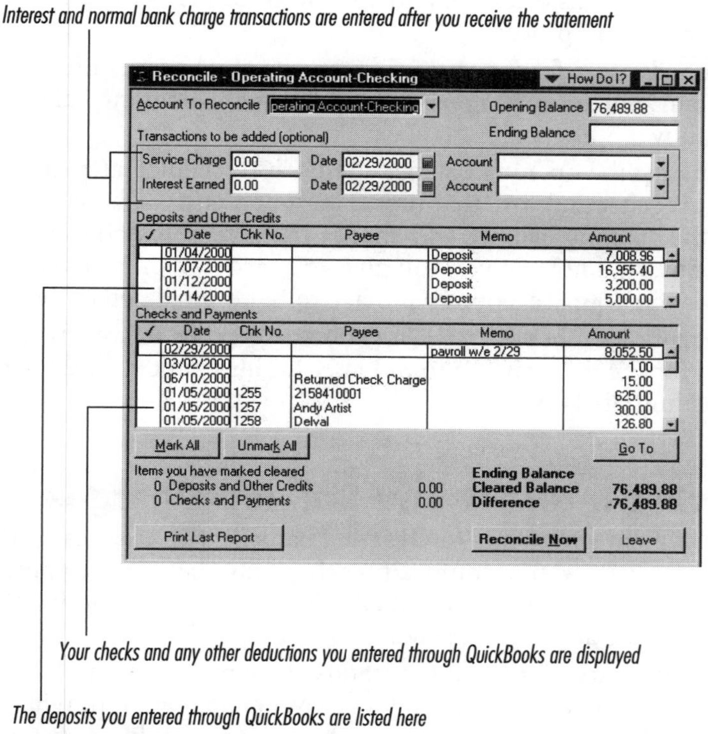

Interest and normal bank charge transactions are entered after you receive the statement

Your checks and any other deductions you entered through QuickBooks are displayed

The deposits you entered through QuickBooks are listed here

FIGURE 12-1 The Reconcile window is crammed with data, but it's easy to sort it all out

trial balance, the account balance on the day you started your QuickBooks setup, or any other scheme you used to get started in QuickBooks. The bank is using a running total that began way back when, starting when you first opened that bank account. The only QuickBooks users who have it easy are those who opened their bank accounts the same day they started to use QuickBooks. (A minuscule number of people fit that description.)

If you entered a beginning balance for your checking account during the QuickBooks setup procedure, you'll notice that the offsetting entry is your equity account. This opening bank balance frequently doesn't match the statement's opening balance. In fact, one big difference is probably the date— your opening balance date is not the same as the opening balance date on the statement (which is a date within the past month).

You cannot change the opening balance directly in the Reconcile window. However, you can change the opening balance in your account register, or you can let QuickBooks create an adjustment to reconcile the difference during the reconciliation process.

Personally, I prefer the latter choice—it's much less confusing to your accountant. But since it is possible to change the opening balance, I'll explain how.

To change the opening balance to match the bank statement, move to the account register and find that first transaction entry. Change the amount to match the opening balance and change the date to match the statement date. Write yourself a note so you can give your accountant a coherent explanation because your equity account will have to be recalculated at the end of the year.

Information on how to tell QuickBooks to make an adjusting entry to account for the difference is found later in this chapter, in the section named "Reconciling the Difference."

Entering Interest and Service Charges

Your statement shows any interest and bank service charges if either or both are applicable to your account. Enter those numbers in the appropriate fields in the section of the window named "Transactions to be added," and make sure the appropriate account is linked.

By "bank charges" I mean the standard charges banks assess, not special charges for bounced checks (yours or your customers'), purchase of checks or deposit slips, or other similar charges. Those should be entered as discrete transactions, making them easier to find in case you have to talk to the bank about your account.

Adding Transactions During Reconciliation

While you're working on the reconciliation, if you find a transaction on the statement that you haven't entered into your QuickBooks software (probably one of those ATM transactions you forgot to enter), you don't have to shut down the reconciliation process to remedy the situation.

Choose Lists | Chart of Accounts from the QuickBooks menu bar. Then double-click the account you're reconciling and record the transaction. Return to the Reconcile window, where that transaction is now listed. Pretty nifty! Check it off as cleared, of course, since it was on the statement.

You can switch between the Reconcile window and the register for the account you're reconciling by clicking on the windows. (Ah, the wonders of multitasking.) If one of the windows is hidden, use the Window menu on the QuickBooks menu bar to move between them.

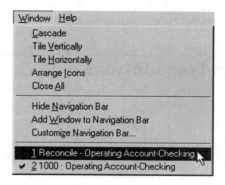

 TIP: I automatically open the register of the account I'm reconciling as soon as I start the reconciliation process. In addition to making it easier to enter those transactions I missed, it's a quick way to look at details when I see a transaction that puzzles me ("Why did I write a check to Joe Fool?").

Deleting Transactions During Reconciliation

Sometimes you find that a transaction that was transferred from your account register to this Reconcile window shouldn't be there. The most common occurrence of this is an ATM withdrawal that you entered twice. Or perhaps you forgot that you'd entered a direct deposit the day you made it, and a couple of days later you entered it again. Whatever the reason, there are occasionally transactions that should be deleted.

To delete a transaction, move to the account register and select that transaction. Choose Edit | Delete Transaction. Instead of "Transaction," the Edit menu names the transaction type, such as "Check" or "Deposit."

When you return to the Reconcile window, the transaction is gone.

Editing Transactions During Reconciliation

Sometimes you'll want to change some of the information in a transaction. For example, when you see the real check, you realize you'd made it out to Sam Smith, but your account register says Stan Smith. Or perhaps the amount on the check is wrong. You might even have the wrong date on a check. (These things only happen, of course, if you write checks manually.)

Whatever the problem, you can correct it by moving to the account register and selecting the transaction. Right-click anywhere on the transaction line and choose the Edit command on the shortcut menu. Record the necessary changes, which are reflected when you return to the Reconcile window.

Clearing Transactions

After you've cleaned up the transactions (missing, duplicated, and erroneous), it's time to tell QuickBooks about the transactions that have cleared. All the transactions that are on your bank statement are cleared transactions. If the transactions are not listed on the statement, they have not cleared.

 N O T E : The only transactions displayed in the Reconcile window are those that have not yet cleared. Any transactions you've cleared in previous months are permanently cleared—they won't appear in the window. This makes it easier to work with this window.

Clear all the transactions that are on the statement by clicking in the column with the check mark (to the left of the transaction). A check mark appears in that column to indicate that the transaction has cleared the bank.

 T I P : If you mark a transaction in error, click again to remove the check mark—it's a toggle.

As you check each cleared transaction, the difference amount in the lower-right corner of the Reconcile window changes.

Reconciling the Difference

If this isn't the first reconciliation you're performing, there's a good chance that there's no difference between the Ending Balance and the Cleared Balance in the Reconcile window. If this *is* the first reconciliation and you changed the opening balance in the account register (as explained earlier in this chapter), you probably have no difference showing.

If that's true, you've finished this part of the reconciliation. Click Reconcile Now and read the section "Printing the Reconciliation Report." If you do have a difference, read on.

Pausing the Reconciliation Process

If there are differences and you don't have the time, energy, or emotional fortitude to track them down at the moment, you can stop the reconciliation process without losing all the data you entered and the transactions you cleared.

Click the Leave button in the Reconcile window and do something else for a while. Go home and have dinner, play with the cat, help the kids with homework, whatever.

When you return and bring up the Reconcile window again, you'll have to re-enter the amounts in the Ending Balance field, as well as the Service Charge and Interest Earned fields. Everything else will be exactly the way you left it.

Finding and Correcting Problems

If there's a difference that has to be cleared up, here are some guidelines for finding the problems:

- Count the number of transactions on the statement and make sure the same number of transactions are cleared in your Reconcile window. (Look in the lower-left corner of the window—the number of cleared transactions is displayed.) If the numbers differ, there's a missing transaction in your QuickBooks records, a transaction you should have cleared but didn't, or a transaction you cleared that you shouldn't have.

- Check the amount of each transaction against the amount in the bank statement.

- Check your transactions and make sure a deposit wasn't inadvertently entered as a payment (or vice versa). A clue for this is a transaction that's half the difference. If the difference is $220.00, find a transaction that has an amount of $110.00 and make sure it's a deduction if it's supposed to be a deduction.

- Check for transposed figures. Perhaps you entered a figure incorrectly in the register, such as $549.00 when the bank clears the transaction as $594.00. A clue that a transposed number is the problem is that the reconciliation difference can be divided by nine.

If you find the problem, correct it. When the difference is zero, click Reconcile Now.

 TIP: You might want to let somebody else check over the statement and the register, because sometimes you don't see your own mistakes.

Permitting an Adjusting Entry

If you cannot find the problem, you can tell QuickBooks to make an adjusting entry to force the reconciliation to balance. The adjusting entry is placed in the register and if you ever do figure out what the problem is you can make the proper adjustment transaction and delete the adjusting entry.

To have QuickBooks create an adjusting entry, click Reconcile Now even though there's a difference. A message appears similar to the one shown in the following illustration. Click OK to permit the adjusting entry.

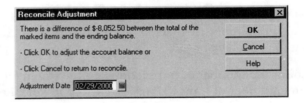

Printing the Reconciliation Report

When you have a balanced Reconcile window, QuickBooks offers congratulations and offers to print a reconciliation report.

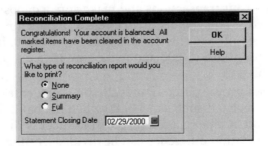

It's not necessary to print a reconciliation report, but some people file it away as a handy reference. And some accountants want to see these reports when they make periodic visits to inspect your books and give advice.

You can print two types of report:

- The Full Report lists all the transactions that are cleared and all the transactions that haven't cleared ("in transit" transactions) as of the statement closing date. Any transactions dated after the statement closing date are listed as being "new transactions."
- The Summary Report breaks down your transactions in the same way, but shows only the totals for each category.

Make your choice and click OK.

 TIP: Back in your account register, all the cleared transactions are distinguished by a check mark in the column that has a check mark as the column name.

Using Budgets

In this chapter, you will learn to...

- Configure a budget

- Create different kinds of budgets

- Report on budgets vs. actual figures

- Export budgets

A budget is a tool for tracking your progress against your plans. A well-prepared budget can also help you draw money out of your business wisely, because knowing what you plan to spend on inventory, staff, or equipment prevents you from carelessly withdrawing profits and living high on the hog whenever you have a good month.

Budgeting Income and Expenses

The most common (and useful) budget is based on your income and expenses. After you've set up a good chart of accounts, creating a budget is quite easy.

To create a P&L (Profit & Loss) budget, choose Company | Set Up Budgets from the QuickBooks menu bar. A blank Set Up Budgets window appears, ready to receive your configuration options (see Figure 13-1).

Entering the Budget Figures

Click the arrow to the right of the Account text box and choose the account you want to budget. (For a P&L budget, select income and expense accounts.) Then, enter the budget amount for that account for the first month.

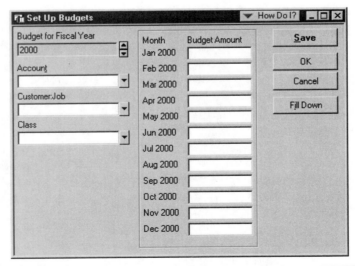

FIGURE 13-1 Budgets start in the Set Up Budgets window

You don't have to type the amounts for the other 11 months—you can use QuickBooks' nifty Fill Down feature. Click the Fill Down button to see the Fill Down window.

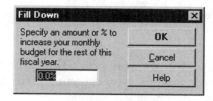

- Enter the per-month growth or reduction that you want to plan on for your chosen account. You can use an amount, such as $1,000, or a percentage.
- Type the % symbol if you want to budget by percentage.
- Use the minus sign (–) if you're working with an account in which you plan to reduce the amount.
- Leave the amount at 0 if you just want to fill in each month with the same number.

For instance, Figure 13-2 shows a company with a budgeted income from consulting fees of $25,000 in the first month, and then an 8 percent growth per month.

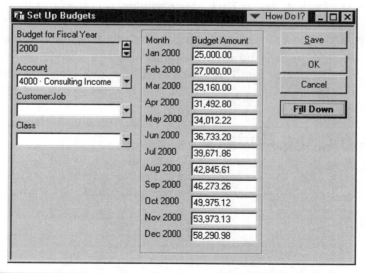

FIGURE 13-2   This company is looking for monthly measured growth of 8 percent over the preceding month

C A U T I O N : Since it's almost impossible to predict balance sheet accounts (assets, liabilities, and equity accounts), don't include them in your budget. In fact, predicting and planning balance sheet account figures is so complicated that it's generally only performed as part of a thesis for an MBA degree—or for a complicated study from a Wall Street acquisitions and merger firm.

The Fill Down feature works from the current month (the one you're using to enter a figure) down, so you can enter static numbers for a couple of months, and then budget in automatic changes.

Click Save to record the budget for that account, and repeat the procedure for the next account. Click OK when you have finished entering figures for all the accounts you want to budget.

T I P : It's common to budget using only certain P&L accounts instead of budgeting for every income and expense account. Many people skip the accounts over which they have little or no control (for instance, rent or mortgage).

Changing the Fiscal Year

If the first month in the Set Up Budgets window isn't the first month of your fiscal year, you must change your company information. Close the Set Up Budgets window and choose Company | Company Information from the menu bar.

When the Company Information window appears (see Figure 13-3), move to the field called First Month In Your Fiscal Year and select the correct month. Then click OK.

Viewing the Budget

After you select the accounts and figures you want to use for your budget, take a look at it. Click the Reports listing in the Navigation Bar to open the Report Finder. Choose Budget as the report type and select P&L Budget Overview.

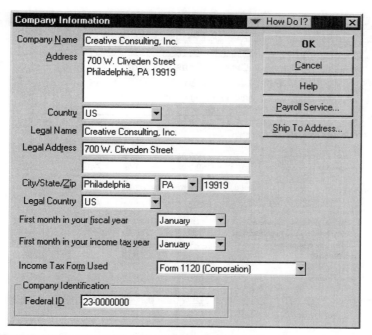

FIGURE 13-3   Your company profile includes fiscal year information

Your budget appears as a report (see Figure 13-4) in the Profit & Loss Budget Overview window.

- If you use subaccounts in your budget, you can click the Collapse button in the budget window to see only the parent account totals. The button changes its name to Expand after you click it.
- To condense the numbers, change the interval in the Columns drop-down list box. The default is Month, but you can choose another interval, and QuickBooks will calculate the figures to fit. For example, you might want to select Quarter to see four columns of three-month subtotals.

You can make changes to the budget by repeating the steps for creating it—the same budget appears, and you can change amounts or add/remove accounts.

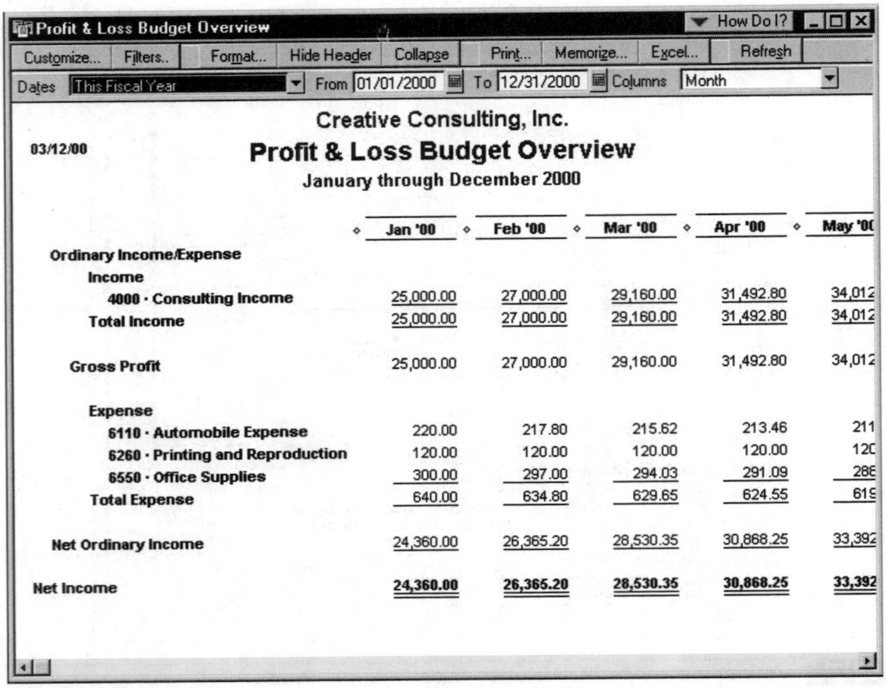

Creative Consulting, Inc.

03/12/00 Profit & Loss Budget Overview

January through December 2000

	Jan '00	Feb '00	Mar '00	Apr '00	May '0
Ordinary Income/Expense					
Income					
4000 · Consulting Income	25,000.00	27,000.00	29,160.00	31,492.80	34,012
Total Income	25,000.00	27,000.00	29,160.00	31,492.80	34,012
Gross Profit	25,000.00	27,000.00	29,160.00	31,492.80	34,012
Expense					
6110 · Automobile Expense	220.00	217.80	215.62	213.46	211
6260 · Printing and Reproduction	120.00	120.00	120.00	120.00	120
6550 · Office Supplies	300.00	297.00	294.03	291.09	288
Total Expense	640.00	634.80	629.65	624.55	619
Net Ordinary Income	24,360.00	26,365.20	28,530.35	30,868.25	33,392
Net Income	24,360.00	26,365.20	28,530.35	30,868.25	33,392

FIGURE 13-4 Scroll through the report to see all the budget figures you created

Comparing Your Budget with Reality

When you create a P&L budget, you can run Budget vs. Actual reports, which means you can see how your real numbers stack up compared to your budget figures. The report will also display the difference between the two.

View the Budget Comparison Report

In the Report Finder, choose Budget as the report type and select P&L Budget vs. Actual. When the report appears, you can scroll through it to look at the month-by-month details.

Customize and Memorize the Budget Comparison Report

The first thing you'll notice in the report is that all the accounts in your general ledger are listed, regardless of whether you included them in your budget. However, only the accounts you used in your budget show budget figures. You can change that by customizing the report to include only your budgeted accounts. Click the Customize button. In the Customize Report window that opens, click the Advanced button to open the Advanced Options window. Click the option labeled Show Only Rows And Columns With Budgets.

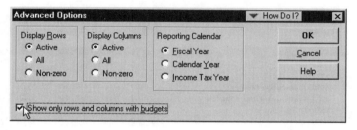

Click OK to return to the Customize Report window, and then click OK again to return to the Profit & Loss Budget vs. Actual report window. The data that's displayed is only that data connected to your budgeted accounts (see Figure 13-5).

You can also use the options in the Customize Report window to make other changes:

- Change the report dates.
- Change the calculations from Accrual to Cash (which means that unpaid invoices and bills are removed from the calculations, and only actual income and expenses are reported).

You should memorize the report so that you don't have to make these customization changes the next time you want to view a comparison report. Click the Memorize button at the top of the report window, and then give the report a meaningful name.

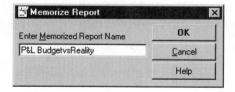

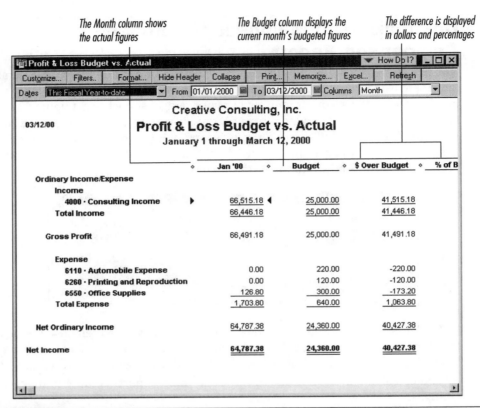

The Month column shows the actual figures

The Budget column displays the current month's budgeted figures

The difference is displayed in dollars and percentages

FIGURE 13-5   Generate a Budget vs. Actual report to see how closely your real numbers match your budget

Budgeting by Customer or Job

If you have a customer or project that you want to track, create a budget for it. While it's useful to create budgets if you think there might be a problem with costs, it's equally valid to create a budget just for the information you gain. For example, if you're beginning to accept projects on which you'll have to submit a bid or an estimate, tracking the first few jobs with a budget may produce an important pattern. Perhaps you always under-budget one item or over-budget another. Use the information you gather to bid and estimate in a smarter fashion.

Creating Specific Budgets for Customers and Jobs

You start customer and job budgets the same way you start P&L budgets, by choosing Company | Set Up Budgets from the QuickBooks menu bar. This brings up the Set Up Budgets window.

Click the arrow to the right of the Customer:Job field and select either a customer or a job. Configure the budget with the following guidelines:

- To track everything (income and expenses) for this customer or job, you can skip the accounts and just enter a budget amount in each month. Part of the Budget vs. Actual report will show the net income against the net budget amount.
- To track an entire project when you don't care about the month-by-month details, enter the entire budget amount in the first month.
- To track only certain accounts for a customer or job, select the accounts and enter a monthly budget amount for each account.

When you're finished filling out the fields, click OK to save the budget.

Creating Budgets for Multiple Customers or Jobs

QuickBooks only recognizes one Customer:Job budget. You can, however, track multiple customers and/or jobs. The quick way to create multiple budgets for different customers is to finish the first customer's configuration and click Save instead of OK. Then, choose another customer or job and configure that one. Continue until you've created budgets for all the customers and jobs you need. Then click OK.

Viewing Customer and Job Budget Reports

To see your budget, open the Report Finder and choose Budget as the report type. Then choose P&L Budget By Job Overview from the Reports listing on the Navigation Bar. When the report opens, don't be surprised if you don't see information about customers and jobs, because this report needs some customization to do its job properly. Click the Customize button to use the Customize Report window, shown in the following illustration, to set up the report layout properly.

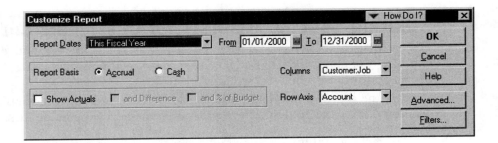

- Click the arrow to the right of the Columns box and select a time period (month, year, and so on).
- Click the arrow to the right of the Row Axis box and select Customer:Job.
- Then click OK to see your budget.

To see a Budget vs. Actual report, choose the P&L Budget vs. Actual By Job report. Unfortunately, this report shows you all customers, not just the customers you included in your budget. To confine the report to budgeted customers, make the same changes to the columns and rows as mentioned in the preceding list.

Copying Budgets

If you want to use the same budget for the next year, you can copy the budget to the next year, but this isn't a one-step procedure. In fact, you're not making a copy at all; you're exporting the budget to another software program, changing the year field, and then importing the budget back into QuickBooks (where it replaces the original budget). This procedure exports all the budget information; you have no chance to select specific budget accounts.

Copying to Microsoft Excel

If you use Microsoft Excel, you can click the Excel button on the budget button bar. QuickBooks asks whether you want to use a new Excel spreadsheet for this budget or send the budget to an existing spreadsheet. In this case, choose a new spreadsheet.

Microsoft Excel launches, and your budget appears on the screen, where you can make whatever changes you need to. See Appendix C for more information about using QuickBooks with Microsoft Excel.

Exporting to Another Software Program

You can copy the budget to any software program that lets you manipulate documents of this type. Here are all the steps for copying budgets to another year:

1. Choose File | Utilities | Export from the QuickBooks menu bar.
2. When the Export dialog box opens, it displays all the QuickBooks lists. Select the item named Budgets and click OK.
3. Another Export dialog box opens (it looks like the Save dialog box you're used to seeing in Windows software). Select a folder in which to save this exported file, or leave it in your QuickBooks folder. I usually change the folder to the location where I keep files for the program I'm going to use for the exported file.
4. You must also give this exported list a filename with an .iif extension ("Budgets.iif" is the most logical).
5. Click Save. QuickBooks displays a message telling you that your data has been exported successfully. Click OK.

 C A U T I O N : When you enter the filename, don't forget to delete the asterisk (*) that QuickBooks placed in the field.

Now, you must open the software in which you want to make the change in the date (your best bet is a spreadsheet program). Then, you must import the .iif file into the software:

1. Click the Open icon in the software you're using. When the Open dialog box appears, move to the folder where you stored your .iif file.
2. In the Files of Type field of the Open dialog box, change the specification to All Files (otherwise, you won't see your .iif file in the listings).
3. Double-click your exported .iif file to open it.
4. Your software application should recognize that this file doesn't match its own file type, and therefore begin the procedures for importing a file. In case your spreadsheet software doesn't figure it out, your .iif file is a tab-delimited file.
5. When the import procedures are completed, your budget is displayed in the window of your software program.

6. Move to the column labeled STARTDATE, and update the dates for the following year.

7. Save the spreadsheet (it must have an .iif extension in the filename) and close the software.

Okay, the year is changed; now you have to import the budget, with its new year, back into QuickBooks:

1. Open QuickBooks and choose File | Utilities | Import from the menu bar.

2. When the Import dialog box opens, double-click the file you saved in your spreadsheet software.

3. QuickBooks flashes a message to tell you the import was successful. Click OK.

Now open a budget report and change the Date fields to reflect the new year. Instead of blank lines, you have figures displayed, duplicating last year's budget.

You can, of course, export your budgets at any time and for any reason—you don't have to wait until you need a copy of the budget for next year. You can use spreadsheet software to play "what if" games with the figures, or add fields and calculations that don't exist in QuickBooks. The more comfortable you are with spreadsheet software, the more power you'll gain from your budgets.

Using Journal Entries

In this chapter, you will learn to...

- Enter the opening trial balance
- Make adjustments to the general ledger
- Depreciate fixed assets
- Journalize outside payroll services

As you work in QuickBooks, the amounts involved in the financial transactions you complete are transferred to your general ledger. In addition to transaction totals, numbers can be placed into the general ledger directly. This is called making a *journal entry*.

Journal entries shouldn't be made without a specific purpose, and usually that purpose is to add figures that cannot be added to an account via a standard transaction such as an invoice or a check.

Entering the Opening Trial Balance

If you opted to skip entering opening balances during your EasyStep Interview when you first started using QuickBooks, eventually you'll need to enter the opening balances for your company. All that's necessary is the opening balances for the balance sheet accounts. Then you can add all the transactions that took place since the beginning of the year to create a thorough history of transactions while you're posting the current year's activity to the general ledger.

QuickBooks does not have an item or feature called the "opening balance," per se. However, every account register is sorted by date, so using the first day of your fiscal year creates an opening balance automatically.

1. Click Banking on the Navigator Bar, then click the Make Journal Entry icon to bring up the General Journal Entry window.

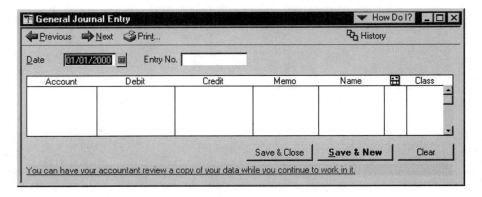

2. You can enter a number in the Entry No. field if you want to track all your journal entries.
3. Click in the Account column, and then click the arrow to see a display of your chart of accounts. Choose the account you need.

4. Move to the Debit or Credit column (depending on the account you're using), and enter the amount of the opening balance.

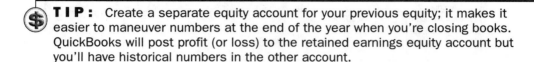

TIP: Create a separate equity account for your previous equity; it makes it easier to maneuver numbers at the end of the year when you're closing books. QuickBooks will post profit (or loss) to the retained earnings equity account but you'll have historical numbers in the other account.

The remaining columns are not needed for the opening balance journal entry but I'll describe them because you'll be looking at them when you create journal entries:

- Use the Memo column to write a comment about the amount on this line of the entry.
- Use the Name column to assign a customer, vendor, employee, or other name to the amount on this line of the entry.
- The column with the icon is a "billable" flag. It means that the amount is billable to the name in the Name column. Click the column to put a line through the icon to prevent making this a billable entry. This column is only available if you are using an expense account and you enter a customer name in the Name column.
- If you are using the Classes feature, you can link this line of the entry to a class. (See Chapter 21 for information about classes.)

The truth is, there is really no reason to use any of those columns, because journal entries shouldn't be used in place of transactions, and these columns are connected to transaction issues.

As you enter each item in the opening trial balance, QuickBooks presents the offsetting total. For example, if the line items you've entered so far have a higher total for the debit side than the credit side, the next entry presents the balancing offset (see Figure 14-1).

There are a couple of problems you may run into that aren't well explained by QuickBooks as they occur.

First of all, a journal entry can use only your A/P account or your A/R account; you cannot use both of those accounts in the same journal entry. You'll get an error message that says "you cannot use more than one A/R or A/P account in the same transaction" (which is not a clear explanation). This restriction makes no sense,

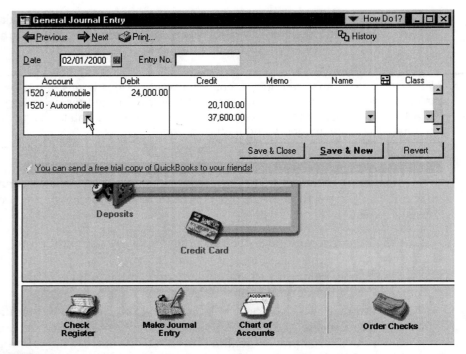

FIGURE 14-1 QuickBooks keeps the running offset figure available—you'll be able to use it for the last entry

and if your opening balance has both A/R and A/P totals you're going to have to fake it. Check with your accountant first, but here's my solution:

1. Create another account to replace either the A/R or A/P account. For instance, if you're replacing A/P, create a current liability account named "Stand-In for AP." If you're replacing A/R, create an asset account (I usually use the type "other current asset").
2. Enter the appropriate amounts.
3. Create another journal entry, also dated the first day of your fiscal year, and move the total from the ersatz account to the real account.

Another problem you're going to have is that QuickBooks insists that you must attach a customer or vendor name to the entry if you're making a journal entry that involves your A/R or A/P account. If you'd planned to enter discrete invoices or bills for customers or vendors, those totals will already be applied.

Here's the best solution to both problems: Enter your opening trial balance without the A/R and A/P entries. Adjust the equity account if your accountant preconfigured the opening trial balance for you.

Then enter the open invoices for customers and vendors as of the opening balance date as transactions and let QuickBooks post the totals to the general ledger. You can create one comprehensive invoice per customer/vendor and pay it off if you don't want to bother with the individual invoices that created the opening balance.

Making Adjusting Entries

There are some circumstances, such as changing accounts and tracking depreciation, that require adjusting entries to your general ledger. Read on to find out how to handle these situations.

Making Journal Entries for Changed Accounts

I've had many clients who decided, after they'd been using QuickBooks for a while, that they wanted to track income differently. Instead of one income account (income received), they opted for separate income accounts that are more specific. For example, an income account for fees and another income account for products sold. This made business analysis easier.

This transaction is quite simple. Create the new account and then take the appropriate amount of funds out of the original account and put them into the new account:

1. Debit the original account for the amount that belongs in the new account.
2. Credit the new account for that same amount.

Then, of course, you'll have to go to the items list and change the necessary items to reflect the new income account so you don't have to keep making journal entries.

The same decision is frequently made about expenses, as business owners decide to split heretofore comprehensive accounts. Perhaps Insurance should be Car Insurance, Equipment Insurance, Building Insurance, Malpractice Insurance, and so on.

For expense accounts, the journal entry goes to the opposite side of the ledger:

1. Credit the original expense account for the amount you're taking out of it and putting into the new account(s).
2. Debit the new account(s) for the appropriate amount(s).

If you have an asset account named Automobiles and want to divide your tracking into more specific accounts (track the truck separately from the car, for instance), make a journal entry. You should also separate out any accumulated depreciation so it's assigned to the correct asset. (You can get that information from your tax returns, or ask your accountant.) You can make the same separation for automobile expenses.

Making Depreciation Entries

Depreciation is a way to track the current value of a fixed asset that loses value as it ages. The loss of value can be viewed as just part of aging or because the asset probably won't last more than a given number of years (it either becomes obsolete or just doesn't work anymore). The basis of an asset's depreciation from an accounting point of view, however, is really determined by a complicated set of rules. The IRS has a great deal to do with these rules and the rules change frequently. Your accountant should determine the amount of any asset's depreciation; the details of your depreciation deductions are part of your business tax return.

Depreciation is a journal entry activity. Most companies enter the depreciation of their assets at the end of the year, but some companies do perform depreciation tasks monthly or quarterly.

Depreciation is a special journal entry because the accounts involved are very restricted—this is not a "free choice, I'll decide which account I want to use" entry.

- The account that is being depreciated must be a fixed asset.
- The offset entry is to an account named Depreciation Expense (or Depreciation), and it is in the expense section of your chart of accounts.

I'm assuming that you've created your fixed asset account and that the assets you've purchased have been posted there. You might have multiple fixed asset accounts if you want to track different types of fixed assets separately. (For instance, my chart of accounts has three fixed asset account sections: equipment, furniture & fixtures, and automobiles.)

When it comes to accounting procedures that have a direct bearing on my taxes and for which I might need information at a glance (especially if I'm called upon to explain it), I like to be very explicit in the way I work. Therefore, for every fixed asset account in my chart of accounts I have families of accounts for depreciation. I create a parent (account) and children (subaccounts) for each type of fixed asset. For example, the fixed asset section of a chart of accounts I create would look like this:

```
Equipment Assets (Parent)
     Equipment (Subaccount)
     Equipment-Accum Depr (Subaccount)
Furn & Fixture Assets (Parent)
     Furn & Fixtures (Subaccount)
     Furn & Fixtures-Accum Depr (Subaccount)
Automobile Assets (Parent)
     Automobiles (Subaccount)
     Automobiles-Accum Depr (Subaccount)
```

Each account has an account type of Fixed Asset.

If you use numbers for your chart of accounts (actually, I do), create a numbering system that makes sense for this setup. Here's an example:

```
1500-Equipment Assets
     1501-Equipment
     1502-Equipment Accum Depr
1510-Furn & Fixtures Assets
     1511-Furn & Fixtures
     1512-Furn & Fixtures Accum Depr
1520-Automobile Assets
     1521-Automobiles
     1522-Automobiles Accum Depr
```

By now, you've probably guessed that I post asset purchases to the asset subaccount and that I make my journal entry for depreciation in the Accum Depr subaccount. There are several reasons for this:

- Both the asset subaccount and the depreciation asset subaccount are "pure." I can look at either one to see a running total instead of a calculated net total.
- Tracing the year-to-year depreciation is easy. I just open the depreciation asset subaccount and each line represents a year.
- It's just plain easier and quicker to open the depreciation asset subaccount if I'm asked about the depreciation total (handy if you sell the asset and have to add back the depreciation).

The net value of my fixed assets on the balance sheet is correct. And even though the asset subaccount doesn't have the decreases in it so that I can see its current value, I don't care. I don't know anyone who's ever needed that information. If I ever do need it, I can get a quick balance sheet report from QuickBooks, and the net number for each asset is displayed (see Figure 14-2).

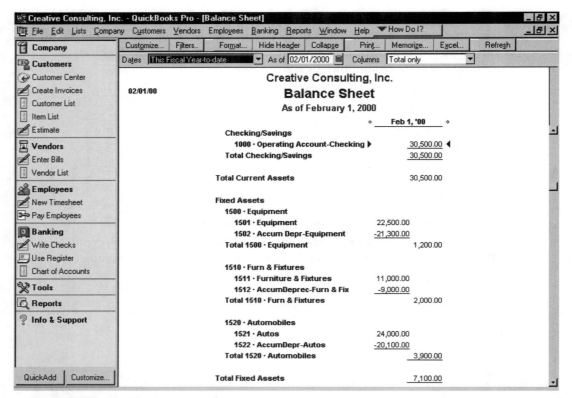

FIGURE 14-2 A detailed display of your depreciation procedures appears on the balance sheet if you have separate depreciation subaccounts

Here's how to make your depreciation entry:

1. Click the Banking item on the Navigation Bar, and then click the Make Journal Entry icon.
2. Choose the depreciation subaccount.
3. Enter the depreciation amount in the Credit column.
4. Choose the next asset depreciation subaccount and enter its depreciation amount in the Credit column.
5. Continue until all your depreciation figures are entered in the Credit column.
6. Choose the Depreciation Expense account.
7. The total amount of the credits is automatically placed in the Debit column.
8. Click Save & Close to save the journal entry.

Journalizing Outside Payroll Services

If you have an outside payroll service, you have to tell QuickBooks about the payroll transactions that took place. You get a report from the service, so all the numbers are available. It's just a matter of entering them.

It's common for businesses to perform this task via a journal entry (even businesses that don't use computers and have to haul out the big ledger books). Like all other journal entries, this one is just a matter of entering debits and credits.

There are three parts to recording payroll:

- Transferring money to the payroll account
- Entering the payroll figures
- Entering the employer expense figures

Transferring Money to the Payroll Account

You must have a separate bank account for payroll if you have an outside payroll service—in fact, a separate payroll account is a good idea even if you do your own payroll with QuickBooks.

Outside payroll services reach into your checking account (in fact, they have checks) and you certainly don't want to be giving away checks for your regular operating account. Another reason for a separate payroll account, even if you do your own payroll, is the discipline involved in holding on to your employee withholdings until you pass them along to insurance companies, other vendors, and the government—*especially* the government. The money you withhold and leave in your bank account until you're ready to transmit it to the government is not your money. You cannot spend it. It doesn't matter if you need the money to save your business from total bankruptcy—you cannot spend the money. People have done that and gotten into serious trouble, including jail. Keeping all the money associated with payroll in a separate bank account removes it from the amounts you have available for running your business.

To transfer the money you need for this payroll, choose Banking | Transfer Funds from the menu bar. Then transfer the money from your regular operating account to your payroll account (see Figure 14-3).

Be sure to transfer enough money for the gross payroll plus the employer payroll expenses. These include:

- Employer matching contributions to FICA and Medicare
- Employer matching contributions to pension plans

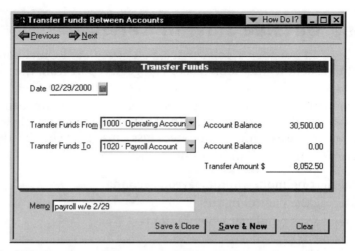

FIGURE 14-3 A transfer is really a journal entry, crediting the sending account and debiting the receiving account

- Employer matching contributions to benefits
- Employer state unemployment assessments
- Employer FUTA
- Any other government or benefit payments due

Even though some of these aren't transmitted every payday, you should transfer the amounts. Then, when it's time to pay them, the correct amount of money will have been amassed in the payroll account.

Recording the Payroll

The *payroll run* (jargon for "printing the paychecks") itself produces a fairly complicated set of debits and credits. Many businesses record a journal entry for the run, then a separate journal entry for the employer expenses when they're transmitted.

If your payroll service takes care of remitting employer expenses, you can journalize the payments. If you do the employer reports yourself and send the checks directly, your check-writing activity will record the payments.

Here's a typical template for recording the payroll run as a journal entry:

ACCOUNT	DEBIT	CREDIT
Salaries & Wages (Expense)	Total Gross Payroll	
FWT (liability)		Total Federal Withheld
FICA (liability)		Total FICA Withheld
Medicare (liability)		Total Medicare Withheld
State Income Tax (liability)		Total State Tax Withheld
Local Income Tax (liability)		Total Local Tax Withheld
State SDI (liability)		Total State SDI Withheld
State SUI (liability)		Total State SUI Withheld
Benefits Contrib (liability)		Total Benefits Withheld
401(k) Contrib (liability)		Total 401(k) Withheld
Other Deductions (liability)		Total Other Ded Withheld
Payroll Account (asset)		Total of Net Payroll

It's possible that you don't have all the expenses shown in this list (for instance, not all states have employee unemployment assessments). And, you may have additional withholding such as union dues, garnishments against wages, and so on. Be sure you've created a liability account in your chart of accounts for each withholding category you need, and a vendor for each transmittal check.

Recording Employer Payments

You need to record the employer payments if your payroll service is taking care of them for you (if you do it yourself, just write the checks from the payroll account). Typically, the journal entry looks something like this:

ACCOUNT	DEBIT	CREDIT
Federal Payroll Expenses (expense)	FICA and Medicare Employer Matching Total	
Federal Withholdings (liability)	All individual withholding totals (FIT, FICA, etc.)	
State & Local Withholdings (liability)	All withholding totals (taxes, SDI, SUI, etc.)	
SUTA (expense)	Employer SUTA	
FUTA (expense)	FUTA	
Employer Contributions (expense)	All benefit, pension, other contributions	
Payroll Account (asset)		Total of checks written

The entry involving the transmittal of withholdings is posted to the same account you used when you withheld the amounts. In effect, you "wash" the liability accounts; you're not really spending money.

You can have as many individual employer expense accounts as you think you need, or you can post all the employer expenses to one account named "payroll expenses."

 REMEMBER: Don't have your payroll service take their fee from the payroll account. Instead, write them a check from your operating account. The service is not a payroll expense; it's an operating expense.

Reconciling the Payroll Account

The problem with journal entries for payroll is that when the bank statement comes for the payroll account, reconciling it is a bit different. When you open the payroll account in the Reconcile window (see Figure 14-4), you see the journal entry totals instead of the individual checks.

Reconciling Outside of QuickBooks

You have the report from the payroll service, listing each check number. You can therefore reconcile the account outside of the Reconcile window (using a manual system or creating a spreadsheet in your spreadsheet software).

Reconcile - Payroll Account ▼ How Do I? _ □ ✕

Account To Reconcile | 1020 · Payroll Account ▼   Opening Balance | 0.00

Transactions to be added (optional)   Ending Balance | |

Service Charge | 0.00   Date | 02/01/2000 ▦   Account | ▼

Interest Earned | 0.00   Date | 02/01/2000 ▦   Account | ▼

Deposits and Other Credits

✓	Date	Chk No.	Payee	Memo	Amount
	02/29/2000				8,052.50

Checks and Payments

✓	Date	Chk No.	Payee	Memo	Amount
	02/29/2000				7,895.60

| Mark All | Unmark All | | | Go To |

Items you have marked cleared

0 Deposits and Other Credits	0.00	**Ending Balance**	
0 Checks and Payments	0.00	**Cleared Balance**	**0.00**
		Difference	**0.00**

Print Last Report   **Reconcile Now**   Leave

FIGURE 14-4   No check numbers or amounts appear in the Reconcile window

 N O T E : Most people find that the payroll checks themselves are cashed quickly and clear rapidly, which always makes reconciliation easier. Payments to government agencies may not clear quite as fast.

Entering Fake Payroll Checks

If you feel you really need to perform the reconciliation in QuickBooks, you could enter the checks without posting them to an account, instead posting them back to the payroll account. (The journal entry took care of all the real postings.) You have a little bit of setup to do, then you can perform this task every payday.

Create a name, "Payroll," with a type Other Name. (Choose Lists | Other Names List from the menu bar.) You can use this name for every check.

Or, you could create a name for each employee in the Other Name list, using initials, last name only, or some other name that isn't the same as the original employee name. The reason you have to create these fake names is that QuickBooks will not let you write a direct check to a real employee. Employee checks can only be written via the real Payroll feature. The only reason to go through this work is if you feel you must have all the details in your QuickBooks register instead of looking up the check number and employee name in the payroll service report you received.

Now you have a payee name for the payroll checks. Grab the report from the payroll service and enter the individual checks:

1. Open the account register for the payroll account.
2. On the next available transaction line, enter the payroll check date.
3. TAB to the Number field and enter the first check number on the payroll service report.
4. Enter the payee Payroll (unless you've entered all your employee names as Other Name types, in which case enter the appropriate name).
5. Enter the amount of the net paycheck.
6. In the Account field, choose the Payroll account. QuickBooks will flash a message warning you that you're posting the payment to the source account. Click OK. (In fact, you might want to click the check box that tells QuickBooks to omit this warning in the future.)

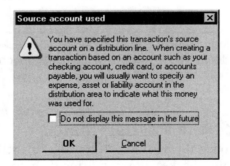

7. Click the Record button to save this check, and then enter the next check.

Continue the process until all the checks are entered. You can also enter the checks the payroll service wrote to transmit your withholdings or pay your taxes. As long as the postings were entered into the journal entry you can post everything back to the payroll account. You're "washing" every transaction, not changing the balance of the account. Then, when you want to reconcile the payroll account, the individual checks are there. The fact is, this procedure is quite easy and fast and you only have to do it on payday (or once a month if you want to wait until the statement comes in).

Using Journal Entries to Produce Business Reports

Thelma and Louise have a bookkeeping business. Their clients are local small businesses, none of which own computers. This means that producing reports about income and expenses is time-consuming for the clients. None of their clients have employees so there aren't any payroll issues.

Both women installed QuickBooks on their laptop computers and travel to the clients' offices, where they produce reports for the clients' accountants. This is much cheaper for their clients than having their accountants visit and do the same work the women can do easily with QuickBooks. (Luckily, QuickBooks permits multiple company files.)

All the work is done via journal entry, one journal entry per month. Here are the details:

- All the deposit slips are added up and the total is posted as a debit to the bank account. The deposit slips are marked with a "Q" for QuickBooks, so none will be accidentally entered again next month.
- All the checks that were written are totaled and the total is entered as a credit against the bank account. Each check stub is marked with a "Q" for QuickBooks as it's added to the total so next month it's clear which checks have not yet been accounted for.
- Each check stub is marked with an account code and the amount of the check is debited against the appropriate account in the journal entry window. Most of the checks are for expense accounts, but some are for the purchase of equipment or other assets, and some are posted to Owners Draw, which is an equity account.
- If there's a question about how to post a check, it's posted as a debit to an expense account named "To Be Resolved" and a note is left for the client to call the accountant for instructions. Then, next month, a separate journal entry is used to credit the "To Be Resolved" account and debit the correct account.

When the journal entry is completed and saved, everything necessary for a Balance Sheet, a Profit and Loss statement, and a Trial Balance is in the QuickBooks files.

Running General Ledger Reports

In this chapter, you will learn to...

- Report the trial balance
- Create a balance sheet
- Create a profit & loss statement
- Create an accountant's review copy

If QuickBooks is your first accounting software program and you've been using manual bookkeeping procedures, you've already discovered how much easier it is to accomplish bookkeeping tasks. However, even with the ease and power you've gained with QuickBooks, bookkeeping probably isn't fun. I can't give you any QuickBooks tips to make it fun (it isn't—it's precise, repetitive work), but I can tell you how to feel better about all the work you do in QuickBooks.

It's the reports you get out of the software that make the work worthwhile. These are reports you'd have to spend hours on in a manual bookkeeping system. And you can change, customize, and manipulate those reports to get all sorts of information about your business. Most of the results you obtain from QuickBooks reports couldn't be gained from a manual system. (Well, maybe they could, if you made a lifetime career out of it and spent weeks on each report.)

Reporting the Trial Balance

A *trial balance* is a list of all your general ledger accounts and their current balances. It's a quick way to see what's what on an account-by-account basis. In fact, you can use the individual totals and subtotal them to create a balance sheet and a profit & loss (P&L) statement. However, you don't have to do that because both of those important reports are also available in QuickBooks.

To see a trial balance, choose Reports | Accountant & Taxes | Trial Balance from the QuickBooks menu bar.

The trial balance is displayed on your screen and looks similar (in form, not content) to Figure 15-1. You can scroll through it to see all the account balances. The bottom of the report has a total for debits and a total for credits and they're equal.

Click the Print button on the report's button bar to print the report.

Configuring the Trial Balance Report

You can change the way the trial balance is reported with the configuration options available for this report. Click the Customize button on the report's button bar to bring up the Customize Report window.

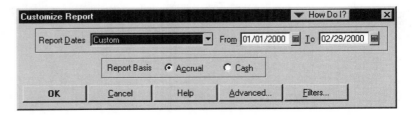

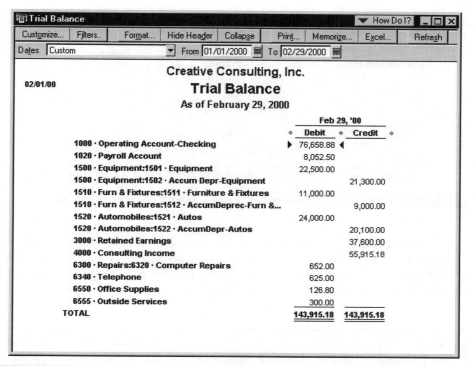

FIGURE 15-1 The trial balance presents the current balance for each account

Accrual vs. Cash Trial Balance

The important control in the Customize Report window is the Report Basis selection. QuickBooks can show you your balances on an accrual basis or on a cash basis:

- Accrual numbers are based on your transaction activity. When you invoice a customer, that amount is considered to be revenue. When you enter a vendor bill, you've entered an expense.
- Cash numbers are based on the flow of cash. Revenue isn't real until the customer pays the bill, and your vendor bills aren't expenses until you write the check.

By default, QuickBooks, like most accounting software, displays accrual reports. It's generally more useful as you analyze your business.

Filtering the Data

Click the Filters button in the Customize Report window to open the Report Filters window seen in Figure 15-2. You can also reach this window with the Filters button that's on the report button bar.

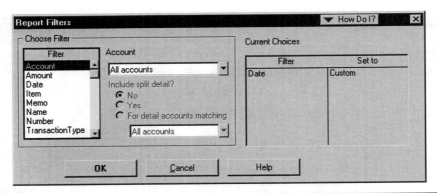

FIGURE 15-2   Change what's reported and how it's reported by filtering information

Select a category from the list in the Filter box and decide how each category should be displayed. You can also exclude category data with filters. Different categories have different filtering criteria. For instance, you can filter amounts that are less or greater than a certain amount.

 C A U T I O N : Once you start filtering accounts and amounts, you probably will have a trial balance that no longer balances. At that point you can't call it a trial balance; you're creating a list of account balances.

Setting Advanced Options

Click the Advanced button in the Customize Report window to see the Advanced Options window. The two display choices (Rows and Columns) change the criteria for displaying information.

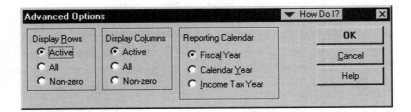

- Select Active to see rows or columns for accounts that had activity during the date range you've selected.

- Choose All to see everything, whether or not there was activity for the account during the date range. This means that every account is listed on the trial balance report (and many of them may show a zero balance).
- Choose Non-zero to see only those rows or columns that had activity and also have a closing amount that isn't zero.

The Reporting Calendar option can change the ending balance for the account if your company preferences are not set for a fiscal year and a tax year that coincide with the calendar year.

Click OK to return to the Customize Report window, then click OK again to put all your configuration changes into effect.

Memorizing a Customized Trial Balance

I find that I like to glance at the trial balance report occasionally, just to see what certain totals are. Calling up the trial balance to view five or six account balances is faster than opening five or six account registers to examine the current balance. I only need to see the accounts that have a balance; I have no interest in zero balance accounts.

 TIP : Balance sheet accounts display their current balances in the Chart of Accounts List window.

My accountant, on the other hand, likes to see all the accounts. He finds significance in some accounts being at zero.

The solution to providing both of us with what we want is in memorizing a configuration that's been customized.

After you've configured the report to display the information you want, in the manner in which you want it, click the Memorize button on the report's button bar. The Memorize Report window appears so you can give this customized format a name.

Memorize Report	✕
Enter Memorized Report Name	**OK**
TB for Accountant	Cancel
	Help

REMEMBER: Be sure to use a reference to the report type in the memorized name. If you use a name such as My Report, you'll have no idea what the report is about.

You can recall a memorized report by choosing Reports | Memorized Reports from the QuickBooks menu bar.

Creating a Balance Sheet

A balance sheet report is specifically designed to show only the totals of the balance sheet accounts from your chart of accounts. It's really a report on your financial health.

The reason a balance sheet balances is that it's based on a formula:

Assets = Liabilities + Equity

Before you glance at the trial balance you just printed and prepare to write me a note saying "Excuse me; you don't know what you're talking about. I just added those accounts up and it doesn't balance," let me redefine one of the terms: equity.

When you generate a balance sheet report, the equity number is a calculated number, and is arrived at with these steps:

1. All the income accounts are added up.
2. All the expense accounts are added up.
3. The expense total is subtracted from the income total.
4. The result of the calculation in step 3 is added to the totals in existing equity accounts (which could be Opening Balance Equity, Prior Retained Earnings, Retained Earnings, and so on).
5. The total that's calculated in step 4 becomes the figure for equity in a balance sheet report.

If you have more expenses than you have income, you're operating at a loss, and consequently it's a negative number that is combined with the existing equity accounts. This means that the equity number that appears on your balance sheet could be lower than the equity number that shows on your trial balance.

To create a balance sheet report, click the Reports listing on the Navigation Bar, and then choose one of the Balance Sheet reports from the Report Finder.

Balance Sheet Standard

The standard balance sheet reports the balance in every balance sheet account (unless the account has a zero balance), and subtotals each account type: asset, liability, and equity. The report is automatically configured for year-to-date figures, using your fiscal year. The fiscal year is the same as the calendar year for most small businesses.

Balance Sheet Detail

This report is similar to a detailed general ledger transaction report, showing every transaction in every balance sheet account. By default, the report covers a date range of the current month to date. Even if it's early in the month, this report is lengthy. If you change the date range to encompass a longer period (the quarter or year), the report will go on forever.

If you want to see a balance sheet only to get an idea of your company's financial health, this is probably more than you wanted to know.

Balance Sheet Summary

This report is a quick way to see totals. All the account types are listed and subtotaled, as shown in Figure 15-3.

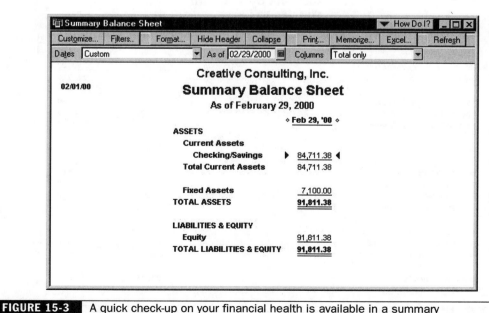

FIGURE 15-3 A quick check-up on your financial health is available in a summary balance sheet

If you miss seeing the details, hold your mouse pointer over any total (your pointer turns into a magnifying glass) and double-click. An itemized list of the transactions for each account represented by that total appears. For example, Figure 15-4 shows the display that appears when I double-click the total for Fixed Assets.

Close the detail report to return to the summary balance sheet.

Balance Sheet Previous Year Comparison

The comparison balance sheet is designed to show you what your financial situation is compared to a year ago. There are four columns in this report:

- The year-to-date balance for each balance sheet account
- The year-to-date balance for each balance sheet account for last year
- The amount of change between last year and this year
- The percentage of change between last year and this year

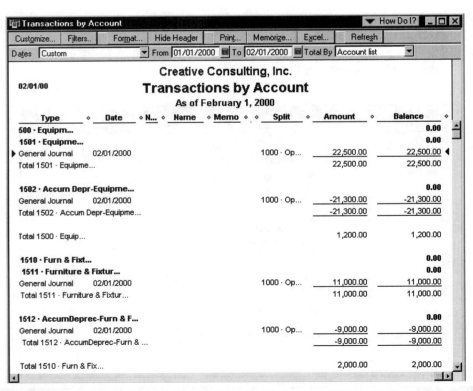

FIGURE 15-4   More details are available for any total in the balance sheet report

If you've just started using QuickBooks this year, there's little reason to run this report. Next year, however, it'll be interesting to see how you're doing compared to this year.

Customizing and Memorizing a Balance Sheet

When your balance sheet is on the screen, you can use all of the customization features mentioned for the trial balance. Then, when you have the configuration you need, memorize the report.

Creating a Profit & Loss Statement

Your P&L report is probably the one you'll run most often. It's natural to want to know if you're making any money. A P&L report is also called an *income report*. It shows all your income accounts (and displays the total), all your expense accounts (displaying the total), and then puts the difference between the two totals on the last line. If you have more income than expenses, the last line is a profit.

The P&L Reports are available in the Report Finder, which you open by clicking the Reports item in the Navigation Bar.

Profit & Loss Standard Report

The standard P&L report is a straightforward document, following the normal format for an income statement:

- The income is listed and totaled.
- The Cost of Goods Sold accounts are listed and the total is deducted from the income total in order to show the gross profit.
- The expenses are listed and totaled.
- The difference between the gross profit and the total expenses is displayed as your Net Income.

 N O T E : If you don't sell inventory items you probably don't have a Cost of Goods Sold section in your P&L.

However, while the format is that of a normal income statement, the end result isn't. The default date range for the QuickBooks standard P&L is the current month to date. This is not a year-to-date figure; it uses only the transactions from the current month. Click the arrow to the right of the Dates field and change the date range to This Fiscal Year to Date. The resulting display is what you want to see—a normal income statement for your business for this year.

Profit & Loss Detail Report

This report is for terminally curious people. It lists every transaction for every account in the P&L format. It goes on forever (see Figure 15-5).

This report shows an audit trail, and it's good to have if you notice some numbers that seem "not quite right" in the standard P&L. I don't recommend it as the report to run when you just need to know if you're making money.

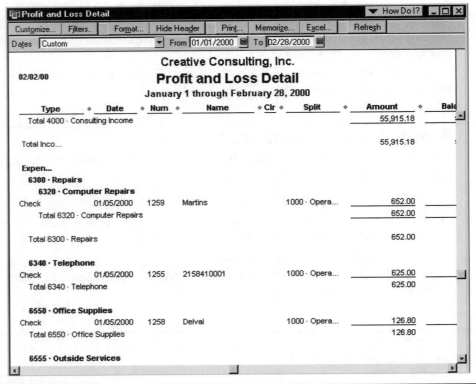

FIGURE 15-5 Use the scroll bar to see everything that happened in every income and expense account

Profit & Loss YTD Comparison Report

The YTD (year-to-date) comparison report compares the current month's income and expense totals with the year-to-date totals. Each income and expense account is listed.

Profit & Loss Previous Year Comparison Report

If you've been using QuickBooks for more than a year, this is a great report! If you recently started with QuickBooks, next year this will be a great report!

This is an income statement for the current year to date, with a column that shows last year's figure for the same period. This gives you an instant appraisal of your business growth (or ebb).

So you don't have to tax your brain doing the math, there are two additional columns: the difference between the years in dollars and the difference in percentage.

Profit & Loss by Job Report

This report presents a year-to-date summary of income and expenses posted to customers and jobs. In effect, it's a customer P&L. Scroll through the columns to view the total profit (or loss) for each customer (see Figure 15-6).

Customizing and Memorizing P&L Reports

Use the QuickBooks Customize feature to tailor P&L reports so they print exactly the way you want to see the information. You might want to customize several formats: for you, for your accountant, and perhaps for your bank (your bank also wants to see a balance sheet report). Then memorize the perfect customization you achieve.

Creating an Accountant's Review

Many accountants support QuickBooks directly, which means they understand the software and know how to use it. In fact, they help clients through the setup procedures. In fact, they have a copy of QuickBooks on their own computer system.

At various times during the year, your accountant might want to look at your books. There might be quarterly reports and adjustments, a physical inventory that resulted in serious changes in your balance sheet, expenses that should be

Creative Consulting, Inc.
Profit and Loss by Job
January 1 through February 28, 2000

02/02/00

	AlphaEng	DatabaseTraining (BillsCafe)	Installation (BillsCafe)	Total BillsCafe
Ordinary Income/Expense				
Income				
4000 · Consulting Income ▶	8,955.40 ◀	1,052.66	3,200.00	4,252.66
Total Income	8,955.40	1,052.66	3,200.00	4,252.66
Expense				
6555 · Outside Services	0.00	300.00	0.00	300.00
Total Expense	0.00	300.00	0.00	300.00
Net Ordinary Income	8,955.40	752.66	3,200.00	3,952.66
Net Income	**8,955.40**	**752.66**	**3,200.00**	**3,952.66**

FIGURE 15-6 In addition to per-customer and per-job totals, I can see the profits for individual service items

reappropriated, or any of a hundred other reasons. Almost definitely this will occur at the end-of-year process you have to go through in order to close your books for the year.

This could result in your accountant showing up and sitting in front of your computer, making the necessary changes (almost always journal entries), moving this, reversing that, and generally making sense out of your daily transaction postings. By "making sense," I mean putting transaction postings into categories that fit your tax reporting needs.

While your accountant is using the software, you can't get much accomplished. You could say "excuse me, could you move, I have to enter an invoice," but remember, you're paying for the accountant's time.

Or if your accountant doesn't want to visit, he or she may request printouts of various reports, then write notes on those printouts: "Move this, split that, credit this number here, debit that number there." Or you receive a spreadsheet-like printout with an enormously long and complicated journal entry, which means you have to stop entering your day-to-day transactions to make all those changes.

QuickBooks has a better idea. Give your accountant a disk with a copy of your QuickBooks records. Let your accountant do the work back at his or her office. When the disk comes back to you, the necessary changes have been placed on the disk. QuickBooks merges the changes into your copy of the software. It's magic!

 CAUTION: While your accountant is working on your records, QuickBooks locks certain parts of the database so you can't make changes that would affect what the accountant is working on. You can continue to enter transactions; you just can't make changes to some of the basic items in the database. After the accountant's changes have been merged, all of your data is available to you again.

Creating an Accountant's Review Copy

You can create the accountant's review copy on a floppy disk, or save it to a file and send it to your accountant via e-mail.

Choose File | Accountant's Review | Create Accountant's Copy from the QuickBooks menu bar. The Save Accountant's Copy To dialog box appears so you can save the information for your accountant.

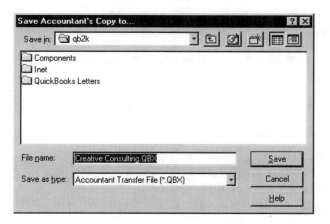

Change the location to your floppy drive if you plan to send a floppy disk to your accountant. If you're going to transmit the file via e-mail, you'll save some time searching for the file if you save it in the folder that your e-mail software uses as the default location.

The filename must have an extension of .qbx. You can change the name of the file if you want to, but generally it's a good idea to keep the filename QuickBooks suggests (which is based on your company name).

Click Save to create the accountant's copy. When the process is completed, QuickBooks notifies you of success. If the file won't fit on a floppy disk, you'll be asked to insert a second floppy disk to complete the process.

Working During the Accountant's Review

Because parts of your QuickBooks data have been locked, it's important to know what you can and cannot accomplish until you receive data back from your accountant.

- You can do anything you need to do with transaction windows. You can create, change, or delete any transaction.
- You can add entries to any list, or change information for a list entry, but you cannot delete any entries in a list.
- In your chart of accounts, you cannot change an account to a subaccount or change a subaccount to a parent account.
- You cannot change the name of any item in a list.

These restrictions aren't a real hardship, so long as your accountant returns your files in a timely fashion. (I won't attempt to define "timely" because it might not match your accountant's definition.)

Incidentally, your accountant also has restrictions on manipulating your files:

- No list entries can be deleted or made inactive.
- No transactions can be created except for journal entries.

Here are some of the things your accountant might do:

- Add accounts to your chart of accounts
- Edit account names
- Change account numbers (if you use numbers for your chart of accounts)
- Edit tax information for accounts
- Make journal entries
- Adjust inventory quantities and values
- Print 1099 Forms
- Print 941 Forms
- Print 940 Forms
- Print W-2 Forms

Unlocking Your Files Without a Review

If you make an accountant's review copy in error, or if your accountant tells you there are no changes to be made, you can unlock your files. This puts everything back as if you'd never created an accountant's review copy.

Choose File | Accountant's Review | Cancel Accountant's Changes. QuickBooks asks you to confirm your decision.

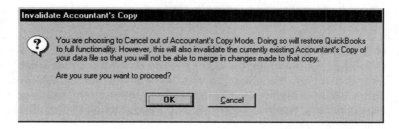

Click OK. You'll have to re-create the accountant's review copy the next time you want to use this feature.

Merging the Accountant's Changes

When your accountant returns your files to you, the changes have to be imported into your QuickBooks files.

1. Place the floppy disk you received from your accountant into the floppy drive. If you received the file via e-mail, note the location and filename used to store it on your hard disk.
2. Choose File | Accountant's Review | Import Accountant's Changes.
3. QuickBooks insists on a backup before importing. Click OK and proceed with the backup as usual.

TIP: I usually choose a folder on my hard disk for this backup so I don't have to remove the accountant's floppy disk (for my daily backup, I *never* use the hard drive). The Back Up window probably selects Drive A, but you can change the target to your QuickBooks folder. QuickBooks will ask you to confirm the fact that you want to back up to your hard drive.

4. When the backup is complete, QuickBooks automatically opens the Import Changes from Accountant's Copy window. Make sure the Look In field at the top of the window matches the location of the accountant's review file.

5. Choose the import file, which has an extension of .aif, and click Open (or double-click on the .aif file).

Your QuickBooks data now contains the changes your accountant made and you can work with your files normally.

REMEMBER: Make sure your accountant sends you a note or calls to tell you about the changes. QuickBooks does not indicate what has changed after the import. If you want to see the changes, you can view them in a spreadsheet program. Open the spreadsheet program and import the file (it's tab-delimited). See Appendix C to learn about using Microsoft Excel with your QuickBooks data.

Using Online Banking Services

In this chapter, you will learn to...

- Set up a connection to QuickBooks on the Web
- Set up online bank accounts
- Perform online transactions

If you have a modem attached to your computer you can use the wide range of online services offered by QuickBooks. In fact, you can register your software, get updates, find information about using QuickBooks more efficiently, and perform banking chores.

It's the banking chores that are the subject of this chapter. You'll discover that QuickBooks and its parent company, Intuit, have used the Internet to make banking a snap. You can sign up for online banking, which means you can view the status of your account, see which transactions have cleared, and generally maintain your account via your modem. You can also sign up for online payments, which means you send money to vendors via your modem. The money is deposited directly into your vendor's bank account, or a check is automatically generated (depending upon the way your vendor works).

Setting Up a Connection

Before you can use the QuickBooks online services, you have to let the software know how you get online. If you aren't currently online, but you have a modem, you can let QuickBooks set up your online services.

Choosing an Online Access Method

The first step is to let QuickBooks know how you reach the Internet. Choose Help | Internet Connection Setup from the menu bar. This launches the Internet Connection Setup Wizard, which presents a question in the first window (see Figure 16-1).

The choices on the first wizard window cover all the possibilities. One of them fits your situation, and here's the explanation for each of the choices.

- **I have an existing dial-up Internet connection**   You have a way to connect to the Internet using your modem. This connection could be through an ISP (Internet Service Provider), which you reach using the dial-up capabilities built into your operating system (Dial-Up Networking). Or you may have a connection through a proprietary software program that connects you to a particular host such as CompuServe or America Online. These proprietary programs first connect you to their host server, where there are preconfigured sections of information. Then, the systems permit you to wander off on your own on the Internet.

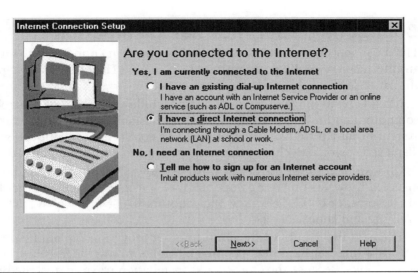

FIGURE 16-1 The first step is to determine how you reach the Internet

- **I have a direct Internet connection**   You have a direct connection through a network. Your network has a host, or server, that is connected to the Internet (usually through an ISP). You don't need a modem for this connection, you just need to access a resource on your network server and then use the server's capabilities to reach the Internet.
- **Tell me how to sign up for an Internet account**   You're not connected to the Internet, but you do have a modem. This choice leads to an explanation that you must sign up for Internet service before using the Internet Connection Setup wizard. After you're signed up, you can use the ISP for any sort of Internet meanderings, not just for reaching the QuickBooks Internet sites.

Using AOL from QuickBooks

QuickBooks 99 comes with a setup program for America Online. You can use it to open a new account on AOL, or to set up an existing AOL account on the computer that contains your QuickBooks software.

Use the Start menu and look in the QuickBooks Program group for the listing named AOL & Internet FREE Trial. Open that program and follow the instructions.

Configuring Your Internet Connection

The most common connection method is a modem connection to an ISP or an Internet service. I'll go over those steps here. (The other choices present similar tasks.)

Click Next to move to the next wizard window. QuickBooks searches your computer and finds any connections you've established through your operating system's Dial-Up Networking features. The connection or connections are displayed so you can choose the one you want to use (see Figure 16-2).

Choose Next to see the next wizard window. QuickBooks has found all the installed browsers on your computer (which usually means Internet Explorer, or Netscape, or both). Select the one you want to use to travel to the QuickBooks Web site and choose Next.

The next two windows are about Internet browsers, explaining that you must use Internet Explorer version 4 or higher to use the features offered by QuickBooks. Because the QuickBooks installation program installed IE 5, select that browser.

The next wizard window is an offer to have QuickBooks check the condition of the data exchange process when you go online for banking transactions (see Figure 16-3).

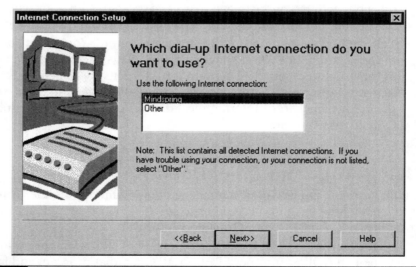

FIGURE 16-2 If you have more than one Internet connection, choose the one you want to use; QuickBooks inserts a connection named "Other" in case you don't have a connection

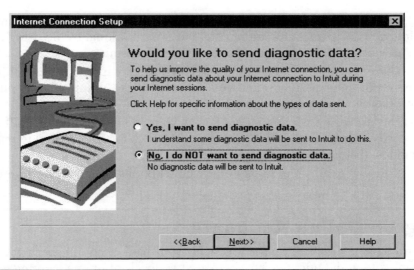

FIGURE 16-3 QuickBooks offers to test the quality of your communication with the Internet

Here are some things to think about before making this decision.

Phone lines sometimes have problems, especially with static noise. The noise can be caused by an overburdened phone system, squirrels gnawing on the insulation around the telephone wires, a thunderstorm anywhere between you and the other computer, and any number of noise-producing situations. This noise gets mixed in with data (which is transferred over the modem as a series of noises) and can corrupt the data. Most modem communication involves a quick check of the data to see if there are problems and, if there are, the data is sent again. If the problems are persistent, it takes forever to exchange the data (although eventually you'll probably see an error message indicating the modem has given up). Or worse, a problem isn't detected and the data that's exchanged is corrupt.

If you select the option to let QuickBooks send diagnostic data across the lines, some information about your computer, your connection, and your QuickBooks software is transmitted. None of this information is deeply personal nor does it contain any information about your bookkeeping data. Some of the information sent to QuickBooks during the diagnostic process includes your ISP name, the telephone number you use to reach your ISP, the version of QuickBooks you're using, the version of Windows you've installed on your computer, and the name and model of your modem. While these aren't intensely personal, private issues, it bothers some people to have a host computer peek into their computers.

QuickBooks says that running the intermittent diagnostic procedures won't slow down the transmission of data, but it *is* additional traffic using up bandwidth that would otherwise be used to transmit your data.

There's no correct answer here. If you normally have clean telephone lines and clean transmissions when you exchange files and information on the Internet, you probably can say No.

The last wizard window shows you all your configuration choices. If everything is correct, click Finish. If something's amiss, click the Back button to return to the window that needs to be changed.

Now you're all set to use all of the QuickBooks online services you need.

Setting Up Online Accounts

You have to establish online access for your bank accounts, both with your bank and with QuickBooks. There are two levels of online banking:

- Online account access
- Online bill paying

You can sign up for either or both of these services. The process for enabling online banking has three steps:

1. Apply for online services with your bank.
2. Receive a Personal Identification Number (PIN) from your bank.
3. Enable a QuickBooks bank account (or multiple accounts) for online services.

Explanations and instructions for all of these processes are contained in this section.

Understanding Online Account Access

If you sign up for online account access, you have the ability to connect to your bank's computer system and look at your account. Once you're plugged in to your account records online, there are a number of tasks you can accomplish:

- Check your balance as of this moment.
- Transfer money between accounts. (Both accounts must be at this bank and enabled for online services.)
- Download information about all the cleared transactions to your computer. The information is automatically placed into your QuickBooks bank register.

One of the nifty advantages of this system is that you can do all these things at your own convenience; the bank's hours of operations have become irrelevant for you. If you want to do your banking in the middle of the night, you can. Check with your bank, however, to see if there's a time period when online access isn't permitted (usually in the wee hours of the morning). Some banks reserve a few hours each night to perform maintenance tasks on their computers.

Understanding Online Bill Paying

You can pay your bills online, transferring money directly from your account to your vendors. This point-and-click method of paying bills is certainly a lot easier than writing out checks. If you don't have printed checks, I can't imagine not using online payment, because writing out a check manually is a whole lot of work! Even if you do have printed checks, you might want to consider online payments because it's usually easier and quicker than mailing checks.

When you make an online payment, the following information is transmitted to your vendor in addition to money:

- The date and number of the invoice(s)
- Information about any discounts or credits you've applied to the invoice(s)
- Anything you inserted as a memo or note when you prepared the payment

If the vendor is set up to receive electronic payments, the money is transferred directly from your bank account to the vendor's bank account. Incidentally, being set up to receive electronic payments does not mean your vendor must be using QuickBooks; there are many and varied methods for receiving electronic payments and many companies have these arrangements with their banks.

If the vendor's account is not accessible for online payments, your bank writes a check and mails it, along with all the necessary payment information.

Finding Your Bank Online

You may already have learned about your bank's online services—many banks enclose information about this feature in the monthly statements, or have brochures available when you visit the bank. (If you've already applied for online services you can skip this part and move to the section "Enabling Your Online Bank Accounts").

Before you run to the neighborhood bank branch to sign up, you can find out what your bank expects from you by going online. In fact, you may be able to sign up online. The wonders of a modem!

Choose Banking | Set Up Online Financial Services from the menu bar. The submenu has three commands:

- **Apply For Online Banking**, which opens a wizard that lets you find your bank on the Internet and fill out an application.
- **Online Financial Institutions List**, which opens an Internet window in your browser so you can see the list of participating financial institutions.
- **About Online Banking**, which displays QuickBooks explanations of the services offered online.

Check the Online Financial Institutions List

If you haven't discussed online services with your bank, you can choose Online Financial Institutions List to see if your bank participates. QuickBooks launches your Internet connection, opens your browser, and travels to the Financial Institutions Directory Web site (see Figure 16-4).

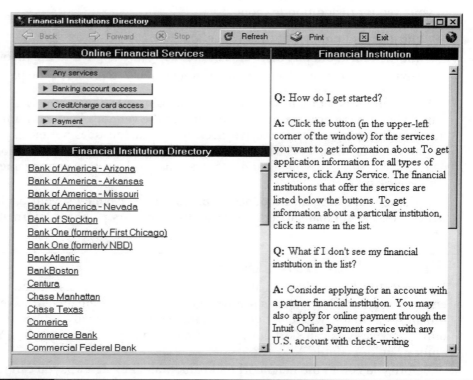

FIGURE 16-4 Select a banking service to see the list of institutions that support that service

Scroll through the list to find your bank, then click that listing. The right pane of your browser window displays information about the bank's online services, along with a link to its online Web site. Many banks also display a button titled Apply Now, and clicking it opens an application.

Apply for Online Services

If you already know that your bank has online services, but you haven't filled out an application, you can apply online by selecting the command Apply for Online Banking from the Set Up Online Financial Services submenu. The Online Banking Setup Interview Wizard seen in Figure 16-5 appears to guide you through the process.

Click Next to move to the next window, and click the Apply Now button. QuickBooks launches your Internet connection, opens your browser, and takes you to the Financial Institutions Directory Web site, which is the same location as described in the previous section (and shown in Figure 16-4).

Scroll through the list to find your bank and click on its listing. In the right pane, click the Apply Now button (if there isn't one, follow the instructions your bank has placed in the right pane).

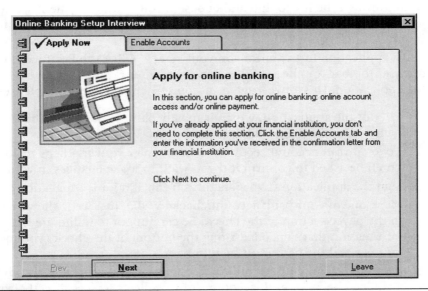

FIGURE 16-5 Use the Online Banking Setup Interview to complete your bank's application online

C A U T I O N : You may see a warning that you are about to send information to an Internet zone in which it might be possible for other people to see the data you send. Select Yes to continue (you might want to select the option not to be warned in the future). If this makes you nervous, forget online banking, because there's no guaranteed security on the Internet—even though Intuit makes every possible effort to keep data secure.

When your bank's application form appears in the browser window, fill it out and submit it. Your bank will send you information about using its online service, along with a PIN that's been assigned. All banks provide a method of changing the PIN to one of your own choosing. In fact, many banks insist that you change the PIN the first time you access online services.

Using the QuickBooks Online Payment Service

If your bank doesn't participate in online services, and if your prime motivation for banking online is paying your bills via the Internet, you can sign up for that service directly with QuickBooks/Intuit.

When the Financial Institutions list is displayed in your browser window, scroll through the list to find and choose Intuit Online Payment service in the left pane. QuickBooks travels to the Intuit Online Payment Service site on the Internet. Click Apply Now.

An application form appears on your screen. Click the Print icon on your browser toolbar (or choose File | Print from your browser menu bar) to print the application. (It's a two-page print job.) Then take these simple steps:

1. Fill out the application, which is mostly basic information about your name, company name, address, and so on.
2. To keep your account secure, you must enter your mother's maiden name. You'll be asked to confirm it if you want to make changes in your account.
3. Sign the application (two signatures if this is a joint application).
4. Mark one of your bank account checks VOID. Just write the word "VOID" in the payee section of the check. Be careful not to obliterate the important information that's encoded along the bottom of the check (your account number and the bank routing number).
5. If you are signing up for online payment for multiple bank accounts, send a voided check for each account. Intuit collects its fees directly from your checking account, so indicate which bank account is the billing account by writing "billing account" on the back of the appropriate check.

6. Mail your completed, signed application, along with the check(s) to:

> CheckFree Corp.
> P.O. Box 3128
> Lisle, IL 60532-9729

In a couple of weeks you'll receive all the information you need to begin paying your bills online.

Enabling Your Online Bank Accounts

After you've signed up with your bank and have your secret PIN, you must configure your QuickBooks bank account(s) for online services.

 N O T E :   Some banks use passwords instead of PINs.

Choose Banking | Set Up Online Financial Services | Apply for Online Banking. The Online Banking Setup Interview Wizard appears, and this time you should click the Enable Accounts tab. Follow the instructions and answer the questions as you proceed through the wizard. (Click Next to keep moving along.)

As you go through the steps in the wizard, you'll create a QuickBooks bank account that's configured as an online account. You'll be asked to select the online services you'll use with this account. Choose online account access, online payments, or both.

You can create online bank accounts in QuickBooks for as many accounts and different financial institutions as you need.

Performing Online Transactions

After you've set up your online banking permissions with your financial institutions and established your online bank account(s) in QuickBooks, you're ready to do your banking on the Internet.

Accessing Your Bank Account Online

You can dial into your online bank records and check the balance and activity of your account.

When you're online viewing your account, the list of transactions can be downloaded to your computer in order to update your QuickBooks register.

(You'll have to enter your PIN or password, of course, to view your account). Follow the directions on the screen to place the information into your QuickBooks system.

Transferring Money Between Accounts Online

If you have multiple accounts at your financial institution, you can transfer money between those accounts. For example, you may have a money market account for your business in addition to your checking account.

To transfer money online, you must have applied at your financial institution for online banking for both accounts. You'll probably have a unique PIN for each account. To make your life less complicated, you should make changes while you're online to ensure both accounts have the same PIN. In addition, you must have enabled both accounts for online access within QuickBooks.

There are two methods you can use to transfer funds between online accounts: Use the transfer funds function, or use the register for either account.

Using the Transfer Funds Function

The simplest way to move money between your online accounts is to use the QuickBooks Transfer Funds Between Accounts window, which you reach by choosing Banking | Transfer Funds from the menu bar.

Specify the sending and receiving accounts (remember, both must be enabled for online access) and enter the amount you want to transfer. Click Save & Close. Then choose Banking | Online Banking Center, make sure the transaction has a check mark, and click Send.

Using the Bank Register to Transfer Funds

You can enter a transfer directly into the account register of the bank account from which you are sending the money. The significant data entry is the one in the check number column; instead of a check number, type the word **send**. Don't enter a payee, enter the amount, and enter the receiving account in the account field.

Then choose Banking | Online Banking Center, make sure the transaction has a check mark, and click Send.

Paying Bills Online

You can pay your bills in QuickBooks, then go online to send the payments to the payees. You may either use your own bank (if it's capable of working with QuickBooks) or use the QuickBooks bill paying service. In this section, when I say "bank," you can mentally substitute the QuickBooks service if that's what you're using.

If your vendor can accept electronic funds, this is a breeze. What happens is that your bank's software transmits the payment electronically, and the vendor's bank uses its software to accept it. No paper, no mail, no delays.

If your vendor cannot accept electronic funds, your bank actually prints a check and mails it, and there's a four-day delay in the delivery of the funds. Personally, I don't understand why this would be better for you. The delay and risk of lost mail is no different than if you wrote the checks and mailed them yourself. In addition, you have to pay a service charge to have the bank mail each check. If you absolutely hate writing checks, I guess this might be the price you're willing to pay.

There are three different methods for creating the transaction in QuickBooks:

- Use the Write Checks window.
- Use the Pay Bills window.
- Use the register for the online account you use for online payments.

I think the easiest is way is using the Write Checks window. Here's how it works:

1. Press CTRL-W or choose Banking | Write Checks from the menu bar.
2. Select the vendor.
3. Enter the delivery date, which is the date on which you want the funds to be delivered.

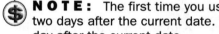 **NOTE:** The first time you use online bill paying, the default delivery date is two days after the current date. Thereafter, the default delivery date will be one day after the current date.

4. Enter the amount of the online payment.
5. Enter an optional memo if you want to include a message to the vendor.

CAUTION: A memo can only be delivered as a voucher or stub, which means that your payment will not be made electronically even if the vendor is able to accept electronic payments. Instead, a check is sent, which delays the payment.

6. Assign the expense account (or item sale) in the line item section of the window.
7. Repeat this process for each payment you're making.

Finally, go online to transmit the information to the Online Banking Center. Choose Banking | Online Banking Center. In the Online Banking Center window, click Send. Your payments are sent to the big bill-paying machine on the Net.

Creating Online Transaction Reports

You can track your online activities using the available QuickBooks reports. The quickest way to see your online transactions is to click the Reports listing on the Navigation Bar. Choose Accountant & Taxes as the report type, then select the Transaction Detail by Account report.

In the report window, click the Filters button to open the Report Filters window (see Figure 16-6).

In the Choose Filter list box, select Online Status, then select the online status option you need:

- **All** reports all transactions whether they were online transactions or not (don't choose this option if you're trying to get a report on your online transactions).
- **Online to send** reports the online transactions you've created but not yet sent online.
- **Online sent** reports only the online transactions you've sent.
- **Any online** reports on all the online transactions you've created, both sent and waiting.
- **Not online** excludes the online transactions from the report. (Don't choose this option either.)

After you've set the filter options, click OK to return to the report window.

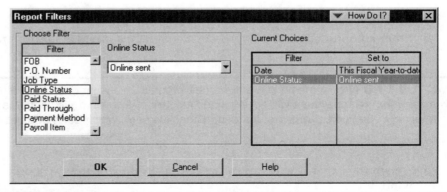

FIGURE 16-6   Select the status option you need for the report you're creating

Doing Business with Big Business

Jerry's Computer Upgrades is a thriving small business, specializing in adding memory, peripherals, gizmos, and doodads to PCs. Jerry buys lots of memory chips, and his supplier has offered a 10 percent price reduction if Jerry will deposit his payments electronically (and on time, for which Jerry already gets a 2 percent deduction in the bill amount).

The supplier explained that online payments are much less work because they eliminate the labor and time involved in opening mail, crediting Jerry's account, writing a deposit slip, and taking the check to the bank. Jerry called around and asked other vendors if they had the ability to accept online payments. Many of them did (but nobody else offered Jerry a discount for using online bill paying).

Jerry went to his bank and opened a separate account for his online bill paying. He also enabled online transactions for his regular operating account so he could transfer money into the online bill-paying account as he needed it.

Now Jerry can hold onto his money until the day the payment is due to his vendors (why should they get the interest?) instead of sending checks several days ahead in order to insure that his 2 percent discount for timely payment is valid.

His normal procedure is to go online, upload the checks he's written for online bill paying, and then transfer the appropriate amount of money from his operating account to his bill-paying account.

Because the accounts are separate, generating reports about his online transaction activity is easy. Because he doesn't have to sign checks, put them in envelopes, place stamps on the envelopes, and take the envelopes to the mailbox, Jerry is saving time. And Jerry, like all good business people, believes that time is money.

Year-End Procedures

In *this chapter, you will learn to...*

- Run reports on your financial condition

- Print 1099 Forms

- Make year-end journal entries

- Get ready for tax time

- Close the books

Chapter 17

The end of the year is a madhouse for bookkeepers, and that's true for major corporations as well as small businesses. There is so much to do, so many reports to examine, corrections to make, entries to create—whew!

You can relax a bit. You don't have to show up at the office on January 1st (or the first day of your new fiscal year if you're not on a calendar year). Everything doesn't have to be accomplished immediately. QuickBooks is date-sensitive so you can continue to work in the new year. As long as the dates of new transactions are after the last day of your fiscal year, the transactions won't work their way into your year-end calculations.

Running Year-End Financial Reports

The standard financial reports you run for the year provide a couple of services for you:

- You can see the economic health of your business.
- You can examine the report to make sure everything is posted correctly.

To run financial reports, click the Reports listing on the Navigation Bar. The Report Finder window offers several types of reports—you can see the list by clicking the arrow to reveal the drop-down list.

For year-end reports you'll need to access several of these types of reports.

Running a Year-End P&L Report

Start with a Profit & Loss Standard report (also called an *income statement*), which is one of the reports in the Company & Financial listing. Set the date range as This Fiscal Year (you can set the date range on the Report Finder window or on the report window). Voilà! The report displays the year-end balances for all the income and expense accounts in your general ledger that had any activity this year (see Figure 17-1).

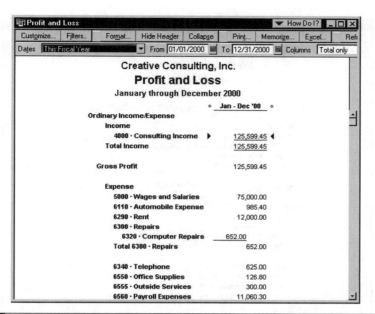

FIGURE 17-1 Quick! Scroll to the bottom to see if there's a profit or a loss

Examine the report and if anything seems totally out of line, double-click the total to see the postings for that account. You can double-click on any of the posting lines to see the original transaction.

If there's a transaction that now looks as if it's in error, you can take corrective action. You cannot delete or void a bill you paid, nor a customer invoice for which you received payment, of course. However, you might be able to talk to a customer or vendor for whom you've found a problem and work out a satisfactory arrangement for credits. Or you may find that you posted an expense or income transaction to the wrong general ledger account. If so, make a journal entry to correct it (see the section on making journal entries later in this chapter). Then run the year-end P&L report again and print it.

Running a Year-End Balance Sheet

Your real financial health is demonstrated in your balance sheet. To run a year-end balance sheet, select Balance Sheet Standard from the Report Finder and set the date range for This Fiscal Year. Your year-end balance sheet figures appear in the report (see Figure 17-2).

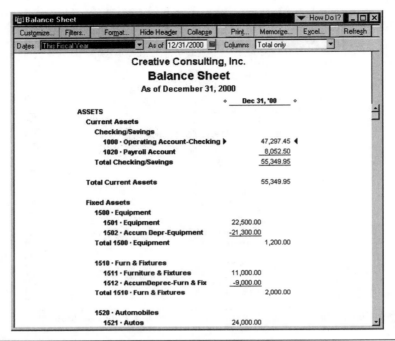

FIGURE 17-2 The balance sheet figures reveal the health of your business

The balance sheet figures are more than a list of numbers; they're a list of chores. Check with your accountant first, but most of the time you'll find that the following advice is offered:

- Pay any payroll withholding liabilities with a check dated in the current year in order to clear them from the balance sheet and gain the expense deduction for the employer taxes.
- Pay some bills ahead of time. For example, pay your rent or mortgage payment that's due the first day of the next fiscal year during the last month of this fiscal year. Enter and pay vendor bills earlier than their due dates in order to pay them this year.

Printing 1099 Forms

If any vendors are eligible for 1099 Forms, you need to print the forms and mail them. First, make sure your 1099 setup is correct by choosing Edit | Preferences and moving to the Tax: 1099 tab (see Figure 17-3).

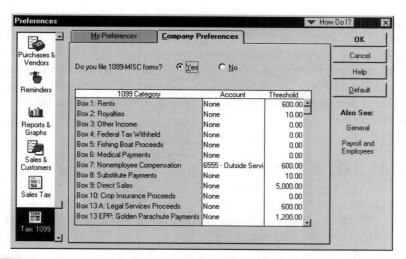

FIGURE 17-3 Check the threshold and account information in your 1099 preferences

Check the latest IRS rules and make any changes to the threshold amounts for the categories you need. Also assign an account to each category.

 REMEMBER: You cannot assign the same account to more than one category.

Run a 1099 Report

Before you print the forms, you should print a report on your 1099 vendors. To accomplish this, select the Reports listing on the Navigation Bar. When the Report Finder opens, choose the Vendors & Payables report types from the drop-down list. Then select one of the 1099 reports:

- **1099 Summary** lists each vendor eligible for a 1099 with the total amount paid to the vendor.
- **1099 Detail** lists each transaction for each vendor eligible for a 1099.

You can make adjustments to transactions, if necessary, in order to make sure your 1099 vendors have the right totals.

It's also a good idea to go through your entire Vendor list to find any vendors who did not appear on the 1099 report but who should be receiving 1099s. If you find any, edit the Vendor record to make sure the 1099 option is selected on the Additional Info tab. You must also have an identification number for the vendor, either a Social Security number or a Federal EIN number if the vendor is a business (proprietorship or partnership—corporations do not receive 1099s).

Print 1099 Forms

To print the 1099 Forms, click the Vendors listing on the Navigation Bar. Then click the Print 1099s icon to open the Print 1099 Forms window. The specific type of 1099 Form that's offered depends on the preferences you set for 1099s and vendors. Most of the time you'll use the 1099 MISC form.

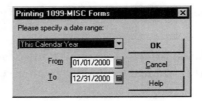

1. Be sure the dates are correct in the Printing 1099 Forms window, and click OK.
2. When the list of 1099 recipients appears, any vendor who is over the appropriate threshold should have a check mark.
3. Click Preview to see what the form will look like when it prints. Make sure your company name, address, and EIN number are correct. Click Close on the Preview window to return to the 1099 window. Then load the 1099 Forms into your printer and click Print.
4. If you're using a laserjet or inkjet printer, set the number of copies so you have enough for your own records—you'll need three. Dot matrix printers use multipart forms.

When the forms are printed, send one to the vendor, one to the government, and put the third copy in your files. You must deliver the forms to vendors by January 31.

Repeat these procedures for each type of 1099 Form you are required to print (most business only need to worry about the 1099-MISC Form).

Making Year-End Journal Entries

There are probably a couple of journal entries your accountant wants you to make before you close your books for the year:

- Depreciation entries
- Prior retained earnings moved to a different account
- Any adjustments needed for cash vs. accrual reporting (these are usually reversed on the first day of the next fiscal year)

 N O T E : Chapter 14 has detailed information about making journal entries.

You can send the P&L and balance sheet reports to your accountant, and you'll receive journal entry instructions. Or you can send your accountant an accountant's review copy of your company data and import the changes. See Chapter 15 to learn how to use the accountant's review copy feature.

Running Tax Reports

You can run tax reports whether you prepare your own taxes, or your accountant prepares them. Before you can run accurate reports, you must make sure your data is configured properly for taxes.

Check Tax Line Information

Every account in your chart of accounts that is tax related must have the right tax form in the account's tax line assignment. QuickBooks tells you if tax line assignments are missing in the Income Tax Preparation report:

1. Click the Reports listing on the Navigation Bar.
2. Choose Accountant & Taxes as the type of report.
3. Choose Income Tax Preparation.

When the report appears, all your accounts are listed, along with the tax form assigned to each account.

If you created your own chart of accounts, the number of accounts that you neglected to assign to a tax form is likely to be quite large, as seen in Figure 17-4.

It isn't necessary to enter tax form information if you don't plan to prepare your own taxes, but if you change your mind you must edit each account. To do so, double-click the account to open its account window and select a form from the Tax Line entry drop-down list (see Figure 17-5).

 TIP: One of the selections in the drop-down list is Not Tax Related, which may be appropriate for some accounts.

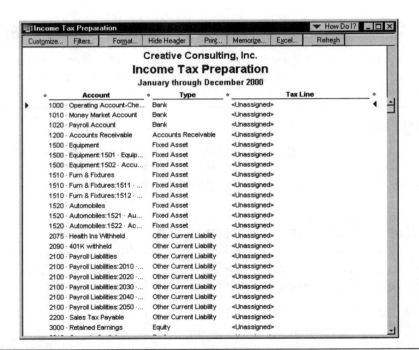

FIGURE 17-4 Look what happens when you don't take the time to assign tax forms as you create accounts

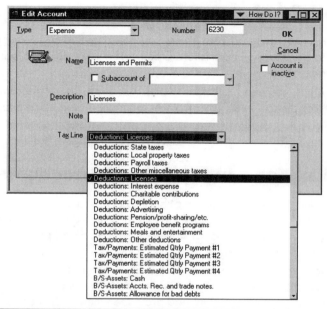

FIGURE 17-5 Scroll through the list to find the right tax form for this account

Calculate Other Important Tax Information

There are some taxable numbers that aren't available through the normal QuickBooks reports. One of the most common is the report on company officer compensation if your business is incorporated.

If your business is a C corporation, you file tax form 1120, while a Subchapter S corporation files tax form 1120S. Both of these forms require you to separate compensation for corporate officers from the other employee compensation. You will have to add those totals from payroll reports (either QuickBooks payroll or an outside payroll service).

You can avoid the need to calculate this by creating a separate Payroll item called Officer Compensation and assigning it to its own account (which you'll also have to create). Then open the Employee card for each officer and change the Earnings item to the new item.

Putting QuickBooks to Work

Using Turbo Tax

If you purchase Turbo Tax to do your taxes, you don't have to do anything special in QuickBooks to transfer the information. Open Turbo Tax and tell it to import your QuickBooks company file.

Almost everything you need is transferred to Turbo Tax. There are some details you'll have to enter directly into Turbo Tax (for example, home office expenses for a Schedule C form).

Linking Tax Form Information to Accounts

Ray's Snow Plowing Co. (a proprietorship) had a good year. (Mother Nature cooperated and luckily she's not on commission.) All the income and expenses were straightforward. There were no unusual transactions. Customers were billed and paid on time. Vendors were paid. There is no inventory.

Ray has decided to do his own taxes, but when he set up his company he created his own chart of accounts (at that time he thought he'd ask his accountant to do the taxes). He used the account list his accountant had provided when he first started the business, at which time he was doing his bookkeeping manually.

When Ray ran the Income Tax Summary report, there was practically no tax information on it; almost everything was unassigned. He started to edit the accounts to add tax information, but figuring out which tax form went with which account was just too complicated.

Ray created a new company in QuickBooks. He chose File | New Company from the menu bar and began filling out the EasyStep Interview.

1. He answered the first few questions, filling out the name of a fake company.

2. He chose Consulting as the company type because it seemed to be the closest to his own situation.

3. He saved the company information to a file as instructed.

4. He told the EasyStep Interview Wizard to create a chart of accounts.

5. He clicked Leave and stopped the interview.

That's all Ray had to do to get most of the information he needed. When the new company was opened in QuickBooks, he chose List | Chart of Accounts from the menu bar. He clicked the Account button at the bottom of the Chart of Accounts window and chose Print List.

When the chart of accounts printed, the report had a column named Income Tax Line. Almost all of the accounts had associated tax information displayed.

Ray has several choices as he attempts to determine whether unassociated lines need to be edited:

- He can call his accountant and ask.
- He can call the IRS service office and ask.
- He can buy a book.
- He can go to the library.

Closing Your Books

After all the year-end reports have been run, any necessary journal entries have been entered, and your taxes have been filed (and paid), it's traditional to go through the exercise of closing the books.

Typically, closing the books occurs some time after the end of the fiscal year, usually within the first couple of months of the next fiscal year (right after the tax forms have been sent to the government).

The exercise of closing books is performed in order to lock the books. No user can change anything. After taxes have been filed based on the information in the system, nothing can be changed. It's too late, this is it, the information is etched in cement.

Understanding Closing in QuickBooks

QuickBooks doesn't use the traditional accounting software closing procedures. In most other business accounting software, closing the year means you cannot post transactions to any date in that year, nor can you manipulate any transactions in the closed year. Closing the books in QuickBooks does not etch the information in cement; it can be changed and/or deleted by users with the appropriate permissions.

QuickBooks does not require you to close the books in order to keep working in the software. You can work forever, year after year, without performing a closing process. However, many QuickBooks users prefer to lock the transactions for a year as a way to close the books for that year.

The QuickBooks closing (locking) procedure is tied in with the users and passwords features that are part of the software. This is so that closing can lock some users out of changing anything in last year's books and still permit an administrator (and selected users) to do so. If a restricted user attempts to change (or delete) a transaction in the closed period, an error message appears telling the user he or she is denied access.

 T I P : If you haven't yet set up users, read Chapter 21.

Closing the Year

You can reconfigure user rights to enable or prevent entry into closed transactions with the following steps:

1. Choose Company | Users from the QuickBooks menu bar.
2. When the User List window opens, click Closing Date.
3. Enter the closing date and click OK.

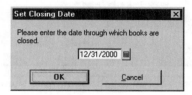

Now the fiscal year that ended on the closing date you entered is closed. If your fiscal year is different from a calendar year, don't worry about payroll. The payroll files and features (including 1099s) are locked into a calendar year configuration and closing your books doesn't have any effect on them.

Changing User Access to Closed Books

If you want to check, and perhaps change, user rights in order to keep some users from changing transactions in the closed year (or to permit them to), you can view and edit the current user rights.

Choose Company | Users from the QuickBooks menu bar. When the User List opens, select the user you want to work with. Click View User to see whether or not the user has rights in closed transactions (see Figure 17-6).

Click Leave to return to the User List. If you want to change this user's access, click Edit and make the necessary changes.

The truth is, nobody should mess around with transactions that are in a closed year—not even you.

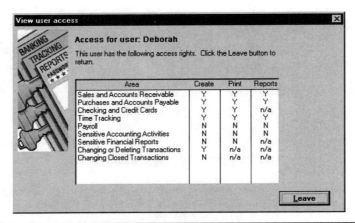

FIGURE 17-6 The last entry in this user's list of rights shows she cannot access closed transactions

Creating a Year-End Backup

After all the numbers are checked, all the journal entries are made, and the books have been closed by entering a closing date as described in the previous section, do a separate backup. Don't put this backup on one of the floppy disks you're using for your normal backups. If you use other removable media for backups (such as Zip or Jaz drives) use a fresh disk or create a folder on the removable drive for this backup. Label the disk (or folder) Year End Backup 2000.

Using Time and Billing

Lots of service businesses sell time; it's the most important commodity they have. Actually, most service businesses are really selling knowledge and expertise, but nobody's ever figured out how to put a value on those assets. The solution, therefore, is to charge for the time that it takes to pass along and use all that expertise.

If you've installed the Time and Billing features of QuickBooks, Part Three of this book covers all the steps you need to take to set your system up for maximum efficiency and accuracy. Then we'll discuss all the ways you can use the functions and tools that are available within the system.

Part Three

Using Time Tracking

In this chapter, you will learn to...

- Configure time tracking

- Fill out timesheets

- Edit timesheets

- Bill for time

You can track time just to see how much time is spent completing a project or working for a customer, or you can track time for the purpose of billing the customer for the time. In fact, time tracking does not have to be connected to time billing. In and of itself, time tracking is a way to see what everyone in your company is doing, and how much time they spend doing each thing. Some of those activities may be administrative and unconnected to customers.

You can use this information in a variety of ways, depending on what it is you want to know about the way your business runs. If you charge retainer fees for your services, time tracking is a terrific way to figure out which customers may need to have the retainer amount raised.

Configuring Time Tracking

When you first install QuickBooks Pro, and whenever you create a new company, you're asked if you want to track time. If you respond affirmatively, QuickBooks Pro turns on the time-tracking features.

If you opted to skip time tracking, you can turn it on if you change your mind later. In fact, if you did turn it on, you can turn it off if you find you're not using it.

If you're not sure whether you turned on time tracking when you installed your company, choose Edit | Preferences from the QuickBooks menu bar. Select the Time Tracking icon and click the Company Preferences tab. Make sure the Yes option button is selected.

Configuring Your Work Week

By default, QuickBooks Pro assumes your work week starts on a Monday. However, if your business is open every day of the week, you might want to use a standard Sunday-to-Saturday pattern for tracking time.

You can turn on, turn off, or configure time tracking quite quickly:

1. Choose File | Preferences from the menu bar.
2. When the Preferences window opens, scroll down in the left pane to find the Time Tracking icon and click it.
3. Click the Company Preferences tab to open the Preferences window shown in the following illustration.

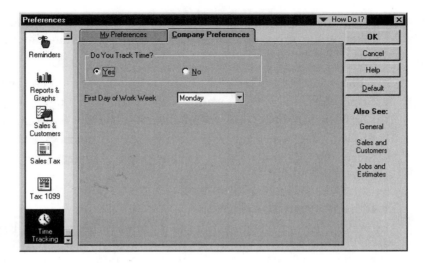

4. Specify the first day of your work week.
5. Click OK.

TIP : If you've been tracking time and decide you don't want to bill customers for time any longer, you can turn off time tracking. Any time records you've accumulated are saved nothing is deleted. If you change your mind again later and turn time tracking back on, the records are available to you.

Configuring the Workers

If you're tracking time for your employees, outside contractors, or yourself, everybody who must keep track of his or her time must exist in the system. Each person must also fill out a timesheet.

Tracking Employee Time

If you are running the QuickBooks payroll feature, you already have employees in your QuickBooks system. You can track the time of any employee who fills out a timesheet (covered later in this chapter).

You can also use the timesheet data to pay the employee, using the number of hours reported in the time-tracking system to determine the number of hours for which the employee is paid. However, for this to work the employee must be linked to his or her timesheet. To do this, you must modify the employee record:

1. Choose Lists | Employee List from the menu bar to open the Employee List.
2. Select the employee you want to link to time tracking.
3. Click the Employee button and choose edit to open the employee record.
4. Move to the Payroll Info tab of the employee record (see Figure 18-1).
5. Select the Use Time Data To Create Paychecks check box.
6. Click OK.

Tracking Vendor Time

Any vendor in your system who is paid for his or her time can have that time tracked for the purpose of billing customers. Most of the time these vendors are referred to as outside contractors, or subcontractors. You don't have to do anything to the vendor record to effect time tracking; you merely need to record the time used as the vendor sends bills.

Tracking Other Worker Time

You may need to track the time of people who are neither employees nor vendors. The word "employees" should be taken literally, meaning you have

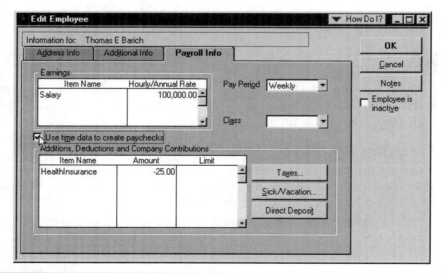

FIGURE 18-1 Link an employee to the time-tracking system so you can use timesheets to calculate the payroll

established QuickBooks payroll services. If you have employees, but you don't use QuickBooks payroll, they're not employees to your QuickBooks software.

QuickBooks provides a system list called Other Names. You use this list to amass names or descriptions that don't fit in the other QuickBooks lists. You can track time for people by entering their names into the Other Names list. Here are some situations in which you'll need to use the Other Names feature:

- *You have employees and use QuickBooks payroll but you are not an employee because you take a draw instead of a paycheck.* In this case, you must add your own name to the Other Names list if you want to track your own time.
- *You have employees and are not using QuickBooks payroll so there is no Employees list in your system.* You must add each employee name to the Other Names list in order to track employee time.
- *You have no employees and your business is a proprietorship or a partnership.* Owner or partner names must be entered into the Other Names list in order to track time.

Configuring the Tasks

Most of the tasks you track already exist in your system as Service items. These are the items you use when you bill customers for services. However, because you can use time tracking to analyze the way the people in your organization spend their time, you may want to add service items that are relevant to non-customer tasks.

For example, if you want to track the time people spend performing administrative tasks for the business, you can add a service item called Administrative to your items list. If you want to be more specific, you can name the specific administrative tasks you want to track (for example, Bookkeeping, Equipment Repair, New Sales Call, and so on).

To enter new items, choose Item List from the Navigation Bar. When the Item List window opens, click the Item button and choose New to open a new item form. Select Service as the item type and name the new item. Here are some guidelines for administrative items:

- *If you're specifying administrative tasks, create a service named Administration, and then make the specific items subitems of Administration.*
- *Don't put an amount in the Rate box.* You're not charging a customer for this service and you can calculate the amount you're paying the recipient when you make the payment (via payroll or vendor checks).
- *Because you must assign an account, choose an innocuous revenue account (such as Other Revenue). No money is posted to the account.*

Configuring User Permissions

If you're using multiple user and password features in QuickBooks, you must edit each user to make sure people can use the time-tracking forms. See Chapter 21 for detailed information about setting up users and permissions.

Using Timesheets

QuickBooks offers two methods of recording the time you spent on work: Single Activity and Weekly Timesheet.

Single Activity is a form you use to enter what you did when you perform a single task at a specific time on a specific date. For example, a Single Activity form may record the fact that you made a telephone call on behalf of a customer, or you repaired some piece of equipment for a customer, or you performed some administrative task for the company which is unrelated to a customer.

Weekly Timesheet is a form in which you indicate how much time and on which date you performed work. Each Weekly Timesheet entry can also include the name of the customer for whom the work was performed.

Your decision about which method to use depends on the type of work you do and on the efficiency of your workers' memories. People tend to put off filling in Weekly Timesheets and then they attempt to reconstruct their activities in order to complete the timesheets. This frequently ends up being less than accurate as an approach. The method only works properly if everyone remembers to open the timesheets and fill them in as soon as they complete each task. Uh huh, sure.

 TIP: If you fill out a Single Activity form, when you open a Weekly Timesheet form any single activity within that week is automatically inserted into the Weekly Timesheet.

Using the Single Activity Form

Use the Single Activity form when you need to record one event you want to track:

1. Choose Employees | Time Tracking | Time/Enter Single Activity from the menu bar to open the Enter Single Activity window (see Figure 18-2).
2. The Date field is automatically filled in with the current date. If this activity took place previously, change the date.

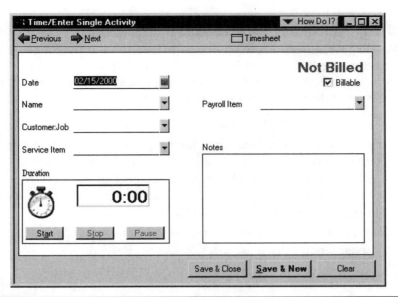

FIGURE 18-2   Everything related to the way you spend time can be entered in the Single Activity form

3. Click the arrow to the right of the Name field and select the name of the person who performed the work from the list. The list contains vendors, employees, and names from the Other Names list.

4. If your time was spent working on a task for a customer, rather than performing an administrative task, select the customer or job in the Customer:Job field. Do this whether or not the customer is going to be billed for the time.

5. In the Service Item field, select the task.

6. Enter the duration of time you're reporting.

7. If this time is billable, the Billable check box should be marked (it is by default). If the time is not going to be billed to the customer, click the box to remove the check mark.

8. If the Payroll Item field appears, select the payroll item that applies to this time (for example, salary or hourly wages). This field only appears if at least one employee has been linked to the time-tracking system, as explained earlier in this chapter.

9. Click in the Notes box to enter any comments or additional information you want to record about this activity.

10. Click Save & New to fill out another Single Activity form, or click Save & Close to finish.

Using Weekly Timesheets

A Weekly Timesheet records the same information as the Single Activity form, except that the information is recorded in week-at-a-time blocks. To use this form, choose Employees | Time Tracking | Use Weekly Timesheet to open the Weekly Timesheet window (see Figure 18-3).

1. Select the name of the person for whom the timesheet is being created.

2. If you want to enter time for a different week, click the Set Date button and enter the first day of any week for which you want to enter activities.

3. Click in the Customer:Job column to display an arrow, which you click to see the Customer list. Select the customer connected to the activity.

4. Enter the service item that describes your activity.

5. If you're an employee, select the Payroll Item that fits the activity.

6. Enter any notes or comments you feel are necessary.

7. Click the column that represents the day for which you are entering a timesheet activity and enter the number of hours worked on this task.

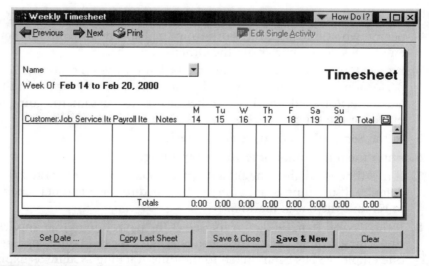

FIGURE 18-3   QuickBooks assumes you want to enter information for the current week

8. Move to the beginning of the next row to enter the next timesheet entry, repeating until you've accounted for your time for the week.

9. For each row, use the TAB key to move to the last column and indicate whether the time is billable. By default, all time entries are billable (the icon is a sheet of paper that's supposed to look like an invoice). Click the icon to put an X over it if the time on this row is not billable.

10. Click Save & New to use a timesheet for a different week. Click Save & Close when you are finished entering time.

 TIP: If this week's timesheet has the same entries as the last timesheet this person filled out, click Copy Last Sheet to move the entries into this timesheet.

Reporting Timesheet Information

Before you use the information on the timesheets, you can check the data and the other important elements (for example, whether billable and non-billable items are accurate). You can edit information, view and customize reports, and print the original timesheets.

Running Timesheet Reports

To run reports on timesheets, choose Reports | Jobs & Time from the QuickBooks menu bar. Use one of the four reports listed at the bottom of the submenu:

- Time by Job Summary reports the amount of time spent for each service on your customers and their jobs.

- Time by Job Detail reports the details of the time spent for each customer and job, including dates and whether or not the time was marked as billable (see Figure 18-4).

- Time by Name reports the amount of time each employee or subcontractor spent on work for your customers and their jobs.

- Time by Item provides a quick analysis of the services your company is providing, and to whom.

If you've made it a practice to encourage people to enter comments in the Notes section of the timesheet, you should change the report format so it

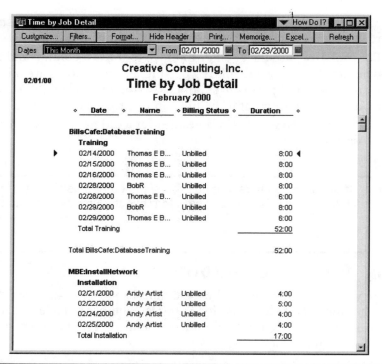

FIGURE 18-4 All the details from timesheets are provided in the Time by Job Detail report

includes those comments. You can do this only in the Time by Job Detail report (refer to Figure 18-4):

1. Open the report and click the Customize button on the button bar.
2. In the Customize Report window, select Notes from the Columns list.

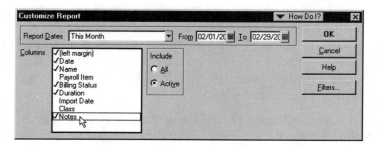

3. Click OK.

To make sure you always see the notes, you should memorize this report. Click the Memorize button on the report button bar and name the report. Hereafter, it will be available in the Memorized Reports list.

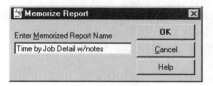

Editing Timesheet Entries

While you're browsing the report, double-click an activity listing to see the original entry, an example of which is seen in Figure 18-5. You can make changes on the original entry if necessary.

In fact, before you use the timesheets for customer billing or payroll, it's a good idea to examine them and make any corrections that are needed. The common revision is the billable status. If you have outside contractors or employees filling out timesheets, it's not unusual to have some confusion about which customers receive direct time billings. In fact, you may have customers

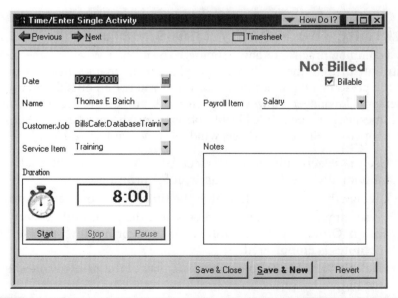

FIGURE 18-5 Check the original entry to see any details not shown in the report

to whom you send direct time bills only for certain activities and provide the remaining activities as part of your basic services.

If you check the timesheets regularly, double-checking them isn't terribly onerous or time-consuming. Just open a timesheet and select the person connected to the timesheet you want to inspect. Use the Prev Week, Next Week, or Set Date button to move to the correct Weekly Timesheet. Then edit the information as necessary:

- You can change the number of hours for any activity item.
- Click the icon in the Billable column (the last column) to reverse the current status (it's a toggle). Line entries that are not billable have an X over the icon.
- To view (and edit if necessary) any notes, first click in any of the weekday columns to activate the Edit Activity button. Then click the Edit Single Activity button at the top of the timesheet window to see the entry as a single activity, with the entire note available for viewing or editing.

 CAUTION: If you've already used the timesheet data to bill the customer or pay the employee, the changes you make are useless. It's too late. Customer invoices and payroll records are not updated with your edits.

Printing the Weekly Timesheets

It's a common practice to have employees print their Weekly Timesheets and distribute them to the appropriate people. Usually that means your payroll person (or the person who phones in the payroll if you use an outside payroll service) or a personnel manager. However, you may want to designate one person to print all the timesheets. Choose File | Print Forms | Timesheets from the QuickBooks menu bar to open the Print Timesheets window shown in Figure 18-6.

- Use the selection buttons to select All or None, or check each name individually to select that timesheet for printing.
- Change the date range to match the timesheets you want to print.
- To see any notes in their entirety, select the Print Full Activity Notes option. Otherwise, the default selection to print only the first line of any notes is empowered.
- Click Preview to see an onscreen display of the printed timesheets (see Figure 18-7).

When the Print window opens, you can change the printer or options. One selection you probably should make is to change the default number of copies if you plan to distribute the printed timesheets to multiple people.

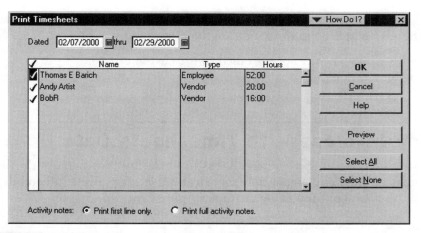

FIGURE 18-6 You can print all the timesheets and distribute them

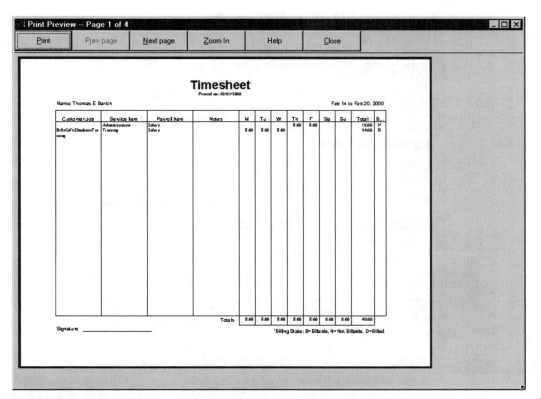

FIGURE 18-7 Each person's timesheet starts on a fresh page, so use the Next Page button to move to the next timesheet

One thing you should notice about printed (or previewed) timesheets is that there's a single column to indicate the billing status. The entries are codes:

- B = billable, but not yet billed to the customer
- N = not billable
- D = billed to the customer

Creating Invoices with Timesheets Data

After you've configured QuickBooks to track time, you can use the data you amass to help you create customer invoices quickly. For a full and detailed discussion about invoicing customers, please turn to Chapter 3.

Plugging in Time Charges

When you're ready to bill customers for time, click Create Invoices on the Navigator Bar:

1. When the Create Invoices window opens (see Figure 18-8), select the customer or job.

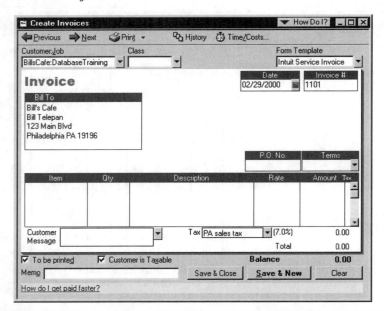

FIGURE 18-8 The customer, job, and date of the invoice determine which time-tracking activities are available for this invoice

Using Timesheets for Internal Controls

In addition to billing his clients from timesheets, attorney Ernie Esquire uses the information to track the activities of his employees, all of whom are salaried (which means he doesn't use timesheet hours for payroll).

Ernie has two office rules and they both influence the way timesheets are configured and filled out:

- Billing time is entered in ten-minute blocks. This policy isn't uncommon in professional offices; it means that no matter how much time is spent on a client's work, the employee must round it up to the next ten-minute figure on the timesheet.
- An employee's day belongs to the company. Every moment of the eight-hour day for which the employee's salary is designated must be reported.

The billing time minimum means that when Ernie examines timesheets he frequently finds many more minutes (or even hours) listed than the actual time the employee spent at work. Within a real ten-minute period, an employee who completes a quick activity for each of three clients can enter 30 minutes on the timesheets.

To permit employees to track their nonclient-related time, Ernie has created a number of additional activity/service items: Lunch, Personal, Thinking. When he set up these items, he configured them for zero value and posted them to a miscellaneous expense account (it doesn't matter because there will never be an invoice for the services, so nothing will ever post). He uses the information he garners from the timesheets to analyze the way employees work and to decide whether or not his employees need assistants.

Because Ernie congratulates employees for effective use of time, including personal and thinking time, there's no particular threat in being honest when they fill in the timesheets. In fact, one of the interesting byproducts of his system is that there are notes frequently appended to the Lunch activity ("Sat near Judge Johnson's clerk at the corner deli and heard that the Judge is planning a long vacation in June, and since we're trying to avoid him for the Jackson case, let's press for a June date"). Similarly, employees sometimes enter notes about their thinking time ("We need more chocolate choices in the vending machine").

2. Enter the date of this invoice (if it isn't today, which is the date that appears by default). Unbilled activities up to and including the invoice date are available for this invoice.

3. Click the Time/Costs button on the invoice form to open the Choose Billable Time and Costs window. Click the Time tab to see the entries from timesheets, as seen in Figure 18-9.

4. Select the entries you want to include on this invoice.

5. If you don't want to change any options (see the following discussion), click OK to transfer the items to the invoice.

Click Save & New to continue to the next invoice, or Save & Close if you are finished creating invoices.

Changing Options for Time Charges

There are a number of changes you can make in the way you transfer data from the timesheets to the invoice. All the necessary tools for accomplishing this are on the Choose Billable Time and Costs window that opens when you click the Time/Costs button on the Create Invoices window.

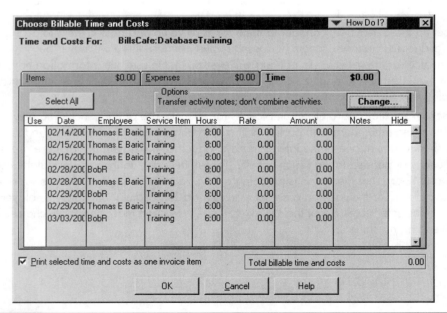

FIGURE 18-9 The timesheet entries for this customer are collected and displayed so you can choose the ones you want to include on the invoice

Print One Invoice Item

Click the check box next to the selection named Print Selected Time And Costs As One Invoice Item. Instead of individual items, the total charges to the customer are printed in a single line item on the invoice. The name and description of the line are taken from your Group entry in your items list. See Chapter 2 for information on creating items.

This one will drive you crazy unless you take the word Print literally. After you make the selection and return to the invoice form, you see every individual item listed on the invoice, with individual totals for each item. The only thing that's different is that the top line has the name of your Group entry, although there's no amount displayed for that line item.

Don't worry, it prints as one item; the onscreen invoice is not the same as the printed invoice any more. If you're a skeptic, click the Preview button to see what the printed invoice will look like (told ya so!).

Combine Service Items

In the Options section of the window, click the Change button to change the way data is transferred to the invoice (see Figure 18-10).

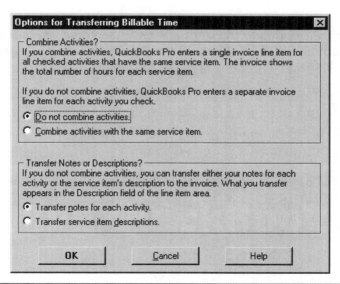

FIGURE 18-10 You can change the way the timesheet information is transferred to an invoice

Select one of the options in the Combine Activities section of the Options window:

- If you do not combine activities, there's a separate line item on the invoice for each activity.
- If you do combine activities, a total for each activity type is placed on one line item in the invoice. For example, if you have Consulting and Training as services, and there are several activities for each of those services, the invoice will have a line item for Consulting and another line item for Training. Each line will have the total for that service.

In the Transfer Notes or Descriptions section of the Options window, you can choose what is printed in the Description column of the invoice:

- Select the option to transfer notes if you want the Description field to contain the notes from the timesheet entry.

 CAUTION: Don't transfer notes unless you check every timesheet to make sure an employee hasn't entered a note you'd prefer the customer didn't see. Delete any such notes from the activity window when you edit the timesheets.

- Select the option to transfer the service item description if you want the Description field filled in with the description attached to the service item.

Using Timesheets for Payroll and Job Costing

In this chapter, you will learn to...

- Configure payroll records
- Run payroll checks
- Configure services and reports for job costing

When you turn on time tracking, you can connect it to your QuickBooks payroll functions. This ability to track the information on the timesheets and transfer it to payroll does more than create paychecks—you can use it for job costing by tracking your payroll expenses against jobs.

Setting Up Timesheet Data

You must tell the QuickBooks payroll function about every employee you want to link to timesheets. Actually, QuickBooks offers some assistance for configuring existing employees when you first begin using timesheets.

The first time you enter an employee's name on a timesheet (either a single activity form or a weekly timesheet), QuickBooks asks you if you want to use the data from timesheets to pay this employee.

- If you answer Yes, the employee's record is marked for time tracking.
- If you answer No and later decide that wasn't the correct answer, you must manually configure the employee record.

Configuring the Employee Record

To link an employee to time tracking, you must select the time-tracking option on the Payroll Info tab of the employee record (see Figure 19-1).

To accomplish this for an existing employee, open the Employee List and select the employee. Click the Employee button and choose Edit to open the record. Move to the Payroll Info tab.

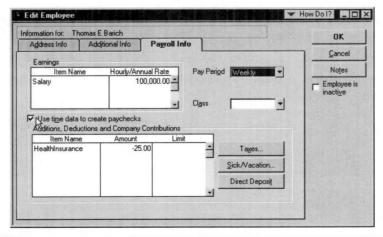

FIGURE 19-1   Link an employee's paycheck to his or her timesheets

When you enter a new employee, remember to select the link to time tracking when you enter information on the Payroll Info tab. To do this, click the check box next to the "Use time data to create paychecks" option.

 TIP: Link salaried employees to time tracking to create reports on job costing.

Configuring Payroll Preferences

If your time tracking is just as important for job-costing analysis as it is for making payroll easier, you can configure your payroll reporting for that purpose:

1. Choose Edit | Preferences from the menu bar.
2. Move to the Payroll section and click the Company Preferences tab.
3. At the bottom of the window (see Figure 19-2), enable the reporting of payroll taxes by Customer:Job, Service Item, and Class. If you're not using Classes, that option isn't available.
4. Click OK to save your preferences.

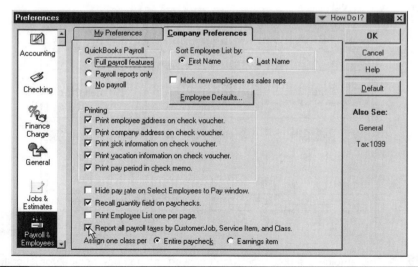

FIGURE 19-2 You can sort the information about the cost of payroll to aid in your job-cost analysis efforts

Training Employees to Use Timesheets

If your employees only keep timesheets to indicate the billable work they do, that's not going to do much to automate the payroll process. Few employees will have a full 40-hour week (see Figure 19-3), and you'll have to fill in the remaining information manually when you create the paycheck.

- Create at least one payroll item to cover nonbillable work. You can call it administration, in-office, or any other designation. No customers are attached to these entries.
- Make sure employees account for every hour of the day and every day of the week.
- Have employees fill in days for sick pay or vacation pay on their timesheets. Those items are probably already part of your payroll items.

Running Payroll with Timesheets Data

When it's time to run the payroll, you can use the data from the timesheets to create the paychecks:

1. Click the Pay Employees item on the Navigation Bar.
2. When the Select Employees To Pay window opens (see Figure 19-4), select the option to enter hours and preview the check.
3. Select the employees to pay.
4. Click Create.

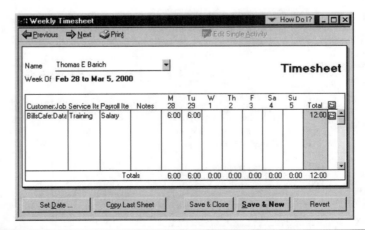

FIGURE 19-3   This employee's timesheet won't convert to a full paycheck automatically—the hours don't add up

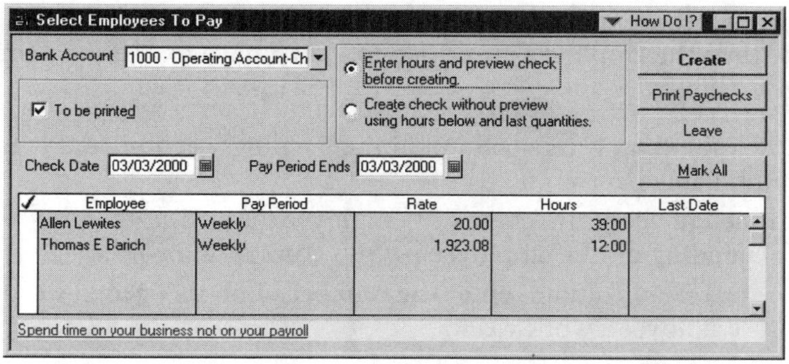

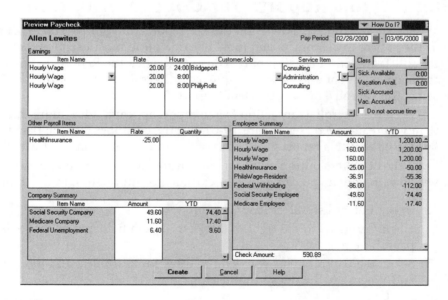

FIGURE 19-4 Select the option to preview the checks

Each employee's paycheck is previewed. Some hourly employees will have billable hours that filled their week, and other employees may have administrative tasks that filled their week (see Figure 19-5). Still others will have entered only the billable hours, and you'll have to fill in the rest yourself.

FIGURE 19-5 You can adjust the number of hours to make sure the employee's paycheck is for the correct amount

If the timesheet data that is transferred to the paycheck doesn't account for all the time the employee is entitled to, you'll have to add the administrative items yourself:

1. Click the Item Name column in the Earnings section, and enter a nonbillable payroll item.
2. In the Rate column, enter this employee's annual rate or hourly rate (depending on the employee payroll configuration).
3. In the Hours column, enter the number of hours needed to complete this employee's work week.
4. Click Create.

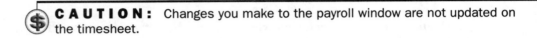

CAUTION: Changes you make to the payroll window are not updated on the timesheet.

See Chapter 8 for detailed information about creating payroll checks.

Running Payroll Reports for Cost Information

When you use time tracking, you can see reports on your payroll expenses as they relate to customers and jobs. The one I find most useful is the Payroll Transaction Detail report. To get to it, click the Reports listing on the Navigation Bar and choose Employee & Payroll as the report type. Then, select the Payroll Transaction Detail report.

When the Payroll Transaction Detail report appears, it has more information than you really need (see Figure 19-6), but the customer and job data is there. I've found that this report needs a bit of customization to make it useful.

Click the Filters button on the report buttonbar to open the Report Filter window, in which you can get rid of extraneous information in this report:

1. In the Filters list, select Payroll Item.
2. Click the arrow to the right of the Payroll Item field and choose Selected payroll items.
3. Select the payroll items you want to track for customers and jobs; Salary and Wages are the ones I find useful.
4. Click OK.
5. I also find it useful to click the Customize button and deselect the Wage Base column, because it's not important to me.

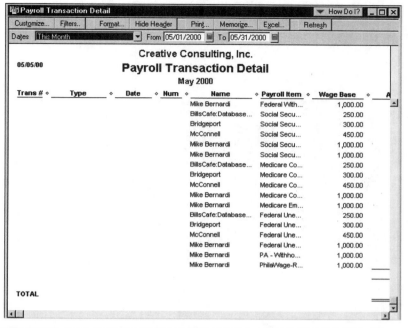

FIGURE 19-6 Every detail about each paycheck is noted, including the amounts charged to customers and jobs

Click the Memorize button to make this configuration permanent, giving it a name that reminds you of why you need the report.

Now you're all set! You can get the information you need whenever you need it.

Using the Onscreen Timer

In this chapter, you will learn to...

- Install Timer

- Make copies for others

- Use Timer

- Export activities

- Export information to Timer users

- Import files from Timer

If you have QuickBooks Pro, you can install a Timer program that permits you and other people connected to your company to track time automatically. It works by providing an onscreen clock that ticks away as you perform tasks. Each time you start a task you tell Timer what you're doing and the program keeps track of the amount of time it takes to complete each task.

Installing Timer

The Timer software must be installed separately; you can perform the installation when you first install QuickBooks or wait until you have your QuickBooks system up and running properly. You can also give copies of the program to employees, subcontractors, or anyone else whose time you must track in order to send invoices to customers or to perform cost analysis. Those folks do not have to have QuickBooks installed on their computers.

The Timer program works separately; you cannot launch it from within QuickBooks Pro. It has its own menu choice on your computer's Program menu.

You can interact with Timer from QuickBooks, importing and exporting files between QuickBooks Pro and the Timer software.

Installing the Program Files

To use Timer, you must install it on your computer. Before you begin the installation, close any programs that are open. Then open the QuickBooks CD-ROM and choose Install QuickBooks Pro Timer.

 TIP: If you installed QuickBooks from floppy disks, there are separate floppy disks for Timer. Start with Disk #1 (there are three disks). Choose Run from the Start menu and enter **a:install.exe**.

The installation program displays the directory into which Timer will be installed. If you have some reason to move the software to a different directory, choose Browse and select another location.

Click Next to see the next installation window, which is where the installation program displays the location of the Start menu folder that will contain the Timer program. This should be the QuickBooks section of the Start menu, but it doesn't matter—what's important is that a program item will appear on your menu. Click Next to approve the choice.

The files are transferred to your hard drive, which takes only a short time. (If you're installing from floppy disks, you'll be prompted to change disks as necessary.) Then the installation program notifies you that the files have been installed, and you must restart your computer to use the software. Choose Yes or No, depending on whether you want to restart your computer immediately or do it yourself later, and then click Finish.

After you've restarted the computer, the Timer software is on your Programs menu, in the submenu under your QuickBooks menu item.

Creating Disks for Others

Everybody who performs work for you should have a copy of the Timer program. (This is perfectly legal and your QuickBooks Pro Timer software license permits it.) As they track their activities, the data is saved in files that you can import to fill out timesheets. The information in the files includes the customer for whom the work is being performed, the amount of time, and all the other information a timesheet should track. Using Timer is far more efficient and accurate than relying on everyone's memory.

The folks you distribute this software to do not have to have QuickBooks on their computers. Timer is an independent program.

If you installed Timer from a floppy disk, make a copy of each disk for each person who needs the software. Be sure to write accurate information on the label of each copied disk (Disk #1, Disk #2, and so on) so the recipients know which disks are which.

If you installed Timer from your QuickBooks CD-ROM, Timer includes a program that lets you create disks for the distribution of the Timer program:

1. Label three blank formatted floppy disks (one for each disk number).

 T I P : Be sure you indicate the word "Timer" on the floppy disk labels; it's confusing to your recipients to have a disk labeled #1 without a software name indicated.

2. Put the QuickBooks CD-ROM in the CD-ROM drive. If it starts the installation program automatically, click the X in the upper-right corner of the window to close the program.
3. Put the disk labeled Timer Disk #1 into your floppy disk drive.

4. Click the Start button on your taskbar and move to Programs. Then move to the QuickBooks Pro program item to display the submenu. Click the submenu program item named Create Timer Install Disks.

The wizard asks questions and provides instructions, all of which are easy to handle. Just keep going until the three disks are created. It takes a while, by the way, and part of the reason is that CD-ROMs aren't as fast as hard drives and floppy disk drives are slower than snails.

After the first set of floppy disks is created you can either repeat the process, or use the disks themselves to make copies.

Installing Timer Disks You Receive

On the receiving end, the installation of Timer disks is straightforward and easy. You can give these directions to your recipient. Or perhaps you are your own recipient—you might have multiple computers in your office and want to install the Timer program on a computer that is used by an employee to track his or her time.

1. Put floppy Disk #1 into your floppy disk drive and click the Start button on the taskbar.
2. Choose Run from the Start menu.
3. In the Open text box enter **a:\install**.
4. Click OK.

At this point, everything is the same as I described earlier in this chapter in the instructions for installing the Timer software. Well, there is one difference—if QuickBooks isn't installed on this computer, the Programs menu listing won't be placed in the QuickBooks menu group (since it doesn't exist). Instead, a discrete menu entry is added to your Programs menu for Timer. Remember that you'll have to restart your computer after the installation is complete in order to use the Timer program.

Exporting Data Lists to Timer Users

You must export information from your company files to the Timer program so the program has data to use. The information is the data in your lists: employees, customers (and jobs), vendors, and service items. If you're using classes in QuickBooks, that data is also exported.

1. Choose File | Timer | Export Lists for Timer from the QuickBooks menu bar.
2. The Export Lists for Timer window opens, as seen in Figure 20-1.
3. Click OK to begin the export process.

The graphic describes the processes between QuickBooks and Timer.

Click OK to begin exporting the data.

Click here if you want to skip this explanatory window the next time you transfer data.

FIGURE 20-1 Export the data needed by Timer users to a file

When the Export window opens (see Figure 20-2), choose a location for the file and give the file a name, using the following guidelines:

- *If you are creating the export file for your own use, save it in a folder on your hard drive.* The default folder is your QuickBooks folder, which is as good a choice as any.
- *If you are creating an export file on a floppy disk for another user, click the arrow to the right of the Save In field and choose your floppy drive.* Make sure you have a blank, formatted floppy disk in the drive.
- *If you are creating the export file for another user and you're going to send it via e-mail, you can save it to any folder on your hard drive.* However, it's faster if you save it to the default folder that is selected by your e-mail software when you choose to upload a file.
- *Give the file a name that will remind you of the company to which the data is attached.* For instance, if the company name is A.J. Backstroke, Inc. you might want to name the export file AJB.
- *Don't forget to delete the asterisk (*) that QuickBooks places in the filename box.*
- *Make sure the file extension is .iif.*

Click Save to save the export file. QuickBooks displays a message announcing that the data has been exported successfully. Now you can use the file and give it to any Timer user.

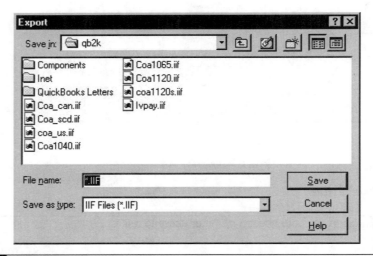

FIGURE 20-2 Give the export file a name and save it to a folder or a floppy disk

Incidentally, you only have to save this file once, even if you're shipping it to multiple Timer users. You can make your own copy, saving it on your hard drive. Then copy that file to a floppy disk as many times as you need to, or upload it via e-mail.

Using Timer

You use Timer to track your work and report the time you spend on each task. In order to report your time, the Timer software keeps a data file. That file can be brought into QuickBooks and imported into a timesheet. Then, you get paid for the time.

You don't have to have QuickBooks installed on your computer to use Timer. You do, however, have to have information about the company for which you're doing the work. That information is contained in files you import to your Timer software (the same files I discussed in the previous section). Then, when you use Timer, you can configure your tasks to tell the software who you are, what services you're performing, and which customer is being serviced.

Using Timer for the First Time

The first time you use Timer you have a little setup work to do, after which you can go onto autopilot.

Start Timer by choosing Start | Programs | QuickBooks Pro Timer. When the software opens for the first time, there's no file established for saving the data. Timer offers three choices for remedying this problem, as shown in the following illustration.

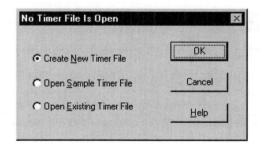

Select Create New Timer File. Then click OK.

TIP: QuickBooks provides a sample data file you can use to explore and play with, but this software is easy enough to use that you can jump right in and create your own file.

When the New Timer File window opens (see Figure 20-3), enter a filename for your personal Timer data. It's a good idea to use your name or initials, because Timer files are connected to a specific user. If you expect to keep files for multiple companies, make the filename a reflection of both the company name and your own name. For example, if your name is Debby Doright and you perform tasks for companies named Creative Consultants and WeAreWidgets, you might create one file named DDCC and another file named DDWAW.

The filename must have an extension of .tdb.

The newtimer file is a template used by Timer; you cannot open it.

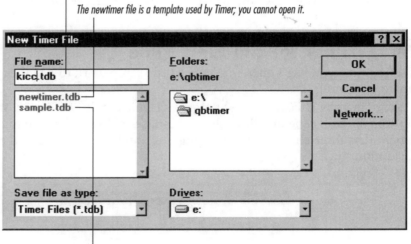

The sample file can be used to play around in Timer and get used to it.

FIGURE 20-3   This filename reflects the company and my initials

Click OK to save the filename. Timer displays a message telling you that you must import company information before you can use your new file and offering to open a Help file that explains how to perform this task. You can click No, because the instructions are available right here.

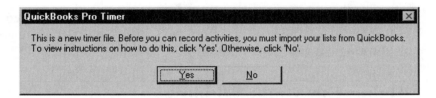

The Timer window is on your screen and the name of your file is on the title bar. However, because no data file is attached to it (yet), the important menu items aren't accessible.

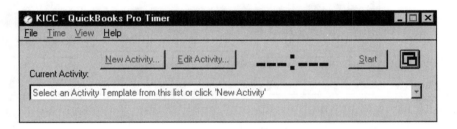

Luckily, since you read the explanation about how to create the data file earlier in this chapter, a file with the needed data has been created and exported so you can import it (when you control all sides of this process, it's terribly efficient).

1. Choose File | Import QuickBooks Lists from the menu bar of the Timer window to open the Import QuickBooks Lists window (which is the same window you saw when you created the export file).
2. Click Continue to display the Open File For Import window.
3. If the folder displayed in the right pane of the window is not the location of the exported file, move through your computer's drives and folders to choose the right folder. If the file is on a floppy disk, click the arrow to the right of the Drives field and select the floppy disk drive.
4. Select the file that has been prepared for you and click OK.

TIP: Make sure the person who prepared the file for your Timer software tells you the filename, because there may be multiple export files (files with .iif extensions) in a folder.

Timer displays a message telling you that the file was imported successfully. Click OK to clear the message from the screen. Now it's time to go to work—and track your time as you work.

Using the Timer Window

The Timer software window opens and now all the menu items are accessible. However, you have to set up an activity before the software can do its job.

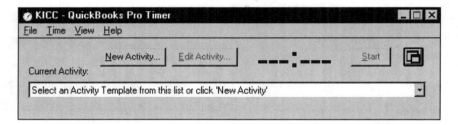

Setting Up an Activity

Click the New Activity button to open the New Activity window (see Figure 20-4) so you can establish an activity.

The date is automatically filled in with the current date, and all the other fields are very easy to fill in. You just have to click the arrow to the right of each field to see the list that's been imported from the company you're working with. (Of course, there's no preconfigured list for the Notes field, which you can use to make comments.) If the activity is billable to the customer, be sure that option is selected.

 TIP: Your name must be in the list that appears in the Your Name field, which means you've either been established as an employee, a vendor, or an "other name" in the original company's files.

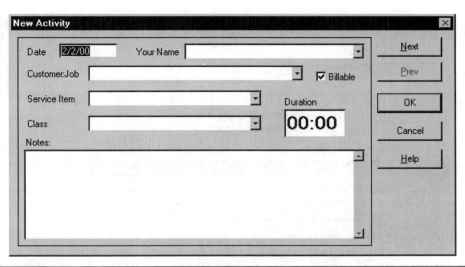

FIGURE 20-4 Designing an activity means specifying who, for whom, and what

CAUTION: There is no option to add a new item to any list; you can only work with the items provided by the company's imported file.

After you've configured this activity, click Next to set up another activity or click OK to finish entering activities and return to the Timer window. Now the Timer window is ready to let you work (see Figure 20-5).

TIP: Whether you leave the Timer window at its opening size, or reduce it to a little square digital readout of time (like a digital clock), you can move it to a corner of your screen by dragging the title bar.

The activity you design acts like a template. It's available all the time and when you use it to time your activities, a copy of the template is loaded and that copy is used for today's work (Timer works by the day).

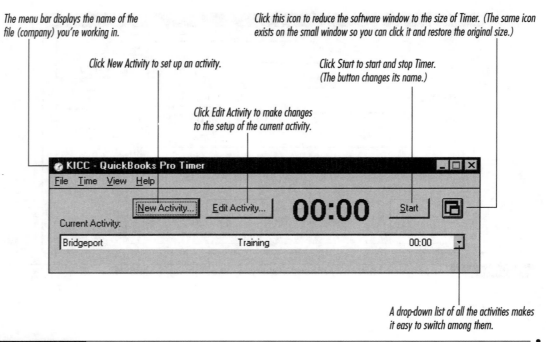

The menu bar displays the name of the file (company) you're working in.

Click New Activity to set up an activity.

Click Edit Activity to make changes to the setup of the current activity.

Click this icon to reduce the software window to the size of Timer. (The same icon exists on the small window so you can click it and restore the original size.)

Click Start to start and stop Timer. (The button changes its name.)

A drop-down list of all the activities makes it easy to switch among them.

FIGURE 20-5 The Timer window is ready to go!

Editing the Activity

Click the Edit Activity button to open a window with the original fields for the current activity. Then make the changes you need to make. Commonly, the changes involve a different service item or a change as to whether or not this is billable work.

Timing Your Work

Go to work. That might mean you're doing research, making telephone calls, building an ark, writing a white paper, or anything else for which the company pays you (and probably bills its customers).

1. Choose the activity from the Activity bar.
2. Click the Start button. The Activity bar indicates that timing is activated, and the elapsed minutes appear on the Timer window.

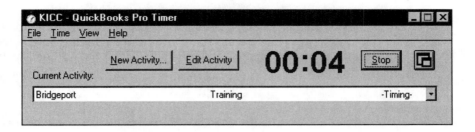

3. If you need to stop working for a while, click the Stop button. The button changes its name to Resume.

4. If you stop working because you've finished the task, you can create another activity, choose a different activity from the Activity bar, or close the software.

Each day, as you work with Timer, you can choose an activity from the Activity bar. As you switch from activity to activity in the same day, you're resuming the activity, not starting a new one. In fact, when you return to an activity any time in the same day, the Resume button is active.

Setting Timer Preferences

After you've used Timer for a while you may want to set preferences so the software works the way you prefer. To accomplish this, choose File | Preferences from the Timer menu bar to display the submenu.

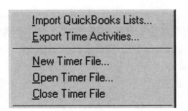

The most useful preference is the one that enters a default name every time you create a new activity. That name, of course, should be your own name. When you select this option, the Choose a Default Name window opens so you can select your name from the list. You can also set a default option for whether or not your work is billable to customers.

TIP: If more than one person uses Timer on your computer, it's probably better not to enter a default name. However, if you do enter a default name, the other user just has to choose the activity and click the Edit Activity button to change the name.

Exporting Your Time Files

When you've completed your tasks or stopped for the day, you can send the company the information about your working hours. Some companies may want daily reports; others may want you to wait until you've completed a project.

Viewing the Log

Before you send your files back to QuickBooks, you should take a look at the information. Choose View | Time Activity Log from the Timer menu bar. When the Time Activity Log window opens, it shows today's activities (see Figure 20-6).

If you wish, you can view a larger range of activities by changing the dates covered by this log. Click the arrow to the right of the Dates field and choose a different interval.

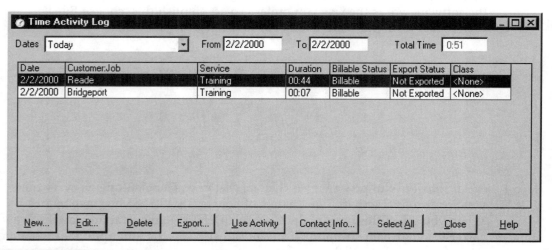

| **FIGURE 20-6** | What did you do today? |

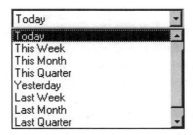

You can also enter dates directly in the From and To fields.

Editing an Entry

You can change the information in any entry by selecting it from the list and clicking the Edit button (see Figure 20-7). The most common reason to do this is to change the time, especially if you worked on this activity away from your computer. Enter the new time in the Duration field in the format *HH:MM* and click OK.

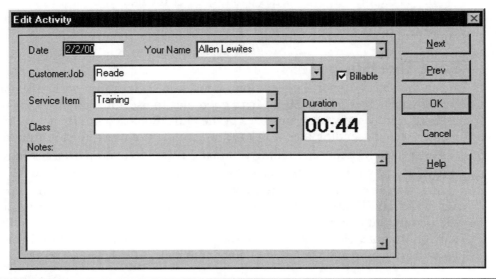

FIGURE 20-7 You can make adjustments or add notes before you export an activity

Creating an Export File

If you want to get paid, you must export your information to QuickBooks so your timesheet reflects your work. You can either choose specific entries for export, or export all the information in your Timer system.

Choose Specific Entries

You might want to choose only specific entries for export:

1. Open the Time Activity Log.
2. Click the first entry you want to export.
3. Hold down the CTRL key as you click any additional entries.
4. Choose Export from the Time Activity Log window.

Send All Your Entries

You could also choose to export everything:

1. Choose File | Export Time Activities from the Timer menu bar.
2. Click Continue if the opening explanation window is displayed. (Remember, you can select the option to stop showing this window.)
3. In the Export Time Activities window enter the date you want to use as the cut-off date for selecting activities.
4. Click OK.

Save the File

When the Create Export File window opens, select a location for the file and give it a name (see Figure 20-8). It's a good idea to use your initials in the name so there won't be any problems back at the QuickBooks computer if multiple Timer users are sending files. Click OK when you've entered the information.

Timer displays a message telling you that the file was exported successfully. When you view your activity log, it reflects the export process (see Figure 20-9).

After you've exported an activity, it's still available in the Activity bar for the rest of the day (it disappears tomorrow). Don't use it. Even though QuickBooks will permit you to export it again with the new number for time spent on the activity, it's not a clean way to work (although you do get a warning). Instead, open the template and start a new Timer activity.

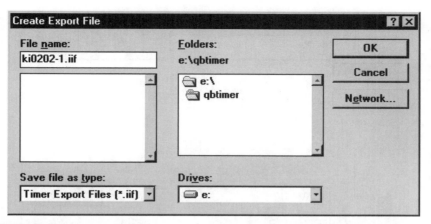

FIGURE 20-8 Save the export file that will be imported into QuickBooks

Importing Timer Files into QuickBooks Pro

When you receive Timer files from employees and subcontractors, you must import them into QuickBooks. This is a simple process, and QuickBooks takes care of putting the information you've received into the appropriate files.

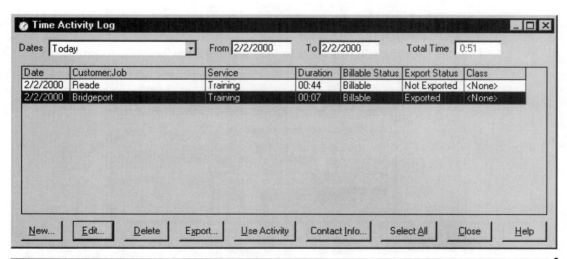

FIGURE 20-9 The activity log tracks your exports

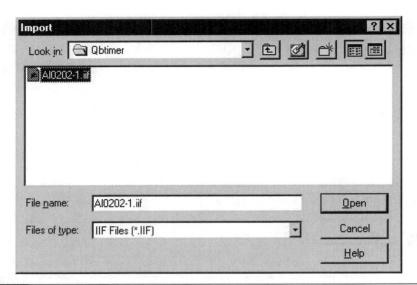

FIGURE 20-10 Select the folder or drive that contains the export file you've received

Importing the File

On the QuickBooks menu bar, choose File | Timer | Import Activities from Timer. This opens the Import window, and you must specify the location of the file in the Look In field in order to see the exported files that are available (see Figure 20-10).

Double-click the file you want to use. It takes a few seconds to import the file, then you're notified that the data has been imported successfully.

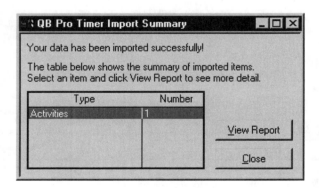

Handling Multiuser Activities in Timer

ABC Engineers is a consulting firm, and most of their work is as a subcontractor to another company. One of their clients uses QuickBooks Pro and ABC has received the Timer software, along with instructions to use it for tracking the time they spend working for this client company.

Three of the ABC employees are assigned to this client and each employee installed the Timer software on his own computer. The Names list on the file that was imported from the client contained a listing for ABC Engineers and all three employees made this name the default for all activities.

As work is completed on the computer, on paper, and via telephone calls (they track the time used in conversations with the client), Timer runs.

Every Friday afternoon each employee exports a file that covers all unexported activities up to the current date and sends it back to the client company via e-mail. The filename contains the employee initials, so three separate files are received by the client.

Back at their client company, the files are imported into QuickBooks Pro. This automatically places the information into timesheets. Since ABC Engineers is a vendor/subcontractor, there are no payroll issues to worry about.

In the Payroll and Time tab of the Navigation Bar, the QuickBooks user goes to the Reports listing and clicks the Project icon. Then the Time by Name report is run so that the information on time is sorted by the name of the person who performed tasks with Timer. The ABC timesheet entries are displayed, along with a total.

A customer invoice is created. Clicking the Time/Costs button on the Invoice window produces a list of all the timesheets entries connected to the customer on the Time tab. Some of the entries are from in-house employees and were accumulated through the use of a timesheet. Other entries have been imported from the Timer program. The appropriate charges are marked for billing and the invoice is completed automatically.

If you want to see details, select an item and click View Report to see a Timer Import Detail report, as shown in Figure 20-11.

You can double-click on a line item in the report to see even more details.

Using Timesheets with Timer Data

What makes all of this seem almost miraculous is the way you can use this data without doing anything. It's just there, waiting for you. Timer data is sent to the user's timesheet and from there on, everything is on autopilot.

- *Open the Weekly Timesheets and select the name of the person who sent you the Timer file.* Voilà! Everything's there.

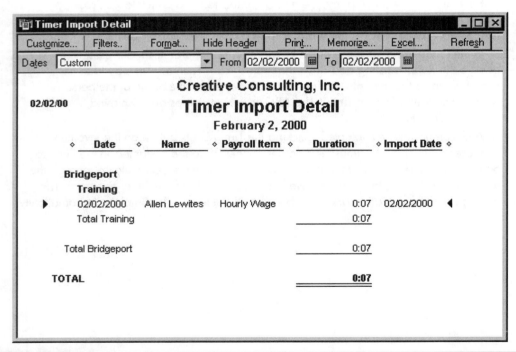

FIGURE 20-11   The report lists the activities that are in the Timer file

- *Skip the timesheets and head right into the Create Paychecks program.* Once again, everything's there (having been transferred from the timesheets).

See Chapter 18 for more information about using timesheets, and Chapter 19 for information about integrating timesheets with payroll.

Managing QuickBooks

All software needs TLC, and accounting software needs regular maintenance to ensure its accuracy and usefulness.

In Part Four of this book, you'll learn how to customize QuickBooks so it works more efficiently, matching the way you like to work. The chapters in Part Four cover the features and tools you can use to make QuickBooks even more powerful. In addition, you'll learn how to maintain the file system, create additional company files, and use QuickBooks in network mode (so more than one person can be working in QuickBooks at the same time).

Of course, I'm going to cover backing up your data, which is the most important maintenance task in the world. Once you put your accounting data into QuickBooks, your business life depends on it. Hard drives die, motherboards freak out, power supplies go to la-la land, and all sorts of other calamities are just waiting to happen. We'll discuss the preventive measures you can take to make sure your business continues to live after your computer dies.

Part Four

Customizing
QuickBooks

n this chapter, you will learn to...

- Change general preferences
- Customize the Navigation Bar
- Create users and passwords
- Use QuickBooks on a network
- Create classes

QuickBooks, "out of the box," is set to run efficiently, providing powerful bookkeeping tools that are easy to use. However, you may have specific requirements because of the way you run your company, the way your accountant likes things done, or the way you use your computer. No matter what your special requirements are, it's likely that QuickBooks can accommodate you.

Changing Preferences

The preferences you establish in QuickBooks have a great impact on the way data is kept and reported. It's not uncommon for QuickBooks users to change or tweak these preferences periodically. In fact, the more you use QuickBooks and understand the way it works, the more comfortable you'll be about changing preferences.

You can reach the Preferences window by choosing Edit | Preferences from the QuickBooks menu bar. When the Preferences window opens, the General section of the window is selected (see Figure 21-1).

The My Preferences tab is where you configure your preferences as a QuickBooks user. Each user you create in QuickBooks can set his or her own preferences, and QuickBooks will remember them when that user logs in to the software.

The Company Preferences tab is the place to configure the way QuickBooks accounting features work for the current company.

As you select options and move from one section of the Preferences window to another, you'll be asked to save the changes in the section you just completed.

Setting General Preferences

Since the Preferences window starts us in the General section, let's begin there. Like all the other sections, the General section offers two tabs:

- My Preferences, which sets preferences for your entire QuickBooks system.
- Company Preferences, which sets preferences for the current company. You can have entirely different preferences for each company you create in QuickBooks.

TIP: Most of the sections in the Preferences window have options available only on one tab, not both.

Click these icons to move to sections of the Preferences window.

Each section contains two tabs (but not all sections have options available on both tabs).

The Default button resets everything to its out-of-the-box configuration.

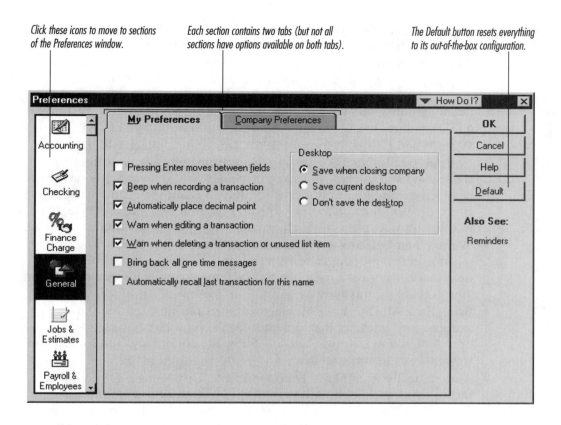

FIGURE 21-1 Use the Preferences window to choose the options you need to use QuickBooks

Setting My Preferences for the General Section

The My Preferences tab of the General section offers a number of options you can select:

- **Pressing Enter Moves Between Fields** This option exists for people who constantly forget that the normal key for moving from field to field in Windows software is the TAB key. Of course, when they press ENTER, the record they're working on is saved even though they haven't finished filling out all the fields. Rather than force users to learn Windows procedures, QuickBooks lets you change the procedures to match your instincts.

- **Beep When Recording A Transaction** This is inaccurate; it's not a beep you hear, it's the *ka-ching!* noise of a cash register. Deselect the option to turn it off.

- **Automatically Place Decimal Point**   This is a handy feature if you can get used to it. It means that when you enter numbers in a field (usually dollar amounts) a decimal point is placed to the left of the last two digits. Therefore, if you type 5421, when you move to the next field the number automatically becomes 54.21. It means that if you want to type in even dollar amounts, you have to enter the zeros, as in 6500, which becomes 65.00 (without this feature, entering 65 would result in 65.00).

- **Warn When Editing A Transaction**   This option, which is selected by default, tells QuickBooks to flash a warning when you change any transaction and then try to close the window without explicitly saving the changed transaction. This means you have a chance to abandon the edits. If you deselect the option, the edited transaction is saved, unless it is linked to other transactions (in which case the warning message appears).

- **Warn When Deleting A Transaction Or Unused List Item**   This option, when selected, produces a warning when you delete a transaction or an item that has not been used in a transaction. (Actually it's a message asking you to confirm your action.)

- **Bring Back All One Time Messages**   One-time messages are those introductory windows that include a Don't Show This Message Again option. If you've selected the Don't Show Me option, select this check box to see those messages again.

- **Automatically Recall Last Transaction For This Name**   This option means that QuickBooks will present the last transaction for any name (for instance, a vendor) in full whenever you use that name. This is useful for repeating transactions, but you can turn this off if you find it annoying.

There are also some choices for the way you want QuickBooks to present the desktop (the QuickBooks window):

- **Save When Closing Company** means that the state of the desktop is remembered when you close the company (or exit QuickBooks). Whatever QuickBooks windows were open when you left will reappear when you return. You can pick up where you left off.

- **Save Current Desktop** lets you save the configuration of the QuickBooks desktop as it is at this moment and use it as the opening desktop when you work in this company. If you choose this option (not really a terrific idea) an additional choice named Keep Previously Saved Desktop appears on the window.

- **Don't Save The Desktop** tells QuickBooks to display an empty QuickBooks desktop when you open this company.

Setting Company Preferences for the General Section

The Company Preferences tab in the General section has three choices:

- **Time Format**   Select a format for entering time, choosing between Decimal (for example, 11.5 hours) or Minutes (11:30).
- **Always Show Years As 4 Digits**   If you prefer to display the year with four digits (1/1/2000 instead of 1/1/00), select this option.
- **Never Update Name Information When Saving Transactions**   By default, QuickBooks asks if you want to update the original information for a list item when you change it during a transaction entry. For example, if you're entering a vendor bill and you change the address, QuickBooks offers an opportunity to make that change back on the vendor record. If you don't want to be offered this opportunity, select this option.

Setting Accounting Preferences

Click the Accounting icon on the left pane of the Preferences window to move to the Accounting preferences. There are only Company Preferences available for this section; the My Preferences tab has no options available (see Figure 21-2).

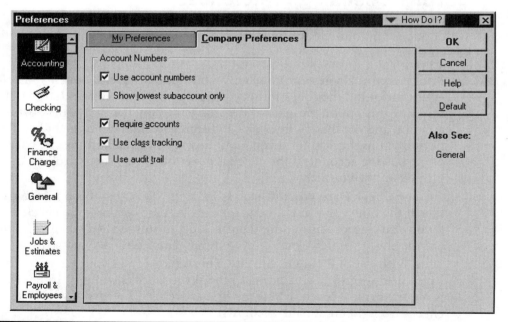

FIGURE 21-2   Choose the accounting options you need to run your company efficiently

- **Use Account Numbers**   Choose this option if you want to use numbers for your chart of accounts in addition to names.
- **Show Lowest Subaccount Only**   This option is useful because it means that when you see an account name in a field (in a transaction window), you only see the subaccount. If the option is not selected you see the parent account followed by the subaccount, and since the field display doesn't show the entire text unless you scroll through it, it's hard to determine which account has been selected.
- **Require Accounts**   Select this option to require that every transaction you enter in QuickBooks has to be assigned to an account.
- **Use Class Tracking**   This option turns on the Class feature for your QuickBooks system (which is discussed later in this chapter).
- **Use Audit Trail**   Select this option to keep a log of changed transactions (not a log of all transactions, just those that are changed after they're first entered). What's important about this option is that deleted transactions are listed in the audit trail. To see the audit log, click the Reports listing on the Navigation Bar. Choose the Accountant & Taxes report type, then choose Audit Trail.

Setting Checking Preferences

This section, in which only Company Preferences is available, is concerned with options for your checking accounts. Some of them may be more important to you than others:

- **Print Account Names On Voucher**   This option is useful only if you print your checks and the check forms you purchase have vouchers (stubs). If so, selecting this option means that the stub will show the Payee, the posting account, and the first 16 lines of any memo you entered on the bill you're paying. If the check is for inventory items, the item name appears instead of the posting account. If the check is a payroll check, the payroll items are printed on the voucher.
- **Change Check Date When Check Is Printed**   Selecting this option means that at the time you print checks, the current date becomes the check date. If you don't select this option, the check date you specified when you filled out the check window is used (even if that date has already passed).
- **Start With Payee Field On Check**   This option forces your cursor to the Payee field when you first bring up the Write Checks window. If the option is off, the bank account field is the first active field (needed if you write checks from different bank accounts).

- **Warn About Duplicate Check Numbers** When this option is selected (which it is, by default) QuickBooks will warn you if a check number you're filling in already exists.

- **Autofill Vendor Account Number In Check Memo** Most vendors maintain an account number for their customers, and your account number can be automatically printed when you print checks. In order for this to occur, you must fill in your account number in the Vendor card (on the Additional Information tab).

Setting Finance Charge Preferences

Another section with Company Preferences only, this is the place to turn on, turn off, and configure finance charges (see Figure 21-3).

Finance charges can get a bit complicated, so read the complete discussion about this topic in Chapter 5.

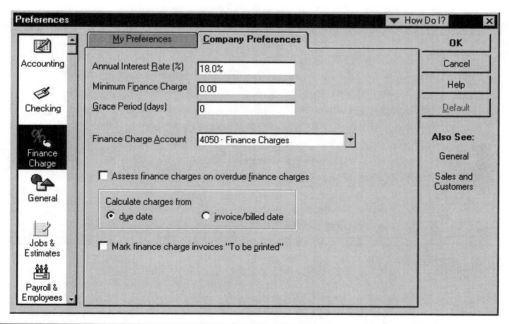

FIGURE 21-3 Configure the way you want to impose finance charges on your customers

Setting Jobs & Estimates Preferences

For QuickBooks Pro, you can configure the way your estimates and invoices work, as shown in Figure 21-4.

Setting Payroll & Employees Preferences

Use the Company Preferences tab of this section of the Preferences window to set all the configuration options for payroll (see Figure 21-5).

Read Chapter 8 to understand the selections in this window.

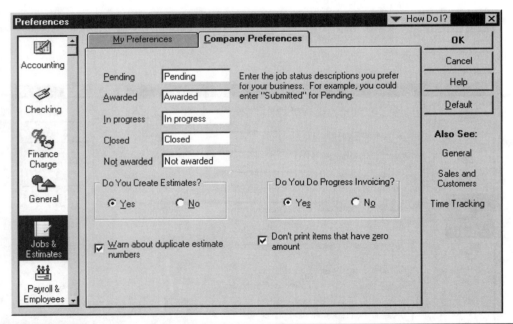

FIGURE 21-4 Turn estimating on and off, and configure the lingo you want to use

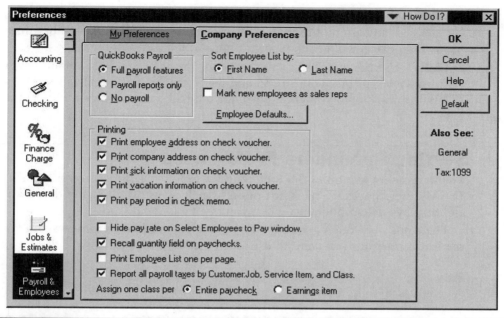

FIGURE 21-5 You'll probably return to this window many times to reset options as you fine-tune the payroll feature

Setting Purchases & Vendors Preferences

The Company Preferences tab has several configuration options for using purchase orders and paying vendor bills:

- **Inventory And Purchase Orders Are Active** Select this option to tell QuickBooks that you want to enable the inventory features; the purchase orders are automatically enabled with that action.
- **Warn If Not Enough Inventory To Sell** This option turns on the warning feature that is useful during customer invoicing. If you sell ten widgets and your stock of widgets is fewer than ten, QuickBooks displays a message telling you there's insufficient stock to fill the order. (You can still complete the invoice; it's just a message, not a limitation.)

- **Warn About Duplicate Purchase Order Numbers** When this option is enabled, any attempt to issue a purchase order with a P.O. number that already exists will generate a warning.
- **Bills** Use the options in this section of the window to set default payment terms for vendors (you can change the terms for individual vendors) and to issue a warning if you enter a vendor bill (the same invoice number) twice.

Setting Reminders Preferences

The Reminders section of the Preferences window has options on both tabs. The My Preferences tab has one option, which turns on the Reminders feature and displays a Reminders list when you open a company file.

The company Preferences tab enumerates the available reminders and you can select the ones you want to use (see Figure 21-6).

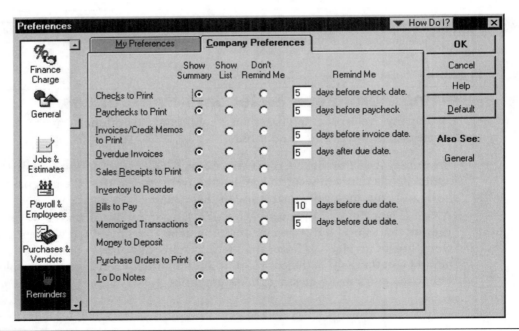

FIGURE 21-6 Design the list of chores you want to be reminded about

For each item, decide whether you want to see a summary (just a listing and the total amount of money involved), a complete detailed list, or nothing at all. You can also determine the amount of lead time you want for your reminders.

 TIP: If you choose Show Summary, the Reminder list itself has a button you can click to see the details.

Setting Reports & Graphs Preferences

This is another section of the Preferences window that has choices on both tabs, so you can set your own user preferences, and then set those options that affect the current company.

Use the My Preferences tab (see Figure 21-7) to configure performance issues for graphs.

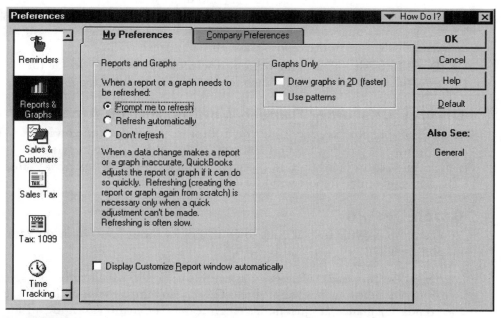

FIGURE 21-7 Set the parameters you want to use when you create reports and graphs

Updating Reports and Graphs

While you're viewing a report or a graph, you can make changes to the format or to the data behind it. Most of the time, QuickBooks automatically changes the report/graph to match the changes. However, if there is anything else going on (perhaps you're also online, or you're in a network environment and other users are manipulating data that's in your report or graph), QuickBooks stops making changes automatically. The reason for the shut-down of automatic refreshing is to keep your computer running as quickly and efficiently as possible. At that point, QuickBooks has to make a decision about when and how to refresh the report or graph. You must give QuickBooks the parameters for making the decision to refresh.

- **Prompt Me To Refresh**   Choose this option to see a message asking you whether you want to be reminded to refresh the report or the graph after you've made changes to the data behind it. It's just a reminder—you initiate the Refresh feature yourself by clicking the Refresh button on the report/graph window.
- **Refresh Automatically**   Select this option if you're positively compulsive about having up-to-the-second data and don't want to remember to click the Refresh button. If you work with QuickBooks on a network, this could slow down your work a bit because any time any user makes a change to data that's used in the report/graph, it will refresh itself.
- **Don't Refresh**   This is the option to select if you want to decide for yourself, without nagging, when to click the Refresh button.

Display Customer Report Window Automatically

If you find that almost every time you ask for a report you find you have to customize it, you can tell QuickBooks to open the Customize window whenever a report is brought to the screen. Click the check box next to the "Display Customize Report window automatically option."

Graph Design

You can also provide instructions to QuickBooks about how you want your graphs created:

- **Draw Graphs In 2D (Faster)**   Select this option to have graphs displayed in two dimensions instead of three. This doesn't impair your ability to see trends at a glance; it's just not as "high-tech." The main reason to consider this option is that the 2D graph takes much less time to draw on your screen.

- **Use Patterns** This option tells QuickBooks to draw the various elements in your graphs with black-and-white patterns instead of colors. For example, one pie wedge may be striped, another speckled. This is handy if you print your graphs to a black-and-white printer.

Setting Company Report Preferences

Move to the Company Preferences tab of the Reports & Graphs window to set company preferences (see Figure 21-8).

- **Summary Reports Basis** Specify whether you want to see summary reports as accrual-based or cash-based.
- **Aging Reports** Specify whether you want to age A/R and A/P aging reports using the due date or the transaction date.
- **Reports—Show Accounts By** Specify whether you want accounts listed by their account names, their descriptions, or both.

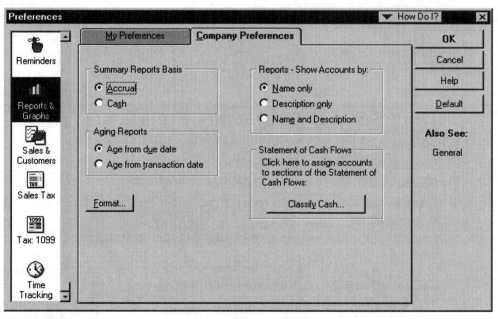

FIGURE 21-8 Configure the options for reporting on your finances

Setting Report Format Defaults

You can set the default formatting for reports by clicking the Format button and making changes to the default configuration options.

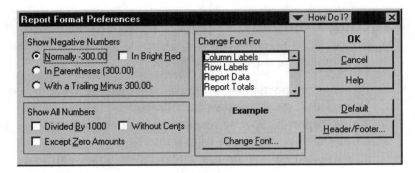

Configuring the Cash Flow Report

A cash flow report is really a complicated document, and before the days of accounting software, accountants spent many hours creating such a report. QuickBooks has configured a cash flow report format that is used to produce the cash flow reports available in the list of Company & Financial reports.

You can view the format by clicking the Classify Cash button, but you shouldn't mess around with the selections in the window that appears unless you check with your accountant.

Setting Sales & Customers Preferences

You can set a few options as defaults in the Sales & Customer section of the Preferences window:

- Set the default shipping method.
- Set the default markup percentage. This is used for items that have both a cost and price.
- Set the FOB statement for invoices. FOB (Free On Board) is the location from which shipping is determined to be the customer's responsibility. This means more than just paying for freight; it's a statement that says "at this point you have become the owner of this product."
- **Track Reimbursed Expenses As Income**   This option changes the way your general ledger handles payments for reimbursements. When this option is enabled, the reimbursement can be assigned to an income account (which you should name "reimbursed expenses"). When the option is not

enabled, the reimbursement is posted to the original expense account, washing away the expense.

- **Automatically Apply Payments** This option tells QuickBooks to apply payments automatically to open invoices. If the payment amount is an exact match for an open invoice, it is applied to that invoice. If the payment amount is smaller than any open invoice, QuickBooks applies the payment to the oldest invoice. Without this option, you must manually apply each payment to an invoice (which is the way I work, because frequently the customer's check stub indicates the invoice the customer wants to pay even if it's not the entire amount).

- **Warn About Duplicate Invoice Numbers** This option tells QuickBooks to warn you if you're creating an invoice using an invoice number that's already in use.

Setting Up Sales Tax Preferences

This is one section of the Preferences window that is easy to configure, because you're bound by laws and rules. Select the options that your government sales tax agency lays out. Figure 21-9 shows my configuration; yours may differ.

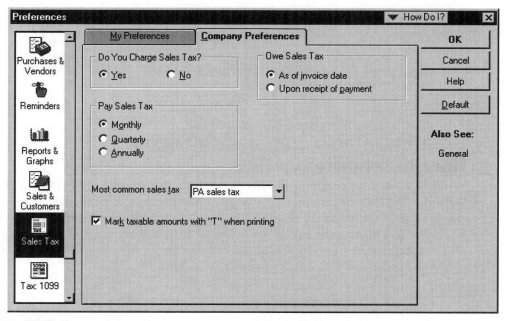

FIGURE 21-9 Sales tax preferences are a matter of state law

Setting 1099 Form Preferences

Use this section of the Preferences window to establish the 1099 Form options you need. For each type of 1099 payment, you must assign an account from your chart of accounts. You cannot assign two payment types to the same account.

Setting Time-Tracking Preferences

Use this section to turn on Time Tracking and to tell QuickBooks the first day of your workweek (which really means the first day listed on your timesheets). Read all about tracking time in Chapter 18.

Working with Multiple Users

The first time you used QuickBooks, the EasyStep Interview program asked if other people use your computer to perform work in QuickBooks. If you answered Yes, you were asked to provide names and passwords for each person. After the additional users are configured, you, as the administrator, can determine who can use the various features in QuickBooks. You can add users, delete users, and change access permissions at any time. Only the administrator can perform these tasks.

If you said No during the interview, you can change your mind and set up multiple users now.

Creating, Removing, and Changing User Information

When you want to create or modify users, choose Company | Set Up Users from the QuickBooks menu bar. If you are setting up multiple users for the first time, QuickBooks displays the Set Up QuickBooks Administrator window. You must have an administrator (I'm assuming it's you) to manage all the other user tasks.

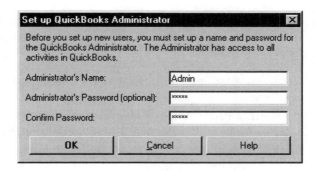

It's a good idea to leave the name as Admin. Then use the TAB key to move to the password box and enter a password and then confirm it. You won't see the text you're typing; instead, the system shows asterisks as a security measure (in case someone is watching over your shoulder).

 TIP: While the use of a password is optional, omitting passwords altogether can put at risk your whole system's security.

Creating a New User

If you already set up the configuration option to have multiple users, selecting Company | Set Up Users displays the User List window.

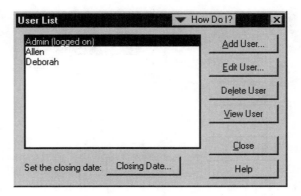

To add a new user to the list, click Add User. This launches a wizard that assists you in setting up the new user. In the first wizard window (see Figure 21-10), fill in the necessary information.

1. Enter the user name, which is the name this user must type to log in to QuickBooks.
2. If you want to establish a password for this user (it's optional), press the TAB key to move to the Password field, and enter the user's password.
3. Press the TAB key to move to the Confirm Password field and enter the same password to confirm it.
4. Click Next to set up the user's access to QuickBooks features. See the section "Setting User Permissions," a bit later in this chapter.

TIP: Make a note of all user passwords and keep that list in a safe place. Inevitably, a user will come to you because he or she cannot remember a password.

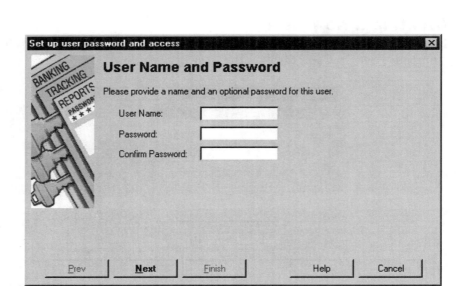

FIGURE 21-10 The first step is adding the user's name and password

Deleting a User

If you want to remove a user from the User List, select the name and then click the Delete User button. QuickBooks asks you to confirm your decision.

Editing User Information

You can change the configuration options for any user. Select the user name in the User List window and click Edit User. This launches a wizard similar to the Add User wizard, and you can change the user password, access permissions, or both.

Setting User Permissions

When you're adding a new user or editing an existing user, the wizard walks you through the steps for configuring the user's permissions. Click Next on each wizard window after you've supplied the necessary information.

The first permissions window asks if you want this user to have access to selected areas of QuickBooks or all areas. If you want to give the user full permission to do everything, you're asked to confirm your decision. After that, there's no further work to do in the wizard.

Configuring Rights to Individual Areas of QuickBooks

If you want to limit the user's access to some areas of QuickBooks, select that option and click Next. The ensuing wizard windows take you through all the QuickBooks features (Accounts Receivable, Check Writing, Payroll, and so on) so you can establish permissions on a feature-by-feature basis for this user. You must configure permissions for every component of QuickBooks that you installed.

For each QuickBooks component, you can select from these permission options:

- **No Access** The user will be denied permission to open any windows in that section of QuickBooks.
- **Full Access** The user can open all windows and perform all tasks in that section of QuickBooks.
- **Selective Access** The user will be permitted to perform tasks as you see fit.

If you choose to give selective access permissions, you'll be asked to specify the rights this user should have. Those rights vary slightly from component to component, but generally you're asked to choose one of these permission levels:

- Create transactions

- Create and print transactions
- Create transactions and create reports

 TIP: You can select only one of the three levels, so if you need to give the user rights to more than one of these choices, you must select Full Access instead of configuring Selective Access.

Configuring Special Areas of QuickBooks

There are two wizard windows for setting permissions that are not directly related to any specific area of the software: sensitive accounting activities and sensitive accounting reports.

Sensitive accounting activities are those tasks that aren't directly related to specific QuickBooks features:

- Making changes to the chart of accounts
- Manipulating the register for any balance sheet account
- Using online banking
- Transferring funds between banks
- Reconciling bank accounts
- Creating journal entries
- Preparing an accountant's review
- Working with budgets

Sensitive financial reports are those reports that reveal important financial information about your company, such as:

- Profit & Loss reports
- Balance sheet reports
- Budget reports
- Cash flow reports
- Income tax reports
- Trial balance reports
- Audit trail reports

Configuring Rights for Existing Transactions

If a user has permissions for certain areas of QuickBooks, you can limit his or her access to manipulate existing transactions within those areas (see Figure 21-11).

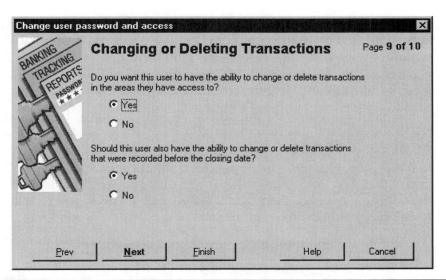

FIGURE 21-11 Even if you permit users to work in specific areas of QuickBooks, you can limit their ability to change or delete existing transactions

It's generally not a good idea to let users other than the administrator (that's probably you) work in closed books. In fact, it's generally not a good idea for a software program to permit anyone to mess around in a closed year, but since QuickBooks does permit this, you should limit the permissions severely.

When you have finished configuring user permissions, the last wizard page presents a list of the permissions you've granted and refused. If everything is correct, click Finish. If there's something you want to change, use the Prev button to back up to the appropriate page.

Configuring Classes

QuickBooks provides a feature called Classes, that permits you to group items and transactions in a way that matches the kind of reporting you want to perform. Think of this feature as a way to "classify" your business activities. To use classes, you must enable the feature, which is listed in the Accounting section of the Preferences window.

Some of the reasons to configure classes include

- Reporting by location if you have more than one office.
- Reporting by division or department.
- Reporting by business type (perhaps you have both retail and wholesale businesses under your company umbrella).

You should use classes for a single purpose; otherwise, the feature won't work properly. For example, you can use classes to separate your business into locations or departments, but don't try to do both.

When you enable classes, QuickBooks adds a Class field to your transaction windows. To fill it in, you must create the classes you want to use.

Adding a Class

To create a class, choose Lists | Class List from the QuickBooks menu bar to display the Class List window. (Remember that you must enable Classes in Preferences to have access to the Class Lists menu item.) Press CTRL-N to add a new class. Fill in the name of the class in the New Class window.

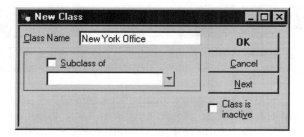

Click Next to add another class, or click OK if you are finished. It's a good idea to create a class called Other. This gives you a way to sort transactions in a logical fashion when there's no link to one of your real classes.

Using a Class in Transactions

When you're entering transactions, each transaction window provides a field for entering the class (see Figure 21-12).

TIP: Your invoice form adds a Class field (next to the Customer:Job field) so you can assign the invoice to a class. However, you can also link a class to each line item of the invoice (if you expect the line items to require separate links to classes). You must customize your invoice forms to add classes as a column. When you do, you should add the column to the screen form, but not the printed form. Your customers don't care. See Chapter 3 to learn how to customize invoice forms.

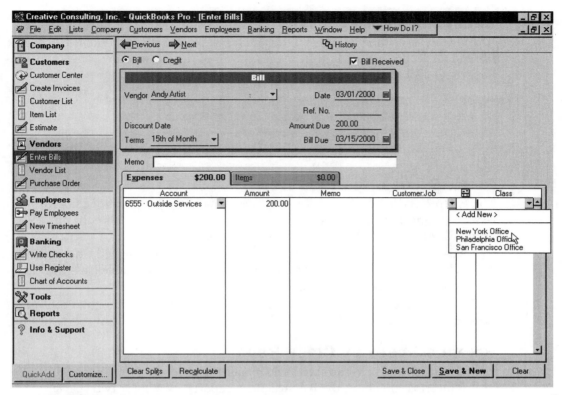

FIGURE 21-12 Link a transaction (even an individual line item) to a class

Reporting by Class

There are two types of reports you can run for classes:

- Individual class reports
- Reports on all classes

Reporting on a Single Class

To report on a single class, follow these simple steps:

1. Open the Classes list and select the class you want to report on.
2. Click the Reports button on the bottom of the window and choose QuickReport (or press CTRL-Q instead of clicking the Reports button).

When the Class QuickReport appears you can change the date range or customize the report as needed.

Reporting on All Classes

If you want to see one report in which all classes are used, open the Classes list and click the Reports button at the bottom of the list window. Then choose Reports On All Classes to see a submenu of available reports.

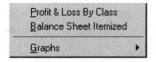

Profit & Loss by Class Report

The Profit & Loss By Class report is the same as a standard Profit & Loss report, except that each class uses a separate column. The Totals column provides the usual P&L information for your company.

Totals for items not assigned to a class appear in a column called Unclassified. This is likely to be a rather crowded column if you chose to enable class tracking after you'd already begun using QuickBooks.

You can find detailed information about running and customizing Profit & Loss reports in Chapter 15.

Balance Sheet by Class Report

This report is similar to the standard Balance Sheet report (see Chapter 15 for lots of information about the Balance Sheet report), except for two special characteristics:

- The report is itemized by transaction instead of reporting totals for each balance sheet account.
- A column indicates the class to which each transaction is linked.

Graphs That Use Class Data

You can also display a graph for Income & Expenses sorted by class, or one that compares budget versus actual figures sorted by class.

Customizing Other Reports for Class Reporting

Many of the reports you run regularly can also be customized to report class information (for example, aging reports). Use the Filters button to add all, some, or one class to the report.

Using Classes to Track Partners

Carl, Pete, and Lucy are veterinarians with a busy practice. Before they formed their partnership, each of them had practiced independently. They each brought a certain amount of equity into the partnership (including cash, equipment, and patients) and they want to track the individual equity amounts by using the profits each provides. In effect, each of their examining rooms is run as an individual profit center.

Each partner name is established as a class, and there are two additional classes:

- Other, which is used to mean "this particular item is practice-wide."
- Split, which is used to mean "add this up at the end of the year and assign a percentage to each partner."

All revenue transactions are assigned to a partner class. Each line item on every vendor bill is assigned to a class, as follows:

- Certain overhead items such as rent, utilities, and so on are assigned to Other.
- Consumable overhead items, such as towels, syringes, and medical supplies are assigned to Split.

At the end of the year, when the reports are run, the totals for the Split class are reapportioned with a journal entry. The percentage of income is used as a guideline for the percentage of the split, because the assumption is that a partner with a certain amount of revenue must have used a certain amount of consumable items in order to produce that revenue. While this system isn't terribly exact, it is as ingenious and fair as a system could be.

When the year is closed, a percentage of the retained earnings figure is posted to each partner's equity account. The profit for each partner is the revenue, less the expenses incurred by each partner (including the Split class percentage).

This system also provides a nifty way to figure end-of-year bonuses, since the partners can base the amount of the bonus (a draw) on the amount of the current year retained earnings for each partner.

Using QuickBooks on a Network

If you're using QuickBooks Pro, you and other users can use the software on a network. Multiple users can be working in QuickBooks at the same time.

You must purchase a separate copy of QuickBooks Pro for each user who will access the network files and install that copy on the user's computer. Look for special network packages of QuickBooks Pro, with special pricing (for example, the five-user pack).

Setting Up the Network Installation

The first thing you must do is install QuickBooks Pro on every computer that will be involved in this network setup. One of those installed copies becomes the main network copy. That copy can reside on a network server or on a user's computer (if you're using Windows 95, Windows 98, Windows NT, or Windows 2000). If you're running on NetWare or Lantastic, your system administrator can set up QuickBooks Pro (the possible combinations and permutations are too numerous to cover here).

Setting Up a Shared Resource

If you're using Windows 95, Windows 98, Windows NT, or Windows 2000, here's an overview of network setup:

1. Install QuickBooks Pro on every user's computer.
2. On the computer that will act as the QuickBooks server, open Windows Explorer and right-click on the folder into which you installed QuickBooks Pro 6.
3. Choose Sharing from the shortcut menu to open the Folder Properties dialog box.
4. Select Shared As. The folder name is automatically entered as the Share Name, and that is probably a good choice. However, you can change the name of the share if you wish.
5. Set permissions for Full Control. (The User setup is the place to set restrictions on users, as described earlier in this chapter.)
6. Click OK.

If you're using Windows 95 or Windows 98, the permissions are configured on the Sharing tab of the Properties dialog box. If you're using Windows NT or Windows 2000, click the Permissions button on the Sharing tab to use the Permissions dialog box.

Mapping the Shared Resource as a Drive on the Other Computers

It's a good idea to map the shared resource as a drive on the other users' computers. It's not necessary, but it speeds up access to the company files:

1. Open Network Neighborhood and select the remote computer that's acting as the server for QuickBooks Pro.
2. Right-click the shared resource for QuickBooks.
3. Choose Map Network Drive from the shortcut menu.
4. In the Map Network Drive dialog box, select a drive letter for this resource.
5. Select the Reconnect at logon option.
6. Click OK.

C A U T I O N : The Reconnect At Logon option works only if the computer that has the shared resource boots up before the other machines when you turn on your computers in the morning. Otherwise, the user computers won't be able to find the resource and map it. If that happens, just repeat the steps to map the drive before using QuickBooks.

Switching Between Multiuser Mode and Single-User Mode

On the computer that's acting as the host/server, you must enable multiuser mode before other users can access the data files. To accomplish this, make sure the company you want users to work in is the current company. Then choose File | Switch to Multiuser Mode from the QuickBooks menu bar.

All the QuickBooks windows are closed while the switch is made. Then a message appears to tell you that the company files are in multiuser mode.

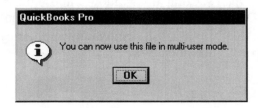

If you need to return to Single-User Mode, use the File menu, where the command has changed to Switch to Single-User Mode. A number of administrative tasks must be performed in single-user mode:

- Backing up
- Restoring
- Compressing files
- Deleting items from lists
- Exporting or importing accountant's review copies
- Certain other setup tasks (QuickBooks displays a message telling you to switch to single-user mode when you access those setup tasks)

 T I P : The first time you log in to the network, choose Files | Preferences and set your personal preferences in the My Preferences window. See the discussion about preferences earlier in this chapter.

Using QuickBooks Pro in Multiuser Mode

Users at computers other than the QuickBooks host/server computer can reach the network data easily:

1. Launch QuickBooks Pro (from the Program menu or a desktop shortcut).
2. Choose File | Open Company/Login from the QuickBooks menu bar.
3. Click the arrow to the right of the Look In field to display a hierarchy of drives and shared resources.
4. Select the drive letter if the resource is mapped.
5. If the resource is not mapped, select Network Neighborhood. Then select the host computer and continue to make selections until you find the shared folder.
6. In the Open A Company window, choose the company you want to use and click Open, or double-click the company name.
7. When the QuickBooks Login window appears, enter your login name and password. Then click OK.

C A U T I O N : Your login name must be unique, and if anyone is already accessing the files with that name you are told to use a different name or try later.

Customizing the Navigation Bar

New to QuickBooks 2000, the Navigation Bar provides an easy-to-use selection process for the most common tasks in QuickBooks. You can change the appearance of the Navigation Bar. More important, however, is the fact that you can customize the program so that your common tasks are not the same as my common tasks. To make QuickBooks efficient for each of us, you can add or remove items from the Navigation Bar.

Changing the Appearance of the Navigation Bar

By default, the QuickBooks Navigation Bar has the following characteristics:

- It's positioned on the left side of your QuickBooks window.
- It displays both icons and text for each listing.

To change those settings, click the Customize button at the bottom of the Navigation Bar to open the Customize Navigation Bar window shown in Figure 21-13.

- Select Show Minimized to reduce the width of the Navigation Bar so that only the icons display on your window. Select Show Maximized to increase the width of the Navigation Bar.
- Select Slide Open so that when you place your mouse pointer over it, the Navigation Bar gracefully slides open to display the names of the icon. Deselect the option if you want the Navigation Bar to pop open when you place your mouse pointer over it.
- Select Right to move the Navigation Bar to the right side of your QuickBooks window.

If you want to hide the Navigation Bar (perhaps you prefer to use the menu system and want more desktop real estate for your QuickBooks windows), choose Window | Hide Navigation Bar from the menu bar. To return the Navigation Bar to your screen, choose Window | Show Navigation Bar.

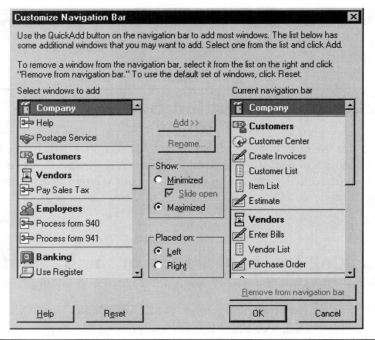

FIGURE 21-13 Change the way the Navigation Bar displays by using the options in the middle of the Customize window

Customizing the Navigation Bar Contents

You can add or remove listings to make the Navigation Bar a totally customized tool. You'll probably change your mind a lot, adding and removing listings as you continue to use QuickBooks.

Adding Listings to the Navigation Bar

You can add a QuickBooks task listing to the Navigation Bar in two ways: Add the listing from the Customize Navigation Bar window, or add the listing when you're using the window for the task you want to add.

To add listings from the Customize Navigation Bar window, select the listing in the left pane and click Add to move the listing to the right pane. The right pane holds the contents of the Navigation Bar.

To add a listing for a task you're currently performing, click the QuickAdd button on the bottom of the Navigation Bar to add the current window to the listings (see Figure 21-14).

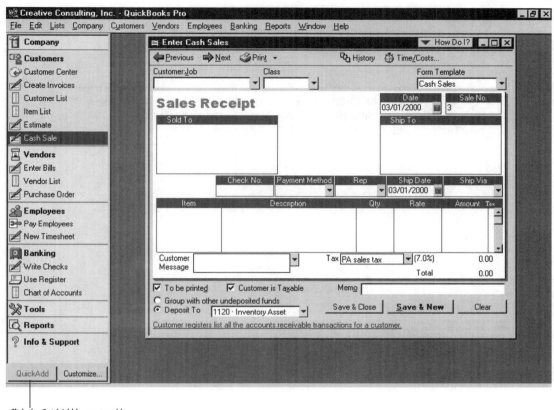

Click the QuickAdd button to add
this task to the Navigation Bar

FIGURE 21-14 While the Enter Cash Sales window is open, the QuickAdd button was
clicked to add Cash Sale to the listings on the Navigation Bar

Renaming Listings on the Navigation Bar

You can change the name of any item on the Navigation Bar in the Customize
Navigation Bar window. Select the item in the right pane and click Rename.
Enter the new name in the Rename Navigation Bar Item window and click OK.

Removing Listings from the Navigation Bar

If you decide you don't use an item often enough to let it take up space on your
Navigation Bar, open the Customize Navigation Bar window and select that

item in the right pane. Click the Remove From Navigation Bar button at the bottom of the right pane. The item doesn't disappear; instead, it moves back to the left pane so you can restore it in the future if you wish.

 TIP: If you decide you really didn't mean to add items to or delete items from the Navigation Bar, click Reset to put everything back the way it was the day you first started using QuickBooks.

Managing Your QuickBooks Files

Chapter 22

In this chapter, you will learn to...

- Back up and restore company files
- Condense data
- Import and export data
- Update QuickBooks software

Creating Companies in QuickBooks

You can create as many companies in QuickBooks as you wish. You can have your business in one company, your personal finances in another company, volunteer to run the local community association, open a second business, keep your mother-in-law's books, or create companies for any of a zillion reasons.

To create a new company, choose File | New Company from the QuickBooks menu bar. This opens the EasyStep Interview wizard (you saw this wizard the first time you ever used QuickBooks). You don't have to go through the entire EasyStep Interview, but you should fill out the General sections, which are represented by tabs across the top of the window (see Figure 22-1).

The questions are easy to answer, and you just need to keep clicking Next to move through all the sections of the interview.

If you don't want to go through the interview process, the third window has an escape hatch in the form of a button named Skip Interview. Click it to use the shortcut method of creating a company, which begins with the Creating New Company window, shown in Figure 22-2.

Click Next to see a list of company types, and select the one that comes closest to this company's mission. QuickBooks uses this information to create a chart of accounts for the company.

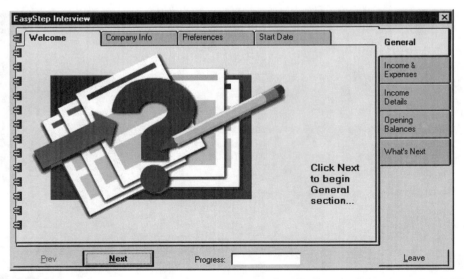

FIGURE 22-1 Creating a company starts with the EasyStep Interview wizard

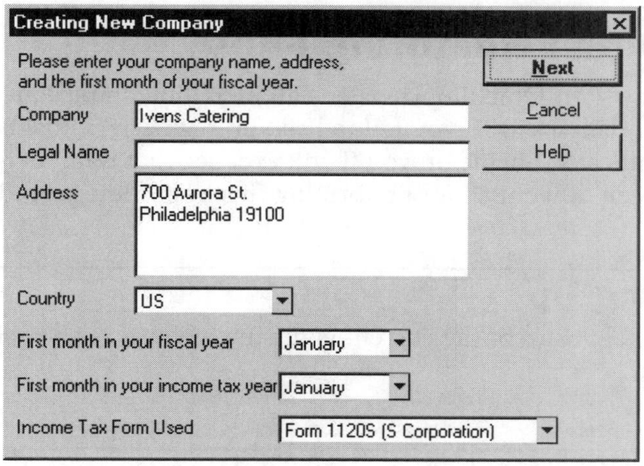

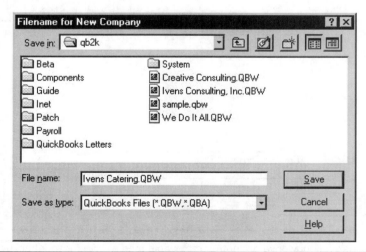

FIGURE 22-2 Answer a slew of questions in one fell swoop in the Creating New Company window

Click Next to save the information in a company file (see Figure 22-3). QuickBooks suggests a filename based on your company name, but you can invent your own filename if you wish. Click Save to make this company a file in your QuickBooks system.

QuickBooks loads the new company as the current company, and you can start setting preferences, entering data, and doing all the other tasks involved in creating a company. Read Chapters 1 and 2 for setup help.

FIGURE 22-3 As soon as you save the information in a file, you can begin working in the new company

Backing Up and Restoring Files

Backing up your QuickBooks data is an incredibly important task and should be done on a daily basis. If you fail to back up regularly, QuickBooks will remind you periodically. Shame on you if you ever see that reminder—it means you haven't been diligent about performing this important procedure.

Backing Up

To create a backup of the current company, choose File | Back Up from the menu bar.

 TIP: QuickBooks may display a message explaining that there's a remote data storage facility you can use as a repository for your backup files. If you want more information, QuickBooks will launch your Internet connection and travel to the Web where the information resides.

Choose a location for the backup file (see Figure 22-4) and click Save. QuickBooks names the backup file for you.

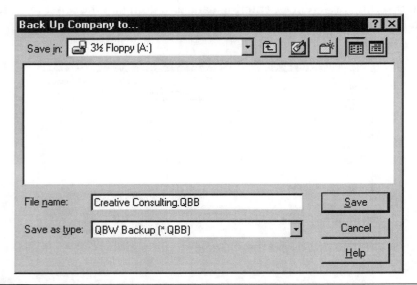

FIGURE 22-4 Use a floppy drive or another removable media drive for your backup

Never back up onto your local hard drive. Use removable media, such as a floppy drive or a Zip drive, because the point of backing up is to be able to get back to work in case of a hard drive or computer failure. If you're on a network, you can back up to a remote folder on the computer that's backed up every night. QuickBooks won't use a network path (UNC), so you must map the remote folder.

QuickBooks compresses the data in your files to create the backup file, but if you have a great many transactions, you may be asked to put a second floppy disk in your drive to complete the backup. If so, be sure to label the floppy disks so you know which is the first disk. (You must start with the first disk if you need to restore the backup.)

Don't back up on top of the last backup, because if something happens during the backup procedure, you won't have a good backup file to restore. The best procedure is a backup disk (or set of disks) for each day of the week. If you're using expensive media, such as a Jaz drive, and you don't want to purchase that many disks, have one disk for odd days and another for even days. When you use a disk that's already received a backup file, QuickBooks will ask if you want to replace the existing file with the new one. Click Yes, because the current backup file is newer and has up-to-the-minute data. The old file is at least two days old, and perhaps a week old, depending on the way you're rotating media.

Periodically (once a week is best, but once a month is essential), make a second backup copy on a different disk and store it off-site. Then, if there's a catastrophe at the office, you can buy, rent, or borrow a computer, install QuickBooks, and restore the data.

Restoring

You just turned on your computer and it sounds different, noisier. In fact, there's a grinding noise. You wait and wait, but the usual startup of the operating system fails to appear. Eventually, an error message about a missing boot sector appears (or some other equally chilling message). Your hard drive has gone to hard-drive heaven. You have invoices to send out, checks to write, and tons of things to do, and if you can't accomplish those tasks, your income suffers.

Don't panic; get another hard drive or another computer (the new one will cost less than the one that died). If you buy a new hard drive, it will take some time to install your operating system. If you buy a new computer, it probably comes with an operating system installed.

Take another few minutes to install your QuickBooks software. Now you're ready to go back to work and make money:

1. Start QuickBooks. It tells you there's no company and suggests you create one.
2. Ignore that message. Put the disk that contains your last good backup into the floppy (or other removable media) drive.
3. Choose File | Restore from the QuickBooks menu bar.
4. When the Restore From window appears, change the location in the Look In box to your floppy (or other removable media) drive (see Figure 22-5). Look! The Look In box is displaying a filename. That's your company data.
5. Click the filename and click Open (or double-click the filename).
6. In the Restore To window, choose the folder that holds the QuickBooks software, and click Save.
7. If your backup occupies multiple floppy disks, you'll be prompted to insert the next disk.
8. You did it! Aren't you glad you back up regularly? Click OK and go to work!

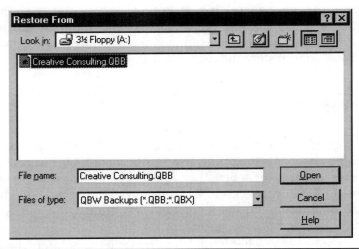

FIGURE 22-5 Your data is safe and sound

> **TIP:** If this backup wasn't saved yesterday, you must re-create every transaction you made between the time of the last backup and the last time you used QuickBooks.

Condensing Data

QuickBooks provides a feature that enables you to condense certain data in your company file in order to make your file smaller. You can use it to make backing up faster (using fewer disks) or to save room on your hard drive. While this seems to be a handy feature, it carries some significant side effects in the loss of details about transactions. Before using this feature, consider other ways to survive with a very large file.

Alternatives to Condensing Data

Condensing data is a last-resort solution to a problem that might be resolved by other means. If your intent is to make the backup faster by eliminating the need to insert additional floppy disks, consider getting removable media that is larger in capacity. Drives such as Iomega Zip (the disks hold 100MB or 250MB of data) and Iomega Jaz (the disks hold 1GB or 2GB of data) are terrific for backing up. You can also install a tape backup system that holds gigabytes of data.

> **WEBLINK:** You can get more information about Jaz and Zip drives at www.iomega.com.

If your problem is a lack of sufficient hard disk space, do some housekeeping on your hard disk. Get rid of temporary files, especially those stored by your browser when you visit the Internet. All browsers provide a menu command to empty the temporary files directory (sometimes called the *cache*).

Understanding the Condensing Procedure

If none of these suggestions is workable, and you feel your file size has gotten out of hand, you should condense your data. Consider this solution only after you've been using QuickBooks for more than a year or so, because you don't want to lose the details for the current year's transactions.

Choosing a Condensing Date

When you condense your data, QuickBooks asks you for the date you want to use as the cutoff date. Everything you no longer need before that date is condensed. No open transactions are condensed; only those data items that are completed, finished, and safe to condense are targeted. Also, any transactions before the condensing date that affect current transactions are skipped and the details are maintained in the file.

Understanding Summary Transactions

The transactions that fall within the parameters of the condensing date are deleted and replaced with summary transactions. A journal entry transaction shows the totals for the transactions, one for each month that is condensed. The following rules apply:

- The account balances are not changed by condensing data, because the summary transactions maintain those totals.
- Inventory transactions are never condensed.

In addition to transactions, you can configure the condensing feature to remove unused list items.

Understanding the After-Effects

You won't be able to run detail reports for those periods before the condensing date. However, summary reports will be perfectly accurate.

You will be able to recognize the summary transactions in the account registers because they will be marked with a transaction type GENJRNL.

Condensing Your File

The steps needed to condense your file are quite simple:

1. Close any transaction windows that are open (choose Windows | Close All from the menu bar to accomplish this quickly).
2. Choose File | Utilities | Condense Data from the menu bar.

3. When the Condense Data window appears, it displays the last day of the previous year as the condensing date (see the illustration). You can use this date or choose an earlier date (a date long past, so you won't care if you lose the transaction details). Be sure to choose the last day of a month.

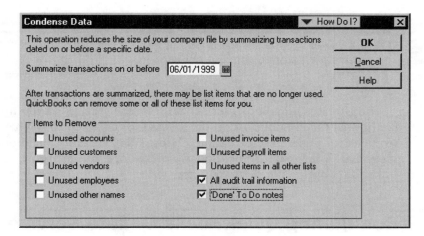

4. Select any items you want removed in addition to the transactions that meet the criteria.
5. Click OK.

QuickBooks walks you through a backup before beginning the process of condensing your data. You can use this backup to find details that will be missed from your condensed data. In fact, you might want to change the name of the backup file, so that if you need to load it to see details, you don't replace your current condensed files. Don't change the file extension.

After a few minutes, you're told that the condensing of your data files is complete.

Updating QuickBooks

QuickBooks provides an automatic update service you can use to make sure your QuickBooks software is up to date and trouble-free. This service provides you with any maintenance releases of QuickBooks that have been created since you purchased and installed your copy of the software. A maintenance release is distributed when a problem is discovered and fixed. This is sometimes necessary, because it's almost impossible to distribute a program that is totally bug-free (although my experience has been that QuickBooks generally releases without any major bugs, since Intuit does a thorough job of testing).

The Update QuickBooks service also provides notes and news from Intuit so you can keep up with new features and information for QuickBooks.

 C A U T I O N : This service does not provide upgrades to a new version; it just provides updates to your current version.

The Update QuickBooks service is an online service, so you must have configured QuickBooks for online access (see Chapter 16). When you want to check for updated information, choose File | Update QuickBooks from the menu bar. The Update QuickBooks window opens (see Figure 22-6), displaying links to set options or download updates.

Configuring QuickBooks Update Service

Click the Options link to configure the Update feature. As you can see in Figure 22-7, you have several choices for updating your software components. You can freely change any options you set, because nothing is etched in stone.

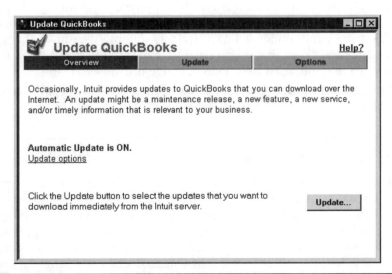

FIGURE 22-6 Configure update options or check for updates from the opening Update QuickBooks window

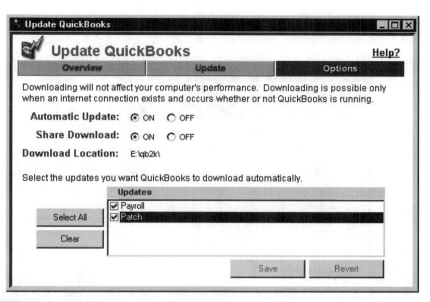

FIGURE 22-7 Set up the Update QuickBooks service

Automatic Updates

You can take advantage of automatic updates, which allow QuickBooks to check the Intuit update site on the Internet periodically while you're connected to the Internet. QuickBooks doesn't have to be running for this function to occur. If new information is found, it's downloaded to your hard drive without notifying you. If you happen to disconnect from the Internet while updates are being downloaded, the next time you connect to the Internet, QuickBooks will pick up where it left off.

Sharing Updates on a Network

If you're using QuickBooks in Multi-User mode, across a network, you must configure the Update QuickBooks service to share downloaded files with other users. The process of updating places the downloaded files on the computer that holds the shared QuickBooks data files. For this to occur, every user on the network must open his or her copy of QuickBooks and configure the Update options for Shared Download.

Determining Update Status

Click the Update link at the top of the page to open the Update QuickBooks window, which displays information about the current status of the service.

If you've configured QuickBooks for automatic downloading, you see the results of the last Internet check.

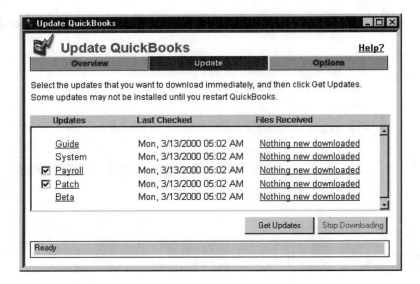

If you aren't using automatic downloading, you can click any listing to tell QuickBooks to check the Internet immediately and bring back any files. After files are downloaded, click the listing to see more information about that download. Most of the time, the files are automatically integrated into your system. Sometimes, the information box tells you that the files will be integrated when you exit QuickBooks.

Appendices

Technical and instructional books always have at least one appendix. Those of us who write computer books include them so we can organize the books in a way that lets you jump right into the software starting with Chapter 1.

However, for most computer software, there's either an installation routine or a configuration routine that must be handled before you dive into using the software, and we use the appendices to instruct you on the appropriate methods for accomplishing these chores.

For accounting software, the installation and setup procedures are far more important than for any other type of software. If the structure isn't right, the numbers won't be right.

You must read Appendix A before you do anything. In fact, you should read it and use the suggestions in it before you even install QuickBooks. That's why I named it "Do This First!" The rest of the appendices can be used as you need them.

Do This First!

Before you do anything with your QuickBooks software, you have to do three things:

- Decide on the starting date for your QuickBooks records.
- Find all the detailed records, notes, memos, and other items that you've been using to track your financial numbers.
- Create an opening trial balance to enter into QuickBooks.

If you don't prepare your records properly, all the advantages of a computer bookkeeping system will be lost to you. The information you enter when you first start using QuickBooks will follow you forever. If it's accurate, that's great! It means you have the right foundation for all the calculations that QuickBooks will perform for you. If it's not accurate, it will come to haunt you in the worst sense of the word.

It's not that you can't change things in QuickBooks; it's that if you start with bad numbers you frequently can't figure out which numbers were bad. Your inability to trace the origin of a problem is what makes the problem permanent.

So get out that shoebox, manila envelope, or whatever container you've used to keep numbers. We're going to organize your records in a way that makes it easy to get QuickBooks up and running—accurately.

Deciding on the Start Date

The start date is the date on which you begin entering your bookkeeping records into QuickBooks. Think of it as a conversion date. In the computer consulting field we call this "the date we go live." Things went on before this date (these are historical records and some of them must be entered into QuickBooks), but from this date on, your transactions go through QuickBooks.

This is not a trivial decision. The date you select has an enormous impact on how much work it's going to be to set QuickBooks up. For example, if you choose a starting date in September, everything that went on in your business prior to that date has to be entered into your QuickBooks system before you start entering September transactions. Okay, that's an exaggeration, because you can enter some numbers in bulk instead of entering each individual transaction, but the principle is the same.

If it's March, this decision is a lot easier, because the work attached to your QuickBooks setup is less onerous.

Here's what to think about as you make this decision:

- The best way to start a new computer accounting software system is to have every individual transaction in the system—every invoice you sent to customers, every check you wrote to vendors, every payroll check you gave an employee.

- The second best way to start a new computer accounting software system is to have running totals, plus any open transactions, in the system up to a certain date (your starting date), and then after that every single transaction is in the system. Open transactions are unpaid bills (either customer or vendor).

There is no third best way, because any fudging on either of those choices makes your figures suspect. There's no point in doing all the setup work if it means the foundation of your financial house is shaky.

If it's the first half of the year when you read this, make your start date the first day of the year and enter everything you've done so far this year. It sounds like a lot of work, but it really isn't. When you start entering transactions in QuickBooks, such as customer invoices, you just pick the customer, enter a little information, then move on to the next invoice. Of course, you have to enter all your customers, but you'd have to do that even if you weren't entering every transaction for the current year. (Chapter 2 is all about entering lists: customers, vendors, and so on.)

If it's the middle of the year, toss a coin. Seriously, if you have goo-gobs of transactions every month, you might want to enter large opening balances and then enter real transactions as they occur beginning with the start date.

If it's late in the year as you read this, perhaps September or October or later, and you usually send a lot of invoices to customers, write a lot of checks, and do your own payroll, think about waiting until next year to start using QuickBooks.

Gathering the Information You Need

You have to have quite a bit of information available when you first start to use QuickBooks, and it's ridiculous to hunt it down as each particle of information is needed. It's much better to gather it all together now, before you start working in QuickBooks.

Cash Balances

You have to tell QuickBooks what the balance is for each bank account you use in your business. Don't glance at the checkbook stubs—that's not the balance I'm talking about. The balance is the reconciled balance. And it has to be a reconciled balance as of the starting date you're using in QuickBooks. So if you haven't balanced your checkbooks against the bank statements for a while, do it now.

Besides the reconciled balance, you need to know the dates and amounts of the transactions that haven't yet cleared.

Customer Balances

If any customer owes you money as of your starting date, you have to tell QuickBooks about it. You have a couple of ways to do this:

- During the QuickBooks setup procedure (the EasyStep Interview), tell QuickBooks the total amount owed to you by each customer. The amount is treated as one single invoice and payments are applied to this invoice.
- Skip the customer balance information during the QuickBooks setup procedure. Then enter each unpaid customer invoice yourself, giving the real dates for each invoice. Those dates must be earlier than your QuickBooks start date.

This means you have to assemble all the information about unpaid customer invoices, including such details as how much of each invoice was for services, for items sold, for shipping, and for sales tax.

Vendor Balances

This is like the customer balances. You have the same chores (and the same decisions) facing you regarding any unpaid bills you owe to vendors. If they're not a lot, it might be easiest to pay them, just to avoid the work.

Asset Balances

Besides your bank accounts, an asset I've already covered, you have to know the state, as of the starting date, of all your assets. You'll need to know the current value, and also what the accumulated depreciation is.

The A/R asset is determined automatically by the customer balances you enter.

Liability Balances

Get all the information about your liabilities together. Your A/P balance is determined automatically by the open vendor bills you enter.

You'll need to know the current balance of any loans or mortgages. If there are unpaid withholding amounts from payroll, they must be entered. (Now there's an item that's easier to pay instead of entering.)

Payroll Information

If you do the payroll instead of using a payroll service, you'll need to know everything about each employee: social security number, all the information that goes into determining tax status (federal, state, and local), and which deductions are taken for health or pension. You have all this information, of course; you just have to get it together. If your employees are on salary, you've probably been repeating the check information every payday, with no need to look up these items. Dig up the W-4 forms and all your notes about who's on what deduction plan.

You also need to know which payroll items you have to track: salary, wages, federal deductions, state deductions (tax, SUI, SDI), local income tax deductions, benefits, pension, and any other deductions (garnishments, for example). And that's not all—you also have to know the name of the vendor to whom these withholding amounts are remitted (government tax agencies, insurance companies, and so on).

My advice is that you do not enter a year-to-date amount for your payroll as of your QuickBooks start date. This is one place where you should go back to the beginning of the year and enter each check. If you enter one total amount for each payroll item, and your starting date is July, what will you do when somebody asks "Can I see your first quarter totals?" If the "somebody" is the IRS, they like a quick, accurate answer.

Inventory Information

You need to know the name of every inventory item you carry, how much you paid for each item, and how many of each item you have in stock as of the starting date.

Other Useful Bits of Paper

Find last year's tax return. QuickBooks is going to want to know which tax forms you use. Also, there's usually other information on the tax forms you might need (depreciation schedules, for example).

If you have a loan or mortgage, have the amortization schedule handy. You can figure out the year-to-date (the date is the QuickBooks starting date) principal and interest amounts.

Opening Trial Balance

Your opening trial balance, which probably should be prepared with the help of your accountant, almost creates itself during the setup process. If your QuickBooks start date is the beginning of the year, it's a snap. The opening trial balance for the first day of the year has no income or expenses. It should look something like this:

ACCOUNT TYPE	ACCOUNT	DEBIT	CREDIT
Assets	Bank	$10,000	
	Fixed Assets	$50,000	
	Accumulated Depreciation/ Fixed Assets		$5,000
Liabilities	Loan from Corner Bank		$15,000
Equity	Opening Balance		$50,000
	Equity	$70,000	$70,000

Notice that there is no inventory figure in this opening balance. The reason is that you want to receive the inventory into your system so there's a quantity available for each inventory item. Otherwise, no matter what you want to sell, QuickBooks will think you don't have it in stock. As you bring the inventory in and assign it a value, your inventory asset will build itself.

If your QuickBooks starting date is any other date except for the beginning of the year, your trial balance will contain information about sales and expenses.

You're now ready to install QuickBooks and fire it up!

Installing QuickBooks

Before you begin installing QuickBooks, make sure you have closed any software applications that are running. Then turn off any virus detection software that's running.

Start the Installation Program

If you purchased QuickBooks on a CD-ROM:

- Put the CD-ROM in the CD-ROM drive. The installation program should start automatically.
- If the CD-ROM doesn't automatically start, see the instructions that follow for floppy disk installation.

If you purchased QuickBooks on floppy disks:

1. Put Install Disk #1 into your floppy disk drive.
2. Click the Start button and choose Settings | Control Panel from the Start menu.
3. When the Control Panel window appears, open the Add/Remove Programs application and click Install. The Install program checks the floppy drive and the CD-ROM drive to find a program named Setup.exe. Don't worry, it will find it and start the installation.

Begin QuickBooks Setup

When the QuickBooks Setup program launches, click Install to begin the installation. The Setup program displays a series of windows in which you must enter information or select options.

Enter Your Key Code

The first thing you must do is enter the Installation Key Code that came with your software. This code is unique and you must use it if you ever have to reinstall the software, so put it in a safe place (and remember where you put it).

If you've purchased multiple copies of QuickBooks Pro because you plan to use the network features that are available, you must follow these rules when you enter the key code:

- If you've purchased a 5-User Value Pack, you must use the same key code for each of the five installation procedures.

- If you've purchased a Value Pack and also purchased several additional copies of QuickBooks Pro, you must use the individual key codes for the additional copies.

Choose a Folder and Program Item

You must tell the Setup program where you want to install the software. If you don't want to use the suggested folder, click Browse and select a folder. You can enter the name of a folder in the Path field and QuickBooks will create the folder if it doesn't exist.

Setup adds a folder for QuickBooks to your Program menu instead of a plain icon, because there are submenu items installed. The Select Program Folder window appears to show you what the new folder will be named (see Figure B-1). You can accept the name, change it, or double-click an existing folder to have the QuickBooks program objects placed within it.

The only reason to consider placing the QuickBooks program folder within another, existing program folder is if you've created special program folders to hold items. (Some people do this to keep the Program menu short.)

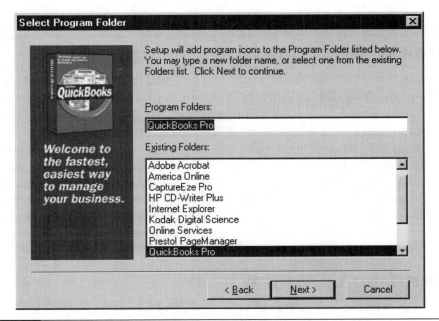

FIGURE B-1   The Program menu item for QuickBooks will be a folder, which means it will have submenu items

Relax While the Files Are Copied

After the Setup program shows you a dialog box that confirms the choices you've made, your configuration efforts are complete (click Back to make changes, Next to continue). It takes a few minutes to copy the software files to your hard drive, and the Setup program tracks the progress for you.

When the files are all copied to your hard drive, the Setup program asks if you want a shortcut to QuickBooks on your desktop (say Yes), then it tells you that installation is complete. Click Finish. You must restart your computer before you can begin using the software, and QuickBooks offers to perform this task.

Choose Other Installation Options

During the installation, QuickBooks asks if you want to install the software for AOL. If you want to use AOL for online access, complete the installation. You can use the installed software to open a new AOL account or access an existing AOL account. If you have QuickBooks Pro, you also have the option to install the Timer.

QuickBooks also installs Internet Explorer 5.0. If you already have Internet Explorer 5.0 on your system, you may be asked if you want to reinstall it. Say No.

Registering QuickBooks

When you first use QuickBooks you'll be asked to register the software. You can accomplish this by going online or by calling QuickBooks on the telephone.

You do not have to register immediately, but QuickBooks will periodically remind you that you haven't completed the registration process.

You will only be able to open QuickBooks 25 times without completing the registration. After that, the software will refuse to run if it's not registered.

You can begin the registration process by responding to the registration reminder notice, or by using the menu items in QuickBooks. To do the latter, choose File | Register QuickBooks from the menu bar. When the Product Registration window opens (see Figure B-2), choose Online or Phone.

Register by Modem

If you choose Online, QuickBooks will walk you through a configuration process. It needs to know the name of your Dial-Up Networking connection and the browser you want to use.

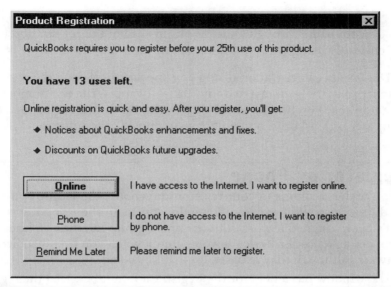

FIGURE B-2 Registration is mandatory for QuickBooks

Then your Dial-Up Networking connection is dialed so you can get to the QuickBooks Web site.

Once you're connected to the Internet, QuickBooks opens your Web browser and travels to the QuickBooks Online Registration site. A registration form is displayed that you must fill out. Make your selections and click Next to go to the next page. When you have completed all the fields in the registration form, there's a short wait while the QuickBooks registration database collects the information. Then your registration number is inserted into your software.

QuickBooks Online displays a list of available Internet addresses you might want to consider if your company doesn't have a Web page. This is part of the QuickBooks Site Builder feature, which is discussed in more detail in Appendix D.

You have the following options for this page:

- Close Internet Explorer and wait until later to decide whether you want to use the QuickBooks Web page feature (the best approach).
- Select a suggested Internet address and click Next to begin the process of joining QuickBooks Online.
- Enter a name for your Web site to have QuickBooks check to see if it's available.

- Select the option My Business Already Has a Domain Name to register your domain name through QuickBooks instead of the registration entity you are currently using (I cannot think of any reason to do this).

The Product Registration dialog box appears displaying the registration number that has been inserted into the software. Write the number down and save it in case you have to enter it again should something happen to your computer or hard drive and you have to reinstall the software.

Register by Phone

If you prefer to phone in your registration, choose the Phone option from the Product Registration window. A window opens to show you the serial number that's been assigned to your software and a group number. Neither of these numbers matches the key code you entered when you first installed the software (although they're based on that key code).

The window has a field for the Registration number. Dial the registration telephone number (it's in your QuickBooks documentation and also on your Help menu when you select "registering" in the index). Give the serial number and group number to the person who answers the telephone. In return, you'll be given the registration number. Write it down on a piece of paper so you have a permanent record of it. Then enter it in the field and click OK. Now you won't be nagged about registration anymore.

Integrating QuickBooks Pro with Other Programs

If you're using QuickBooks Pro, you can integrate your QuickBooks system with other software you may have installed. This brings more power to both your QuickBooks installation and the other software, including:

- Automated integration with Microsoft Excel
- Automated mail merge with Microsoft Word
- Automated synchronization of contact information with Microsoft Outlook and Symantec ACT!

This appendix provides an overview of these powerful features.

Automated Integration with Excel

Integration with Excel is available automatically in many cases, such as the ability to export any report to Excel. Look for the Excel button on the top of the report window. When you click it, your report is exported, Excel opens automatically, and you can make changes to the figures that were brought in from your QuickBooks Pro data.

This is a great way to play "what if" games, to see the effect of rising costs, higher salaries, more benefits, or any other change in your finances.

Mail Merge with Word

Need to send letters to some or all of your customers? Now it's easy, because QuickBooks Pro and Microsoft Word work together to enable this feature.

QuickBooks Pro provides a number of prewritten letters for you to use, or you can design your own letter. In fact, you can use an existing Word document for your mail merge activities.

To get started, choose Company | Write Letters from the QuickBooks menu bar.

Using a QuickBooks Pro Letter

When you open the Write Letters window, you see three choices for letter types (see Figure C-1). This is a wizard, so you fill out each window and click the Next button to move along.

If you're sending a collection letter, the next window asks you to define the criteria for adding a customer to the mail merge list (see Figure C-2).

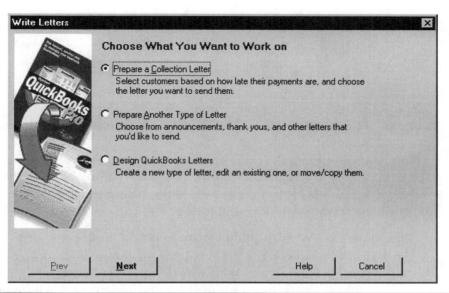

FIGURE C-1 Select the type of letter you want to use for your mail merge

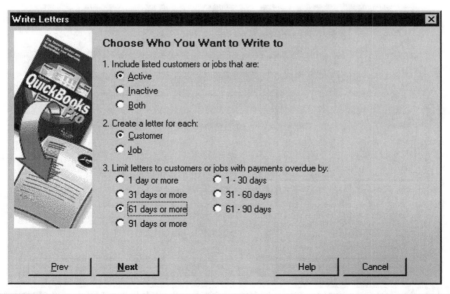

FIGURE C-2 I think that any customer who is at least two months late needs to hear about it

NOTE: If any customers who fall within the criteria have unapplied credits, QuickBooks reminds you of that fact. You can cancel the wizard and apply the credits if you wish to.

The list of customers who match your criteria appears, along with their balances (see Figure C-3). You can deselect any customer you don't want to send your letter to.

Now, you can choose the collection letter you want to send. QuickBooks has created a number of different collection letters, as you can see in Figure C-4.

You might want to look at each of the letters before you make your selection, and you can accomplish that with these steps:

1. Open Microsoft Word (you don't have to close QuickBooks).
2. Click the Open icon on the Word toolbar (or choose File | Open).
3. In the Open dialog box, use the arrow to the right of the Look In text box to move to the folder that holds the QuickBooks letters. You'll find it in a folder named QuickBooks Letters, under the folder in which you installed the QuickBooks software.

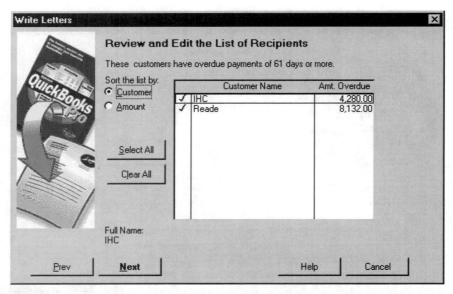

FIGURE C-3   You may have a reason to take a particular customer off your collection letter list

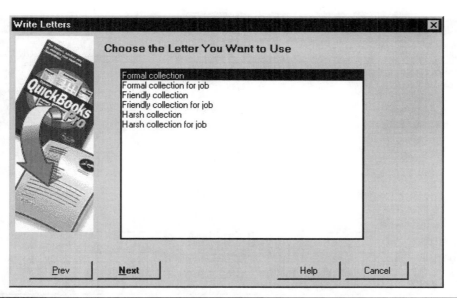

FIGURE C-4 Do you want to be gentle, firm, or downright nasty?

4. There's a folder for each type of QuickBooks letter (see Figure C-5). Open the Collection Letters folder and then open each letter to see which one you prefer to use.

CAUTION: The letter has codes; don't make any changes to them, or your mail merge may not work properly.

5. Close Word and return to QuickBooks.

The next wizard window asks you to fill in your name and title, the way you want it to appear in the letter. After you complete that information, click Create Letters.

QuickBooks opens Microsoft Word, and all of your letters are displayed in the Word window. Here are some guidelines for using this mail merge document:

- There's a page break at the end of each individual letter.
- If you want to make a change in the text, you must change each individual letter.

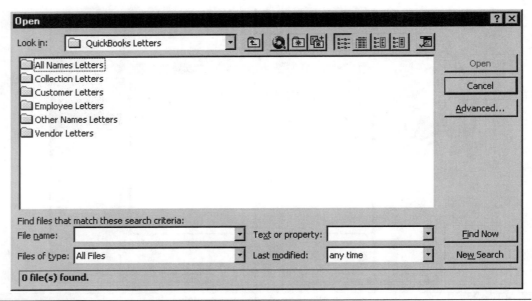

FIGURE C-5 Open the folder that holds the type of letter you're writing

- Changes you make to the text are not saved back to the original QuickBooks letter.
- You don't have to save the mail merge document unless you think you're going to resend the same letter to the same people (which would be unusual).

When it's all perfect, print the letters.

Using Your Own Letter

You can use your own text if you don't want to use a QuickBooks form letter, either writing one from scratch or using an existing QuickBooks letter as the basis of your new document.

When the first wizard window appears, select Design QuickBooks Letters and choose Next. Then, select the method you want to use to create your letter (see Figure C-6).

After you make your selection, choose Next and follow the instructions to complete your task.

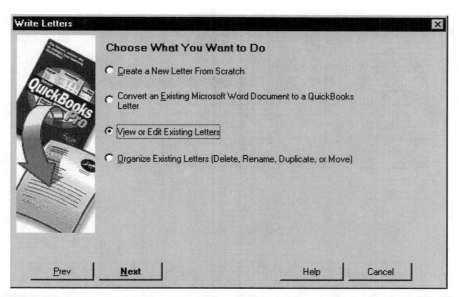

FIGURE C-6   You have plenty of options for using the QuickBooks Write Letters feature

Sending Letters to Vendors, Employees, and Others

You're not restricted to customers for mail merge; you can send mail to lots of different names in your QuickBooks files. Just select Prepare Another Type of Letter in the first wizard window and choose Next. Then, select a Name List and a type of letter (see Figure C-7).

The more you use the mail merge feature, the more creative you'll become.

Synchronizing Contacts

If you use Microsoft Outlook or Symantec ACT! to manage information about business (or personal) contacts, you can synchronize the data in your contact program with QuickBooks. This means you don't have to enter information about customers, vendors, or other contacts in both programs. Synchronization makes even minor changes easier to handle. If a vendor's telephone number changes, you can enter the new information in either program, and then update both programs.

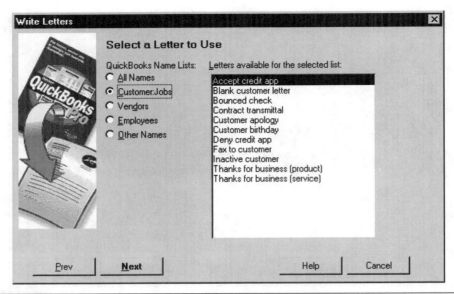

FIGURE C-7 The letter types change depending on the list you select

Understanding the Synchronization

You can synchronize the following data:

- Customer contact information, with the QuickBooks Customer:Job List.
- Vendor contact information, with the QuickBooks Vendor List.
- Other contact information, with the QuickBooks Other Names List.

 CAUTION: QuickBooks names that are marked Inactive are never involved in the synchronization process (in either direction).

You can establish synchronization as a one-way process, which is useful when you first begin to use this feature because most of your contact data likely is in one software application. The one-way direction will depend on whether you installed your contact management program before or after you installed QuickBooks.

Synchronizing the Data

Before you begin, back up your QuickBooks files and your contact software files. Then, choose Company | Synchronize Contacts from the QuickBooks menu bar. QuickBooks displays a message urging you to stop before you synchronize, to perform a backup. If you've just backed up, click Continue. Otherwise, click Cancel, perform the backup, and then return to the synchronization feature.

Synchronization is performed with the help of a wizard, which means you click Next to move through all the windows:

1. The first wizard window asks you to select your contact management program. Choose Outlook or ACT!, depending on the software you use.
2. The next window asks for the path and name of the database. Unless you have an excellent memory, click the Browse button to navigate through your computer to find and select the database.
3. Select the QuickBooks lists you want to synchronize with your database.

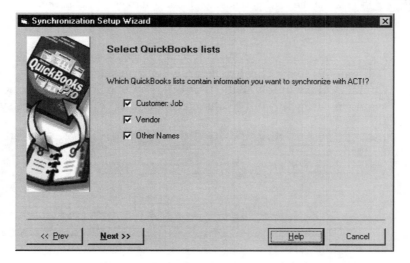

4. Tell QuickBooks how to handle conflicts (see Figure C-8).
5. Click Sync Now to perform the synchronization, or click Sync Later to exit the Synchronization Setup Wizard and do the file transfers at a later time.

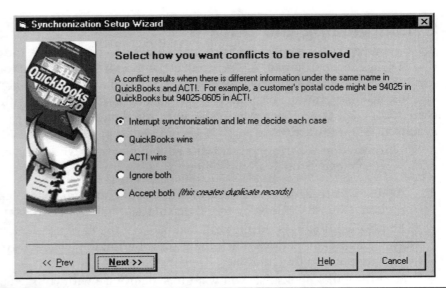

FIGURE C-8 Select the conflict resolution mode you're comfortable with

If you opt to synchronize later, when you select Company | Synchronize Contacts, the window that opens offers a chance to enter the Setup program again (in case you want to change something) or perform the synchronization.

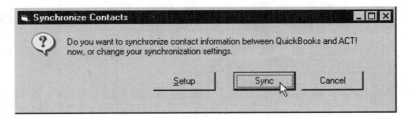

Now, you can use your contact program to track conversations and correspondence with your QuickBooks contacts.

Using QuickBooks Extras

QuickBooks isn't limited to the dull, number-crunching functions involved with bookkeeping. You have a wide choice of extra goodies you can use to enhance the way you run your business. All of the features discussed in this appendix require online access.

QuickBooks Site Builder

Add to your sales and marketing toolbox by creating a Web site for your company through QuickBooks. For a small monthly fee (the first six months are free) you can maintain your own, personalized Web site.

 N O T E : The option to set up your personalized site is available when you register your copy of QuickBooks, but most people prefer to wait until they've finished setting up the bookkeeping basics before looking into the Site Builder feature.

Creating a Company Web Site

To begin setup, choose Company | My Company Web Site | View Web Site from the menu bar. QuickBooks authenticates your copy of the software (checks to see that you registered it), and then launches the wizard that takes you through all the steps of the setup process (see Figure D-1). Fill in the information on the first wizard page and click Next.

 N O T E : If you're not already connected to the Internet, QuickBooks will open your connection before launching the wizard.

It takes a few minutes for QuickBooks to check the Internet to see if there are domain names that are relevant to your company name available. Then some suggested names are displayed for your consideration (see Figure D-2).

If you don't like any of the suggested names, enter your own suggestion so QuickBooks can search the Internet to see if it's available. Avoid capital letters, spaces, and punctuation within the name. If the name isn't available, you're returned to the same page—try another name.

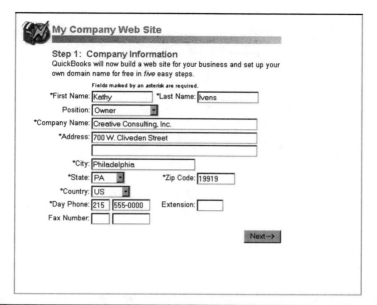

FIGURE D-1 QuickBooks uses the information you enter to set up a domain and choose a domain name for your company

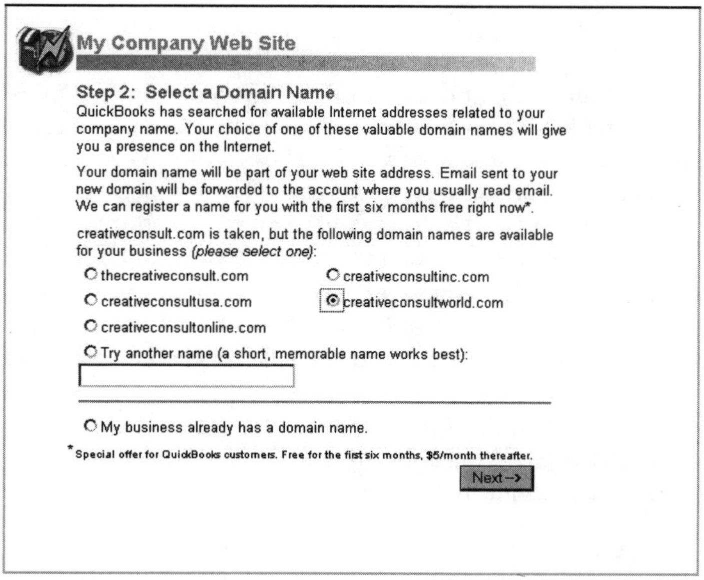

FIGURE D-2 Pick a suggested domain name, or enter one of your own

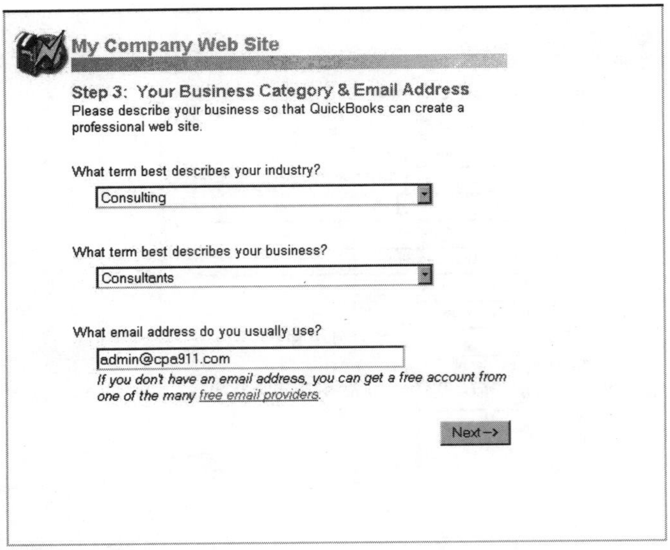

My Company Web Site

Step 3: Your Business Category & Email Address
Please describe your business so that QuickBooks can create a
professional web site.

What term best describes your industry?

Consulting

What term best describes your business?

Consultants

What email address do you usually use?

admin@cpa911.com

*If you don't have an email address, you can get a free account from
one of the many free email providers.*

Next→

FIGURE D-3   QuickBooks sets up a Web site based on the type of business

 N O T E : If you already have a domain name for your business and want to transfer the domain hosting chores to QuickBooks, select that option.

Enter information about the type of business you run, so QuickBooks can put relevant information on your Web site (see Figure D-3). You can change the text and graphics on your site whenever you choose. Supply your e-mail address so QuickBooks knows where to forward messages from people who visit your site and want to contact you. If you don't have an e-mail address, click the link to free e-mail providers and select a home site for an e-mail address.

QuickBooks now shows you a graphic that illustrates the way your site will look. Depending on the type of business you specified, you may have a choice of graphic styles. If so, pick the one you like best (remember, you can change it later).

The Terms and Conditions under which your Web site is created and maintained is displayed for your approval. Read every word of it so you understand exactly what it is you're agreeing to.

- If you agree with the terms, click I Accept.
- If you have a problem with any of the terms, click I Don't Accept, which terminates the setup program.

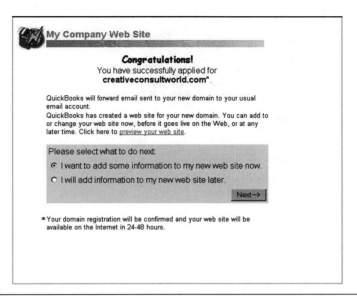

My Company Web Site

Congratulations!
You have successfully applied for
creativeconsultworld.com*.

QuickBooks will forward email sent to your new domain to your usual
email account.
QuickBooks has created a web site for your new domain. You can add to
or change your web site now, before it goes live on the Web, or at any
later time. Click here to preview your web site.

Please select what to do next:

⦿ I want to add some information to my new web site now.

○ I will add information to my new web site later.

Next→

*Your domain registration will be confirmed and your web site will be
available on the Internet in 24-48 hours.

FIGURE D-4   You did it!

Congratulations, you're done. As you can see in Figure D-4, you can visit
your site to preview it, or edit it to add information. If you're not ready to add
information to your site, edit it later by following the instructions in the next
section "Editing Your Company Web Site."

Almost immediately, you receive e-mail from The QuickBooks Team,
congratulating you on your new site and explaining how it all works. The
most important information is that after your free period ends, you'll be asked
to give QuickBooks a credit card number in order to continue using your site.

It takes about 48 hours for information about the location of your site to
work its way throughout the Internet. After that, anyone entering your domain
name into a browser will reach your site.

Editing Your Company Web Site

When QuickBooks builds your Web site, it uses *placeholder* text—that is,
sample text that occupies an area of the page. The placeholder text should
be replaced by text related to your company and its services or products.

To change the placeholder text to real text, and make any other changes to
your site, connect to the Internet and choose Company | My Company Web
Site | Edit Web Site from the menu bar. The QuickBooks administrative window
opens to present your editing choices (see Figure D-5).

FIGURE D-5 Being a Webmaster is easier when your chores are listed for you

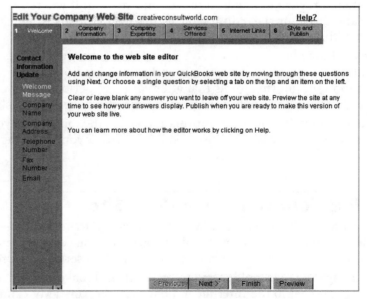

FIGURE D-6 Move through the pages to add and change the information on each page

Editing the Content of Your Company Web Site

If you opt to edit the content, QuickBooks displays an easy-to-use format, which you can see in Figure D-6.

Each page in your Web site is represented by a box on the top of the Edit window. As you select a page, a Table of Contents for that page is displayed on the left side of the window. To make changes to the selected page, click Next and work your way through the contents (noted on the left). Click Preview to see the way the page looks, and click Finish to make your changes permanent.

E-Stamps

After you create and print invoices for your customers, and write or print checks to pay the bills from your vendors, you have to put each item into an envelope and then affix a stamp to each envelope. When you run out of stamps you have to go to the post office and stand in line to buy another roll (there's always a line at my local post office). No, wait, scratch that last part, you don't have to travel to the post office, much less stand in line. One of the products offered as a result of the boom in Internet buying is postage.

As a QuickBooks user, you can take advantage of e-stamps, and even save some of the up-front costs. You can use e-stamps while you're working in QuickBooks, or many other software applications. Here are some of the important things you should know:

- There's a small surcharge for using an e-stamp, so weigh that against the time, energy, and gasoline you expend for trips to the post office.
- The software runs on your local computer; you do not connect to the Internet to use it (which is a security measure).
- Technical support and software updates are available online.

Signing Up For E-Stamps

You can get information about e-stamps and sign up for the service by choosing Company | Postage Service from the QuickBooks menu bar. The QuickBooks Postage Service window opens, as seen in Figure D-7.

Click the link Sign Up Now to open the sign-up page, which displays an explanation of the process as well as a form you must fill in to use the service. After you submit the form, you have to answer a few questions from the United States Postal Service.

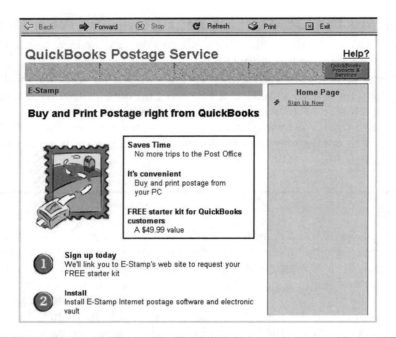

FIGURE D-7   You can sign up for e-stamps right from your QuickBooks software

Using E-Stamps

Soon after you submit your form, you'll receive an e-stamp kit that includes instructions and software. Installing the software adds the postage feature to a number of software programs you may be running, including QuickBooks. In addition, the software runs as a stand-alone application. An e-stamp icon appears on your taskbar.

When you prepare invoices for your customers, click the e-stamp icon to copy the customer's address to the e-stamp software. The e-stamp software prints envelopes and stamps at the same time.

QuickBooks Merchant Card Account Services

If you want to accept credit card payments from customers, you can let QuickBooks set up your merchant card account, and then process the credit card sales directly through your QuickBooks software.

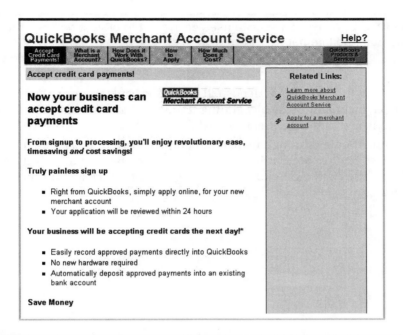

Start here if you want to use the QuickBooks credit card services

Signing Up for Merchant Card Services

To set up credit card services, choose Customers | Accept Credit Card Payments | Learn About the Merchant Account Service from the QuickBooks menu bar. The QuickBooks Merchant Account Service page displays, as seen in Figure D-8. Use the links on this page to travel to an information page, or to the sign-up page.

After you fill out the application, the financial institution QuickBooks uses will review your application and send you e-mail to tell you how to use the merchant card services.

Using the Merchant Card Services

After you create an invoice for a customer who pays with a credit card, choose Customers | Accept Credit Card Payments from the QuickBooks menu bar. You're taken to a secure Web site where you fill in the credit card information.

N O T E : A secure Web site uses encryption to protect data as it travels to and from the Internet.

When the payment is deposited into your bank account, you can download the payment, automatically adding it to your account balance. All that's left to do is match the payment against the invoice to mark the invoice as paid.

QuickBooks, through its parent company, Intuit, is putting more and more services on the Internet for QuickBooks users. Be sure to visit the QuickBooks site at http://www.quickbooks.com regularly to learn about other online features.

Index

NOTE: Page numbers in *italics* refer to illustrations or charts.

• M

THIS BOOK DOESN'T STOP HERE!

Visit cpa911.com™ for more information on QuickBooks

Stay on Top of Changes in QuickBooks 2000

QuickBooks software is updated periodically. Download the updates from Intuit, then download the new instructions and information from **cpa911.com** to ensure that your copy of *QuickBooks 2000: The Official Guide* is always current!

Additional Information, Tricks, and Tips

There's lots of information on QuickBooks features and functions on **cpa911.com™**, so you're sure to find just what you're looking for. If you don't, use the e-mail feature to ask your question or to request more information about a feature.

Information for Accountants

Accountants can find information about using QuickBooks, supporting QuickBooks, becoming a QuickBooks consultant, and using other software (like Excel) to analyze and manipulate QuickBooks client data.

Newsletter for QuickBooks Users

Sign up for the **cpa911.com™** free newsletter, bringing information, tips, tricks, and shortcuts right to your mailbox.